# Employment Law

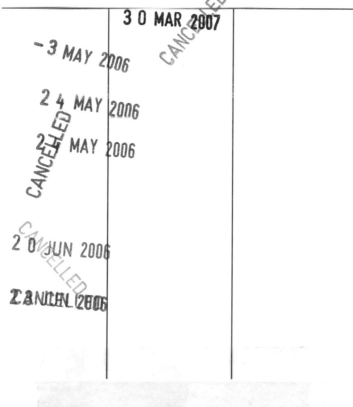

# Employment Law

## John Duddington

Head of the Law School
Worcester College of Technology

**PEARSON**
**Longman**

Harlow, England • London • New York • Boston • San Francisco • Toronto
Sydney • Tokyo • Singapore • Hong Kong • Seoul • Taipei • New Delhi
Cape Town • Madrid • Mexico City • Amsterdam • Munich • Paris • Milan

**Pearson Education Limited**

Edinburgh Gate
Harlow
Essex CM20 2JE
England

and Associated Companies throughout the world

*Visit us on the World Wide Web at:*
www.pearsoneduc.com

First published 2003

© Pearson Education Limited 2003

The right of John Duddington to be identified as author of this work
has been asserted by him in accordance with the Copyright, Designs
and Patents Act 1988.

ISBN 0 582 42376 7

**British Library Cataloguing-in-Publication Data**
A catalogue record for this book is available from the British Library

10   9   8   7   6   5   4   3   2   1
08   07   06   05   04   03

Typeset in 10.5/12.5pt Minion by 35
Printed in Great Britain by Henry Ling Ltd., at the Dorset Press, Dorchester, Dorset

*The publisher's policy is to use paper manufactured from sustainable forests.*

# Contents

# Preface

Employment law, like the Roman God Janus, faces two ways. One way points to a seemingly arid mass of regulatory detail which is being added to in a never-ending stream. The other way points, as I hope this book does, to a fascinating subject in which the law blends with history and politics to produce a study full of contemporary relevance. Of all legal subjects, this one above all has the combination of practical relevance and a contemporary flavour largely but not entirely unencumbered by the concepts of the past. There are also some tough technical issues for the mind to grapple with.

In writing this book I set myself three aims: first, to produce an account which is understandable; secondly, to deal adequately with technical and difficult areas; and, thirdly, to attempt to locate employment law in its contemporary setting in society today. If it has a theme, it is that employment law has come of age. One senses that the main areas of the subject are well settled and that changes of government are unlikely to alter its shape. Now is the time to focus on the details of the present law and to look to its future development, especially in the light of the UK's membership of the European Community and of the incorporation of the European Convention on Human Rights into UK law.

Employment law is of interest to two groups: to lawyers and law students and to personnel officers and others who need a working knowledge of the law. I have tried to deal adequately with all topics which appear in assessments so that the book should be an adequate text for those preparing for degree and professional examinations. I have also included some specimen examination questions and points for inclusion in answers to make the book more useful to students. On the other hand, there should be sufficient detail, especially on the newer areas such as family and parental rights, to meet the needs of personnel officers and others. I hope that the inclusion of diagrams and flow charts aids both groups in understanding what has become, in many cases, a very complex branch of the law.

There is never an ideal time to write a book on any aspect of law, least of all employment law, but I think that this book appears at a reasonably opportune moment. I have been able to deal with the Employment Act 2002, which will bring about something of a sea change in the law of unfair dismissal as well as affecting various other areas. The Fixed-Term Employees Regulations 2002 will regulate the rights of these employees for the first time and I have also been able to mention the proposed changes to the Transfer of Employment (Protection of Employees) Regulations (TUPE), the new draft Regulations on discrimination on the grounds of sexual orientation, religion and belief, age and other changes, both recent and impending.

The staff at Pearson Education have shown a degree of patience going well beyond the call of duty in waiting for the manuscript and especial thanks are due to Pat Bond, who originally commissioned it, Lissa Matthews, who has kept me going in the later stages and Anita Atkinson and Michelle Gallagher. In addition, Juliet Doyle has been an eagle-eyed editor who has kindly allowed me to add material received at a late stage. My wife Anne has, as with all of my writing over many years, been the rock on which this project was built and both she and my daughter Mary have been avid proof readers and custodians of my style and grammar. Both of them and my son Christopher have been a constant source of inspiration and it is, of course, to my family that this book is dedicated. My colleagues at Worcester Law School have provided cheerful and stimulating company and I have been fortunate to be able to draw on the excellent resources of the Law Library there.

Any preface must contain two essential items: the statement that any errors are my own responsibility and the date at which the information in this book is believed to be correct: in this case it is 6 August 2002, although I have been able to add details of statutory material, especially on the Employment Act and on equal opportunities legislation received after that date. Nor is this all, because the publishers have agreed to add a website to this book available at www.booksites.net/duddington, which will be updated quarterly, so that the usual reluctance of authors to let the proofs of a book go, especially on a subject such as employment law, is tempered by the thought that it can be kept up to date so easily.

*Worcester, 6 August 2002*                                                     *John Duddington*

## Note

Since this preface was written the flood of cases has continued unabated and amongst the most significant which have been reported by January 2003 are: *Young v Post Office* [2002] IRLR 660 (employer's liability for stress at work), *Goodwin v UK* [2002] IRLR 664 (ECtHR holds that lack of recognition of the new genetic identity of a transsexual is in breach of Articles 8 and 12 of the ECHR) and *Rutherford v Towncircle Ltd and Secretary of State for Trade and Industry (No. 2) and Bentley v Secretary of State for Trade and Industry* [2002] IRLR 768 (decision of an ET that excluding those over 65 from the right to claim for unfair dismissal and redundancy is indirect discrimination against men and contrary to EU law). In addition, the CA has held in *Sainsbury's Supermarkets Ltd v Hitt* [2003] IRLR 23 that the range of reasonable responses test applies to the question of whether the investigation into suspected misconduct was adequate as well as to the question of whether the employer had reasonable grounds to believe the employee guilty of that misconduct. All of these cases and others will, of course, be noted in the first quarterly update of this book on its website.

# Acknowledgements

We are grateful to the Employment Tribunals Service for permission to reproduce forms IT1 and IT3.

# Keeping up to date with employment law

Any book on employment law can only hope to give an indication of likely changes in the law and therefore it is vital to know how to keep up to date. Anyone with access to the internet really has no excuse for not knowing where the law is going as there are several excellent websites, the addresses of which are set out below. Indeed, browsing the net looking for recent legal developments has become a favourite hobby of mine whilst writing this book and I hope that readers will find equal enjoyment!

In addition to the websites, there are the following sources of printed information:

- **The Industrial Relations Law Reports** are published monthly and have the judgments in full of all major employment law cases. There is also a useful commentary at the beginning of each issue on the cases in that issue.
- **The Industrial Cases Reports** are the other main series of reports and are equally useful.
- **The Industrial Law Journal** is the leading journal on employment law. It is published quarterly and contains, besides articles, notes on recent cases and legislation as well as European developments.
- **Income Data Services** publish a fortnightly IDS Brief giving details of current developments which is written in a most readable style. It also publishes handbooks on particular topics, such as unfair dismissal, which are full of useful information.
- **Harvey on Industrial Relations and Employment Law** is a looseleaf encyclopaedia currently running to six parts which is regularly updated and has monthly bulletins which are invaluable as a first point of reference in checking on current developments.
- **Labour Market Trends** is published monthly and is full of statistics on current trends as well as containing invaluable articles extrapolating the information in them. This is a must for anyone (surely everyone?) who wishes to evaluate the impact of legislation on the labour market.

# Useful websites

Employment law is such a fast changing subject that the internet is a really useful tool. I have set out the websites which I have found especially useful but it may be that readers find other favourites of their own. As many sites have links to others, it is easy to find more sites.

The most useful sites for keeping up to date are, I think, the following:

- **www.dti.gov.uk** This is the website of the Department of Trade and Industry and has a great deal of information on both recent and proposed changes to the law. It has consultation papers and the text of the White Paper *Fairness at Work*. Try to look at it once a week.
- **www.peoplemanagement.co.uk** is the website of the Chartered Institute of Personnel and Development and contains a useful section on current legal issues. The other sections of this website are also worth reading, as it is important to look at the total picture of employment relations and not only the law.
- **www.incomesdata.co.uk** Another invaluable resource for keeping up to date on all aspects of employment relations and has some excellent features on, for example, recent cases.

Other invaluable websites are:

- **www.hmso.gov.uk** (has the texts of legislation).
- **www.courtservice.gov.uk** (has judgments of the courts).
- **www.bailii.org** (another source of up-to-date judgments).
- **www.acas.org.uk** (ACAS website).
- **www.eoc.org.uk** (Equal Opportunities website).
- **www.cre.gov.uk** (Commission for Equal Opportunities website).
- **www.drc-gb.org** (Disability Rights Commission).
- **www.employmentappeals.gov.uk** (Employment Appeal Tribunal).
- **www.europa.eu.int** (European Union).
- **ilj.oupjournals.org** (Industrial Law Journal).
- **www.dwp.gov.uk** (Department for Work and Pensions – useful for updating on social security benefits).
- **www.dataprotection.gov.uk** (especially useful at present in view of current developments).

# Table of cases

# Table of statutes

# Table of statutory instruments

# Table of European legislation

# Table of statutory rights

A large number of statutory rights have been described in this book and readers may find the following table useful as a short guide to the main ones.

| Right | Statute | Time limit | Qualifying period | Remedy |
|---|---|---|---|---|
| Unfair dismissal | Part X ERA 1996 | 3 months | One year | Reinstatement, re-engagement, compensation |
| Unfair dismissal by reason of a business transfer (TUPE) | Transfer of undertakings regulations (reg.8) | 3 months | One year | Reinstatement, re-engagement, compensation |
| Unfair dismissal for taking part in protected official industrial action | S.238A TULRCA 1992 | 6 months | None | Reinstatement, re-engagement, compensation |
| Unfair dismissal for a reason connected with pregnancy, childbirth maternity leave, parental leave, dependant care leave | S.99 ERA 1996 | 3 months | None | Reinstatement re-engagement, compensation |
| Redundancy payments | Part X1 ERA 1996 | 6 months | 2 years | Statutory redundancy payment |
| Sex discrimination | SDA 1975 | 3 months | None | Compensation order declaring rights recommendation |
| Race discrimination | RRA 1976 | 3 months | None | As for sex discrimination |
| Disability discrimination | DDA 1995 | 3 months | None | As for sex discrimination |
| Equal pay | EqPA 1970 | 6 months | None | Arrears of pay for up to 2 years |

| Right | Statute | Time limit | Qualifying period | Remedy |
|---|---|---|---|---|
| Unlawful deduction from wages | Part 11 ERA 1996 | 3 months | None | Payment of wages deducted |
| Guarantee payment | Ss.28–35 ERA 1996 | 3 months | None | Payment of guarantee pay |
| Right to an itemised statement of employment particulars | Ss.8–12 ERA 1996 | 3 months | 2 months | ET may decide what should be in the particulars or amend inaccurate ones |
| Right not to suffer detriment as a result of being a union member or taking part in union activities | S.146 TULRCA 1992 | 3 months | None | Compensation |

*Note*: The phrase 'time limits' in the above table needs clarification, as the time limits run from different starting points.

(a) **Unfair dismissal.** Time runs from the 'effective date of termination' of employment. This is defined by s.92(6) of ERA 1996 as the date when notice of termination expires, or, where the contract is terminated without notice, when termination takes effect. However, in the case of dismissal for taking part in protected official industrial action, the phrase is 'date of dismissal' (s.238(5) of TULRCA), which has the same meaning. In all of these cases the employment tribunal has power to extend the time limit if it feels that it was not reasonably practicable to present a complaint in time.

(b) **Redundancy payments.** Time runs from the 'relevant date', which is defined by s.145 of ERA 1996 in identical terms to that of 'effective date of termination'.

(c) **Discrimination legislation.** The phrase is 'the date of the act complained of' and the employment tribunal has power to extend the time if it considers it just and equitable to do so'. In *equal pay claims* the phrase is 'termination of employment'.

(d) **Unlawful deduction from wages.** Time runs from the date of the last deduction by the employer and this can be extended if the employment tribunal considers that it is just and equitable to do so.

(e) **Guarantee payment.** Time runs from the day for which payment is claimed with the same extension of time if it is just and equitable.

(f) **Right to an itemised statement of employment particulars.** Time runs from the day on which employment ceased with the same extension of time if just and equitable.

(g) **Right not to suffer for trade union activities etc.** Time runs from the last day when there was either an act or a failure to act with the same extension of time if just and equitable.

# Abbreviations used when referring to judges

As we shall see, the judgments of individual judges are of great importance both in the interpretation of statutes and other statutory materials, such as Regulations, and also in directly making law through the system of precedent. When referring to the judgments of individual judges, standard abbreviations are used to indicate particular members of the judiciary. These are as follows and the imaginary name of Smith in this context is used to make the examples clearer.

| | |
|---|---|
| Smith J | Mr or Mrs Justice Smith, a judge of the High Court. |
| Smith LJ | Lord Justice or Lady Justice Smith, a judge of the Court of Appeal. |
| Lord Smith | A Law Lord, i.e. a member of the House of Lords who sits as a judge to hear appeals. |
| Smith P | The President of the Employment Appeal Tribunal, who is also a judge of the High Court. |
| Smith MR | The Master of the Rolls, the presiding judge of the Court of Appeal, Civil Division. |
| Smith LCJ | The Lord Chief Justice, the presiding judge of the Court of Appeal, Criminal Division. |
| Smith LC | The Lord Chancellor, who, amongst other functions, sits as a judge in the House of Lords. |

# Chapter 1

# Employment law and the English legal system

## INTRODUCTION

This chapter aims to show briefly how employment law is located in the legal system. The phrase 'English legal system' has been used, but in fact the legal system extends to Wales also. It is different in Scotland although many of the statutory provisions apply there also.

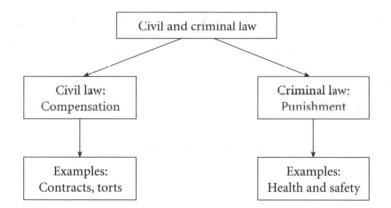

*Note*: the word 'tort' means a wrong which can be redressed by the payment of compensation or some other civil remedy. The tort featured most often in this book is the tort of negligence, which is fully explained in Chapter 8.

The above examples are oversimplified, but they indicate the fundamental distinction in the law between those matters where it is left to the individual to seek redress and those where the state takes a hand. In general, employment law (or labour law or industrial law as it is sometimes called) is far more concerned with civil matters such as actions for compensation for unfair dismissal and claims for unpaid wages. Criminal law plays a relatively small part, being mainly confined to prosecutions under health and safety legislation.

The other feature of the legal system is that law is made in the following ways:

1. By Parliament in the form of statutes and regulations made under them. Codes of practice, e.g. issued under the Disability Discrimination Act, together with guidance are also influential but in general they only have the status of the Highway Code: they are taken into account in legal proceedings but are not the law.
2. Decisions of the courts have been enormously influential in shaping the law and where the law has been developed by the courts it is known as common law. The fundamental principles of English law, as contained in, for example, the law of contract, owe their origin to the courts, although statute law has built on them. Chapter 5, dealing with the contract of employment, is a good example of the interplay between the courts and statute law.
3. Decisions of the courts have also been especially significant in interpreting statutory provisions. Examples are found throughout this book, but an especially good one is *Western Excavating v Sharp* (1978), interpreting the part of the law on unfair dismissal known as constructive dismissal.
4. European Community law and the European Convention on Human Rights are dealt with in subsequent chapters.

## DISPUTE SETTLEMENT IN EMPLOYMENT LAW

Some disputes, for example those involving a breach of a contract or a claim for unpaid wages, go to the civil courts, although claims for a breach of contract of employment can be brought in an employment tribunal, where the amount claimed is £25,000 or less.

**Diagram of the civil courts**

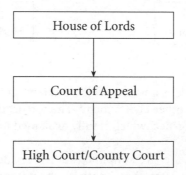

Civil claims begin in either the High Court or the County Court, according to their monetary value and their complexity. Appeals go to the Court of Appeal, with a further appeal, generally only on a point of law of general public importance, to the House of Lords. The involvement of the European Court of Justice

(ECJ) is dealt with in Chapter 2 and that of the European Court of Human Rights (ECtHR) in Chapter 3.

**Claims brought in employment tribunals**

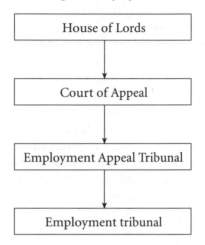

Employment tribunals hear all the statutory claims for unfair dismissal, redundancy payments, discrimination and other matters dealt with in these chapters. In addition, they can also hear contract claims as indicated above. In 2000/01 they heard 130,408 claims, an increase from 91,913 in 1998/99. They have a legally qualified chairman who sits with two others drawn from both sides of industry.

Employment tribunals were originally known as industrial tribunals and their object has been to provide a relatively straightforward means of hearing employment claims. Although to the layperson they do not seem very different from a court, they are not subject to the rules of evidence to the same degree and the procedural rules and forms are simplified from those of the courts. Claims are brought by the issue of form ITI and the person bringing the claim is known as the applicant. The present government briefly considered a proposal that a fee of perhaps £100 should be payable on the issue of an ITI but, like their predecessors in 1996, they rejected it. The other party is known as the respondent, who has 21 days to reply to the claim by means of an IT3. Both of these forms are set out at the end of this chapter. Tribunals have, to an extent, become victims of their own success and the vast increase in the amount of legislation in this area. Thus the number of claims has increased so that in 2000/01 there were 130,408 claims registered with tribunals as compared to 34,697 in 1990/91. This has led both to changes in the tribunal system and to an attempt to direct some of the claims to other channels. One example is the introduction of new procedures in the Employment Act 2002 designed to encourage more disciplinary and grievance issues to be settled within the workplace rather than be the subject of a complaint to an employment tribunal (these are dealt with in Chapter 11). Another important change has been the rule introduced in 1993 that where an applicant is considered at a pre-hearing to have no reasonable prospect of success, then a deposit of £500 might be required from them as a condition of continuing with the application. Costs can also be awarded where a party has been warned at a pre-hearing that the case has no reasonable prospect of success but still continues. This has been taken further by a provision in the Employment Act 2002 which clarifies the rarely used power to strike out cases which are obviously very weak. It is also intended that the power to award costs should be used more frequently and s.22 of the Employment Act 2002 contains a provision enabling costs to be awarded against a representative because of his or her conduct. Even so, the fact remains that the rule in civil actions that the loser is almost always ordered to pay the winner's costs does not apply in tribunals.

The Employment Rights (Dispute Resolution) Act 1998 contained power for ACAS (see below) to conduct binding arbitrations in unfair dismissal claims provided that the parties agreed. Any decision of the arbitrator is final subject to an appeal on either a point of EC law or the European Convention on Human Rights (ECHR). Power was given to ACAS to prepare a scheme under which the system would operate and this came into effect in May 2001. There is anecdotal evidence that the takeup of it has so far been small. In addition, the provisions of the Employment Act 2002 dealing with statutory disciplinary dismissal and grievance procedures (see Chapter 11) may reduce the number of claims. In line with the trend to encourage the settlement of claims by conciliation, s.24 of the Employment Act 2002 provides that tribunals have the power to postpone a hearing in order to give time for conciliation.

## Employment Appeal Tribunal

This hears appeals from employment tribunals and has the same status as the High Court. It is headed by a President who is a High Court judge and cases are heard by a judge and two laypersons from opposite sides of industry.

## Other institutions of employment law

The work of other institutions will be considered at various points in this book but the main ones are, in brief, as follows:

### Advisory Conciliation and Arbitration Service (ACAS)

This is a statutory body which has the following general functions:

- Conciliation in individual disputes. Any settlement reached when a claim is brought but then settled after the intervention of ACAS and recorded on the appropriate form is binding and the claim cannot be proceeded with to the tribunal.
- Conciliation in collective disputes between employers and unions.
- Preparation of codes of practice. The most important one is the Code on Disciplinary and Grievance Procedures (see Chapter 11).

- Designating an independent expert to prepare a report in equal value claims (see Chapter 9).
- Providing information and advice on employment matters.

## Central Arbitration Committee

This is a permanent body, independent of government, employers and unions, which deals with disputes and other matters relating to collective aspects of employment law. It has a major role in trade union recognition matters and applications by unions for the disclosure of information for collective bargaining purposes, discussed in Chapter 13. It also provides voluntary arbitration in industrial disputes. With the revival of trade union recognition and collective aspects of employment law, the Committee has itself been revived from its somewhat moribund state in much of the 1980s and 1990s.

## Certification Officer

This officer has the role of certifying whether a trade union is independent (see Chapter 13) and, if so, granting certificates of independence. The grant of such a certificate is a prerequisite to the exercise of most trade union rights.

## Equal Opportunities Commission, Commission for Racial Equality, Disability Rights Commission

These three bodies are concerned with the Sex Discrimination Acts, Race Relations Acts and the Disability Discrimination Act. They have the general duty of working towards the elimination of discrimination and they monitor the operation of the Acts as well as generally promoting equality of opportunity. Their work is dealt with in Chapter 9.

## Application to an Employment Tribunal

Received at ET

Case number

Code

Initials

♦ If you fax this form you do not need to send one in the post.
♦ This form has to be photocopied. Please use CAPITALS and black ink (if possible).
♦ Where there are tick boxes, please tick to one that applies.

1 Please give the type of complaint you want the tribunal to decide (for example, unfair dismissal, equal pay). A full list is available from the tribunal office. If you have more than one complaint list them all.

4 Please give the dates of your employment

From _____ to _____

5 Please give the name and address of the employer, other organisation or person against whom this complaint is being brought

Name

Address

Postcode

Phone number

Please give the place where you worked or applied to work if different from above

Address

Postcode

2 Please give your details

Mr ☐ Mrs ☐ Miss ☐ Ms ☐ Other _____

First names

Surname

Date of birth

Address

Postcode

Phone number

Daytime phone number

Please give an address to which we should send documents if different from above

Postcode

3 If a representative is acting for you please give details (all correspondence will be sent to your representative)

Name

Address

Postcode

Phone | Fax

Reference

6 Please say what job you did for the employer (or what job you applied for). If this does not apply, please say what your connection was with the employer

IT1(E/W)

7   Please give the number of normal basic hours worked each week

    Hours per week

9   If your complaint is not about dismissal, please give the date when the matter you are complaining about took place

8   Please give your earning details

    Basic wage or salary

    £          :          per

    Average take home pay

    £          :          per

    Other bonuses or benefits

    £          :          per

10  Unfair dismissal applicants only

    Please indicate what you are seeking at this stage, if you win your case

    ☐  Reinstatement: to carry on working in your old job as before (an order for reinstatement normally includes an award of compensation for loss of earnings).

    ☐  Re-engagement: to start another job or new contract with your old employer (an order for re-engagement normally includes an award of compensation for loss of earnings).

    ☐  Compensation only: to get an award of money.

11  Please give details of your complaint

    If there is not enough space for your answer, please continue on a separate sheet and attach it to this form.

12  Please sign and date this form, then send it to the appropriate address on the back cover of this booklet (see postcode list on pages 13-16).

    Signed

    Date

IT1(E/W)

*Source*: Employment Tribunals Service

**EMPLOYMENT TRIBUNALS**

Notice of Appearance by Respondent

In the application of

**Case Number**
(please quote in all correspondence)

\* This form has to be photocopied, if possible please use Black Ink and Capital letters
\* If there is not enough space for your answer, please continue on a separate sheet and attach it to this form

**1. Full name and address of the Respondent:**

Post Code:

Telephone number:

**2. If you require documents and notices to be sent to a representative or any other address in the United Kingdom please give details:**

Post Code:

Reference:

Telephone number:

**3. Do you intend to resist the application?** (Tick appropriate box)

YES     NO

**4. Was the applicant dismissed?** (Tick appropriate box)

YES     NO

Please give
reason below

Reason for dismissal:

**5. Are the dates of employment given by the applicant correct?** (Tick appropriate box)

YES     NO

please give correct dates below

| Began on | |
| --- | --- |
| Ended on | |

**6. Are the details given by the applicant about wages/salary, take home or other bonuses correct?** (Tick appropriate box)

YES     NO

Please give correct details below

| Basic Wages/Salary | £ | per |
| --- | --- | --- |
| Average Take Home Pay | £ | per |
| Other Bonuses/Benefits | £ | per |

**PLEASE TURN OVER**

For office use only
Date of receipt     Initials

**Form IT3 E&W - 8/98**

7. Give particulars of the grounds on which you intend to resist the application.

8. Please sign and date the form.

Signed                                    Dated

DATA PROTECTION ACT 1984
We may put some of the information you give on this form on to a computer. This helps us to monitor progress and produce statistics. We may also give information to:
* the other party in the case
* other parts of the DTI and organisations such as ACAS (Advisory Conciliation and Arbitration Service), the Equal Opportunities Commission or the Commission for Racial Equality.

Please post or fax this form to : The Regional Secretary

* IF YOU FAX THE FORM, DO NOT POST A COPY AS WELL
* IF YOU POST THE FORM, TAKE A COPY FOR YOUR RECORDS

Form IT3 E&W 8/98

*Source*: Employment Tribunals Service

# Chapter 2

# Employment law and European Community law

## INTRODUCTION

The significance of EC law can be best appreciated by the following example, which is based on the case of *Macarthays Ltd v Smith* (1980).

*Example*

X, a man, was employed as the manager of a warehouse stockroom at a wage of about £60 per week. He left in October 1975. Four months later, Y, a woman, was appointed to what was really the same post but on a wage of £50 per week. Could Y claim equal pay with X?

As we shall see in Chapter 9, the Equal Pay Act 1970 gives a right to equal pay for 'like work'. The work of Y was certainly 'like work' to that done by X but the problem was that they were not working at the same time. The Court of Appeal held that the Equal Pay Act did not cover this situation and, had this been the only legal authority, Y would have lost her claim.

However, the European Court of Justice (ECJ) held that what was Article 119 of the EC Treaties (now Article 141) covered a situation where a woman received less pay than a man who had *previously* worked for the same employer and where they both did equal work. Accordingly, the Court of Appeal decided the case in accordance with the ruling of the ECJ and Y eventually succeeded in her claim.

This example illustrates the following points:

1. The supremacy of EC law over national law. Where, as here, there is a conflict between the two, then national law must give way. This principle is given statutory force in the UK by s.2 of the European Communities Act 1972. The difference between this straightforward principle and the complex way in which the European Convention on Human Rights is given effect in UK law, as described in the next chapter, is striking.
2. The fact that the basic principles of EC law are derived from the EC Treaties, as explained below.
3. The relationship between national courts and the ECJ. Where, as here, a national court has a case turning on the interpretation of the EC Treaties then, under Article 234 (formerly 177) of the EC Treaty, the national court

may refer the question to the ECJ and the national court must then decide the case in accordance with the interpretation given by the ECJ. This is what happened in the above case.

4.  The fact that EC law, like Continental legal systems, works in broader concepts than UK law. Under Article 119 (now 141) of the EC Treaty, the term used is 'equal work', whereas the Equal Pay Act used the term 'like work', which, as we shall see in Chapter 9, is a rather more technical term.

EC law has had a considerable effect on UK employment law and this is growing. This chapter will first look at the sources of EC law and will then consider the general thrust of EC employment law. Detailed accounts of the impact of EC law will be found in chapters dealing with particular topics.

## SOURCES OF EC LAW

1.  The EC Treaties. These are the primary sources of EC law and include the Treaty of Rome (1957), the Maastricht Treaty (1992) and the Treaty of Amsterdam (1997). The treaties provide a framework within which legislation can be implemented.
2.  EC Regulations. These are automatically binding in all Member States of the EC and, in contrast with Directives (see below) they become law without the need for any intervention by Member States, who are effectively bypassed.
3.  EC Directives. These lay down particular objectives to be achieved but, in contrast to Regulations, they leave it to Member States to decide how actually to implement them. A good example is the Working Time Directive, which was implemented in the UK by the Working Time Regulations 1998 and 1999. Another is the Framework Directive, under which Member States must introduce legislation prohibiting discrimination on grounds which go further than, for example, existing UK legislation by including age, sexual orientation and religion or belief.
4.  EC Decisions. These are addressed to individual Member States, individuals or organisations and are binding on those to whom they are addressed.

## THE EXTENT TO WHICH EC LAW IS BINDING ON INDIVIDUALS AND CAN BE RELIED ON BY THEM

In some cases EC law has direct effect in Member States. This means that it can be relied on by individuals. The doctrine of direct effect was developed by the ECJ and is not found in the Treaty itself. A provision will have direct effect if it is clear and unambiguous, unconditional and needs no further action by the EC itself or national states to come into force beyond implementation by the state. Where a Treaty provision has direct effect, then this means that it can be relied on by individuals both vertically (in actions against the state and organs of the state) and horizontally (in actions against other individuals). A provision in a Directive which has direct effect only has vertical direct effect and cannot be relied on in actions against other individuals.

A good example of direct effect of a Treaty provision in employment law is Article 141, giving the right to equal pay for equal work, dealt with in Chapter 9, and which has had a great influence in moving UK law forward in this area. An example of the direct effect of a Directive is *Marshall v Southampton and South West Hampshire AHA* (1986), where the ECJ ruled that different retirement ages for women (60) and men (65) were sexually discriminatory and in breach of the Equal Treatment Directive (76/207), which could be relied on as the health authority was an emanation of the state. The significance of the case was that the relevant UK law, the Sex Discrimination Act 1975, did not, by s.6(4), apply to provisions in relation to retirement. The effect was that, as the Directive had no direct effect horizontally, those who worked for the state or emanations of it were able to rely on this ruling but it had no effect in relation to private employers. This unsatisfactory state of affairs had to be put right and this was done by the Sex Discrimination Act 1986, under which differential retirement ages in all employment was brought within the scope of the sex discrimination legislation.

Where EC law does not have direct effect, it may have indirect effect, which means that the courts will interpret national legislation so as to give effect where possible to the provisions of EC law. A good example is the attitude of the courts to the interpretation of the Transfer of Undertakings (Protection of Employment) Regulations (TUPE) and an instance in this context is the decision of the House of Lords in *Litster v Forth Dry Dock and Engineering Co. Ltd* (1989), discussed in Chapter 12.

## THE EC AND EMPLOYMENT LAW

The European Community has its genesis in three treaties which were all broadly economic in effect, and which formed the European Coal and Steel Community, Euratom and the European Economic Community, which is now known as the European Community. This point is important, as it shows that EC intervention in social affairs, such as the details of the employment relationship, was not one of the original concerns of the EC. The first piece of EC legislation to have an impact on employment law was Article 119 (discussed above). This was followed by the Equal Treatment Directive of 1976, which established the principle of equal treatment for men and women which meant that, in the words of the Directive, 'there shall be no discrimination whatsoever on grounds of sex' (see Chapter 9). A year later, in 1977, the Acquired Rights Directive gave rights to workers when the ownership of the undertaking which employed them was transferred. These rights were implemented in the UK by the Transfer of Undertakings (Protection of Employment) Regulations 1981 (see Chapter 12). In 1986 the Single European Act inserted a new Article 118a into the Treaty (now

Article 137), which provides that Member States must pay particular attention to encouraging improvements in the health and safety of workers. What was also significant was that Article 118a provided for qualified majority voting on its implementation, which meant that individual states, and especially, as it turned out, the UK, could not veto them. This was followed by a number of health and safety Directives, the most important being the Framework Directive of 1989 (see Chapter 8).

Much greater impetus to EC regulation of the employment relationship was given by the adoption in 1989 by 11 Member States (not including the UK) of a Social Charter, which was followed by an Agreement on Social Policy in the form of a Protocol attached to the Maastricht Treaty of 1992. The reason for the Protocol was that the UK government had vetoed the inclusion of the so-called Social Chapter in the Treaty itself. This meant that social policy was now firmly at the forefront of EC strategies and in 1997 the incoming Labour government in the UK indicated that it wished to opt into the Agreement on Social Policy. Accordingly, the Treaty of Amsterdam of 1997 incorporated most of the Agreement on Social Policy into the EC Treaty itself, in Articles 136–145. A new Framework Directive on Equal Treatment was agreed in 2000 and a Directive on Rights for Workers Employed on Fixed Term Contracts in 1999 (70/1999). Indeed, it can almost be said that the main impetus today for change in employment law comes from the European Community.

## INTERNATIONAL LABOUR STANDARDS

The International Labour Organisation (ILO) has the general role of promoting fair employment conditions in all member countries. It was established in 1919 and now operates as the specialised agency of the United Nations in promoting social justice and human and labour rights. It has so far produced a total of 183 Conventions setting minimum standards on, for example, the right of free association, equal opportunities and hours of work. Although valuable, they are of limited use, as they are not binding on states and can be denounced even when ratified. The UK has ratified 83 Conventions but the Conservative government of 1979–97 denounced some, including the minimum wage fixing machinery. Indeed, a total of 17 Conventions previously ratified have been denounced. However, their effectiveness should not be underestimated, as, for example, Convention No. 100 of 1951 on equal opportunities was taken into account when the Equal Pay Act 1970 was being framed (see Chapter 9). In addition, the ILO provides training and advisory services to both employers' and workers' associations and is generally active in the field of labour relations.

# Chapter 3

# Employment law and the European Convention on Human Rights

## INTRODUCTION

The European Convention on Human Rights (ECHR) has already had an impact on employment law and this means that, in future, it will be necessary, especially with the passage of the Human Rights Act 1998, to assess the effect of the Convention when advising on any aspect of this area. The scheme of this chapter is to provide a kind of outline map of the Convention, looking at its main features and at how it is incorporated into UK law. Following this, individual chapters will have one or more sections which look at its impact on particular areas.

## THE EUROPEAN CONVENTION ON HUMAN RIGHTS

The ECHR came into effect on 3 September 1953, in the immediate aftermath of the Second World War, when it was felt imperative to enshrine certain fundamental human rights. The mechanism adopted was for countries to sign the Convention as such and to ratify articles of it. The ECHR also established the European Court of Human Rights (ECtHR), which deals with alleged violations of the ECHR. The UK signed the ECHR in 1950 but it did not accept the jurisdiction of the ECtHR until 1966, and only then did the UK accept the right of individual UK citizens to petition the ECtHR. From 1966 until the Human Rights Act 1998 came into force on 2 October 2000, the UK was in a kind of limbo: whilst it had signed the ECHR and accepted that individuals could petition the ECtHR, the Convention was not actually part of UK law. Therefore, the ECtHR could, and did, rule that the UK was in breach of the Convention but the UK government was not legally obliged to take any notice.

The effect of the Human Rights Act 1998 has been to incorporate most, but not all, of the Convention, into UK law. It would be wrong, however, to say that it is part of UK law in the same way as, for example, the Employment Rights Act 1996 is, because:

1. Not all of the ECHR has been incorporated into UK law by the Human Rights Act. Articles 2–12 and 14 have been incorporated and Articles 1–3 of the First

Protocol and Articles 1 and 2 of the Sixth Protocol. (Protocols are simply additions to the Convention.) References in this chapter will, unless stated to the contrary, be references to the ECHR as incorporated into UK law.

2. The way in which the ECHR is part of UK law is not straightforward, as explained below.

3. It is possible for states to enter reservations to the Convention. The concept of a reservation means that the state reserves laws or policies so that they cannot be challenged under the Convention. In the case of the ECHR, there is only one reservation by the UK, relating to the provision of education.

4. It is also possible, under Article 15, for states to derogate from the ECHR in times of war or public emergency. The UK government has used this in relation to Northern Ireland.

From the point of view of employment law, reservations and derogations are not, for the moment, relevant. Moreover, the parts of the Convention which have not been incorporated into UK law are not of great significance in employment law.

## THE ARTICLES OF THE ECHR

Although employment law is only affected by certain articles of the Convention, readers may find it useful to have a summary of the topics covered by all of the articles so as to have an idea of the scope of the Convention. They are as follows:

Article 2: Right to life
Article 3: Prohibition of torture
Article 4: Prohibition of forced labour
Article 5: Right to liberty and security
Article 6: Right to a fair trial
Article 7: No punishment without law
Article 8: Right to respect for private and family life
Article 9: Freedom of thought, conscience and religion
Article 10: Freedom of expression
Article 11: Freedom of assembly and association
Article 12: Right to marry
Article 13: Right to an effective remedy
Article 14: Prohibition of discrimination in the exercise of Convention rights

Furthermore, the Protocols deal with:

Protocol One, Article 1: Protection of property
Protocol One, Article 2: Right to education
Protocol One, Article 3: Right to free elections
Protocol Six: Abolition of the death penalty

All of the articles are incorporated into UK law by Schedule 1 to the Human Rights Act, with the exception of Article 13. A striking feature is the extent to which the articles reflect the prevailing ethos of the post-war period, with the emphasis on political rights and with the need to protect from tyranny very much in mind. What is missing is any clear statement of social and economic rights, such as a right to work, for example, and this inevitably means, as will be seen, that none of the articles deal directly with employment matters. Article 14 might be thought to have a direct bearing on employment law, but this is not so. It does not prohibit discrimination as such but only discrimination in the exercise of Convention rights. This is important, as the article goes much further than UK law does at present because it applies to discrimination not only on the grounds of sex and race but also on grounds of, for example, religious, political or other opinion. However, Article 14 is only internal to the Convention. For example, if the right to education in Protocol One, Article 2 was denied on any of the grounds set out in Article 14, then there would be a breach of the Convention. However, Article 14 does not directly prohibit discrimination in employment on the grounds it sets out. (This topic is considered further in Chapter 9.)

## SCOPE OF THE ECHR UNDER THE HUMAN RIGHTS ACT 1998

The Human Rights Act *does not* simply provide that the ECHR has effect in the same way as a statute. Therefore, a person cannot just say that, as their rights under the ECHR have been broken, they are entitled to a remedy and leave it at that. Nor is it true to say that the ECHR is a kind of higher law, as EC law has become, so that any law in conflict with the ECHR is void. This is not so. The position is as follows:

1. All courts and tribunals must take account, where relevant to proceedings before them, of decisions of the ECtHR and its organs (s.2) (see below).
2. So far as is possible, all legislation, whether existing or future, must be read and given effect to in a way which is consistent with the rights in the Convention (s.3).
3. If it is not possible to read primary legislation in a way that gives effect to the Convention, then the High Court or a superior court has the power to declare that a specific provision in an Act is incompatible with the Convention, but such a declaration does not affect the continued operation of that provision (ss.4–5).
4. It is unlawful for a public authority to act in a way which is incompatible with a Convention right unless it could not have acted differently. Public authorities are broadly defined and include not only courts and tribunals but also private persons when exercising functions of a public nature (s.6). Accordingly, s.7 creates a new right, directly enforceable against public bodies, under which it will be a cause of action against them that they have failed to act compatibly with the Convention. However, this will not apply

to purely private bodies or to private individuals. A public body is merely defined as a body which exercises public functions (s.6(3)(b)), which is not enlightening, but it is clear that central and local government are public bodies and therefore when acting as employers will be directly subject to the ECHR. Bodies which undertake the functions of the state, such as ACAS and NHS trusts, will also be public and so will bodies set up by statute, such as many colleges and universities. In addition, a private employer will cross over and become a public body when it performs public functions. In the House of Lords' debates on the Human Rights Bill, the Lord Chancellor, Lord Irvine, gave as examples where a private security company is engaged to manage security at prisons and where doctors who work for the NHS also take private patients. Where the security firm is managing the prison and where doctors are working for the NHS, they will be public authorities.

5. When considering whether a state is in breach of the Convention, the courts allow it a 'margin of appreciation' whereby the court should give a certain amount of discretion to the state in achieving its particular policy goals.

## Example

Article 11 of the Convention gives the right to form and join trade unions. The UK Parliament passes the Abolition of Trade Unions Act, which prohibits the formation of trade unions. This is obviously contrary to the Convention but the Act is not invalid for this reason. If a prosecution was brought for forming a trade union then the court would make a declaration that the Act was incompatible with the Convention (see point 3 above). It would be up to the government to decide whether or not to ignore this declaration. Clearly, the thinking is that the force of public opinion will in many cases make it difficult for a government to ignore a ruling that it has acted in breach of the Convention.

## Example

The UK Parliament passes the Derecognition of Trade Unions Act, under which the recognition provisions of the Employment Relations Act 1999 are abolished. A union complains that the government has refused to recognise it for collective bargaining purposes and that the Act is in breach of Article 11. The union may make a direct complaint against the government as a public body (see point 4 above) but it will almost certainly lose the action, as the ECtHR decided in *National Union of Belgian Police v Belgium* (1979) that the right to form trade unions did include the right to be recognised. It is this type of case which is most common where the allegation is not that the statute is directly contradictory to the Convention but that the Convention should be interpreted so that it includes a particular right which the statute infringes.

## RELEVANCE OF THE ECHR TO EMPLOYMENT LAW

Although the impact of the ECHR will be examined in detail in the context of individual chapters, the following is an indication of the main areas in which the ECHR has had, or may have, an impact on employment law:

## Article 6 (right to a fair trial)

This affects the procedures of employment tribunals and will have an impact on disciplinary proceedings, as the word 'trial' includes hearings that can determine civil rights or obligations. Thus, where a public authority conducts a hearing, Article 6 will be applicable if that hearing can result in a decision such as suspension or dismissal. If the proceedings are simply investigatory, then Article 6 will not be applicable. An allegation that Article 6 has been broken can be made in judicial review proceedings or the fact of the alleged breach can be relied on in other legal proceedings such as an unfair dismissal claim. Where the employer concerned is a private employer then Article 6 will only have relevance where a statutory provision is relied on which may be alleged to be in breach of the ECHR. The great difference is that it will not be possible to allege that internal disciplinary proceedings conducted by a private employer are illegal because of a breach of Article 6.

## Article 8 (right to respect for family and private life)

This will have an impact on interception of employees' communications and on data protection (see Chapter 5). It may also affect disciplinary proceedings and decisions to dismiss where the private life of the employee is an issue. A good example is *Treganowan v Robert Knee* (see Chapter 11).

## Article 9 (freedom of thought, conscience and religion)

This could be relevant where the employer requires employees to hold certain religious beliefs. This is very relevant to Church of England and Roman Catholic Schools, which normally require applicants for teaching posts to be practising members of their faith. However, s.60 of the School Standards and Framework Act 1998 explicitly allows schools with a denominational character to prefer staff who subscribe to the school's denominational ethos. An interesting point is the extent to which the EC Framework Directive will, when implemented, affect this right. This area is a fascinating example of the interplay between the ECHR and EC law.

## Article 10 (freedom of expression)

This could have been invoked by 'whistleblowers' facing dismissal because they had exposed malpractice within their organisation. However, the Public Interest Disclosure Act 1998 probably gives sufficient protection in these cases. This point is discussed further in Chapter 5.

## Article 11 (freedom of assembly and association)

This is the one article that has a direct bearing on employment law, as it is of great significance in the area of collective employment rights. It affects the right to join trade unions and thus the tortuous UK legislative provisions on trade union membership and the rules on industrial action and picketing need to read in the light of it. The impact of the ECHR is just beginning to be felt in this area with the recent decisions of the ECtHR in the cases of *Wilson v UK* (2002) and *Unison v UK* (2002). These are considered in Chapters 12 and 13.

## Article 14 (prohibition of discrimination)

This has, as explained above, an unusual status in that it is internal to the Convention, but many of the areas which it covers are also included in the EC Framework Directive (see Chapter 9).

# Chapter 4

# The employment relationship

## INTRODUCTION

The subject matter of this chapter is very simple: who is this book about? Clearly it is about employers and employees, but who are they? The notions of an employer and an employee may seem to be straightforward but, as we shall see, they are not. The main problem is with the definition of an employee but that of an employer also causes difficulties.

## EMPLOYERS

The statutory definition of an employer is not enlightening: s.230(4) of the Employment Rights Act 1996 (ERA) provides that an employer 'in relation to an employee or worker, means the person by whom the employee or worker is . . . employed'. This, of course, begs the question of precisely who does employ the employee.

The decision as to who is an employer is important in two situations:

1. Legal documents, such as a claim for unfair dismissal, need to be served on an employer. In this case there may be the practical question of who the employer is where the employer cannot be identified from any Statement of Initial Employment Particulars or written contract of employment because none was issued. In this case the question of who the employer is will come down to a matter of evidence, such as who actually engaged the employee and who paid the wages.

2. Various rights under employment law can only be claimed where the employee has a certain length of continuous employment, such as unfair dismissal (normally one year needed) and redundancy (two years needed). Suppose that an employee has changed employers and wishes to add the length of service with one employer to the length of service with the second. This will depend on whether he can count both employers as associated employers.

*Example*

X began employment with Y Co. on 1 January 1999. On 1 July 1999, X left Y Co. and went to work for Z Co. On 1 January 2000, X was dismissed by Z Co. X wishes to claim unfair dismissal but he only has six months' service with Z Co. However, if he can add the service with Y Co. to that with Z Co. then he will have a year's service. Y Co. and Z Co. are both subsidiaries of the same holding company, W Co.

The details of how to calculate continuous service will be dealt with in Chapter 6, but the important issue for the present is that if both Y Co. and Z Co. count as associated employers, then X will be able to add the service with both companies together and he will be able to claim for unfair dismissal.

Another instance where the question of associated employers is significant is where a redundant employee is made an offer of suitable alternative employment. As will be seen in Chapter 12, the refusal of such an offer can lead to the employee losing any right to a redundancy payment. Section 146(1) of the ERA has the effect that such an offer may be made by an associated employer as well, of course, by the actual employer of the employee.

Section 231 of the ERA 1996 provides that two employers shall be treated as associated if:

(a) one is a company of which the other (directly or indirectly) has control; or
(b) both are companies of which a third person (directly or indirectly) has control.

Three issues arise from this:

1. The concept of an associated employer can only arise when at least one of the employers was a company. This was significant in *Gardiner v Merton London Borough Council* (1981), where it was held that s.231 did not include local authorities and thus an employee could not add service with, in this case, four local authorities to enable him to calculate compensation for unfair dismissal by reference to his service with all of them. However, local government employees are deemed to have continuous employment for redundancy purposes when they move from one local authority to another.
2. However, the person who controls the company in situation (a) above need not be a company and could be a natural person, an unincorporated association, a partnership or any other form of organisation.
3. Section 231 provides that the test for deciding if employers are associated depends on whether the one not actually employing the employee has control of the other. In *Secretary of State for Employment v Newbold* (1981) it was held that control means voting control and therefore a person will be in control – and thus an associated employer – if they control a majority of the votes carried by the shares. An extension to this was suggested in *Zarb and Samuels v British and Brazilian Produce Co. (Sales)* (1978), where the EAT accepted an argument that the word 'control' can include a situation where two or more persons act together and between them own more than 50% of the voting shares. However, in *South West Launderettes v Laidler* (1986) the

21

Court of Appeal declined to follow the approach in *Zarb*, although later cases (such as *Tice v Cartwright* (1999) – a decision of the EAT) have followed *Zarb*. The matter awaits clarification. What can be said is that the concept of control, by focusing on ownership of shares, is narrow and fails to take account of ventures such as franchising and sub-contracting. Furthermore, one may, in practice, control a company without having a majority of the votes at meetings.

## EMPLOYEES

### ■ Introduction – different types of workers

The significance of the term 'employee' lies in the fact that employment law grants a large number of rights to employees which are not granted to workers who are not employees. For example, the right to claim for unfair dismissal and to claim a redundancy payment is only given to employees. The problem is that a satisfactory comprehensive definition has proved to be elusive and therefore, although in most cases it will be clear whether or not a person is an employee, there are a large, and increasing, number of cases where this is not so. What is unfortunate is that, whilst the law has been active since 1963 in giving an increasing number of rights to employees, it has not paid the same attention to the question of who is entitled to those rights.

In all of the following examples the employer, A Co., is a large manufacturing company and each example deals with a particular employee of A Co.

*Example 1*

B is employed on the factory floor assembling components. He works a regular 46-hour week.

*Example 2*

C works as the personal assistant to the managing director and works a regular 42-hour week.

*Example 3*

D works as a receptionist at the factory and her hours of work are 16 a week.

*Example 4*

E works as and when required to conduct parties of schoolchildren round the factory to give them an idea of what life in a factory is like. She has no fixed hours of work.

*Example 5*

F works from home as a designer for the company. She occasionally comes into the office and has no fixed hours of work, although her contract provides that she is to work a 44-hour week.

*Example 6*

G is working as a temporary secretary to cover for absence through illness but she was hired through an agency.

*Example 7*

H runs a taxi hire business which is frequently used by A Co. to transport both staff and visitors to the station and the airport.

The issue in each case is whether the person is an employee or not.

In examples 1 and 2, it is clear that B and C are employees. They work regular hours at the employer's place of business. In example 3, D is an employee although she only works part-time. It is clear that H, in example 7, is not an employee of A Co., as he has a business of his own. The difficult ones are examples 4, 5 and 6. D is a casual worker, E is a homeworker and G is an agency worker. These categories of worker have expanded greatly in recent years and the law has yet to devise a satisfactory way of deciding whether they are employees or not. In this chapter we shall explore how the law has sought to deal with persons in these categories.

## Terminology

The traditional distinction was between an employee and an independent contractor. Thus B, C, and D would be employees and H would be an independent contractor. Another way of putting it was to say that an employee has a 'contract of service', whereas an independent contractor had a 'contract for services'. This makes sense in example 7, where H's taxi firm supplies services in the form of transporting staff and visitors on behalf of A Co. One problem with this terminology is that the word 'service' can lead to an employee being called a 'servant'. The last example of the use of this term by the courts which I have been able to trace is that in the judgment of MacKenna J in *Ready Mixed Concrete (South East) Ltd v Minister of Pensions and National Insurance* (1968). A recent development is to use the term 'worker', which, as we shall see, is being increasingly used in recent legislation; and there is also a tendency in EC law to develop the rights of the 'citizen-worker'. In this chapter the term 'employee' will be used unless the context requires otherwise.

## Why is it important to be able to define who an employee is?

The significance of this was briefly mentioned earlier but the reasons in detail are as follows:

1. The growth in employment protection legislation since the passage of the Contracts of Employment Act 1963 has given employees vastly increased

rights. Not only this, but, as we shall see in Chapter 5, the courts have been active in developing the obligations of the employee at common law.

2. Employers also need to know who is an employee particularly as the common law places obligations on employees as well as employers – for instance, the obligation of confidentiality. Clearly, it is vital for employers to know whether a particular person is bound by this obligation.

3. The change in the composition of the workforce.

4. The growth in the impact of EC law has brought with it the challenge of integrating into UK law ideas derived from a legal system with different concepts.

Points 1 and 2 will become apparent in the course of this book, but we must now look at points 3 and 4 in detail.

## The changing composition of the workforce

### The nature of the change

The challenge to employment law is that the traditional pattern of most employees being in full-time jobs, where their status as employees was clear, is changing and, as the examples above show, it is becoming difficult to fit workers who are in newer patterns of work into the traditional category of employee. As McKendrick puts it:

> The Labour market in Britain is presently undergoing significant structural change. The principal change is a rapid increase in new, flexible forms and patterns of work which depart radically from the standard employment relationship whereby an employee works regularly (that is, full-time) and consistently for his employer under a contract of employment. This new flexible, 'atypical' workforce consists largely of the self-employed, part-time workers, casual workers, 'temps', homeworkers and those working on government training schemes.

(McKendrick, 'Vicarious Liability and Independent Contractors – A Re-Examination' (1990) 53 MLR 770.)

Another area which has grown and where there is an urgent need for clarification of the law is with volunteers. As Debra Morris argues ((1999) 28 ILJ 249), there is 'anecdotal evidence that voluntary organisations are denying benefits previously given to volunteers, in order to prevent their gaining employment rights'. As she puts it: 'Voluntary organisations *may* benefit from informal relationships with their volunteers, but is it not appropriate that volunteers should be able to take advantage of *relevant* employment protection legislation?'

### The statistical evidence

The evidence is that the trend from traditional full-time employment to other patterns of work accelerated greatly in the 1980s. In 'Labour Law in Flux – The Changing Composition of the Workforce' ((1997) 26 ILJ 337) S. Fredman points out that between 1981 and 1987 the number of full-time jobs of indefinite duration fell by 1.1 million from 70% of total employment to 64%. At the same time, non-standard jobs (i.e. of the kind referred to above) increased from 30% to 36% of total employment. Moreover, this trend has continued, as between 1995 and 1996 the number of part-time and self-employed workers increased by 264,000 and the number of temporary employees by 45,000. Looking at the statistics over a longer period, and taking the quarter March to May for comparative purposes, the total number of self-employed was nearly 3.2 million in 2001, a similar figure to that in 1993. However, the number of part-time workers, including both employed and self-employed, rose from just over 6 million in 1993 to just over 7 million in 2001. There is also a discernible increase in the number of workers with second jobs, to nearly 2 million (Labour Market Trends, September 2001 at S18). It must be probable that a number of these jobs are of the non-standard type referred to above.

## The impact of EC law

### The effect of EC Directives

A number of EC Directives apply to employees: Directive 77/187 on transfers of undertakings, Directive 80/987 on the rights of employees when their employer is insolvent, and Directive 91/533 on the information which must be given to employees on their terms and conditions of employment. The term 'employee' is, in principle, to be given the same meaning in a Member State as it has in the national laws of that Member State in accordance with the principle of subsidiarity. However, all of these Directives apply to 'every paid employee having a contract or employment relationship'. As B. Bercusson points out (see *European Labour Law* (London, 1996), especially Chapter 29, to which this account is greatly indebted) the significant point is the use of the phrase 'employment relationship', which obviously means relationships other than those where there is a contract of employment. Independent contractors would seem to be included (although the UK government, in a non-binding minute, said that they would be excluded), and Article 1(2)(b) of Directive 91/533 expressly states that the Directive applies to casual and/or specific workers unless its non-application to those categories is justified. Moreover, the Explanatory Memorandum to Directive 91/533 refers to the development of different work patterns leading, as it says, to 'an erosion of the criteria defining the traditional status of an employee'. Quite clearly, then, the phrase 'employment relationship' was drafted with this problem in mind. While it is true that the term 'employee' will be given the same meaning as it already has in each Member State, it is not clear precisely what 'employment relationship' means. As Bercusson points out, the whole idea of Directive 91/533 is to require information, in the words of Article 2(1), of the 'essential aspects of the employment relationship' and therefore the relationship must, by definition, be one where a certain amount of detail is available. Therefore, the Directive requires details of, for example, the date when the relationship began, how long it is expected to last, normal working time and remuneration. Very casual relationships would thus be excluded, as this detail would not be available.

### The concept of the worker in the Treaty of Amsterdam

Article 39 grants the right of free movement to all workers who have nationality in one of the Member States and who have crossed an internal frontier in order to take up an offer of employment. A well-known example is *Union Royal Belge des Societes de Football Association ASBL v Bosman* (1995), where a footballer successfully argued that this principle of free movement extended to free movement of footballers between clubs in the EC. Furthermore, the ECJ has stated that the concept of a 'worker' must be a Community law concept (*Unger v Bestuur* (1964)), unlike the term 'employee', and therefore the term 'worker' has the potential to develop a life of its own. Indeed, as pointed out by E. Szyszczak (*EC Labour Law* (Harlow: Longman, 2000) Chapter 3 of which is most illuminating on this whole area), 'a person may also be classed as a worker after having left the paid labour market where, for example, he/she takes up a vocational training course' (at p.59).

One can sum up the impact of EC law on the question of employment status by saying that, although it is not hugely significant at the moment, it has the potential to change completely this branch of the law through the increasing influence of the EC on social policy, including employment law.

## ■ The present law

The law at present is a mixture of statute and common law. Statute law will be examined first.

It cannot be said that statute law is particularly helpful. The definitions are not in themselves enlightening and there are a confusing number of them.

The fundamental definition of an employee is found in s.230(1) of the Employment Rights Act 1996 (ERA), which defines an employee as an 'individual who has entered into or works under (or, when the employment has ceased, worked under) a contract of employment'. When one turns to s.230(2) to find out what a contract of employment is, the answer turns out to be that a 'contract of employment means a contract of service or apprenticeship, whether express or implied, and (if it is express) whether oral or in writing'. Although this definition has some value, as we shall see later in this chapter, it does not help in defining the term 'employee', which is why the courts have had such an important role in this area. This definition applies to all claims under the ERA except those under Part II, for example claims for unfair dismissal, redundancy payments, rights to a Statement of Initial Employment Particulars, maternity rights, rights to time off work and guarantee payments.

However, other legislation has used wider terms. Section 230(3) refers to the term 'worker' and provides that a worker is either a person who has entered into a contract of employment or one who has entered into any other contract 'whereby the individual undertakes to do or perform personally any work or services for another party to the contract whose status is not by virtue of the contract that of a client or customer of any profession or business undertaking carried on by the individual'. In *Byrne Bros v Baird* (2002) the use of this definition in the Working Time Regulations (see Chapter 7) was considered and the EAT held that self-employed labour-only sub-contractors were within this definition.

It will be seen that this definition contains three elements:

1. A worker can be a person who has entered into a contract of employment.
2. Alternatively, a worker can be a person who, although not having a contract of employment, still undertakes to perform services personally.
3. A person will not be a worker where he/she is performing services for a professional client.

The important difference between the two definitions is the inclusion of elements 2 and 3 in the definition of a worker in s.230(3), whereas in the definition of an employee in s.230(1) only definition 1 is present. This definition of a worker has been used in trade union legislation for some time (see s.296(1) of TULRA 1992) and it is also used in discrimination legislation (but without element 3). However, here the definition is applied to an employee. (See s.1(6)(a) of the Equal Pay Act 1970, s.82(1) of the Sex Discrimination Act 1975, s.78(1) of the Race Relations Act 1976 and s.68(1) of the Disability Discrimination Act 1995.) It also applies to claims under Part II of the ERA, which deals with deductions from pay, but here the word 'worker' is used. The Health and Safety at Work Act 1974 defines an employee in the narrow sense as used in s.230(1), i.e. someone who works under a contract of service or apprenticeship.

A further definition is contained in the Transfer of Undertakings (Protection of Employment) Regulations 1981, which define an employee as a person who works for another 'whether under a contract of service or apprenticeship or otherwise but does not include anyone who provides services under a contract for services'. This is the narrowest of all the definitions.

It will be seen that, because different definitions are used, it is possible for a person to be able to bring a claim under one part of employment law but not under another. For example, a person will be able to claim under the discrimination legislation provided that he/she works personally for another but an actual contract of employment is needed for a claim for unfair dismissal. There have been few cases under any of these provisions, probably reflecting the fact that they are somewhat general, and therefore the main burden of defining employee status has fallen on the courts. A recent example of the interpretation of statutory provisions, however, is found in *Loughran and Kelly v Northern Ireland Housing Executive* (1998), which involved a claim under the Fair Employment (Northern Ireland) Act 1976, where the phrase 'personally to execute any work or labour' was used. It was held that this covered a solicitor who was a partner in a firm.

It is not easy to see a reason for the different definitions except that Parliament may have felt that, as a matter of policy, discrimination legislation should have the widest possible scope. In the case of trade union legislation the object was to give trade unions immunity from actions in tort (see Chapters 13 and 14) where there was a trade dispute and this could be where the dispute concerned 'workers' as well as employees in the narrow sense. Therefore, the wider the definition of 'worker', the greater protection would be given to trade unions acting on their behalf.

The White Paper *Fairness at Work* (1998) signalled the beginning of an attempt to extend a wider definition of who is entitled to employment protection rights, whether the term 'worker' or 'employee' is used. The White Paper said that the government sought views on whether some or all employment protection rights should be extended to 'all those who work for another person'. There was concern about the use of zero hours contracts, where a person has no set working hours but is required to be available to the employer although there is no guarantee that they will be called on to work. One result was the inclusion in the Employment Relations Act 1999 of s.23, which allows the Secretary of State to extend the scope of employment legislation to groups not already covered by it. Thus, orders can be made providing that individuals can be treated as parties to workers' contracts or contracts of employment and can make provision as to who are to be regarded as the employers of individuals. This power could be used to bring many workers within the scope of employment law whose status at present is doubtful, such as casual workers, homeworkers, agency workers and workers on zero hours contracts. So far it has not been used, but in *Montgomery v Johnson Underwood* (2001) the Court of Appeal felt that it could be used to clarify the status of those who find work through employment agencies.

Recent legislation has tended to be wider in scope anyway. The National Minimum Wage Act 1998 applies to agency workers and homeworkers (see ss.34 and 35) and the Public Interest (Disclosure) Act 1998 applies to groups of workers who are not covered by the term as defined by s.230(3) of the ERA (the wider definition): agency workers; homeworkers; NHS doctors, dentists, ophthalmologists and pharmacists; trainees on vocational or work experience schemes. The Working Time Regulations 1998 also apply to agency workers. However, the definition of an agency worker is different in the Public Interest (Disclosure) Act from those in the other two pieces of legislation.

One possibility is that the government could adopt the proposals in *Working Life*, published by the Institute of Employment Rights in 1996. This suggests that what it calls the 'core of rights' in the employment relationship should apply to all who work under a contract to personally execute any work or labour and who are economically dependent on the business of the other. The effect would be to apply the wide definition of an employee/worker to all 'core' employment protection rights. It further proposes that equal treatment legislation and certain collective rights should also apply to those who normally work and to those seeking work.

## Part-time workers

Part-time workers now have a measure of special protection as a result of the Part-time Workers (Prevention of Less Favourable Treatment) Regulations 2000, which came into force on 1 July 2000. This was passed as a result of the EC Directive on Part-time Work (Directive 97/81/EC) and, as a broad principle, gives a part-time worker the right not to be less favourably treated than a full-time worker. One could say that it prohibits discrimination against part-time workers in the same way as equal opportunities legislation prohibits discrimination on the grounds of sex, race and disability. However, the details are different.

### Which workers do the Regulations apply to?

Regulation 1(2) adopts the definition in s.230(3) of the ERA. Therefore, a worker is anyone who either has a contract of employment or who undertakes to personally perform work for the other party with the usual proviso that this does not include situations where the worker is performing services for a professional client.

### What is meant by a part-time worker?

The Regulations adopt the interesting and novel principle of relying on 'custom and practice' to decide this, rather than complex statutory formulae. One suspects that this is the right approach in that, although it will lead to litigation on the question of 'custom and practice', this will be preferable to adding yet more complexity to employment law.

Accordingly, Regulation 2(2) provides that a worker is part-time if, 'having regard to the custom and practice of the employer in relation to workers employed by the worker's employer under the same type of contract, [he/she] is not identifiable as a full-time worker'. There is a similar definition of a full-time worker in Regulation 2(1) (but stating that the worker by custom and practice is regarded as full-time).

Three points should be noted:

1. The Regulations also add that both sets of workers must be paid wholly or in part by reference to the time they work.
2. A comparison can only be made for custom and practice purposes between workers who, broadly speaking, are employed by the same employer in the same organisation. This point is dealt with in more detail below, but the significant issue here is that the custom and practice of one employer, or in a trade or profession generally, is not relevant: what matters is the custom and practice of the employer against whom the claim is being made.
3. This appears to be the first time that the phrase 'custom and practice' has been used in statute law and any interpretation of it by the courts will be bound to have an effect on the common law of employment.

### How is the comparison to be made?

The Regulations do this in two stages:

(a) Regulation 1(2) lays down the 'pro-rata' principle, which is to apply unless 'it is inappropriate' (Regulation 5(3)). This means that where a full-time worker receives or is entitled to pay or any other benefit, then a part-time worker is entitled to receive that benefit pro-rata according to the number of hours worked by him/her in comparison to those worked by the full-time worker. Regulation 2(3) provides that weekly hours shall be calculated without counting overtime and that, where hours vary, the average shall be taken. However, even though the pro-rata principle applies, it is still open to the employer to argue that the difference in treatment is 'objectively justified' (Regulation 5(2)). This term is intended to have the same meaning as in the Sex Discrimination and Race Relations Acts and its meaning will be discussed in Chapter 9.

(b) Regulation 2(4) then sets out which full-time workers are to be the comparators. There is a three stage test:

(i)   The workers must be employed by the same employer under the same type of contract.

(ii)  They must be engaged in the same or a broadly similar form of work having regard, where relevant, to whether they have similar qualifications, skills and experience.

(iii) The full-time worker must be based at the same establishment as the part-time worker or, if there is no full-time worker based at that establishment, then a comparison may be made with a full-time worker based at another establishment provided always that both employees are employed by the same employer. Accordingly, a comparison cannot be made with a notional full-time worker. The worker must actually exist.

### What benefits can be claimed?

Regulation 5 provides that the right to not less favourable treatment extends to:

1. Treatment according to the terms of the contract. Thus it applies to rates of pay, sick pay and maternity pay, occupational pension schemes, access to training, leave, and career breaks. It also applies to selection for redundancy and therefore part-timers should be treated no less favourably than full-timers (see Chapter 12). (The guidance attached to the Regulations is particularly helpful in giving examples.) Overtime is dealt with by a special provision (Regulation 5(4)), which states that where the part-time worker has completed the number of hours which a full-time worker would need to work to qualify for overtime then the part-time worker will be entitled to overtime. This will be a particularly helpful change for part-timers as at the moment there is no right to overtime once they have worked beyond their normal hours.

2. A right not to be subjected to any detriment by the employer for exercising their rights under the Regulations. This is a similar right to that which exists under other employment protection legislation.

Other provisions:

1. Regulations 4 and 5 deal with the situation where a worker who was full-time and then returns to work part-time (whether or not after absence). They

provide that a worker in these cases has the right to be treated no less favourably than before, although the 'objective justification defence' will apply.

2. Regulation 6 gives a part-time worker who believes that he/she has been treated less favourably under the terms of Regulation 5 the right to receive a written statement of the reasons for this from the employer within 21 days of the request. A failure by the employer to comply can lead the tribunal to draw inferences, including that the employer has infringed the right in question.

3. Regulation 7 gives workers the right to complain to an employment tribunal that his/her rights have been infringed and the tribunal may award compensation as well as make a declaration and recommend that the employer takes action to remedy the adverse effects on the complainant of the unequal treatment, i.e. that the employer treats equally in future. There is no ceiling on compensation. Proceedings must be brought within three months of the date of the less favourable treatment, although there is the usual proviso allowing complaints to be considered out of time if it is just and equitable to do so.

4. An employee who is dismissed shall be regarded as having been unfairly dismissed if the reason or principal reason for the dismissal is that the worker asserted his/her rights under these Regulations. This provision is found throughout employment law but here it includes the seeking of a written statement under Regulation 6.

### Relationship between the Part-time Workers Regulations and the Sex Discrimination Act

As will be seen in detail in Chapter 9, the Sex Discrimination Act 1986 has been used to establish that discrimination against part-timers amounted to indirect sex discrimination because of the considerably larger number of women compared with men employed part-time in many organisations. In future, such claims can be brought instead under these Regulations with the advantage that there will be no need to prove as a first stage that there was an adverse impact on the ground of sex. Therefore, claims will be possible where all or most of the workers in an organisation are women or, for that matter, men.

### Fixed-term employees

Following on from the above Regulations on part-time workers, the Fixed-Term Employees (Prevention of Less Favourable Treatment) Regulations 2002 came into force on 1 October 2002. These were also introduced as a result of an EC Directive, in this case the Fixed Term Work Directive and can be seen as part of a process of attempting to ensure that those engaged in atypical work patterns (i.e. other than full-time work on permanent contracts) are not disadvantaged in their employment rights. The proposed directive on agency work (see below) is part of the same pattern.

The Regulatory Impact Assessment on these Regulations estimated that the number of those working on fixed-term contracts in the UK is between 1.1 and 1.3 million and a higher proportion (just over half of the total) are in the public sector. The public sector accounts for 70% of those who have been in fixed-term contracts for more than two years.

### To whom do the Regulations apply?

The striking difference from the Part-time Workers Regulations is that these only apply to employees and not to workers, as the definition adopted is that in s.230 (1) of the ERA and not that in s.230(3).

### What is meant by a fixed-term employee?

The simple answer is that it is an employee on a fixed-term contract. The Regulations (Regulation 1(2)) define such a contract as either one which is made for a specific term fixed in advance or one which terminates automatically when a particular task is completed or upon the occurrence or non-occurrence of a specific event. It is not clear whether this includes contracts which can be ended by notice before the fixed term is up (this point is considered further in Chapter 11 when discussing dismissal for failure to renew a fixed-term contract). Other employees are defined as permanent and they are the comparators.

### The right not to be less favourably treated

This is contained in Regulation 3 and gives a right not to be less favourably treated than a permanent employee as regards the terms of the contract or being subjected to any other detriment. The general principle for deciding whether less favourable treatment has occurred is the pro-rata one, as for part-time workers, unless it is inappropriate. A fixed-term employee will not be less favourably treated if the difference in treatment is justified on objective grounds (Regulation 4). This means that an employer will establish justification where the contract of the fixed-term employee is, *taken as a whole*, not less favourable than that given to permanent employees. This 'package approach' differs from that adopted in the Part-time Workers Regulations, where a straightforward comparison in terms of the benefits received is made. The intention is to allow the employer and employee to negotiate a total package where greater benefits are received in some areas but less favourable treatment than permanent employees receive is given elsewhere, provided that, as a whole, there is no less favourable treatment. A possible example would be *less* favourable pension benefits but *more* favourable pay rates. The phrase 'as a whole' could lead to some complex cases unless the courts devise a formula that excludes most decisions in this area from the need for judicial scrutiny.

### Employment Act 2002

The right to not less favourable treatment is to be extended to pay and pensions as a result of provisions in the Employment Act 2002.

### Regulation 3(2)

It is specifically provided by Regulation 3(2) that a fixed-timer must not be treated less favourably as regards any periods of service qualification, the opportunity to receive training and the opportunity to secure permanent employment. So far as the last right is concerned, Regulation 3(5) provides that a fixed-timer has the right to be informed of any vacancies in the establishment.

### Regulation 2

The comparison with a permanent employee is, by Regulation 2, to be made with one who is employed by the same employer and engaged in the same or broadly similar work having regard, where relevant, to whether they have the same or similar levels of skills, qualifications and experience. The comparator must be based at the same establishment or, where there is no comparator there, then a comparison can be made with a comparator at a different establishment.

### Regulation 8

One of the most significant provisions is in Regulation 8, which provides that where an employee has been employed under one or more fixed-term contracts for four years or more *and* the employment under a fixed-term contract was not justified under objective grounds, *then* if the contract is renewed or they are re-engaged under a new contract without continuity of employment being broken then the new contract will be a *permanent* one. No period of continuous service before 10 July 2002 counts and so the effect is that the earliest date by which an employee could claim a permanent contract as a result of these provisions is 10 July 2006. It will be possible for a workforce or collective agreement to amend this rule by, for example, specifying different maximum numbers of fixed-term contracts. See Chapter 6 for details of the rules on continuity of employment and Chapter 7 for details of collective and workforce agreements.

### Example

Terry was employed by Ambridge College of Technology as a lecturer under a series of one year fixed-term contracts beginning in September 2002. He is offered another one year fixed-term contract in September 2006. This will now be a permanent contract, as the period for which the fixed-term contracts ran was four years unless the college establishes an objective justification for the fixed-term contract.

Thus, the effect of Regulation 8 is to put a cap on fixed-term contracts of four years unless objectively justified.

### Waiver clauses

Waiver clauses, under which employees employed under a fixed-term contract for two years or more may waive their right to a redundancy payment (s.197(3) ERA), are to be abolished.

### Other provisions

There are the same provisions relating to the right to receive a written statement of reasons for alleged less favourable treatment, complaint to an employment tribunal and dismissal, as are found in the Part-time Workers Regulations.

### Proposed Directive on agency work

The EC is consulting on a Directive which will provide that agency workers shall have the same treatment as permanent workers in the client company unless the difference is objectively justified. The proposal is that equal treatment will not be required for posts of six weeks or less, or where the workers are covered by a collective agreement or where the worker has a permanent post. Also, the government issued a Discussion Paper in July 2002 asking for views on whether ministers of religion (see below) should be granted employment status along with others such as agency workers and homeworkers.

## TESTS USED BY THE COURTS TO ESTABLISH WHETHER AN EMPLOYMENT RELATIONSHIP EXISTS

Given that statute does not provide any detailed guidance on when there is an employment relationship, the focus naturally shifts to the courts, who have over the years highlighted a number of tests to try answer this question. All of these tests still tell us something of value and indeed the first test is illustrated by both the oldest case and the newest case considered below. It should be borne in mind that in cases up to 1968, at least, the word 'servant' or 'workman' was sometimes used but, for consistency, the term 'employee' will be used throughout.

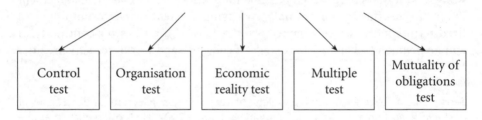

| Control test | Organisation test | Economic reality test | Multiple test | Mutuality of obligations test |

## ■ Control test

In *Walker v Crystal Palace Football Club Ltd* (1909) the issue was whether a footballer was employed by the club so as to enable him to claim compensation under the Workmen's Compensation Act 1906 as a result of an accident whilst playing in a match. It was argued for the club that he was not covered by the Act and reliance was placed on the words of Bramwell LJ in *Yewens v Noakes* (1880), where he defined an employee as 'a person subject to the command of his master as to the manner in which he shall do his work'. The Court of Appeal in *Walker* nevertheless held that it was enough that he was obliged to obey the general directions of the club even though he clearly exercised his own judgement as to how to play.

The recent case of *Motorola v Davidson and Melville Craig Group Ltd* (2001) shows the continuing relevance of the control test. Davidson was recruited by Melville Craig, who ran what amounted to an employment agency and who supplied temporary workers to Motorola. Davidson was accordingly assigned to work at Motorola. His job was as an analyser, repairing mobile telephones. His contract with Melville Craig provided that he was bound to comply with all reasonable instructions and requests made by Motorola. However, Motorola then terminated his assignment and the question was whether he was an employee of Motorola and therefore able to claim unfair dismissal against it. The EAT held that he was an employee of Motorola, relying on Davidson's obligation to obey their instructions which gave them a right of control. In *Montgomery v Johnson Underwood Ltd* (2001) the applicant was registered with an agency but was sent to work for the same client for two years. She subsequently brought unfair dismissal proceedings against both the agency and the client. It was held that the agency did not have sufficient control over the applicant for her to be their employee. The Court of Appeal held that the two essential tests for the existence of a contract of employment were control and mutuality. (The concept of mutuality of obligations is dealt with later in this chapter.) Another recent case involving agency agreements is *Hewlett Packard Ltd v O'Murphy* (2001). A computer specialist set up a company which made a contract with an employment agency under which his services were hired out to another firm (the end-user). The EAT held that he was not an employee of the end-user as there was simply no contract between him and the end-user.

All of these cases can be seen as reflecting social trends. In *Walker* there was clearly a need for the law to move beyond the outdated concept of control set out in *Yewens v Noakes*. In *Motorola* the court recognised that if an employee under an agency agreement could not claim unfair dismissal against the client firm it would be unlikely that he/she could claim successfully against the agency, which would simply say that it had no choice but to comply with the client's request to remove that employee from the client firm. The decision in *Motorola* is thus of considerable significance in extending the rights of agency workers.

## The organisation test

In *Stevenson Jordan and Harrison Ltd v McDonald and Evans* (1952) Denning LJ suggested that a person would be an employee if their work was integrated into the business rather than accessory to it. This test has an attractive simplicity to it and was useful in making it clear at the time that skilled professionals, such as doctors in the NHS, were employees. However, it is not satisfactory when dealing with problems of outworkers and workers employed by sub-contractors. Even so, it still has its part to play.

## The economic reality test

This asks whether the worker is working for himself/herself or is working for another. If the worker takes the risk of making profits or losses then he/she is not likely to be held to be an employee. It appears to originate from decisions in the USA and Canada. In *United States of America v Silk* (1946) the Supreme Court said that the test was whether workers 'were employees as a matter of economic reality'. The test was applied in *Market Investigations v Minister of Social Security* (1969), which concerned an interviewer who worked for the company part-time carrying out market research. She could do the work at whatever time she wished provided that it was done within the allotted time. The High Court held that despite the autonomy given to her in how she actually arranged to do the work, she was not working for herself but for another and thus she was an employee. Cooke J outlined a number of factors to assist in deciding whether a person was in business on his/her own account or not:

> whether the man performing the services provides his own equipment, whether he hires his own helpers, what degree of financial risk he takes, what degree of responsibility for investment and management he has, and whether and how far he has an opportunity of profiting from sound management in the performance of his task.

Furthermore, Cooke J observed that although it may be easier to apply this test where the worker is running an established business of his/her own, a person may still be an independent contractor where he/she does not have an existing business.

Cooke J was, in effect, providing a checklist of factors to decide employee status but the disadvantage of this is that it can encourage a mechanistic approach whereby one simply ticks off factors without looking at the relationship as a whole. Moreover, in *Hall v Lorimer* (1994) Nolan LJ pointed out that the question of whether an person is in business on their own account 'may be of little assistance in the case of one carrying on a profession or vocation. A self-employed author working from home or an actor or singer may earn his living without any of the normal trappings of a business'. In this case the worker was a television technician who worked for about 20 television companies, usually for no more than a day at a time. He was held to be self-employed.

In *Lorimer* the question of status arose in the context of tax, but in the context of liability for injuries to the worker at work the courts may reach a different conclusion. In *Lane v Shire Roofing Co. (Oxford) Ltd* (1995) a roofer who traded as a one-man firm and who was self-employed for tax purposes suffered serious injuries when working for the defendants, who had employed him on a payments by results basis. It was held that he was an employee. Henry J, having outlined various factors in the employee-or-not equation, then remarked that 'these questions must be asked in the context of who is responsible for the overall safety of the men in question'. The decision is therefore clearly a policy one, designed to ensure that, so far as possible, those employing staff are responsible for their safety, and is none the worse for that although the fact that the courts can reach different decisions on employee status depending on the nature of the claim does nothing for clarity in this branch of the law.

## ▉ The multiple test

The leading case is *Ready Mixed Concrete (South East) v Minister of Pensions and National Insurance* (1968). The issue was whether the company was liable to pay national insurance contributions for a lorry driver employed by it. The contract between the driver and the company stated that the driver was self-employed and it obliged him to maintain, repair and insure the lorry, to wear the company's uniform and not to use the lorry except on the company's business. If he was unable to work then a replacement had to be hired by him. He was paid by a rate per mile for a specified quantity of cement delivered. It was held that he was an independent contractor because the contract was one of carriage rather than one of employment: 'The ownership of the assets, the chance of profit and the risk of loss in the contract of carriage are his and not the company's.' A significant factor was that the driver could hire a substitute, albeit with the consent of the company, and one who had to be competent, a point that will be dealt with below, although it must be said that, on the facts, the relationship looks very much like one of employment.

In the course of his judgment, MacKenna J stated that a contract of service existed if:

(a)  the employee agreed in consideration of a wage or other remuneration to provide his own work and skill in the performance of some service for his employer;
(b)  the employee agreed that in the performance of the service he would be subject to the control of the other party sufficient to make him his master;
(c)  the other provisions of the contract were consistent with its being a contract of service.

It may be questioned whether the multiple test and MacKenna LJ's words really add anything to the law on employee status. The term 'wage or other remuneration' is so general that it excludes nothing and the reiteration of the control test tells us nothing new. The final part appears to add nothing, but in *Montgomery v Johnson Underwood Ltd* (2001) Buckley J said that it meant that 'all the terms of the agreement must be considered', which brings in the multiple test. The only significant feature is the emphasis on 'his *own* work and skill' (my italics) which, as we will see, has led subsequent courts down a blind alley. It could be argued that this test says nothing more than is already said by the economic reality test. In essence, the two tests are similar in trying to avoid one all-embracing phrase such as 'control' or 'integration' but they both fall into the trap of appearing to suggest a mechanical 'ticking off of factors' approach. Nevertheless, in the most recent decision of the Court of Appeal, *Montgomery v Johnson Underwood Ltd* (2001), MacKenna J's formulation was approved with the explanation that test (i) means mutuality of obligations (see below) and test (ii) means control. If this is so, then the combination of these two tests may be a useful tool for solving disputes about employment status.

## ■ The mutuality of obligations test

This test has gained currency in recent years in dealing with casual workers and other workers, such as homeworkers, who do not fit into the traditional pattern of employment. It focuses on the obligations which the parties owe each other to decide if there is an employment relationship.

It is worth mentioning at the outset that there are three possibilities in cases of these types of workers, especially casual workers:

1. to decide that the workers are independent contractors;
2. to decide that the workers are employed each time that they are engaged;
3. to decide that they have a global contract, i.e. one which continues even though they are not actually engaged.

The starting point is *O'Kelly and others v Trusthouse Forte plc* (1983). The applicants were 'regular casuals' employed at a hotel who claimed that they had been unfairly dismissed for being members of a trade union and taking part in its activities. They therefore needed to prove that they were employees. The industrial tribunal listed 18 relevant factors and, of these, the following were in favour of employee status: they were not in business on their own account; they were subject to the conditions of the hotel; and they needed permission to take time off from rostered duties. However, two factors were decisive against their claim:

1. The intention of the parties in the light of custom and practice in the hotel industry was not to create a relationship of employer and employee.
2. Mutuality of obligation was missing. As Ackner LJ put it: 'The "assurance of preference in the allocation of any available work" which the regulars enjoyed was no more than a firm expectation in practice. It was not a contractual promise.' Had the applicants refused to accept a particular piece of casual work then they would not have been liable for breach of contract. Therefore, there could not be, in the terminology used above, a global contract of employment.

This decision has been criticised on the ground that the introduction of a requirement of mutual obligations means that employees with irregular or variable contracts will be unable to fulfil this requirement and so lose employee status. It is argued by P. Leighton (at (1984) 13 ILJ 62 and especially 65–66) that a flexible approach to the question of employee status with 'evidence of control coupled with *de facto* interdependence' could mean that workers such as cab drivers, homeworkers, building workers and door-to-door salesmen were employees. The requirement of mutuality could mean that this opportunity is lost.

The concerns expressed by Leighton may have been unnecessary in the case of homeworkers, although not in the case of others, because of the decision of the Court of Appeal in *Nethermere (St. Neots) Ltd v Taverna and Gardiner* (1984). The applicants were homeworkers who made garments for the company and the question was the extent to which there were mutual obligations. The workers could fix their hours of work and vary the number of garments which they took, but Dillon LJ found that the workers were obliged to take a reasonable amount of work and the company was obliged to provide a reasonable amount of work. Neither of these obligations were written down but the course of dealing between the parties over several years gave rise to mutual obligations on both sides sufficient to lead the court to hold that there was a contract of employment. A similar decision had been reached in the earlier case of *Airfix Footwear Ltd v Cope* (1978), where a homeworker who had assembled shoes for the company for seven years was held to be an employee on the basis of the regularity of the relationship over a period of time.

Conversely, in *Wickens v Champion Employment* (1984), the mutual obligations test was used to deny employment status to temporary workers engaged by an employment agency because the agency was not bound to make any bookings for them and they were not bound to accept bookings which were made. A more helpful decision for employees was *McMeechan v Secretary of State for Employment* (1997), in which the Court of Appeal held that an agency worker can have the status of an employee in relation to a particular engagement although there is no employment status under the general terms of the agreement (i.e. no global contract) because of the lack of mutual obligations. On the other hand, in *Clark v Oxfordshire Health Authority* (1998) a 'bank nurse' was denied a 'global' contract of employment as the health authority did not guarantee her any work; she was simply available as and when needed. The question of whether she had a contract of employment each time she worked was remitted to the employment tribunal. Note also the tendency of statute law, as mentioned above, to bring agency workers under its protection in a few recent instances.

It had been hoped that the House of Lords would bring much-needed clarity to this area of the law in its decision in *Carmichael v National Power plc* (1999), but the opportunity was not taken to review the law in detail and to state any general principles. The applicants were guides at power stations who worked on a 'casual as required' basis. They were offered and accepted work as it arose but there was no guarantee of work, nor did they always accept work which was offered. The issue was whether they were employees and so entitled to a Statement of Initial Employment Particulars. The House of Lords held that they did not have a 'global' contract of employment. Irvine LC stated that: 'The parties incurred no obligations to accept or provide work but at best assumed moral obligations of loyalty in a context where both recognised that the best interests of each lay in being accommodating to the other.'

The difficulty is that after more than 20 years of trying to decide on a suitable test for the existence of an employment relationship on the basis of mutual obligations, the law remains in a confused state. This is particularly unfortunate because, as we have seen, this test has been applied in situations, such as agency work, which frequently arise today and where there is accordingly a particular need for clarification. One way forward would be for the courts to recognise that the mutual obligations test has not provided the answer, at least by itself, and to apply another test, such as that of control as well, as suggested in *Montgomery v Johnson Underwood* (2001).

## OTHER POINTS WHICH MAY BE RELEVANT TO THE QUESTION OF EMPLOYMENT STATUS

### The description given by the parties to their relationship

In *Ferguson v John Dawson and Partners (Contractors) Ltd* (1976) the claimant worked on a building site, was subject to the employer's orders as to what he did, and used tools provided by the employer. However, the site agent said in evidence that when the claimant went to work for the company, he said to the plaintiff that 'there were no cards. We were working purely as a lump labour force'. (The term 'lump' meant that the workers were paid a lump sum and it was their job to pay tax and national insurance. The term was frequently used in the building trade.) The Court of Appeal held that on the evidence the claimant was an employee and that any declaration by the parties to the contrary would be disregarded. Megaw LJ said that: 'I find difficulty in accepting that the parties, by a mere expression of intention as to what the legal relationship should be, can in any way influence the conclusion of law as to what the relationship is.'

However, this robust statement by Megaw LJ may have disguised a policy consideration, in that the claim was for injuries sustained at work and to have held that he was not an employee would have deprived him of compensation for his injuries. The decision can thus be viewed in the same light as that in *Lane v Shire Roofing Co. Ltd* (1995), discussed above. Support for this view is given by the decision of the Court of Appeal in *Massey v Crown Life Insurance* (1978). Massey was the branch manager of one of the company's offices and asked to change his status from that of an employee to that of an independent contractor, as this would be to his advantage from the tax point of view. He was later dismissed and sought to claim unfair dismissal. It was held that he had changed his status and therefore could not do so. No doubt the court was influenced by the fact that Massey clearly wanted it both ways: it suited him to say that he was self-employed for tax purposes but it suited him to say that he was an employee when he needed to do so to claim unfair dismissal. Clearly, this would be wrong in principle. There was also a difference on the facts between this case and that of *Ferguson*: in *Ferguson* the worker was simply presented with a statement about his status, the legal significance of which he probably did not appreciate; in *Massey* the worker knew exactly what he was doing and indeed he suggested the change of status.

One can perhaps sum up the law in this area by saying that where it is obvious that a worker is either an employee or an independent contractor then any label attached to the relationship by the parties will be ignored. If, however, the case is borderline then a label will be taken into account, subject always to the nature of the claim being considered.

## The extent to which the worker contracts to perform services personally

*Example*

Y employs X and X agrees with Y that if, for whatever reason, she is unable to perform her duties then she will arrange for someone else to perform them instead. In all other respects X is clearly an employee of Y. Does the inclusion of this term mean that she will not, after all, be classed as an employee? The question is really whether the worker is contracting to provide services which are not necessarily his/her own services.

The starting point is a statement of MacKenna J in *Ready Mixed Concrete (South East) v Minister of Pensions and National Insurance* (1968), a case discussed above. He stated that: 'Freedom to do a job either by one's own hands or by another's is inconsistent with a contract of service though a limited or occasional power of delegation may not be.' It will be recalled that here the driver could hire a competent substitute with the consent of the company and this was one factor in the decision that he was not an employee.

It will be seen that the power to hire a substitute was not absolute: the substitute had to be competent and the consent of the company was needed. A more extreme example of the power occurred in *Express and Echo Publications Ltd v Tanton* (1999). Tanton originally worked for the company as an employee but he was made redundant and he later accepted employment with them as a driver on what he originally accepted was a self-employed basis. A clause in his contract stated that: 'In the event that the contractor is unable or unwilling to perform the services personally he shall arrange at his own expense entirely for another suitable person to perform the services.' Tanton never signed the contract but worked according to its terms and on one occasion did arrange for a substitute. Peter Gibson LJ in the Court of Appeal held that 'where, as here, a person who works for another is not required to perform his services personally, then as a matter of law the relationship between that person and the person for whom he works is not that of employer and employee'.

In the subsequent case of *McFarlane v Glasgow City Council* (2001) Lindsay J in the EAT categorised the clause in *Tanton* as 'extreme': 'The individual there, at his own choice, need never turn up for work. He could, moreover, profit from his absence if he could find a cheaper substitute. He could choose the substitute and then, in effect, he would be the master.' In this case the EAT distinguished *Tanton* on the facts. The applicants were gymnastic instructors and their contracts allowed them, if they were unable to take a class, to arrange for a substitute from a register of instructors maintained by the council. It was held that this was a much more limited power than in *Tanton*, as it only applied if the instructor was actually unable to take a class and did not apply otherwise, thus it would not be possible for the instructors never to turn up, as would theoretically have been the case in *Tanton*. However, although the cases undoubtedly are distinguishable, one cannot help but feel that the EAT in *McFarlane* had no great enthusiasm for *Tanton* and was concerned lest the law got itself into a position where any power to employ a substitute automatically meant that the relationship was not one of employer and employee. In *Byrne Brothers v Baird* (2002) (above) the existence of a clause in the contracts of workers allowing them to engage a substitute with the agreement of the contractor and only where he was unable to provide the service was held not to prevent the workers being classed as such for the purposes of the Working Time Directive.

## IS EMPLOYMENT STATUS A QUESTION OF FACT OR LAW?

Readers may be surprised by this question, given the detailed discussion of decisions of the courts in this chapter. Obviously the law has something to say about employment status. The issue is really whether an appeal tribunal (the EAT, Court of Appeal or House of Lords) can interfere with the decision of the employment tribunal on the facts themselves or whether the role of the appeal tribunal is confined to cases where the employment tribunal has applied the wrong test as a matter of law. The point is important in practice, as s.21 of the Industrial Tribunals Act 1996 provides that appeals only lie from decisions of employment tribunals on a point of law.

In *O'Kelly v Trusthouse Forte* (1984) the Court of Appeal held that the question of employee status was one of mixed law and fact. This was reinforced in *Lee Ting-Sang v Chung Chi-Keung* (1990), where Lord Griffiths said that 'where the relationship has to be determined by an investigation and evaluation of the factual circumstances in which the work is performed', this is a question of fact 'to be determined by the trial court'. The only exception, according to Lord Griffiths, was where the relationship was dependent on the construction of a written document, as in *Davies v Presbyterian Church of Wales* (1986), where the employment status of a clergyman was in issue. In such a case the question would be one of law.

The position therefore seems to be that where the question is purely one of applying established rules to the facts, the decision will be one of fact with which the appellate courts cannot interfere. The problem is that it is often difficult to decide precisely what the established rules are in particular cases, which is why there seems to be no decrease in the number of appeals on the question of employee status. Thus the question of whether employment status is one of fact or law is, given the current unsettled state of the law, less significant than it might be.

## THE STATUS OF PARTICULAR TYPES OF WORKERS

### Company directors

Non-executive company directors will not be employees but an executive or managing director could be an employee. If the director works full-time for the company and is paid a salary then there seems no reason why he/she should not be an employee (see *Folami v Nigerline (UK) Ltd* (1978)) but problems arise where the matter is not so clear cut. In *Parsons v Albert J Parsons & Sons Ltd* (1979) the director worked full-time but he had no written contract of employment and his remuneration was expressed as 'directors fees'. In the most recent case, *Secretary of State for Trade and Industry v Bottrill* (1999), the Court of Appeal held that there was no rule that where a director was the controlling shareholder of a company then he/she could not be an employee. The issue was one of fact in each case. Previously, the EAT had held in *Buchan v Secretary of State* (1997) that the existence of a controlling shareholding did make a difference as, given that in practice there would be little difference between the director and the company, it would be wrong that such a person should be able to claim unpaid wages from the state when he/she had put the company into liquidation. One can certainly see the force of the argument in *Buchan* but for now it does not represent the law.

## Ministers of religion

As a general rule ministers of religion do not have employee status, although there have been attempts to argue the contrary. These have floundered on various grounds. In *McMillan v Guest* (1942) it was held that this was a case of an office rather than employment and in *President of the Methodist Conference v Parfitt* (1984) Dillon J said that 'the minister sets out to serve God as his master; I do not think that it is right to say that in the legal sense he is at the point of ordination undertaking by contract to serve the church or the conference as his master throughout the years of his ministry'. As pointed out by Gillian Evans ('The Employment Status of Ministers of Religion' (1997) Law and Justice 32), the issue of control is not clear cut in the relationship between a clergyman and his/her bishop because a bishop, theologically, has supervision or 'oversight' of his clergy, which is in a way what she calls a 'personal binding of minister to supervisor'.

The issue is important because, as Emma Brodin has said ((1996) 25 ILJ 224): 'There are approximately 10,000 male and female priests in the Church of England. This is a significant number of workers who are denied employment rights and who have no satisfactory alternative procedure.' To this must be added clergy of all other denominations and a sizeable figure then emerges. She points out that the MSF Union has a clergy section and this topic could well see further developments (see the July 2002 Discussion Paper on this, mentioned earlier in this chapter).

## Office holders

This category includes those who have a particular status as the holder of an office. Although there may be doubt as to whether they are employees in the strict sense because they hold an office rather than being employed by someone else, they do have rights under employment protection legislation. Thus in *Miles v Wakefield Metropolitan District Council* (1987) a Registrar of Births, Marriages and Deaths was allowed to claim for unpaid salary, although the claim ultimately failed on other grounds (see Chapter 7). The other point is that office holders may be able to claim public law rights and remedies, such as a claim that their dismissal was in breach of the rules of natural justice (see Chapter 11). In some cases the holder of an office may be paid an honorarium. This is often the position with, for example, clerks to school governors. The existence of this term does not prevent any claim to employment status because, as we saw above, the courts look at the reality of the relationship. In any event, holders of these posts could claim that they are employees.

A special type of office holder is a police officer. They are entitled to public law remedies (see *Ridge v Baldwin* (1964) in Chapter 11) but s.201 of the ERA provides that they have no rights under employment protection legislation except the right to a Statement of Initial Employment Particulars, a minimum notice period and redundancy pay.

## ■ Crown servants

Crown servants are simply those in Crown employment and are commonly known as civil servants. There is a doubt as to whether Crown servants have a contract with the Crown and, even if they do, whether that contract is a contract of employment. In *IRC v Hambrook* (1956) Goddard LCJ said: 'an established civil servant is appointed to an office . . . so that his employment depends not on a contract with the Crown but on appointment by the Crown.' Other judges have, however, held that Crown servants have a contract, even if it is not a contract of employment (see e.g. *Cresswell v Board of Inland Revenue* (1984)). This point is somewhat academic because s.191 of the ERA provides that all of its provisions extend to Crown servants except those giving the right to a minimum period of notice and the right to a redundancy payment. Therefore, a Crown servant can claim compensation for unfair dismissal but not redundancy pay. Indeed, s.159 of the ERA expressly states that civil servants have no right to a redundancy payment. However, they are covered by more generous schemes and so this exclusion does not in reality affect them. A special provision is found in s.245 of the Trade Union and Labour Relations (Consolidation) Act 1992 (TULRCA), whereby Crown servants are deemed to be employees for the purposes of liability for the economic torts. The reason is that trade unions have immunity from actions for the tort of inducement of a breach of contract, one of the economic torts, but this immunity would not exist if a civil servant were not an employee because he/she did not have a contract. This provision therefore protects trade unions rather than civil servants directly. The subject of trade union immunities is dealt with in Chapter 13.

## Trainees

Where a trainee has a contract of apprenticeship, he/she will come within employment protection legislation because s.230(2) of the ERA provides that a contract of apprenticeship is a contract of employment. However, a contract of apprenticeship is a formal agreement between the employer, who agrees to train the apprentice, and the apprentice, who agrees to serve the employer. Not all trainees are apprentices and the number of apprentices is declining because of the increase in training schemes funded by the government. Trainees other than apprentices appear to have no contract (see *Daley v Allied Supplies Ltd* (1980)), but trainees are given the protection of equal opportunities and health and safety legislation although, for example, they have no rights to claim for unfair dismissal.

## CONTINUITY OF EMPLOYMENT

The main reason why it is important to decide whether a worker is an employee is, as we have seen, to establish if he/she is entitled to the benefit of employment protection legislation. However, in certain cases, a person can only claim employment protection rights if, in addition to being an employee, he/she has a certain period of continuous employment. This topic is considered in Chapter 6.

# Chapter 5

# The contract of employment: form and content

## FORM OF THE CONTRACT OF EMPLOYMENT

### ▇ Introduction

Contracts of employment, with a few exceptions, conform to the general rule that no formalities are required for a contract and therefore a contract of employment can be made orally or in writing. The main exception is contracts of merchant seamen, who must have individual written agreements which must then be collected into crew agreements (see s.25 of the Merchant Shipping Act 1995).

However, all employees are entitled to a written statement of initial employment particulars not later than two months after the beginning of employment. This right was first conferred by the Contracts of Employment Act 1963 and this statute began the modern flow of employment protection rights. The right is now contained in ss.1–7 of the Employment Rights Act 1996 (ERA). It is of crucial importance to appreciate that the ERA does not require a written contract of employment but only a written statement of certain terms of employment. The distinction between this statement and a contract will be explored later in this chapter.

Therefore, an employer can do any of the following:

1. Give employees a statement of initial employment particulars with any extra terms, if any, left to an oral agreement.
2. Give employees a written contract of employment which contains the details required to be contained in the statement but also contains other details (see below for examples).
3. Give employees two documents: the statement plus a written contract containing additional matters. This may occur when an employer wishes to insert extra provisions in the contract after the employee has begun work.

In practice, option 2 is quite common, although many employers still just give the statement.

## Contents of the statement

Section 1(3) of the ERA provides that the statement must contain the following details correct at the date of the statement:

(a) the names of the employer and employee;
(b) the date on which the employment began;
(c) the date on which the employee's period of continuous employment began, taking into account any period of employment with a previous employer which counts towards continuity (see Chapter 6 for the details of when this can occur).

Section 1(4) then provides that the statement shall contain the following details, which must be correct at a specified date not more than seven days before the statement is given. (The reason for this provision is that a detail might change in the interval between the issuing of the statement and its receipt and therefore without this rule it would be impossible to issue a statement.)

(a) the scale or rate of remuneration or the method of calculating it;
(b) the intervals at which it is paid (weekly, monthly, etc.);
(c) terms and conditions relating to hours of work;
(d) terms and conditions relating to holidays and holiday pay, sick pay and other terms relating to incapacity for work due to sickness or injury, and pensions and pension schemes;
(e) the length of notice which the employee is entitled to receive and is obliged to give to terminate employment;
(f) the employee's job title or a brief job description;
(g) if the employment is not to be permanent, how long it is to last, or the date when a fixed-term contract ends;
(h) the employee's place of work or an indication that the employee is expected to work at various places if this is so;
(i) any collective agreements which affect the terms and conditions of employment;
(j) where the employee is required to work outside Great Britain for a period of more than one month, the period to be spent abroad, the currency in which remuneration will be paid, any additional remuneration and benefits and any terms and conditions relating to the employee's return to the UK.

Section 3(1)(a) provides that the employer must include a note specifying any disciplinary rules applicable to the employee or referring the employee to a reasonably accessible document containing these. Section 35(2) of the Employment Act 2002 has added a s.3(1)(aa) providing that the employer must specify any procedures applicable to the taking of disciplinary decisions or decisions to dismiss or refer the employee to a reasonably accessible document containing these. The addition of para. (aa) is intended to support the new disciplinary procedures laid down in ss.29–34 of the Employment Act 2002 and the effect is that procedures for dealing with disciplinary matters must be specified in addition to disciplinary rules. The note specified in s.3 must also specify the person to whom an employee can apply if dissatisfied with a disciplinary decision and a person to whom the employee can apply to seek redress of a grievance. If there are further steps following this application by the employee then the note must specify them, although s.3(2) provides that none of the foregoing applies to rules, disciplinary decisions or grievance procedures relating to health and safety at work and s.35(4) of the Employment Act 2002 adds to this disciplinary decisions to dismiss relating to health and safety. An important provision, which only applies to s.3, is that these details need not be given if the total number of employees at the date when the employee's employment began (including those employed by any associated employer) is less than 20. However, s.36 of the Employment Act 2002 provides that this exemption will be removed, although s.36 is not yet in force.

The following matters, which have to be included in the statement, are worthy of mention at this point:

1. A vital point of employment law, which was stressed in Chapter 1, is that the object of the statutory provisions is to provide a floor of rights. Therefore, the statement can, where statute provides for certain rights, either state that those rights shall apply or that the employee shall be entitled to rights in excess of the statutory minimum. For example, it can provide that the employee shall be entitled to notice periods set out in the ERA or to extra notice but not to less notice than the ERA provides for. (The topic of notice is dealt with in Chapter 11.)
2. The requirement to state the job title (s.1(4)(f)) needs to be approached with care by an employer because the more specific the job title is, the more difficult it will be to move the employee from one job to another. It should be noted that there is no requirement to give employees a full job description, although this is becoming increasingly common, but only a brief job description as an alternative to a job title.
3. The requirement to state the place of work is also one to be handled with care, as again the designation of a very specific place of work may make it more difficult to move the employee. (This issue is to some extent bound up with redundancy and is dealt with in Chapter 12.)

## Points arising from the statement

The particulars must be contained in a single document, with the exception of the following, which can either be contained in the statement or specified in other ways as indicated:

1. the note specifying disciplinary rules (see above);
2. particulars relating to sickness, sick pay and pensions, when the statement may refer to a reasonably accessible document;
3. details of notice periods may be given by referring the employee to the general law or to a reasonably accessible collective agreement.

The intention of the Act is not to require all of the terms to exist but, if a term relating to any of the specified matters does not exist, then s.2(1) requires the statement to point this out. Carried to its extreme, however, this could mean that a statement simply stated that there were no particulars at all. Clearly this cannot be so, because a contract with no terms at all would not be a contract. In *Eagland v British Telecommunications* (1990) Wood P, in the EAT, distinguished between mandatory terms (which must be included) and non-mandatory terms (which need not). He found the key to the distinction between mandatory and non-mandatory terms in the words 'any terms and conditions relating to', which clearly envisaged, by the use of the word 'any', a situation where there were none. As will be seen from the above list, this phrase appears in (c) and (d) dealing with terms relating to hours of work, holidays, sickness and pensions. All of the other terms laid down in s.1(3) and s.1(4)(a) (b) (e) and (f) were mandatory, which clearly makes sense as, for example, it would be strange if the statement declined to say who the employer was. At the date of this case, there was no requirement to give details of terms (g)–(k) but it is probable that (g) (temporary employment) and (k) (place of work) are mandatory, whereas (j) (collective agreements) can only apply if there are any, and (k) (employment abroad) appears to be mandatory with the exception of the final part beginning with the words 'any terms and conditions'. Finally, the requirement to give details of disciplinary and grievance procedures is mandatory unless the firm has less than 20 employees, but as explained above, this will shortly be abolished.

It is almost certain that, during the time of the employee's employment, some at least of the particulars will change and s.4 provides that, if this is so, then the employer must give employees a statement containing particulars of any changes not later then one month afterwards. Three particular points arise:

1. the changes must be set out in full and may not be given in instalments;
2. where the original details could be specified either in the statement or in other ways (see above) then the same applies to any changes to these details;
3. where only the name or the identity of the employer changes then, although these changes must of course be notified, a whole new statement need not be issued unless continuity of employment is broken.

## Enforcement of the obligation to give a statement

There is no right to claim compensation for failure to give a statement, although in an action for, for example, unfair dismissal, the tribunal will not take a favourable view of the employer's case if it emerges during the hearing that no statement was ever provided to the employee.

Instead, if an employer does not give a statement or if the statement the employee is given by the employer is deficient then the employee has the right by s.11 to complain to an employment tribunal.

Section 12(1) allows the tribunal, where either no particulars have been given or the particulars were incomplete, to decide what particulars ought to be included, and s.12(2) gives the tribunal power, where the statement is inaccurate, to amend particulars or substitute other particulars.

These provisions have caused some difficulty in interpretation, particularly the words 'ought to be included'. The courts have not interpreted this phrase in any creative sense so as to give a wide power to tribunals to decide what ought to be in the statement, but have instead reserved any creative power to themselves to use when expanding the concept of implied terms of the contract. Thus in *Construction Industry Training Board v Leighton* (1978) Kilner-Brown J, in the EAT, said that tribunals have no power 'to declare what a contract meant or to rectify an error manifest in an otherwise binding contract'. Instead, their function is to find out what has been agreed rather then to invent a term. Thus, in *Leighton* itself, the tribunal had decided that the employee was entitled to a salary increment mentioned in the statement when this was unclear. The EAT held that the tribunal should not have embarked on this exercise and instead left the matter to the civil courts in an action on the contract. A good example of the orthodox view is *Cuthbertson v AML Distributors* (1975), where the tribunal refused to state the amount of notice which would have been reasonable when no statement had been given.

However, in *Mears v Safecor Security Ltd* (1982) the Court of Appeal held that a tribunal does have jurisdiction to hear a complaint that inaccurate particulars have been given. The distinction between deciding whether particulars are inaccurate and rectifying an error, which the Court of Appeal said in *Leighton* was not permissible, is clearly a fine one and this area awaits clarification in a future decision.

### Relationship between the statement and the contract of employment

An employee may, as stated earlier, choose to give a contract of employment which includes the matters which need to be in the statement together with other matters. Obvious examples, which will be considered later in this chapter, are confidentiality clauses, restraint of trade clauses and a clause that the employee must not undertake other work outside working hours without the consent of his/her employer.

The fact that the statement is not by itself the contract of employment is significant because the rule that outside evidence is not normally admissible to add to or vary a written instrument, such as a contract, does not apply to statements. Therefore, it is open to either party to argue that the statement does not reflect what was agreed and this is of particular importance to employees, as the issue of the statement may not have been preceded by any negotiation between the parties.

Therefore, in *Systems Floors (UK) Ltd v Daniel* (1985) the EAT allowed an employer to bring evidence that the correct date when the employee began work was a week later than the statement said. (The point was important in calculating whether the employee had sufficient continuity of employment to claim for unfair dismissal.) As Browne-Wilkinson J put it, the statement 'provides very strong *prima facie* evidence of what were the terms of the contract between the parties, but does not constitute a written contract between the parties'. The employer is placed, he said, under a heavy burden to show that the actual terms are different from those in the statement but the point is that, as the statement is not actually the contract, the employer is at least able to argue that the statement is wrong. So, of course, is the employee, and indeed this case was somewhat unusual in that the employer was arguing that his own statement was wrong. In the case of an employee arguing that the statement was wrong the evidential burden would be less as in *Robertson and Jackson v British Gas Corporation* (1983), where the employee successfully argued that the details of bonus payments in the statement were wrong.

Set against these authorities is the awkward decision of the Court of Appeal in *Gascol Conversions Ltd v Mercer* (1974). The employer gave the employee a new contract of employment dealing with, *inter alia*, hours of work, because the Industrial Relations Act 1971 required these details to be included in statements given to employees, and the employee signed for its receipt as a new contract of employment. The employee later argued that the hours of work stated were wrong. It was held that as he had signed a contract, rather than a statement, he could not later argue that the details were wrong. If it was found that he had simply signed for receipt of the document as a statement then he would not have signed the document as a contract and *could* have argued that the details were wrong. On the facts it is not clear precisely how the parties regarded the effect of the employee's signature but the case stands as a valuable reminder that once a contract is signed as such, it will be very difficult to argue later that any of its contents were wrong.

## CAPACITY TO MAKE A CONTRACT OF EMPLOYMENT

The only important restriction here is that minors' contracts of employment are binding provided that, on the whole, they are for their benefit. An illustration is *De Francesco v Barnum* (1890), where a contract was so one-sided that it was held to be not binding. Detailed discussion of this topic, however, belongs to textbooks on the law of contract.

## CONTENTS OF THE CONTRACT OF EMPLOYMENT

### Introduction

The contract of employment, like all other contracts, is made up of terms, which contain the obligations of the parties. Until 1963, and the passage of the Contracts of Employment Act, the terms of the contract as developed by the courts as common law were virtually the only source of employment rights. Now, with the passage of innumerable statutes and other legislation dealing with employment matters, it might seem that the contents of the actual contract are of little significance. This view would be greatly mistaken, as the courts have been most active in developing the common law of employment alongside the statutory developments.

## Types of contractual terms

Terms come from the following sources:

1. The express terms of the contract as actually contained in the contract, whether orally or written.
2. The implied terms of the contract. These are not contained in the contract itself but are derived from the following sources:
   (a) statute;
   (b) custom;
   (c) the courts;
   (d) collective agreements.

Not only this, but there is a grey area dealing with such matters as work rules and company policies which may in some cases be sources of contractual terms.

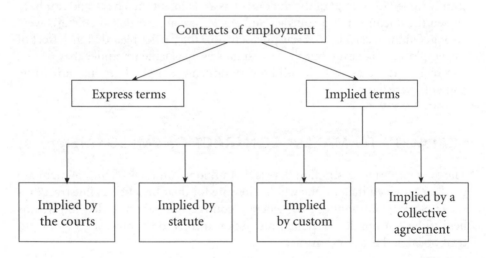

It should be noted that there is a link between implied terms and termination of the contract (see Chapter 11), because a breach of an implied term by the employee may give the employer grounds to dismiss and a breach by the employer may give the employee grounds to claim constructive dismissal as in *Waltons v Morse and Dorrington* (1997) and *WA Goold v McConnell* (1995) (below).

Each of the above sources of terms will now be considered in turn.

### Express terms

This category calls for little comment in itself except to remark that the bald terms of the contract will give little idea of the relationship in practice between the employer and employees nor of how the work is to be done. One can supplement the contract by referring to work rules but work rules are not likely to be held part of the contract, as will appear below. Furthermore, the courts have upheld the idea that there is an area of 'managerial prerogative' which lies beyond the contract and which is seen clearly in cases where the employer wishes to impose changes to the contract on employees. This issue is dealt with in more detail in Chapter 12 in the context of dismissal on a reorganisation of a business.

## Terms implied by statute

A straightforward example is provided by s.1(1) of the Equal Pay Act 1970, which provides that every woman's contract of employment is deemed to include an equality clause under which any term in it which is less favourable than that in the contract of a male employee is modified so that it is not less favourable. (Note that in the Act a woman includes a man.) The effect of this, which is explained in detail in Chapter 9, is to give a woman (or a man) a contractual right to equal pay where the work is, in a broad sense, equal. This type of provision is unusual: the normal method of granting statutory rights is to make enforcement of them independent of the contract.

## Terms implied by custom

The custom of a trade or business may be a source of a term if it is certain and reasonable and applies throughout a particular trade, business or area. A good, if old, example, is provided by *Sagar v Ridehalgh* (1931), where a custom in the Lancashire mills of deducting wages for bad work was held to be binding on an employee. This area of the law needs clarification. For example, Lawrence LJ emphasised that the custom in question had prevailed at the mill where the employee worked for over 30 years, but the essence of custom is that it is observed in a trade rather than just one factory. In addition, Lawrence LJ thought that it did not matter whether the employee knew of the custom or not but in later cases the point has caused a divergence of opinion. In *Marshall v English Electric Co. Ltd* (1945) Lord Goddard thought that a custom was automatically incorporated but du Parcq LJ thought that the employee needed to assent. Certainly a need for assent by the employee is in accord with the trend of modern employment law and it is submitted that it should be required.

## Terms implied by the courts and their importance

This is the most important source of implied terms and will be considered in detail. There is no doubt that the importance of the implied terms has increased enormously in recent years, as a glance at some of the cases discussed below will show. Particularly good examples of recent significant decisions are *Johnstone v Bloomsbury Area Health Authority* (1991) and *Malik v BCCI* (1997). Indeed, in *Johnson v Unisys Ltd* (2001) Lord Hoffmann compared the growth in the common law of employment with the growth in statutory regulation of the employment relationship:

Over the last 30 years or so, the nature of the contract of employment has been transformed. It has been recognised that a person's employment is usually one of the most important things in a person's life . . . Most of the changes have been made by Parliament . . . And the common law has adapted to the new attitudes, proceeding sometimes by analogy with statutory rights . . . The contribution of the common law to the employment revolution has been by the evolution of implied terms in the contract of employment. The most far reaching is the implied term of trust and confidence.

(The term 'trust and confidence' is discussed below.)

### Basis on which the courts imply a term

The classic theory is that the courts imply a term to give effect to the intentions of the parties which they have failed to express in the contract. In *The Moorcock* (1889) Bowen LJ said that the courts must imply terms from the intentions of the parties with the object of giving business efficacy to the transaction. This language clearly reflects the preoccupation of contract law in the nineteenth century with business transactions and may be considered hardly appropriate to modern employment law. In *Shirlaw v Southern Foundries Ltd* (1939) McKinnon LJ put forward the 'officious bystander test', the point of which is that a term will only be implied if an officious bystander suggested it to the parties whilst they were negotiating and it was such an obvious suggestion that they replied that 'of course' it was included.

The basis of both these theories, resting as they do on the supposed intentions of the parties, is undoubtedly narrow and leaves no room for any creativity on the part of the courts. In fact, it has long been recognised that the scope of implied terms is much wider than this and in many cases the courts have, whilst acting under the cloak of giving effect to the intentions of the parties, in fact imposed a term which they feel ought to be included. This has, in recent years, been explicitly recognised by the courts, so that the theory that terms are only implied to give effect to the intentions of the parties no longer represents the law. The difficulty is in stating precisely when the courts will imply a term.

One approach is provided by the words of Slade LJ in *Courtaulds Northern Spinning Ltd v Sibson* (1988), who held that, in deciding whether to imply a term as to the place of work, the courts should imply a term if satisfied that the parties would have agreed to it 'if they were being reasonable'. This is a reflection of the decision in *Liverpool City Council v Irwin* (1977), where the House of Lords emphasised that the question was whether the implication of a term was both reasonable and necessary to the contract, and although that was not an employment case, this seems to represent the law today. A recent example of where the courts have tried to make the position clear is the speech of Lord Bridge in the House of Lords in *Scally v Southern Health and Social Services Board* (1991), where he contrasted the 'search for an implied term necessary to give business efficacy to a particular contract' and a search for 'a term which the law will imply as a necessary incident of a definable category of contractual relationship'.

The position today is that, especially when the courts feel that the common law of employment needs to be advanced and where they are concerned to limit the powers of employers, they may disregard the search for a solution based narrowly on the intentions of the parties. This is particularly true in the case of the development of the implied term of mutual trust and confidence. On the other hand, even in these cases the courts will not imply a term purely because it would be reasonable in a general sense but will ask whether the implication of a term is necessary to the contract. Where, however, the case deals with more basic issues, such as overtime pay, the courts will try to seek the intentions of the parties.

## Implied terms in practice

A good example of an attempt by the courts to imply a term by trying to ascertain the intentions of the parties is *Jones v Associated Tunnelling Co. Ltd* (1981). The employee had been issued with a new written statement, which included a mobility clause which obliged him to work at any place which the employer might decide. He made no protest at the time but when the employers tried to move him to another place of work four years later, he refused and instead claimed that he was redundant. The EAT held that his failure to protest at the time did not necessarily mean that he agreed to the change, as he might not have wished to come into conflict with his employer. It was clearly necessary to imply a term as to place of work in order to give business efficacy to the contract and, although the employer may have intended a term that the employee could be required to move anywhere in the UK, the employee did not intend this. What the court called the 'lowest common denominator' at which the parties would have agreed if asked was that the employee was to be employed within daily travelling distance of home and this term was therefore implied. Another example is provided by *Ali v Christian Salvesen Food Services Ltd* (1997), where a collective agreement provided that employees were entitled to overtime when they had worked 1,824 hours a year. Ali was dismissed before he had worked these hours in a year and he argued that there was an implied term that he would be paid overtime for every hour worked beyond 40 a week. It was held that the fact that the agreement did not mention a right to this did not mean that it should be implied. The fact that this term was omitted was evidence that the parties did not intend it to apply.

On the other hand, in *United Bank Ltd v Akhtar* (1989) the issue of a mobility clause was seen against the duty of mutual trust and confidence (see below) and a different basis was used for the implication of a term. The employee, a bank clerk, had a contract which contained a mobility clause under which he could be required to move to any branch in the UK. He was given six days' notice to move from Leeds to a branch in Birmingham and he left, claiming constructive dismissal. The EAT held that his claim succeeded as there was an implied term in his contract that he would be given reasonable notice of such a move. In the EAT, Knox J, whilst accepting the traditional view that terms should be implied to achieve business efficacy and to give effect to the parties' intentions, added that 'in the field of employment law it is proper to imply an overriding obligation' of trust and respect which is independent of, and additional to, the actual terms of the contract. Therefore, although the employer in this case was entitled by the actual words of the contract to give the order to move with very little notice, this was in conflict with the overriding obligation and thus in breach of contract. The EAT in *White v Reflecting Roadstuds Ltd* (1991) emphasised that the decision in *Akhtar* did not mean that an employee should not simply allege that the employer's actions were unreasonable but that they were in breach of the implied term to treat the employee with trust and respect.

## Relationship between express terms and implied terms

Suppose that an express term of the contract comes into conflict with a term which the courts feel ought to be implied. Which will give way? The question will not normally arise, as terms will not be implied where an express term covers the matter. However, in *United Bank Ltd v Akhtar* (1989), as was seen above, the court held that an express term had to be exercised subject to a fundamental implied term. This, however, was not so much a case of an express term giving way to an implied term but the implied term governing the exercise of the express term.

A clearer case is *Johnstone v Bloomsbury Area Health Authority* (1991). The plaintiff was a junior hospital doctor and his contract provided that, in addition to his standard working week of 40 hours, he should be available on call for an average of another 48 hours a week. He alleged that this was having a detrimental effect on his health, as in some cases he had to work in excess of 100 hours a week and therefore he sued for damages for a breach by his employers of a duty to take reasonable care for his health and safety. The action was heard on an application by the employers to strike it out as disclosing no reasonable cause of action and the Court of Appeal agreed to allow it to proceed. Stuart-Smith LJ held that the express term should be read subject to an implied term that an employer must take reasonable care for the health and safety of employees. The other judges did not go as far. Leggatt LJ, indeed, did not go far at all, holding that the express terms on hours had primacy over any implied term and he would have struck out the action. Browne-Wilkinson V-C took a middle course and held that the agreement to work overtime simply gave the employer a discretion whether to call on employees to do so and this discretion had to be exercised so as to conform with the implied duty to take reasonable care not to do anything to injure the health of employees. With respect, the view of Stuart-Smith LJ seems preferable, as it boldly faces the issue of a conflict between express and implied terms and clearly holds that in some cases an express term may have to give way. In addition, it has been argued that, in so far as the express term was in breach of the duty to take reasonable care for employees' health and safety, it could count as a clause negating the employer's duty of care under the tort of negligence and would be void under s.2(1) of the Unfair Contract Terms Act 1977.

It seems, therefore, that there are certain fundamental implied terms which override express terms either directly, as in *Johnstone,* or by making the exercise of express terms subject to them, as in *Akhtar*. The *Johnstone* case involved terms as to health and safety but another fundamental implied term is that of mutual trust and confidence, which is considered later in this chapter, and which was really the basis of *Akhtar*. However, the relationship between 'fundamental' implied terms and the express terms of the contract is still being worked out. The extent to which the implied duties of the employer and employer can be affected by express terms is not entirely clear, although some of these are so fundamental that no contract of employment could exist without them.

## The implied terms: duties of the employer and employee

The law has long identified certain duties which will be implied into contracts of employment. The relationship between these and the express terms is, as discussed above, not clear but it is probably true to say that, although the actual contract may well modify the *precise contents* of an implied duty, all of these duties must exist in some form in a contract of employment.

## Duties of the employer

### To pay wages

This duty is considered in detail in Chapter 7. Even so, it is needs to be mentioned here if only to emphasise just how fundamental these duties have traditionally been, since clearly there cannot be a contract to work without payment.

### To indemnify the employee against liabilities and losses incurred in the course of employment

An example would be the duty to reimburse the employee for travel expenses incurred in the course of employment. The duty does not extend to taking care of employees' property (*Deyong v Shenburn* (1946)).

### To provide work

The extent of this duty, and whether it even exists, is doubtful. In *Collier v Sunday Referee Publishing Co. Ltd* (1940) Asquith LJ denied that such a duty normally existed: 'Provided I pay my cook her wages regularly, she cannot complain if I choose to take any or all of my meals out.' However, he then recognised certain exceptions to this principle: where payment is by commission or where part of the bargain is publicity for the employee, as with singers or actors. In the latter case, a failure to provide work would mean that the employee might gradually sink into oblivion.

The question is whether there is now a more general duty to provide work. In *Langston v AUEW (No. 2)* (1974) Denning MR proposed overruling *Collier* in cases of skilled employees so that there was a duty to provide them with work. However, this view was not shared by the other members of the Court of Appeal and the National Industrial Relations Court (NIRC), in deciding the case on its facts, did not have to address the general issue. The claim resulted from a refusal by an employee to join a union. The other employees took industrial action as a result of this because there was a closed shop in operation, and he was eventually suspended without pay. The NIRC found that, as he was entitled under his contract to be paid premium rates for night shifts and overtime, the denial of the opportunity to work meant the loss of opportunity to earn these, which was a breach of contract by the employers. In *Breach v Epsylon Industries Ltd* (1976) the EAT held that there may well be exceptions to the general rule that there is no duty to provide work, although precisely what these might be was not specified by the court.

A recent example of the right to be provided with work, which may lead to more general developments in this area, arose in the context of a decision by employers to put an employee on 'garden leave'. In *William Hill Organisation Ltd v Tucker* (1998) a senior employee of a firm of bookmakers had been engaged in developing spread betting, which was a relatively new form of betting. When he wished to leave, his employer tried to impose a six-month garden leave clause. (Such clauses allow employers to impose a long notice period on employees where they are sent home on full pay with a provision that they cannot do any other work during that time. In effect they are paid whilst their skills and knowledge are getting out of date.) In this case the employee successfully challenged the clause on the ground that he needed the opportunity to work as the skills involved in his work required constant practice. This point could, of course, apply to many other employees and this decision may open the way for an expansion of the right to be provided with work. (It should be noted that the garden leave clause was not expressly contained in the contract but simply imposed by the employer. An express garden leave clause would not be easily upset.)

## To take reasonable care for the health and safety of employees

As with the duty to pay wages, this duty is so important that it merits consideration in a separate chapter (Chapter 8), although a clear example is provided by *Johnstone v Bloomsbury AHA* (above). However, it is relevant to mention here that it has been extended to the provision of a working environment which is reasonably safe. In *Waltons and Morse v Dorrington* (1997) the applicant left her employment and claimed constructive dismissal because of the employer's failure to deal adequately with her complaints about being exposed to cigarette smoke from other employees. The EAT upheld her claim and held that the provision of a safe working environment suitable for the performance of contractual duties is an implied term in contracts of employment.

This duty also extends to the taking of reasonable steps to prevent bullying at work and here there is a link with:

(a) constructive dismissal, as a complaint that the employer has breached this duty may lead to a claim for constructive dismissal (see Chapter 11);
(b) sex, race or disability discrimination where the bullying can be said to constitute harassment on any of these grounds (see Chapter 9);
(c) the duty of the employer to take reasonable care for the health and safety of employees (see Chapter 8).

In the context of implied terms, a failure by the employer to deal adequately with bullying can be seen as a breach of the duty of mutual trust and confidence (see below). An interesting point was raised in *McCabe v Chicpak Ltd* (1976), where it was held that if the employee refused to name the alleged bullies then the employer was not liable for failing to take steps other than to speak on general terms to the employee's fellow workers. In *Wigan Borough Council v Davies* (1978) it was held that there was an implied term that employers would take reasonable steps to support employees in their work without harassment or disruption from others and that the onus of proving that no additional steps were practicable lay with the employer. A more recent instance is *Waters v Metropolitan Police Commissioner* (2000), where the House of Lords held that an employer could be liable for psychological harm suffered by an employee when complaints about sexual assaults were not treated seriously and by failing to prevent harassment once the complaint had been made. This case should also be considered alongside the duty of the employer not to subject the employee to undue stress leading to psychological harm, considered in Chapter 8.

## To take reasonable care in the giving of references

It was not until the decision of the House of Lords in *Spring v Guardian Assurance plc* (1994) that the courts expressly accepted that a duty of care in negligence could arise in giving a reference. Until then, the giving of references had been subject to the law of defamation, in that the giver of a reference was (and still is) protected from an action for defamation even if it contains defamatory material provided that the person giving it did not act maliciously.

### Example

X works for Y and then applies for a job with Z. He asks Y for a reference and Y falsely states that X is 'the worst employee I have ever had. He is both dishonest and incompetent'. This is defamatory and, although the giver of a reference, even if it is false, is protected from an action for defamation, this will not be so if it was given maliciously. In this case Y makes the defamatory statement as he has a personal grudge against X, who he believes has had an affair with Y's wife.

However, until the decision in *Spring* there was no liability where a reference was only given negligently and, given that malice can be difficult to prove, it was usually difficult before this decision to make any claim when a reference was wrong. It is now easier to make claims but the law here is developing and there are some doubtful areas.

Liability can arise in the following situations:

1. An employer gives a reference negligently which is acted on by a prospective employer who suffers loss. For instance, the reference might say that the employee is trustworthy when she is not and the new employer subsequently suffers loss when they employ this person who then steals. In *Spring* Lord Slynn observed that the employer would be liable under *Hedley Byrne v Heller* (1964) for negligent misstatement.

2. An employer gives a reference negligently which means that the employee does not get the job. In effect, whereas the reference in 1 above was too good, this one is too bad. This was the situation in *Spring* and it was here that the House of Lords changed the law by holding that liability can arise.

The facts were that Spring worked in insurance and was given a reference which cast doubt on his honesty and ability and was described by the trial judge as 'the kiss of death' to his insurance career. The House of Lords held that the reference was given negligently and the employers were liable. In addition, three Law Lords held that there was also an implied contractual duty to take due care in the preparation of references.

The following points arise from this decision:

1. As Lord Slynn observed, the referee can quite properly state 'the parameters within which the reference is given', so that the reference is limited to knowledge of a person on certain occasions only. However, a disclaimer of liability (e.g. 'we do not accept liability for the contents of this reference') would only be valid if it satisfied the reasonableness test under s.2 of the Unfair Contract Terms Act 1977.

2. It is not clear whether an employer is under a duty actually to give a reference. In *Spring* Lords Hadley and Woolf thought that there was an implied contractual duty where the employee's (present) contract with the employer is of a kind where a reference is normally required. This contractual test makes the requirement to give a reference depend on the type of job which the employee is actually doing, rather than the type of job he/she is applying for. The law will no doubt develop here.

3. An employer may try to safeguard herself by giving a purely factual reference stating certain undoubtedly true facts but no more. In *Bartholomew v Hackney LBC* (1999) the Court of Appeal held that a reference must be in substance true, accurate and fair but not necessarily full and comprehensive. This leaves the point about factual references in doubt: such a reference may be true and accurate but is it fair? In this case the reference stated that disciplinary proceedings for gross misconduct had commenced against the employee when he took voluntary severance but did not state what the misconduct was or that the employee denied it. It was held on the facts that the reference was fair, since knowing the precise details of the misconduct would not have had any effect on a prospective employer and the fact that the employee denied the charge was implicit in the fact that the proceedings were ongoing.

4. What is the position where the employee is being investigated when the reference is given? In *TSB v Harris* (2000) a failure by an employer to tell an employee of complaints about her whilst putting them in a reference was held to be a breach of the duty of trust and confidence. In *Cox v Sun Alliance Life Ltd* (2001) Mummery LJ, in the Court of Appeal, held that any unfavourable statements in a reference should be confined to matters which have been investigated and which the employer had reasonable grounds to believe to be

true. The reference to an investigation clearly implies that the matters have been brought to the employee's attention.

5. The duty only exists when a reference has been given. In *Legal and General Assurance Ltd v Kirk* (2001) an employee claimed that he had been deterred from applying for a reference because of a false allegation that he owed his employers a debt. It was held that a duty only arises when the reference is being given. The particular feature of this case was that there was a rule of the Regulatory Body that a person owing a debt of more than £1,000 could not be employed in certain capacities. One can see the employee's point: there was no point in even applying for the reference unless the allegation was withdrawn or substantiated.

6. A final hurdle which an employee needs to surmount is proving that the negligent reference actually caused his/her failure to obtain the job. This issue of causation may be the most significant barrier in the way of a claim.

7. Does an employee have the right to see references about him/herself? Under the Data Protection Act 1998 (discussed in more detail later in this chapter), although references are personal data to which, by s.7, there is a general right of access, there is a specific exemption in Sch.7, para.1 whereby there is no right of access to references which an employer sends to a prospective employer. An employee could ask the new employer for a copy of a reference supplied to him but this would, under s.7(4), need the consent of the previous employee.

### To take reasonable steps to bring to the attention of employees rights of which they could not have been expected to be aware

An example is *Scally v Southern Health and Social Services Board* (1991). The plaintiffs were doctors employed in the Health Service in Northern Ireland and their employer had failed to tell them of their right to purchase added years to enhance their pension contributions. The House of Lords held that a term would be implied in this case and Lord Bridge laid down the following conditions which need to be satisfied for the implication of such a term:

(a) the terms were not negotiated with the employee but resulted from negotiations with a representative body (e.g. a trade union) or were incorporated by reference;
(b) the employee could only avail himself of the right by taking certain steps himself;
(c) the employee could not, in all the circumstances, reasonably be expected to be aware of the rights unless they were drawn to his attention.

### To deal promptly and effectively with grievances

In *WA Gould (Pearmak) Ltd v McConnell* (1995) two salesmen attempted to raise a grievance resulting from a reduction in their commission due to a change in sales methods. There was no procedure laid down nor were they able to discuss it. They resigned and successfully claimed constructive dismissal. Moreover, the

EAT held that this term was a fundamental one which may put it alongside the other fundamental terms set out above.

## To respect the employee's privacy

This is a recent development and the nature and extent of this duty is not yet clear. In *Dalgleish v Lothian and Borders Police Board* (1991) an injunction was granted to prevent disclosure by the Police Board to the local council of the details of council employees who had not paid the community charge. In *Halford v United Kingdom* (1997) the European Court of Human Rights was asked to consider the applicability of Article 8 (respect for private and family life) of the European Convention on Human Rights (ECHR) in a situation where an employee claimed that her telephone had been tapped. It was held that this was a breach and such claims can be expected to increase with the incorporation of the ECHR into UK law by the Human Rights Act 1998.

### The Data Protection Act 1998

The Data Protection Act 1998 is also relevant in connection with the right of the employee to privacy, although the Act does not refer to privacy as such but regulates the use of information (data) relating to individuals. This Act, which replaces the Data Protection Act 1984 and implements the Data Protection Directive of 1995 (95/46), deals with situations other than employment and refers to data controllers (employers in this context) and data subjects (employees). The terms 'employer' and 'employee' will be used here. The Act applies when-ever data is processed, whether electronically (by computer) or manually (e.g. in a filing system) but it should be noted that certain parts of the Act (e.g. in rela-tion to some manual data) will not be completely in force until 23 October 2007.

The Act places two fundamental duties on employers:

1. To comply with the eight 'data protection principles'. These are set out in Schedules to the Act and, in summary, provide that data shall:
   - Be processed lawfully and fairly. In the employment context, one require-ment here is that the employee must have consented. An employer clearly needs to keep certain data on employees and the easiest way to obtain con-sent is for contracts of employment to state that the employer has permis-sion to process certain data and for the employee to sign that he/she agrees.
   - Only be obtained for lawful purposes. The Schedule provides that an employer may specify the purposes in a notice to the employee.
   - Be adequate, relevant and not excessive in relation to the purposes for which they are obtained. Excessively detailed personal records kept on employees could breach this principle.
   - Be accurate and, where necessary, kept up to date. Data on employees will often have been obtained from others, such as previous employers, and an employer may wish to give employees the chance to check that it is correct.
   - Not be kept for longer then necessary. Records relating to employees should always be kept for at least the length of time after employment ends

during which an employee could bring an action against the employer (the limitation period): the longest period is three years in the case of personal injury at work. An employer may wish to keep data for longer than this for use if a reference is required.

- Be processed in accordance with the rights of data subjects set out in the Act. This would be breached if the employer failed to comply with the rights of employees set out below.
- Take appropriate measures against unauthorised or unlawful processing of data and loss and damage to data. Thus proper security measures are needed and employees with access to records of other employees must maintain confidentiality.
- Not be transferred to a country outside the European Economic Area (the EU plus Iceland, Norway and Liechtenstein) unless that country has adequate protection for the data.

In the case of 'sensitive personal data' there are further restrictions. This is defined by s.2 as data relating to, for example, racial or ethnic origin, political opinions, religious beliefs, trade union membership, health, sexual life, and commission of an offence. The explicit consent of the employee is needed before such data can be processed and this seems to mean that the employer must gain specific consent to the processing of this data and the general consent referred to earlier will not be enough. The eight principles above also, of course, apply to this data as well and it may be that an employer would not be permitted to process it anyway because, for example, it may not be necessary to keep such data.

2. To notify the Data Protection Registrar when they are processing computer records, and certain other records, containing personal data. It is a criminal offence to fail to comply.

Employees have the following main rights:

1. To have access to personal data. The employer is only obliged to supply certain information on receipt of a written request and a fee not normally exceeding £10. There are exceptions to this of which one, as explained above, is that an employee does not have a right of access to a reference about him/her. Failure by the employer to comply gives the employee the right to apply to the county court or High Court for an order requiring compliance.
2. To correct personal data which is in breach of the fourth principle by being inaccurate. The Data Protection Commissioner can be asked to intervene if the employer refuses to correct it.

The Act specifically provides in s.56 that it is a criminal offence for a prospective employer to require a prospective employee to obtain any criminal records which they have or any record of non-payment of social security contributions. In effect, the prospective employer cannot say to the employee 'you have a right of access to this information about yourself and you must exercise it and give me the information'.

### The Regulation of Investigatory Powers Act 2000

The Regulation of Investigatory Powers Act 2000 provides that it is unlawful to intercept communications in the course of transmission by a telecommunications system. This would make it unlawful for an employer to monitor telephone calls made by employees but there are circumstances where this may be needed, as where it is suspected that an employee is sending emails to another employee which may be sexually harassing. The Telecommunications (Lawful Business Practice) (Interception of Communications) Regulations 2000, issued under the above Act, allow interception in certain circumstances, one being where the interception is solely for the purpose of monitoring and recording communications relevant to the needs of the business. Here interception is allowed if the employer has made all reasonable efforts to let users know that communications may be intercepted and the equipment is provided wholly or partly for use in the course of the business. An employer could argue that this allowed the monitoring of all telephone calls and emails but this could be contrary to the Human Rights Act 1998, as Article 8 of the ECHR gives a right to respect for private and family life. A test case is awaited!

### The Access to Medical Records Act 1988

This is an appropriate place to mention the Access to Medical Records Act 1988, which gives employees the right to see medical reports. Although the Data Protection Act also gives this right, it only applies where they are held on computer or on filing systems. The Access to Medical Records Act has no such restriction. Section 1 gives the individual (e.g. employee) access to any medical report relating to him/her which has been prepared by a doctor responsible for his/her medical care. In addition, s.3 provides that an employer shall not request medical reports relating to an individual without that person's consent. Therefore, a prospective employer could not ask for records relating to a job applicant without their consent and an employer could not require an employee's own doctor to supply him with the employee's medical records. However, reports prepared on employees by company doctors or independent doctors, as where an employee may be claiming that he/she is off work through illness, are not within the Act and therefore are available to the employer without the consent of the employee being needed. One exception, however, could be where the company doctor has treated the employee previously, in which case they could be considered responsible for their medical care and would come within s.1 (above). If so, the Act would apply and the individual's consent would be needed before the disclosure of the report.

## ▓ The duty of mutual trust and confidence

This duty is considered between the duties of the employer and employee as it is a duty which, as its title indicates, could fall on either. Nevertheless, the reality is that the duty has a far greater impact on the employer.

The origin of the duty lies in the law of unfair dismissal and, in particular, in constructive dismissal cases where the issue is whether the employer is guilty of a repudiatory breach of the contract, i.e. the employer no longer intends to be bound by one of the essential terms of the contract (see Chapter 11 and especially *Western Excavating v Sharp* (1978)). The courts have developed the law on what constitutes a repudiatory breach so that it encompasses conduct which is a breach of this duty, which really amounts to a duty to treat the employee with respect. The significant point is that now the duty can be used throughout the employer–employee relationship and is not confined to constructive dismissal cases.

One of the earliest examples is in *Isle of Wight Tourist Board v Coombes* (1976), where a director said to another employee that his personal secretary was 'an intolerable bitch on a Monday morning'. The secretary resigned and successfully claimed constructive dismissal. It was held that the relationship between a director and his secretary must be one of complete trust and confidence and this had been shattered by the use of these words.

This decision was confined to a particular relationship but the courts soon began to broaden its application. In *Woods v WM Car Services Ltd* (1981), which also concerned constructive dismissal, Browne-Wilkinson J said that: 'In our view it is clearly established that there is implied in a contract of employment a term that the employers will not, without proper cause, conduct themselves in a manner calculated or likely to destroy or seriously damage the relationship of confidence and trust between employer and employee'. Further examples of this term in practice are *United Bank v Akhtar* (above) and *French v Barclays Bank plc* (1999), where a decision by the bank to change the terms of a relocation loan made to an employee was a breach.

The implied term was thrust into prominence by the decision of the House of Lords in *Malik v BCCI SA* (1997), which concerned a claim by employees that the conduct of their (former) employers in the way they had run the Bank of Credit and Commerce International had breached this implied term and therefore they were entitled to 'stigma damages', being damages for the damage to their future job prospects by their association with the bank. The claim was upheld in what was certainly the first major decision to deal with the implied term of trust and confidence in a situation other than unfair dismissal. Lord Steyn observed that:

> The evolution of the implied term of mutual trust and confidence is a fact . . . It has proved a workable principle in practice. It has not been the subject of adverse criticism in any decided cases and it has been welcomed in academic writings. I regard the emergence of the implied obligation of mutual trust and confidence as a sound development.

Lord Steyn also held that this term could be broken even if the employer's conduct was not aimed at any individual employee and even if the employee did not know that it was happening. This was so in the *Malik* case because the bank was not fraudulently run in order to target any employee, nor did they all know precisely what was going on. What can be said with certainty is that the development of this term will be one area of employment law to watch in the next few years.

## Duties of the employee

### To obey orders and instructions permitted by the terms of the contract

The precise terms of the contract are clearly important here, although many contracts contain a very general clause in addition to specific duties. For example, a teacher's contract, in addition to requiring her to teach, mark and set examination papers etc., will probably also have a clause requiring her to undertake any other tasks associated with the provision of education which her employers may reasonably require. It is this kind of clause which gives rise to difficulties.

The significance of this duty has decreased since the introduction in 1971 of the right to claim for unfair dismissal. Up till then the only claim was for wrongful dismissal and disobedience to a lawful order was, and still is, considered a sufficient breach of contract for summary dismissal. Now the issue, in an unfair dismissal claim, will be the reasonableness of the employer's conduct, a point considered in Chapter 11.

The principle that the employee can be required to obey orders permitted by the contract is subject to two qualifications:

1. The order must not be to perform an illegal act. In *Morrish v Henlys* (1973) the employee was dismissed because he refused to acquiesce in a falsification of records. The employer contended that, as it was common practice to do this, the employee's refusal to agree to it was unreasonable. The NIRC, not surprisingly, rejected this and held his dismissal to be unfair.
2. The employer cannot order the employee to do something which would put him/her in danger. In *Ottoman Bank v Chakarian* (1930) the employee was held to have been justified in disobeying an order to remain in Constantinople where he had previously been sentenced to death and was in danger of a further arrest. However, in *Walmsley v Udec Refrigeration* (1972) an employee was not held to be entitled to refuse an order to go to Eire because of a general fear of IRA activity. The decision in *Chakarian* was referred to by Browne-Wilkinson V-C in the *Johnstone v Bloomsbury AHA* case (above) as authority for the proposition that the employer will safeguard the employee's health even if this conflicts with the express terms of the contract.

Although employees have a duty to obey orders permitted under the contract this goes no further. As Denning MR said in *Secretary of State for Employment v ASLEF (No. 2)* (1972): 'a man is not bound to do more for his employer than his contract requires. He can withdraw his goodwill if he pleases.'

### To adapt to new methods of carrying out the employer's business

The extent of this duty is not entirely clear, but it was the basis of the decision in *Cresswell v Board of Inland Revenue* (1984), where the High Court held that

Inland Revenue employees had a duty to adapt to a new computerised system which replaced the manual system of tax coding. Walton J observed that 'an employee is expected to adapt himself to new methods and techniques introduced in the course of employment'. Nevertheless, he also held that the employer was expected to provide training and, if this involved the acquisition of 'esoteric skills', it might not be reasonable to expect the employee to acquire them.

This topic is related to two others:

1. Dismissal for lack of capability (see Chapter 11).
2. Redundancy, because the question arises whether the changes are such that the employee is being asked to do a new job altogether (see Chapter 12).

### To exercise reasonable care and skill in carrying out the contract of employment

The existence of this duty is so obvious that it needs no justification and, again, the main issues now arise in unfair dismissal claims. The only difficult legal issue arises where the employee, in the course of his duties, injures another person who then claims against the employer as being liable for the employee's actions. The employer pays damages and then seeks to recover these from the employee. It was held in *Lister v Romford Ice and Cold Storage Co. Ltd* (1957) that such a claim could be made, as the employee is under an implied contractual duty to exercise reasonable care and therefore is liable for breach of this duty. The effect was that the employee was liable to indemnify the employer for damages which he had paid for the employee's breach of duty.

*Example*

X is employed by Y as a van driver and negligently injures Z (who happens to be another employee and his father, although the same principle would apply if Z had been a complete outsider). Y pays compensation to Z for the negligence of X and then seeks to recover this from X.

These are the facts of *Lister* (above) where it was held that X would be liable. However, it is very rare for an employer to seek to do this, as insurers nearly always pay any damages and they have agreed amongst themselves not to make these claims.

Even so, there is the possibility that an employer might seek an indemnity but in *Harvey v R.G. O'Dell Ltd* (1958) it was held that the employer's right to do so did not arise where the employee was assisting the employer by performing an act outside normal duties. In this case the employee, who normally worked as a storekeeper, drove his motorcycle on his employer's instructions to do some repair work and was involved in an accident in the course of the journey. It was held that the employee was not obliged to indemnify the employer for damages paid as a result. If there were more claims of this kind it could well be that the courts would limit them by further restrictive decisions such as this.

## To exercise good faith in carrying out the contract

This duty has a variety of names, such as 'fidelity' and 'faithfulness', which have a slightly old fashioned ring to them, and accordingly the term 'good faith' will be used in this book. The remedy for a breach is either dismissal (although if the employee then claims for unfair dismissal the question of reasonableness will arise), or for the employer to claim an account of any secret profits which the employee made through the breach. One example is *Boston Deep Sea Fishing and Ice Co. v Ansell* (1888), where a managing director of a company, who had made secret profits out of his position, was liable to account for them to the company.

A modern example of the duty is *British Telecommunications plc v Ticehurst* (1992), where a manager took part in action including strikes, work to rules and go-slows. The Court of Appeal held that where an employee has a discretion as to what action to take and exercises it so as to cause disruption and inconvenience then the duty is broken. The fact that the employee was a manager was relevant but it is probable that this principle applies to all employees. Again, in *Secretary of State for Employment v ASLEF (No. 2)* (1972) railway workers went on a work to rule and overtime ban in support of a pay claim, causing massive disruption to services, and it was held that this was a breach of contract. Denning MR said that to obey the rule book, if done in good faith without any disruption of services, would be lawful but 'what makes it wrong is the object with which it is done'. Accordingly, the duty can be seen as, in some cases, governing the way in which contractual duties are performed.

The duty of good faith has a number of aspects, which are almost separate duties of their own. These will now be considered in turn.

### Duty not to make secret profits out of the position of an employee

An example is the *Boston Deep Sea Fishing* case (above) but it could be argued that this relates to the special fiduciary duties of company directors. An instance of the duty applying in a more typical case is *Reading v Attorney General* (1951), where an army sergeant was paid £20,000 for agreeing to accompany lorries carrying illicit spirits, his uniform guaranteeing that the lorries would not be inspected. He was arrested and imprisoned and the Crown impounded the £20,000. He claimed it back when he was released but it was held that his claim failed. Lord Porter, in the House of Lords, made the point that whether the employer suffered any loss was irrelevant: the liability to account arose simply because the profit had been made.

### To disclose misdeeds

There are three distinct issues:

### 1. Does the employee have a duty to disclose his own misdeeds?

There is no clear authority here, although it could be argued that the duty of trust and confidence implies an openness in the employment relationship which obliges employees to own up to wrongdoings. In *Sybron Corporation v Rochem*

(1983) the Court of Appeal was bound by the decision of the House of Lords in *Bell v Lever Bros* (1932) that there was no such duty, but *Bell* really dealt with the question of mistake at common law and it has been suggested that at least the employee must not actually mislead the employer about the extent of his misdeeds. The distinction is probably between volunteering information about one's misdeeds, which the law does not require, and deliberately misleading the employer when questioned about them.

### 2. Does the employee have a duty to disclose the misdeeds of fellow employees?

In *Sybron* it was held that there is no general duty to report the misdeeds of fellow employees but the existence of the duty will depend on the circumstances. As Stephenson LJ put it in the Court of Appeal: 'He may be so placed in the hierarchy as to have a duty to report the misconduct of his superior . . . or the misconduct of his inferiors.' An employee may therefore have a duty to report the misconduct of those for whom he is the line manager.

### 3. The effect of the Public Interest Disclosure Act 1998

This deals with the somewhat different situation where the employee knows of wrongdoing being committed within his/her organisation. There is no positive duty to disclose it but suppose that the employee does and is then victimised for so doing. In *Initial Services Ltd v Putterill* (1968) it was held that an employer could not obtain an injunction to restrain an ex-employee from revealing details to a newspaper of unlawful price protection practices contrary to the Restrictive Trade Practices Act 1956. However, legislation was needed to provide protection to those who were still employees and this came about through the passage of the Public Interest Disclosure Act, which was passed because of widespread alarm about cases where workers had been too frightened to voice their concerns of particular dangers. Indeed, this became apparent in many public inquiries, ranging from that into the Zeebrugge Ferry tragedy in 1987 to that into the collapse of BCCI. A noticeable example was that at Bristol Royal Infirmary, where there was concern about high infant mortality rates but a consultant who spoke out had been forced to give up his NHS career. It should be noted that the Act, following a recent trend, operates by making additions to another Act, in this case the ERA 1996, where additions are made in particular to ss.43 and 47.

The scheme of the Act is:

- to provide when a disclosure is 'protected', which means the situations when a worker may make a disclosure and be protected by the Act;
- assuming that the disclosure is protected, to set out what type of disclosures will be protected;
- to provide protection for workers who make 'protected disclosures'.

The 'protected disclosure situations' are those where a worker has a reasonable belief that the disclosure tends to show that a criminal offence has been committed; that there has been a failure to comply with a legal obligation; that a miscarriage of justice has occurred; that health and safety or the environment has been endangered; or that there is evidence tending to show that information relating to any of the above matters has been concealed. In addition, a disclosure will be protected in any of the above situations where it relates to a matter which not only *has happened* (as above) but *which is happening* or is *likely to happen in future*. These situations are referred to in the Act as 'relevant failures'.

The protected disclosure situations are those made in good faith to employers or to persons other than the employer who are believed to be responsible; to legal advisers when legal advice is sought; to a Minister of the Crown when the worker's employer is appointed by the Crown or to any person prescribed by order made by the Secretary of State. In all these cases the disclosure becomes a 'qualifying disclosure'. The idea is that disclosures should normally be made to the person responsible rather than, for instance, to the media, and this makes it advisable that employers should have a policy for dealing with whistle-blowing matters internally.

It may be that the above disclosure situations are not adequate, as where the person to whom disclosure should be made is the person whose conduct should actually be disclosed, such as where the employee wishes to complain about his/her employer or where the disclosure has been made to the employer who has not taken effective action. In this case the Act provides for two cases where wider disclosures can be made:

1. Where the disclosure is made in good faith, the worker reasonably believes that its contents are true, it is not made for personal gain (i.e. the worker is not receiving sums from newspapers for the disclosure), it is reasonable to make the disclosure (detailed criteria are laid down for deciding this) and any one of the following applies:
   (a) the worker reasonably believes that he would be subject to a detriment by his/her employer if he made the disclosure to him/her or to a person prescribed by the Secretary of State (as defined above); or
   (b) if there is no person prescribed then the worker may make the disclosure if he/she reasonably believes that evidence relating to the relevant failure would be concealed or destroyed if disclosure is made to the employer; or
   (c) if the worker has previously made a disclosure to the employer or to a prescribed person.
2. Where the disclosure deals with a 'relevant failure' of an 'exceptionally serious nature'. There is the same provision that it must not be made for personal gain. Here the worker is not obliged to have gone through an internal procedure, such as going to the employer, but can bring the matter straight to the attention of anyone appropriate. Assuming that the disclosure is protected then the worker is protected from victimisation as a result and any dismissal resulting from making such a disclosure is automatically unfair if the disclosure is the reason for it or the principal reason.

A final point is that any clause in an agreement, which purports to prevent a worker from making a 'protected disclosure', is void. This is particularly aimed at confidentiality clauses in settlement agreements.

### Not to disclose or otherwise misuse confidential information

In *Faccenda Chicken Ltd v Fowler* (1986) the employee, a sales manager, left to set up a rival business and his (former) employer claimed that he had used confidential information relating to the needs of customers and the prices which they paid to the detriment of that employer. It was held that the information was not confidential and thus the action failed, but Neill LJ took the opportunity to lay down the following points about the extent and nature of the duty of confidentiality:

1. One should consider any obligations imposed by the express terms of the contract. There were none in *Fowler*.
2. If there are no express terms then one should consider the effect of the implied term of confidentiality. The extent of the duty will vary with the nature of the contract but Neill LJ specifically held that an employee who copies out, or deliberately memorises, a list of customers for use after he leaves will be in breach. (This was the decision in *Robb v Green* (1895) and this applies even though there is no contractual restriction on the employee doing business with his former employer's customers.)
3. Where the employment has ended, the duty is restricted to one not to disclose trade secrets. In deciding whether a matter is a trade secret one must look at the nature of the employment, the nature of the information, whether the employer impressed on the employee that the information was confidential and whether the information can easily be isolated from information which can be disclosed.

An employer should always deal with confidentiality by an express clause in the contract and this applies particularly to clauses preventing the use of trade secrets after leaving employment. Another possibility is to include a garden leave clause in the contract (see above). The extent to which such clauses can be enforced is considered in the section below on contracts in restraint of trade.

### The employee's duty of good faith and inventions

The common law position is that there is an implied term in employees' contracts that the employer is entitled to the benefit of inventions made by the employee which arise out of employment (*British Syphon Co. Ltd v Homewood* (1956)). This has now been almost entirely overtaken by the provisions of the Patents Act 1977 so that the common law is only relevant where the invention was made before the Act came into force or the employee was not employed in the UK. The Act is considerably more favourable to employees than the common law, which was widely felt to be harsh.

Section 39(1) sets out the circumstances when an invention will belong to the employer:

(a) where the invention was –
  (i) made either in the course of the normal duties of the employee or made in the course of duties which were not normal duties but were specifically assigned to the employee; and
  (ii) an invention might reasonably be expected to result;
(b) where the invention was made in the course of the duties of the employee and, at the time, he had a special obligation to further the interests of the employer's undertaking.

The difference between (a) and (b) is that in (b) the invention belongs to the employer, whether or not an invention might reasonably be expected to result, and it is intended to cover employees such as company directors who have a special obligation to further the interests of the company.

If neither (a) nor (b) apply then s.39(2) provides that the invention shall belong to the employee. Thus the effect of the Act is to replace the previous blanket provisions with two specific cases where the invention shall belong to the employee.

Section 40 of the Act then deals with two other situations:

(a) where the invention does belong to the employer under (a) or (b) below the employee may claim compensation where it has proved to be of 'outstanding benefit' to the employer;
(b) where the invention belonged to the employee under the rules in s.39 (above) but the employee has assigned it to the employer and has, however, received inadequate benefits from it in relation to the benefits received by the employer.

In both cases the employee may make a claim for compensation to the Patents Court or the Patents Office within a year of the patent expiring and may be awarded a 'fair share' of the actual or anticipated benefits.

Section 41 lays down the criteria for deciding this. In the case of (a) it is:

(i) the nature of the employee's duties, his remuneration and any other advantages which he gained from the invention or from his employment in general;
(ii) the employee's effort and skill in making the invention;
(iii) the effort and skill contributed by any third party;
(iv) the significance of any contribution made by the employer.

In the case of (b) it is:

(i) any conditions in any licence granted in respect of the invention or patent;
(ii) the extent to which the invention was made jointly between the employee and a third party;
(iii) the significance of any contribution made by the employer.

The Act contains provisions designed to prevent the employee's rights under it from being taken away by any agreement with the employer. Thus s.42 provides that no contract can take away any of the employee's rights under the Act and s.40(4) provides that the rules on compensation shall likewise not be affected by any agreement made individually by the employee with the employer but that a collective agreement may govern the matter instead. The implication is that an agreement made by the employee's union would be most unlikely to diminish his rights.

In the case of copyright in material, s.11 of the Copyright, Designs and Patents Act 1988 provides that the copyright in works produced by the employee during employment belongs to the employee unless there is any agreement to the contrary. There are no provisions similar to those above dealing with patents and thus an employee who produces a book, film or other work which is copyright is worse off than employees who invent.

### The duty not to damage the employer's business when engaging in other work

This duty is best considered in relation to the doctrine of restraint of trade, which is dealt with below.

### The doctrine of restraint of trade and other restrictions on work carried out by the employee during or after employment

#### Example

X Ltd is an advertising agency. It is concerned about the following situations:

(a) Z works in the accounts department and it is known that at weekends he has assisted at promotional events run by W Ltd, another agency. What can X Ltd do?
(b) Y manages the advertising accounts of a number of major companies. It is known that she is thinking of leaving and going to work for another advertising agency. What action can X Ltd take?

In the case of Z, as he is still an employee, the answer is to be found in the common duty law duty of good faith and, in particular, in the duty not to engage in any outside work that could damage the employer's business.

Y's case is more difficult. Her contract might contain a garden leave clause which would put Y on very long notice during which she would be paid and still be an employee but would not be working. If such a clause did not already exist then X Ltd could unilaterally impose one but this might be held to be invalid, as in *William Hill v Tucker* (see above). Even if the garden leave clause was in the contract it might not be entirely effective, as we shall see. An alternative is that her contract contains a restraint of trade clause under which, on leaving her employment with X Ltd, she agrees not to work for any other advertising agency for, perhaps, one year after leaving the employment of X Ltd. These clauses, if carefully drafted, are effective, but in the absence of such careful drafting they run the risk of being struck down by the courts.

Each of these points will now be considered in turn.

#### The common law duty not to engage in any outside work which could damage the employer's business

The leading case is *Hivac Ltd v Park Royal Scientific Instruments Ltd* (1946), where employees of the plaintiffs, who were engaged on highly skilled work making valves for hearing aids, were employed on exactly the same work for a rival firm outside hours. The two firms were in competition with each other and the court held that an injunction would be granted to restrain the rival firm from employing them in this way. Greene MR observed that 'it would be deplorable if it were laid down that a workman could, consistently with his duty to his employer, knowingly, deliberately and secretly set himself to do in his spare time something which would inflict great harm on his employer's business'. On the other hand, he observed that it would be wrong to place restrictions on employees such as manual workers to make use of their leisure for profit. The vital factors will be the work that the employee does and the pay he receives (see *Nottingham University v Fishel* (2000)). In *Laughton and Hawley v Bapp Industrial Supplies Ltd* (1986) the fact that two employees were intending to leave and set up in competition with their (former) employer was not held to be in breach of the duty of good faith, although there might well be a restraint of trade clause which could apply here. If the employer was, whilst working for his employer, directly soliciting customers to transfer their custom to him when he left, then this could be a ground for dismissal. Clauses restraining employees from working for others may also be expressly inserted into the contract and will be subject to the same principles as stated above.

### Garden leave clauses

These have been discussed above and they are a more straightforward method of protecting the employer's interests as the employee in question remains an employee, and is paid wages, throughout the period of garden leave. However, the courts may not enforce them because the usual method of enforcement, through an injunction, is at the courts' discretion. An example is *Provident Financial Group plc v Hayward* (1989), where a six-month garden leave clause imposed on a financial director was not effective to prevent him from taking up another post towards the end of the period. As Dillon J observed: 'The practice of long periods of garden leave is obviously capable of abuse.' If the other business for which the employee wished to leave and work for before the end of the notice period 'had nothing whatever to do with the business of the employers' then the courts would not enforce a garden leave clause. In addition, as in *William Hill v Tucker* (above), a garden leave clause may infringe the employee's right to be provided with work.

### Contracts in restraint of trade

This somewhat old-fashioned term is a reminder of the fact that these clauses were, and still are, used in quite another connection: where a person has bought a business and paid for the goodwill, he/she may then impose a restraint on the seller of the business preventing her from opening a similar business nearby which competes with the one sold. In the employment context, these clauses usually come into force on termination of employment and restrain the employee from engaging in certain work after leaving employment. As such, they have been viewed with suspicion by the courts as infringing a fundamental right to work for whomever one pleases. It is also possible for these clauses to apply *during* employment where the clause restricts the employee from engaging in certain other work. They are sometimes referred to as *covenants* in restraint of trade. A covenant is a promise contained in a deed, and this reminds us that these agreements, especially if they related to the sale of a business, were generally contained in a deed. The term 'contract' should be used where employee restraints are concerned.

These clauses are void unless proved reasonable in the interests of both the parties and the public and the onus of proving this is on the person seeking to enforce the clause. (Lord Macnaghten in *Nordenfelt v Maxim Nordenfelt Guns and Ammunition Co. Ltd* (1894)). In practice, the courts have stressed the interests of the parties far more than the rather vaguer question of the public interest. However, in *Esso Petroleum Co. Ltd v Harper's Garage Ltd* (1968) the question of public interest was to some extent revived by remarks in the House of Lords and has appeared in some recent cases (see below).

A restraint will only be held reasonable if the employer has an enforceable interest to protect. Such an interest will cover knowledge by the employee of trade secrets, cases where the employee has influence over customers, cases where the employee may, on leaving, solicit other employees to join him in a competing business and other miscellaneous cases dealing mainly with sportsmen and women.

A good, if old, example of knowledge of trade secrets or specialised knowledge of the workings of a business is *Forster and Sons Ltd v Suggett* (1918), where a restraint on an employee, who had knowledge of secret glass manufacturing processes, preventing him from working for a similar firm for five years, was held to be valid. In *Littlewoods Organisation Ltd v Harris* (1978) knowledge by the executive director of a mail order business of the details of how it worked was held to be an interest capable of protection. The principles set out in *Faccenda Chicken v Fowler* (above) may be useful in deciding what information can be protected.

Cases where the employee has influence over customers and where a restraint has been successfully imposed include those on a solicitor's managing clerk (now a legal executive) (*Fitch v Dewes* (1921)), an estate agent (*Scorer v Seymour Johns* (1966)) and a milkman (*Home Counties Dairies v Skilton* (1970)). The employer needs to show that the (former) employee will use his influence over customers to try to persuade them to transfer their custom to wherever he is going to work in future. Thus in *Home Counties v Skilton* the milkman spoke to customers on his milk round telling them that he was leaving Home Counties Dairies and setting up in business on his own, covering exactly the same round. The clear implication was that he hoped that they would follow him.

Cases where the employee is leaving to set up or join a competing business and solicits other employees to come with him, include *Dawnay, Day and Co. Ltd v DeBraconier d'Alphen* (1997), in which it was held that covenants preventing the solicitation of other employees by Eurobond dealers who were leaving to join a competing business were valid. In *TSC (Europe) v Massey* (1999) the High

Court again expressly recognised that an employer has a legitimate interest in maintaining a stable, trained workforce although here the restraint failed on its facts (see below).

If the employer does not have a legitimate interest to protect, then no restraint can be valid. In *Attwood v Lamont* (1920) a restraint on a tailor preventing him from being engaged in various types of outfitters business was invalid, as the only reason for imposing it was that his employer feared him because of his skill and therefore did not want him to work in competition with him. In *Eastham v Newcastle United FC* (1964) the retain and transfer system which prevented footballers from moving to other clubs at the end of their contracts was held void and in *Greig v Insole* (1977) a ban imposed on English cricketers because they had signed to play in matches in Australia organised by a private promoter was held void, as the matches posed no threat to English cricket. The question of public interest was also raised by the court in that the ban would deprive the public of the chance of seeing the cricketers play. A different situation arose in *Kores Manufacturing Co. v Kolok Manufacturing Co.* (1959), where two companies agreed that neither would employ anyone who had been employed by the other for the previous five years, the reason being that it benefited both firms to have a stable workforce. However the court held that this was unreasonable, although in *Esso Petroleum v Harper's Garage* (above) some members of the House of Lords thought that the correct ground for the decision should have been that the agreement was against the public interest as in *Greig v Insole* (above).

Assuming that the employer does have an enforceable interest to protect then the restraint will be valid provided that it is no wider then reasonably necessary to protect the interest. Three issues are looked at:

1. the area the restraint covers;
2. the activities it covers;
3. the time it lasts.

*Example*

X works in a hairdresser's business owned by Y in Worcester and a clause in her contract states that on leaving the business she must not work as a hairdresser or beautician in Worcestershire for a period of five years.

Although Y probably has an enforceable interest to protect, as X may well have some influence over customers, the restraint is certainly invalid on each of the three grounds above: the area is too wide (Worcester would probably be as far as it could stretch), it includes work as a beautician as well as a hairdresser; and five years is far too long. Therefore, the restraint would completely fail. Y could have successfully imposed some restraint but, as she tried to impose too great a restraint, she ends up with nothing.

In *Greer v Sketchleys Ltd* (1978) a restraint was imposed on the director of a dry cleaning company which prevented him, on leaving, from being engaged in a similar dry cleaning business in any part of the UK. As Sketchleys only operated in the Midlands and London, the restraint was too wide, although Denning MR observed that had they operated over the whole of the UK then the restraint might have been upheld. Similarly, in *TSC v Massey* (above) the non-solicitation clause was void as it applied to the solicitation of *any* employee, no matter what their role in the business was, and it applied to those who joined the company after the defendants had left. An extreme case is *Fitch v Dewes* (above), where a lifelong restraint on a managing clerk was valid, a possible reason being that it only applied to practice within seven miles of Tamworth Town Hall.

There has been some discussion as to how far, if at all, the courts can interpret a restraint, which may appear to be too wide on its literal interpretation, so that it accords with the intentions of the party imposing it. In *Littlewoods v Harris* (above) the Court of Appeal considered a restraint which covered working for a subsidiary company of the employer and which was on its face too wide, as the employer had many subsidiaries, some of which had completely different businesses to that of mail order, in which the (ex-)employee had worked. The court was prepared to limit the restraint to those subsidiaries concerned with mail order. Two recent decisions have shown a conflicting approach. In *Hollis v Stocks* (2000) the restraint prevented a solicitor from working within ten miles of the firm's office and 'work' was interpreted as 'work as a solicitor'. Yet in *Wincanton Ltd v Cranny* (2001) a restraint which prevented a manager from being engaged in any business which was in competition with that of his former employer was too wide and the court refused to interpret it so that it was valid. Sedley LJ observed that those who live by these clauses must, if need be, perish by them. If the clause is too wide, so be it!

The doctrine of restraint of trade has also been held to apply to exclusive service contracts where the restraint applies during employment rather than after it. These contracts are found in the music publishing trade and an example is *Schroeder Music Publishing Co. Ltd v Macaulay* (1974), where a contract between a young songwriter and a music publisher provided that the songwriter should give his exclusive services to the publisher for five years without the publisher being under any obligation to publish any of his works. The songwriter was only guaranteed one sum of £50 as an advance against future royalties during that time. The House of Lords held that the agreement was totally one-sided and void. However, as was seen above, restraints on employees during employment can be valid (see e.g. *Hivac v Park Royal Instruments* (1946)), but these are not exclusive service agreements but clauses relating to work which could damage the employer's business.

A contract in restraint of trade may in fact contain more than one restraint and it may be that one or more restraints are valid but others are void. If so, it may be possible to sever the invalid restraint and leave the valid one. A good example is *Scorer v Seymour Johns* (1966), where the problem was that although the employer had a valid reason for imposing some restraint on an estate agent, the restraint applied not only to the area around the office where he worked but also to the area around another office where he did not work. The second restraint was severed and the one relating to the office where he worked was upheld. The court will not re-write the contract nor will severance be appropriate where the whole restraint is invalid as in *Attwood v Lamont* (above).

If the restraint is valid then it can be enforced by damages, where the activities of the ex-employee in breach of the clause have caused loss, and/or an injunction can be sought enforcing the restraint. One problem for employers is that the courts have a general discretion whether to grant an injunction and it is possible that, even if the restraint is lawful, an injunction could be refused if the court felt that it would serve no useful purpose. However, the general practice is to grant injunctions if the restraint is valid.

If an employee is wrongfully dismissed then a restraint clause, even if otherwise valid, cannot be enforced because the employer, by wrongfully dismissing the employee, has repudiated the whole contract, including the restraint clause, which accordingly falls (*General Billposting Co. v Atkinson* (1909)). In *Rock Refrigeration Ltd v Jones* (1997) the court considered the effect of a clause attempting to avoid the effect of *General Billposting* which stated that a restraint clause applied on termination of the contract 'howsoever caused'. It was held that this was ineffective and the restraint clause still falls. An as yet unanswered question is whether the same applies where the employee claims unfair dismissal, the problem being that a finding of unfair dismissal does not involve a finding of breach of contract. It would seem ludicrous that a wrongfully dismissed employee is not bound by a restraint clause yet an unfairly dismissed employee still is and a possible way forward might be for the courts to say in an unfair dismissal case that the conduct of the employer was not only unreasonable but also a breach of contract so as to disentitle him from relying on the restraint. In constructive dismissal cases there is a finding of breach anyway.

## ■ Terms implied by a collective agreement

A collective agreement is one made between an employer or employer's association and a trade union. The object will be to deal with such matters as pay, hours of work and disputes procedures. Such agreements very rarely, if ever, have contractual force (see *Ford Motor Co. v AUEW* (1969), where it was felt that such agreements were reached against a background adverse to enforceability) and are, by s.179 of TULRCA, presumed not to be legally binding unless they are in writing and expressly stated that they are binding. We are here concerned with whether such an agreement can be incorporated in the contracts of individual employees.

There are two possibilities: express incorporation of the collective agreement into contracts of employment; and implied incorporation of the collective agreement into contracts of employment.

### Express incorporation of the collective agreement into contracts of employment

An example is *National Coal Board v Galley* (1958), where the contracts of colliery foremen stated that their contracts were to be regulated by national agreements then in force. A new collective agreement was made under which deputies were required to work on such days as might reasonably be required.

The defendant refused to work on Saturdays and was held to be in breach of contract. An interesting, if controversial, extension of the principle of express incorporation occurred in *Cadoux v Central Regional Council* (1986). The employee's letter of appointment stated that he would be employed subject to national conditions of service, which included a non-contributory pension scheme. The employers then withdrew the scheme and it was held by the Court of Session that they were entitled to do so. Lord Ross said that 'the clear inference from the fact that they are the defendants' rules is that the defendants are entitled to alter them'. The effect was to give the employer the power unilaterally to alter the terms of the contract of employment. On the other hand, in *Robertson v British Gas Corporation* (1983) part of a collective agreement which regulated the amounts payable to employees under a bonus scheme was subsequently terminated by the employer. It was held that the employees were still entitled to the bonus payments as any variation had been agreed by the employers. The court in *Cadoux* distinguished *Robertson* on the basis that in *Robertson* the collective agreement had been made between an employer and a trade union, whereas here the agreement was made through consultations locally, but this seems scarcely satisfactory. A further point is that the decision in *Robertson* is also authority for saying that a collective agreement which is not legally enforceable between the parties can still be a source of binding terms in an individual contract. This view was upheld in *Marley v Forward Trust Group Ltd* (1986).

### Implied incorporation of the collective agreement into contracts of employment

A distinction has been drawn between those terms which are considered suitable for incorporation because it is clear what the parties' intentions are, such as terms relating to hours and pay, and those which are not. In *British Leyland (UK) Ltd v McQuilken* (1978) a provision in a collective agreement that an employer would interview employees to establish whether they wished to take redundancy or be retrained was held inappropriate for incorporation. Actual redundancy selection procedures were held not to be incorporated in *Alexander v Standard Telephones and Cables Ltd (No. 2)* (1991), but a different view was taken in *Anderson v Pringle of Scotland Ltd* (1998), where it was held that a redundancy selection procedure agreement providing that selection would be on the 'last in, first out' principle was suitable for incorporation. It seems that the latter decision is preferable, given the impact that selection procedures have on individuals.

It is noteworthy that in many cases the terms of a collective agreement are incorporated by implied acceptance by employees. Suppose that a collective agreement grants employees a pay rise but also requires them to work more flexible shift patterns. Once employees have accepted the extra pay they can scarcely reject the part obliging them to work the more flexible shifts. It is not possible to choose which parts of an agreement to observe.

Although a union member may, therefore, find that a collective agreement is a source of contractual terms, what of a non-unionist? The point has caused difficulty. In *Singh v British Steel Corporation* (1974) a non-unionist was held not to be bound by a collective agreement, although it has been suggested that the idea that a non-unionist is not bound rests on the theory that the union acts as the agent of its members in making the agreement and this has not always been accepted, as in *Burton Group Ltd v Smith* (1977). The law has never devised a satisfactory conceptual basis for the incorporation of implied terms and, as a result, the position of non-unionists is in theory uncertain. In practice they will normally be bound where, as in the above example, the agreement grants a pay rise which they accept.

A final point is that where a collective agreement contains a no strike clause then, by s.180 of TULRCA 1992, this will not form part of individuals' contracts of employment unless:

(a) the collective agreement is made by an independent trade union and is in writing;
(b) it states that the no strike clause may be incorporated into contracts of employment;
(c) it is reasonably accessible during working hours;
(d) the worker's own contract, expressly or impliedly, incorporates it into his contract.

The object is to prevent individual workers from being sued for damages for going on strike when their union, which called them out on strike, could not be because the collective agreement is not legally binding. It would be most unusual to find a situation where a no strike clause *was* incorporated into individual contracts.

## ARE WORK RULES, POLICY HANDBOOKS AND OTHER MANAGERIAL DOCUMENTS INCORPORATED INTO INDIVIDUAL CONTRACTS OF EMPLOYMENT?

Although such rules may be part of the contract where, for example, a contract of employment expressly states that a certain policy is incorporated, otherwise these will not be contractual and therefore can be imposed or altered by the management whenever it wishes. Attempts to argue that they are contractual have included:

1. *Dryden v Greater Glasgow Health Board* (1992), where an employee's claim that the introduction of a non-smoking policy gave grounds for constructive dismissal as being a breach of contract failed because the policy was not contractual and could thus be introduced at will.
2. *Wandsworth BC v D'Silva* (1998), where an argument that a code of procedure on staff sickness could not be unilaterally altered by the employer failed as it was not contractual.
3. *Taylor v Secretary of State for Scotland* (1999), where an equal opportunities policy stating that the employer would not discriminate on the grounds of,

*inter alia,* age was not contractual so that an employee dismissed on this ground could not use it to claim that his dismissal was a breach of contract.

Although the courts have resolutely set their face against incorporation of these documents into the contract, if a claim is brought by an employee for unfair dismissal then, as the basis of the claim is that the employer has acted unreasonably, a failure to observe a code or similar document may well count against the employer.

## TO WHAT EXTENT CAN AN EMPLOYER VARY A CONTRACT OF EMPLOYMENT?

The traditional view that a variation needs the consent of both sides is still true and therefore an employer cannot unilaterally vary a contract. However, two points need to be made:

1. A failure to agree to a variation may, *in some situations*, give the employer grounds for fairly dismissing the employee. This is explored in Chapter 12 and the case of *RS Components v Irwin* (1973) should be particularly noted.
2. An employer may reserve the power in the contract itself to change the contract. However, in *Wandsworth BC v D'Silva* (above) Woolf MR held that clear language was needed to reserve this sort of power and that 'the court is unlikely to favour a variation which does more than enable a party to vary contractual provisions with which that party is required to comply'. The effect of this is that a power to vary provisions to the disadvantage of the employee is unlikely to be accepted unless, at the very least, it is very clearly conferred by the contract.

# Chapter 6

# Continuity of employment

## INTRODUCTION

Some employment rights can be claimed by all employees, such as the rights conferred by sex, race and disabilities legislation. Other rights depend on the employee having a certain amount of continuous employment. One of the main examples is the requirement for an employee claiming unfair dismissal to have one year's continuous employment (although there are exceptions, as we shall see) but there are others: the right to redundancy pay and the amount; the right to a statement of initial employment particulars; and various maternity rights, which all depend on a certain amount of continuous employment.

The reason why certain rights depend on periods of continuous employment whereas others are open to all employees is not easy to find. The origin of the restriction of the right to claim unfair dismissal to employees with a certain amount of qualifying employment appears to be administrative: in 1970 the Department of Employment and Productivity in *Industrial Relations Bill: Consultative Document*, para 53 stated that the initial two-year qualifying period was needed to prevent industrial tribunals (as they were then) being flooded with claims but that the period would be reduced later. This indeed happened, as the period was reduced to one year in 1974 and to six months in 1975. The Conservative government elected in 1979 then saw the ability to bring claims for unfair dismissal as a bar to firms taking on workers and so the period was raised to a year in 1979 and to two years in 1985.

There was also, until 1995, a requirement that employees should, in certain circumstances, have worked for a minimum number of hours a week. The origin of this appears to be found in the Contracts of Employment Act 1963, which gave a right to receive a written statement of terms and conditions of employment and a right to minimum periods of notice to employees who worked at least 21 hours a week. The intention was to exclude employees with spare time or weekend jobs or where the employment was not of substantial importance to the parties. This was carried through into unfair dismissal legislation and, by the 1990s, unfair dismissal could not be claimed (except in certain cases) by employees working for less than 16 hours a week or, where the employee had worked for over five years, eight hours a week. However, by the 1990s, the increase in part-time work and the growing importance attached to statutory rights made this restriction seem anachronistic.

In *R v Secretary of State for Employment, ex parte Equal Opportunities Commission* (1995) the House of Lords held that the restriction to employees with certain hours of work a week and the consequent exclusion of many part-time employees constituted unlawful indirect discrimination against women, given that nearly 90% of employees prevented from claiming were women. Therefore the government removed the restriction by the Employment Protection (Part Time Employee) Regulations 1995. The effect is that the restriction on the number of hours worked has gone but the need for a certain number of weeks' continuity of employment remains.

## THE RULES ON CONTINUITY OF EMPLOYMENT IN OPERATION

*Example*

X was employed by Y from 1 January 2001 until 1 July 2001. He then left and was employed by Z from 1 July 2001 until 2 January 2002. Z then dismissed X and X wished to claim unfair dismissal. He cannot do so (unless he is within the excepted classes) as, although he has over one year's employment, it is not with the same employer. He does not have sufficient continuity of employment.

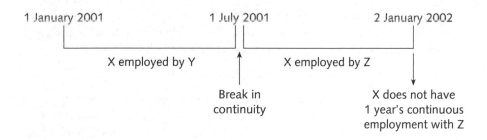

## ◾ Fundamental rule

This is found in s.212(1) of the ERA 1996, which provides that: 'Any week during the whole or part of which an employee's relations with his employer are governed by a contract of employment counts in computing the employee's period of employment.'

The following points emerge from this provision:

1. Only weeks during which the employee is actually employed by that employer count in computing continuity in claims against that employer. This is, however, subject to exceptions where in some circumstances weeks of employment with

one employer can be carried over and added to weeks of employment with another employer when a business is transferred (see below and Chapter 12).

2. Only weeks in which the employee actually has a contract of employment with that employer count. This point is illustrated by *Carmichael v National Power plc* (1999), which was discussed in Chapter 4. Had the power station guides claimed for unfair dismissal on the basis that they had acted as guides for a certain number of years, their claim would have failed because it was held that they did not have a contract of employment when not acting as guides, although they may have had such a contract when they did. In *Hellyer Bros v McLeod* (1987) it was held that trawlermen had no continuity of employment as they were employed on a series of crew agreements which lasted for each voyage but were not employed under a global contract. Therefore, they were not entitled to redundancy payments. This case can be set alongside other cases on employment status such as *Nethermere v Taverna and Gardiner* (1983) and *O'Kelly v Trusthouse Forte* (1983) as an example of the problems which the courts have had in defining employment status. Where, however, there is a contract of employment then continuity is not affected by the fact that the duties may not often be performed. In *Colley v Corkindale* (1995) an employee only worked one shift every fortnight but had continuity as her contract gave her continuity.

3. Section 212(1) simply refers to the employee's relations with the employer being governed by 'a' contract of employment and this means that continuity will be preserved even though an employee may have several different contracts with the same employer. The point was well put by Denning MR in *Wood v York City Council* (1978): 'even though a man may change his job from, say, manual work to clerical work, even though he may change the site of his work from one place to another . . . as long as he is with the same employer all the way through, then it is continuous employment.'

Other provisions of the ERA raise the following points:

1. Section 210(5) of the ERA provides a presumption of continuity and therefore an employer alleging that there is no continuity must prove this. However, in *Secretary of State for Employment v Cohen* (1987) it was held that this only applied to employment with one employer and where the issue related to continuity on the transfer of a business then it was for the tribunal to find whether there was continuity. In effect the burden of proof would be neutral.

2. Section 203 of the ERA prevents any agreement from waiving continuity. Therefore, if a new employer on the transfer of a business made employees agree that their service with the previous employer did not count, then it would be for the courts to decide whether it did and the agreement would have no effect. It is, of course, possible for an employer to agree that there *will* be continuity in a case where there might not have been, as this will have the opposite effect as it will give employees rights which they might not have had.

## WEEKS WHICH COUNT TOWARDS CONTINUITY EVEN THOUGH THERE IS NO CONTRACT OF EMPLOYMENT

Until now, the emphasis has been on the need for employees to show that their contract is continuous for a certain period of time and, conversely, that if there is no contract of employment in existence, then continuity will be broken. However, s.212 of the ERA then provides that in certain situations continuity will be preserved even though the contract is not in existence. In effect, these are exceptions to the general rule.

The exceptions are as follows:

### Employee incapable of work through sickness or injury

Continuity will be preserved in any week in which the employee is incapable of work through sickness or injury (s.212(3)(a)) up to a maximum of 26 weeks (s.212(4)).

*Example*

X's contract of employment with Y began on 1 January 2001. On 1 July 2001 X entered hospital for an operation and Y terminated X's contract of employment. On 1 January 2002 X returned to work with a new contract of employment but was dismissed the next day. X has one year's continuous employment because his absence did not last for more than 26 weeks even though he actually only had a contract of employment for one day over six months. Had Y not terminated X's contract of employment on 1 July 2001 then continuity would not have been affected at all, as his contract would have continued. As it is, X is saved by the exception to the basic rule. If, on the other hand, X had not returned to work until 2 January 2002 and he had not had a contract whilst he was away, then continuity would have been broken as his absence would have lasted more than 26 weeks.

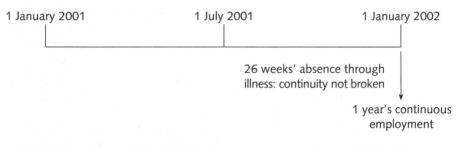

| 1 January 2001 | 1 July 2001 | 1 January 2002 |

26 weeks' absence through illness: continuity not broken

1 year's continuous employment

*Note*: Whether Y should have terminated X's contract when X entered hospital is, of course, a separate question and the whole topic of termination will be dealt with in Chapter 11.

### Employee absent on account of temporary cessation of work

Continuity will also be preserved in any week in which the employee is absent from work on account of a temporary cessation of work (s.212(3)(b)). This time there is no upper limit as there was above and, in theory, the cessation could last for any length of time, although a long cessation would probably not be held as temporary. Once again, it must be remembered that if the contract continues then this provision is not relevant as continuity is preserved anyway.

The following points must be satisfied for this exception to apply:

1. There must be a cessation of work. In *Fitzgerald v Hall, Russell & Co.* (1970) the House of Lords held that the essential requirement is that the employee's actual work must have ceased and this may be even where the employer's business is still continuing.

2. The cessation of work must be temporary. In *Fitzgerald v Hall, Russell & Co.* it was pointed out that this must be looked at with the benefit of hindsight: 'What at the time seems to be permanent may turn out to be temporary, and what at the time seems to be temporary may turn out to be permanent.' Despite this common sense approach, problems have emerged in deciding whether an absence is temporary. In *Ford v Warwickshire CC* (1983) the applicant was a teacher who had been employed under a series of fixed-term contracts each for the academic year from September to July. It was held that the break between them was only a temporary cessation of work and there-fore she had continuity. Lord Diplock said that 'temporary' means 'transient', which itself accords with the general approach in *Fitzgerald*, but he then put forward a somewhat mathematical approach to decide cases where there is seasonal employment followed by breaks such as occur in hotel work. Here he suggested that one should compare the length of the period between the seasonal contracts and the length of the contracts themselves. If the period of the break is short compared with the length of the contract then a cessation could be temporary. In *Flack v Kodak Ltd* (1986) the applicant had been employed for irregular periods of time in the photo-finishing department, with her work varying according to seasonal demand. Woolf LJ, in the Court of Appeal, held that Lord Diplock's mathematical approach was not appropriate to irregular work patterns. Instead, 'it is the whole period of employment which is relevant. In the case of irregular employment, if the periods of employment either side of the dismissal are only looked at, a most misleading comparison would be drawn'. In view of the different approaches in these two cases, the question of how to view the relationship between breaks and periods of work is not settled but it is submitted that the view of Woolf LJ is to be preferred as avoiding what would otherwise be fine distinc-tions based on precise computations of time. In *Sillars v Charrington Fuels Ltd* (1989) it was suggested that the approach in *Ford* could be used where the gaps in employment are regular but that the approach in *Flack* is preferable where there an irregular pattern of employment.

3. The absence must be on account of the cessation of work. In *Roach v CSB (Moulds)* (1991) an employee was dismissed by his employers and then worked for another employer for 12 days and was then re-engaged by his previous employers before finally being dismissed by them. It was held that

continuity had been broken as the 12 days' absence was not on account of a temporary cessation of work.

## Employment regarded as continuing by arrangement or custom

Any week in which by arrangement or custom the employment is regarded as continuing will also count. An example of this might be where the employee is granted leave of absence on compassionate grounds but without pay so that the contract does continue. However, any arrangement to preserve continuity must be agreed on before the absence begins. In *Lloyds Bank Ltd v Secretary of State for Employment* (1979) this provision was used where the employee's contract provided for employment on a one week on, one week off basis but the employee actually had a contract of employment throughout the time. In *Ford v Warwickshire CC* (1983) it was pointed out that none of these exceptions applies where there is an existing contract and so the correctness of the decision in the *Lloyds Bank* case is suspect. Therefore, it could be argued that the employee fell between two stools: she had a contract all the time and so s.212 was inapplicable but her contract contained breaks and so she did not have continuity.

Note that there was a provision that continuity was not affected by absence through pregnancy or childbirth but this has been repealed by the Employment Relations Act 1999, as the contracts of employees now continue through maternity leave.

## WEEKS WHICH DO NOT BREAK CONTINUITY ALTHOUGH THEY DO NOT COUNT TOWARDS PERIODS OF CONTINUOUS EMPLOYMENT

In the above examples all the actual breaks in continuity were treated as if they did not exist and therefore not only did they not break continuity but also the weeks actually counted towards continuous employment. However, in the case of employees on strike there is a kind of halfway house under which weeks do not break continuity but they do not themselves actually count in computing continuous employment and the same may apply where there is a lock-out.

The two cases are set out in s.216 and are as follows.

## Employee taking part in a strike

Any week, or part of a week, where the employee is taking part in a strike does not break continuity (s.216(2)). A strike is defined for this purpose by s.235(5) as where a body of employees acting in combination cease work or where there is a concerted refusal to continue to work with the aim of compelling the employer to accept or not accept terms or conditions affecting employment. It also includes cases where the strike action is taken to aid other employees. This definition of a strike only applies to the continuity of employment provisions and redundancy payments (see Chapter 12). There is another definition of a strike for the purposes of the law on collective action (see s.246 of TULRCA and Chapter 14).

## ◼ Employee locked out by employer

Any week, or part of a week, during which an employee is locked out by the employer does not break continuity (s.216(3)). A lock-out is defined for present purposes by s.235(4) as where an employer closes a place of employment, suspends work or refuses to continue to employ employees with the aim of compelling employees to accept or not to accept terms or conditions affecting employment. It also includes situations where the object of the lock-out is to aid another employer.

In the case of a strike s.216(2) is clear: continuity is not broken, although s.216(1) provides that the weeks on strike do not count towards continuity. In the case of a lock-out s.216(3) states that continuity is not broken but nothing is said about whether the weeks count. The reason is probably that, as a strike is normally a breach of contract (see Chapter 14), it was felt that weeks on strike should not count, but as a lock-out results from action taken by the employer employees locked out will not normally be in breach. The position is probably that where the contract continues when employees are locked out then weeks will count but where it does not then they will not.

*Example*

X's contract of employment with Y began on 1 January 2001. On 1 February 2001 X was called out on strike by his union and did not return to work until 1 March 2001. On 1 February 2002 X was dismissed by Y and asks whether he has one year's continuous employment. The answer is yes. The month on strike did not count but the period before it can be added to the period after it and the result is that X has one year's continuous employment.

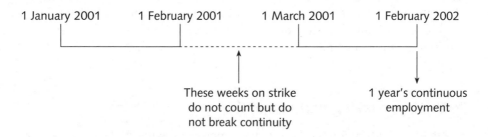

| 1 January 2001 | 1 February 2001 | 1 March 2001 | 1 February 2002 |

These weeks on strike do not count but do not break continuity

1 year's continuous employment

The following other points arise:

1. There is no requirement that the strike be official, although such a distinction is made in deciding whether a dismissal of employees on strike is fair (see Chapter 14).

2. Any period of time after the strike ends but before there is a return to work is likely to be covered by s.212(3)(b) as a temporary cessation of work.

3. Where employees are dismissed whilst on strike continuity will not be affected, as it was held in *Bloomfield v Springfield Hosiery Finishing Co. Ltd* (1972) that s.216 applies to all employees employed at the commencement of a strike. Therefore, if employees on strike are dismissed and then re-engaged continuity will not be broken. Furthermore, s.230(1) provides that the term 'employee' in the ERA includes those who have worked under a contract of employment, which would include employees who have been dismissed in these circumstances.

## CASES WHERE CONTINUITY IS PRESERVED WHEN THE EMPLOYER CHANGES

Section 218 of the ERA deals with continuity in such a case but it is best looked at in conjunction with the Transfer of Undertakings (Protection of Employment) Regulations (TUPE) and the whole topic is considered in Chapter 12.

## ATTEMPTS BY EMPLOYERS TO PREVENT EMPLOYEES GAINING CONTINUITY OF EMPLOYMENT

Although, as we saw earlier, an employer cannot make employees contract out of the rules on continuity (s.203), it is possible for an employer to arrange the contracts of employees so that they do not gain continuity of employment. This happened in *Booth v United States of America* (1999), where workers had contracts with two-week breaks between each contract, so that although the contracts added up to over two years they did not have continuity, as none of the exceptions applied. Morrison P, in the EAT, observed that if there was considered to be a loophole in the legislation then it was for Parliament to deal with it and not the courts, although one might observe that on other occasions the courts have quite readily closed loopholes without waiting for Parliament.

# Chapter 7

# Payment of wages and hours of work

## PAYMENT OF WAGES

The foundation of the right to receive wages is the contract of employment and indeed in this whole area the common law of employment still holds sway, although there is a certain of amount of statutory regulation. The main instances are the statutory rules governing deductions from wages and statutory sick pay and the National Minimum Wage Act 1998.

The nature of the common law obligations regarding wages was expressed succinctly by Lord Templeman in the House of Lords in *Miles v Wakefield MBC* (1987): 'In a contract of employment wages and work go together. The employer pays for work and the worker works for his wages. If the employer declines to pay, the worker need not work. If the worker declines to work, the employer need not pay.'

Although it is clear that an employee who has performed the work is entitled to be paid the wages, two less straightforward issues arise. First, suppose that the employee has failed to complete the work and has instead only performed part of it? Is there a right to part of the wages? The old case of *Cutter v Powell* (1795) held that where the employee fails to complete performance there is no right to any remuneration at all. Thus, when a sailor died during a voyage his widow was not entitled to any wages due to his estate. However, this particular case has generated more heat than light as, for one thing, this situation would now come under the Law Reform (Frustrated Contracts) Act 1943 (see Chapter 11). In any event, it only applies where the contract cannot be divided, in that *one* sum was paid for the whole job. In most employment contracts wages can be deemed to accrue from day to day and s.2 of the Apportionment Act 1870 provides that, *inter alia*, all 'periodical payments in the nature of income' shall be considered as accruing from day to day and shall be apportionable accordingly. The language of the Act, which refers to rents, annuities and dividends, suggests that it was not originally intended to apply to contracts of employment, but in *Sim v Rotherham MBC* (1987) the High Court thought that it applied to the salaries of monthly paid teachers, which could be considered as accruing day by day.

Suppose that a monthly paid employee stopped working half-way through a month, then there would be a right to payment up to the date of death and in any event this would be payable where the cessation was due to the worker's death under the Frustrated Contracts Act. Where the employee was engaged to do a particular job, such as decorating a house, and to be paid a fixed sum on completion, then if performance was not completed the employee might be able to rely on the doctrine of substantial performance as in *Hoenig v Isaacs* (1952). Such a right to wages would be counterbalanced by any right of the employer to claim for damages due to loss caused by the employee's failure to complete. For example, failure to decorate rooms in a hotel as agreed could mean that the hotel suffered loss through being unable to let them.

The second issue which arises is where the employee has refused to perform a particular part of the job rather than failing to complete it. In *Cresswell v Board of Inland Revenue* (1984) the refusal was to adapt to new methods of work and it was held that in such a case the employee would not be entitled to any wages. In a number of industrial disputes where employees have refused to perform particular duties which they were obliged to perform under their contracts, the employer has deducted wages. There are two possibilities: the employer deducts wages only for the time when the employee has refused to perform the particular contractual duties; or the employer declines to pay any wages *at all* for the time when the employee was refusing to perform the duties. The first solution was adopted in *Miles v Wakefield MBC* (1987), where a registrar of births, marriages and deaths refused, as part of industrial action, to conduct weddings on Saturday mornings. He was told that if he was not prepared to work according to his contract on Saturday mornings he need not attend work and would not be paid, but in fact he attended and did other work. The council was entitled to deduct 3/37ths of his salary for the time when he should have been performing weddings. One point, which was left unresolved, was whether he would have a claim in the law of restitution for the value of the work which he *did* perform.

The second solution was adopted in *Wiluszynski v Tower Hamlets LBC* (1989). Local authority employees, as part of an industrial dispute, refused to deal with queries from councillors about their constituents' housing problems and the council refused to pay them at all for the time when they were doing this. Two points emerged: the council had told the employees, before the action commenced, that they would not be paid at all unless they were prepared to carry out their duties in full; but the employees argued that the council had, by not physically preventing them from coming to work, impliedly accepted the work which was done. The Court of Appeal held that the council had not accepted the work. As Nicholls LJ put it: 'a person is not treated by the law as having chosen to accept that which is forced down his throat, despite his objection.' The fact that the council had made the position clear in advance was enough and the result was that the employees received no pay for the month when the dispute lasted, even though the backlog of work through not dealing with complaints was cleared in three hours. In *Ticehurst v British Telecommunications plc* (1992) a similar decision was reached where the employee had a discretion as to how to exercise her duties (see Chapter 5 for a fuller discussion of this case).

An unresolved issue is where the employer is faced with a go-slow or similar action where the extent of the refusal to perform is difficult to quantify. An employer could deduct a reasonable sum representing duties not performed but the easiest way would be to simply declare that any work done during the dispute will be treated as voluntary, in which case under the *Wiluszynski* decision there is no liability to pay anything at all.

## ITEMISED PAY STATEMENT

Section 8 of the ERA 1996 gives employees the right to a written itemised pay statement at or before the payment of wages. This must contain details of:

1. The gross amount of wages and salary.
2. The amounts of any variable deductions from that gross amount and the purposes for which they were made. In the case of fixed deductions it is sufficient to give a standing statement containing the details and then the itemised pay statement need only give the aggregate amount of fixed deductions.
3. The net amount of any wages or salary payable.
4. Where different parts are paid in different ways then the amount and method of each part payment must be specified.

A failure to give this statement is dealt with in the same way as a failure to provide the statement of initial employment particulars (see Chapter 5).

## DEDUCTIONS FROM WAGES

This topic has a long history, beginning with the passage of the Truck Acts in 1831–40, which were designed to stop the practice of employees being paid in tokens which could only be spent on goods produced by the employer. The present law is contained in Part II (ss.13–27) of the ERA 1996 and it is noteworthy that it applies to workers as defined by s.230(3) of the ERA rather than employees.

The first question is what is meant by wages and this is answered by s.27, which gives a detailed list of what counts as wages. The main category is in s.27(a): 'any fee, bonus, commission, holiday pay, or other emolument referable to the worker's employment, whether payable under his contract or otherwise.'

Three points arise from this:

1. Does it include a payment which is stated to be discretionary or ex-gratia where the contract contemplated that it would be made? In *Kent Management Services Ltd v Butterfield* (1992) it was held that it did, so that a refusal by an employer to make such a payment could be challenged as an unlawful deduction.

2. Does it apply where no wages at all are paid rather then a deduction from what *is* paid? In *Delaney v Staples* (1991) the Court of Appeal held that it did and thus a worker who was dismissed when owed £55.50 holiday pay and accrued commission could claim this under these provisions rather than have to make a separate claim for breach of contract. The effect of this decision has been to increase greatly the number of claims alleging unlawful deductions from wages.

3. Does it apply to a claim for wages due in lieu of notice where the worker is dismissed without proper notice? In *Delaney v Staples* (above) the House of Lords answered this in the negative. The worker claimed £82 in lieu of notice and it was held that, as wages are essentially payments due for services rendered and as wages in lieu of notice are not for this (with one exception) such a claim must be brought in an action for breach of contract. The one exception was where wages are due under a 'garden leave' clause (see Chapter 5), where a failure to pay will count as a deduction. However, it must be emphasised that the issue here is not entitlement to wages in lieu of notice but the correct method of asserting that right.

The other categories of wages in s.27 are sums due under various statutory provisions, for example statutory sick pay, guarantee pay, statutory maternity pay and sums payable under orders for reinstatement and re-engagement. The first two are covered later in this chapter, statutory maternity pay in Chapter 10 and the two others in Chapter 11. Certain matters are specifically stated by s.27 not to be wages and thus not subject to the rules on deductions such as pensions and redundancy payments.

Section 13 provides that an employer shall not make a deduction from wages unless:

1. the deduction is required or authorised by statute, e.g. PAYE;
2. the deduction is required or authorised by a provision in the contract provided that the deduction was contained in written terms of the contract of which the employee was made aware, either by being given a copy of the contract or otherwise in writing, before the deduction.
3. the deduction was agreed to by the worker prior to when the deduction is made.

The difference between (2) and (3) is that (2) will usually apply where there is a right under the contract of employment to make the deduction, whereas (3) applies where the worker agrees on the particular occasion to the making of the deduction.

Section 14 then sets out six cases where a deduction can be made even where the requirements in s.13 are not satisfied. Section 14 does not, however, state that deductions in all of the cases below are deemed to be lawful: it was held in *Sunderland Polytechnic v Evans* (1993) that whether a deduction is lawful is a separate issue for the civil courts. Therefore lawfulness will depend on each case and in particular the provisions of the worker's contract. The situations in s.14 are:

1. To cover overpayments of wages or expenses (see below).
2. In consequence of disciplinary proceedings held by virtue of a statutory provision. In *Chiltern House v Chambers* (1990) Wood P said, *obiter*, that this did not cover disciplinary proceedings held by private employers but only, for example, police and fire services.
3. Where there is a statutory requirement to make deductions from wages and to pay the amount over to a public authority, for example, where the worker has had an attachment of earnings order made against him the sum deducted from wages will be paid to the court for transmission to the creditor.
4. Where the worker has agreed in writing that payments can be made to a third party. Deduction of union subscriptions (known as check-off) is dealt with by s.68 of TULRCA 1992, which provides that all such deductions must be authorised by the worker in writing and that this authorisation can be withdrawn by the worker at any time.
5. A strike or other industrial action in which the worker took part.
6. Deductions made in satisfaction of a court or tribunal order requiring the worker to make a payment to the employer, for example, where the employer has sued the worker for a debt.

The one area in the above which has caused difficulty is overpayments. The law of restitution applies here and this is an area which has developed considerably in recent years and is likely to continue to do so in the future. There is a general right to recover overpayments provided that the worker has not changed his/her position in the belief that he/she was entitled to the money. Thus in *Avon CC v Howlett* (1983) a local authority sued a teacher for wages overpaid when he was off sick. It was held that the employer could not recover as the teacher had spent the money and did not know that it was an overpayment. The moral seems to be to spend your wages quickly! In *Howlett* it was also held that the defence of change of position applied even where the worker had only spent *some* of the overpaid wages, as it would be impossible in practice to establish what actual money had been spent.

Where the worker claims that an unlawful deduction has been made, a complaint may be made to an employment tribunal within three months of the last deduction or payment and the tribunal can order repayment of sums wrongly deducted.

## RETAIL EMPLOYMENT

Sections 17–22 of the ERA deal with deductions from the wages of workers in retail employment and provide that any deduction made in respect of cash shortages or stock deficiencies cannot exceed 10% of the gross wages for that day. There appears to be no rule that the deduction can only be made for shortages or deficiencies that are the fault of the employee.

## SICK PAY

There is no general implied term in contracts of employment that workers are entitled to sick pay, although in particular cases one might be implied. In *Mears v Safecar Security Ltd* (1982) the Court of Appeal found that there was no implied term to this effect, as the employer had never paid sick pay and the employee had never claimed sick pay until he had left employment.

This is of less importance now in view of the Statutory Sick Pay (SSP) Scheme, first introduced in 1983 and now governed by the Social Security Contributions and Benefits Act 1992. The main features of the scheme are as follows:

1. The scheme operates, as do many employment rights, to give a basic entitlement which can be added to by the contract. Therefore, the contract may provide both for pay on top of the amount in the scheme and for pay when the employee is no longer covered by the scheme.
2. Self-employed persons are not entitled to SSP and will instead be entitled to incapacity benefit (see below).
3. The employer pays SSP and cannot contract out of liability to pay.
4. The employer cannot recover any of the cost of SSP unless in any income tax month the amount of SSP paid exceeds 13% of the total liability to pay national insurance contributions. If so, the employer can recover the excess over 13%.
5. Employees qualify for SSP if their normal gross weekly wage is at a level to be relevant for national insurance purposes which is currently £75 a week, and they have a contract of employment for over three months.
6. SSP can be claimed for a 'day of incapacity', which is defined as a day in which the employee is incapable by reason of some specific disease or mental or bodily disablement of doing the work which he can reasonably be expected to do under the contract.
7. Assuming that the day is a 'day of incapacity', SSP is paid if the day falls within a 'period of incapacity', which is a period of at least four consecutive days of incapacity including days of the week when the employee does not work, e.g. weekends and holidays. The object is to restrict SSP to absences for at least four consecutive days.
8. Assuming that the 'day of incapacity' does fall within a 'period of incapacity' then SSP is payable if the absence falls within a 'period of entitlement' which begins with the day on which the illness begins and which ends with the day on which the illness ends, *or* after 28 weeks *or* the eleventh week before the expected week of a confinement, *or* when the contract is terminated although the employer cannot terminate simply to avoid liability to pay SSP. The main point to remember is that entitlement to SSP for one spell of sickness ends after 28 weeks at the latest. The position after then is explained below.
9. A final requirement is that the day for which SSP is sought must be a 'qualifying day', i.e. a day when the employee would normally be expected to work.

10. Where the employee is involved in a trade dispute at his/her place of work then there is no right to SSP unless the employee proves that he/she did not participate in the dispute on any day before his illness began.
11. The employee claims SSP by notifying his/her employer and the employer may lay down how this is to be done and a time limit for notification. The employer may refuse to pay SSP for the days by which notification is late.
12. The amount of SSP is at present £63.25, which was set in April 2001, but the exact amount will depend on individual circumstances. If absence is for less than a week then the pay is at a daily rate calculated by dividing the weekly rate by the number of qualifying days.

*Example*

John was absent from 23 January 2002 until 30 January 2002 because of a heavy cold. Is he entitled to SSP? He must prove that he is an employee whose normal weekly wage is at or above the lower limit for NI contributions. All the days will count as days of incapacity but SSP will not be paid for them all, as the first three do not come within a period of incapacity and the period of entitlement to SSP will end on 30 January.

When the employee is no longer entitled to SSP but is still unable to work then he/she is entitled to incapacity benefit, which is paid at different rates depending on whether the incapacity is short term (up to 52 weeks) or long term (over 52 weeks). There are also different rates of short-term and long-term incapacity benefit. As explained above, this benefit is also payable to the self-employed, who are not eligible for SSP. New rules came into force on 8 April 2002 on the extent to which a person can work and still claim incapacity benefit (and some other benefits). There were 907,597 claims for this benefit in 1999/2000 with a total cost of £7m.

## PAYMENT OF WAGES DURING SUSPENSION, LAY-OFF AND SHORT-TIME

### During suspension

What is the position where the employee is suspended from work without pay? Is there a right to wages? In *Hanley v Pease and Partners Ltd* (1915) the employee was suspended for one day for not turning up the previous day as he had over-slept. His action for damages for wrongful dismissal succeeded. In a remarkably clear and straightforward decision for that era, Lush J had no doubt: 'the employers took upon themselves to suspend for one day; in other words, to deprive the workman of his wages for one day, thereby assessing their own damages for the servant's misconduct at the sum which would be represented by one day's wages. They have no possible right to do that.' The message is clear: deprivation of wages by suspension without pay is not lawful. A disciplinary matter should be dealt with by the proper disciplinary route and not by a simple deduction from wages. The only possible time when this might be justified would be where an employee who could be fairly dismissed is offered as an alternative a period of suspension without wages, as, for example, where the employee had a previously unblemished record and many years service. The whole topic of dismissal is considered in Chapters 11 and 12.

## During lay-off

The effect of a lay-off is similar to a suspension, but whereas suspension is used in connection with disciplinary matters, a lay-off occurs when the employer has no work for the employee. We have already seen in Chapter 3 that an employee has no general right to be provided with work, but what is the position where employees are laid off? The straightforward answer is that employees who are laid off are entitled to be paid until their contract is terminated by proper notice but the courts have never stated this principle clearly. The starting point is the contract, which may give a right to wages where there is a lay-off, but otherwise the right will depend on an implied term. In *Devonald v Rosser and Sons* (1906) a tinplate factory was closed because of lack of orders and the employees, who were on piecework, were then given notice. It was held that there was an implied term that, as Alverstone CJ put it, 'the master will find a reasonable amount of work up to the expiration of a notice given in accordance with the contract'. Once work was found then it followed that it must be paid for. The link with the provision of work has muddied the waters somewhat but the duty to find work presumably only applies to piece workers and the law seems to be that in cases where the employee is on a fixed rate then there is a duty to pay when there is a lay-off even though no work can be found. Even with piece workers the duty to find work cannot be absolute but there is a duty to pay.

This last point is shown by the decision in *Minnevitch v Café de Paris Ltd* (1936). Musicians employed at a café were paid according to performance and received nothing when the café closed for six days following the death of King George V. It was held that the owners were entitled to close for two days but the musicians were entitled to payment for the other four days.

A troublesome case is *Browning v Crumlin Valley Collieries Ltd* (1926). Miners were laid off when their mine was closed due to flooding and it was held that the risk of closure of the mine was shared between the mine owner and the miners with the result that there was no right to payment. Greer J said that the question was whether a term should be implied on the basis of *The Moorcock* and he was satisfied that no employer would have consented to pay wages where the mine was closed through no fault of his. This case has not been followed and it is suggested that a future court might distinguish it by using the more modern tests for implying a term on the basis of what is reasonable and necessary (see Chapter 3) rather than a narrow test of intention as here.

## During short-time

There is less authority on this but in principle there seems no reason why the law should be any different from that on payment when laid off. Thus where the contract provides for a minimum number of hours work a week then there is a right to wages for those hours.

## Guarantee pay

This is a statutory right contained in ss.28–35 of the ERA 1996. It gives a right to pay when an employee is laid off and is part of the 'floor of rights' philosophy under which statute sets certain minimum standards with the expectation (not always fulfilled) that employers will exceed them. Therefore, contracts and collective agreements may give a right to a higher level of pay than laid down by the Act. Moreover, these provisions are an exception to the rule that it is not possible to contract out of statutory rights because, by s.35(4), the Secretary of State may issue an exemption order where there is either a collective agreement or an agricultural wages order in force giving a right to guaranteed remuneration. Moreover, this may not be as generous as the amount of guarantee pay, although this is unlikely given the modest rates of guarantee pay.

### Who is entitled to a guarantee payment?

The right is given to employees under the narrow definition in s.230(1) of the ERA, i.e. a contract of employment is required. Such employees must have a period of continuous employment of at least one month, ending with the day before the day on which guarantee pay is claimed. Where an employee has a fixed-term contract or a specific task contract which is for three months he/she does not have a right to guarantee pay unless the employee actually works for more than three months.

### When is guarantee pay to be paid?

Guarantee pay is payable for a 'workless day' but is subject to a statutory maximum, which is at present £17.00 for any five days in a three-month period, which is hardly generous but fits in with the floor of rights philosophy outlined above. The term 'workless day' is defined by s.28 of the ERA as a day when the employee is not provided with work by his employer because either:

1. there is a diminution in the requirements of the employer's business for work of the kind which the employee is normally required to do; or
2. for any other reason affecting the normal working of the employer's business in relation to the kind of work which the employee is employed to do.

Reason (1) is self-explanatory but the significance of (2) is seen when one considers the situations where, despite there being a workless day, the employee is not entitled to a guarantee payment. These are set out in s.29 and are as follows:

(a) Where the failure to provide work is in consequence of a strike, lock-out or other industrial action involving the employer or an associated employer.

(The meaning of the term 'associated employer' was considered in Chapter 1.) Thus, for example, a strike at a completely separate factory would come under (2) and would mean that the employees would be entitled to a guarantee payment, but not a strike within the employer's own factory nor that of an associated employer. Other possible instances of (2) which would entitle the employee to a guarantee payment are a sudden power failure or, for example, where the premises are shut through floods.

(b) Where the employer has offered suitable alternative work but the employee refuses it. In *Purdy v Willowbrook International* (1977) it was held that the alternative work can be work which the employee is not bound to do under his/her contract provided that it is suitable for him/her taking into account their abilities and aptitude for it.

(c) Where the employee fails to comply with a reasonable requirement of the employer designed to ensure that the employee is available for work. For example, supplies of vital materials are late and the employees are asked to wait until they arrive. Some of them, however, do not do so and go home. They would not be entitled to a guarantee payment (see *Meadows v Faithful Overalls Ltd* (1977)).

A workless day must be a day when the employee would normally be required to work. Therefore, where an employee works, for example, from Monday to Thursday and the factory is shut down on Friday, there is no right to guarantee pay. What is the position where the employee works a shift that spreads over two days, for example, from 10 p.m. to 6 a.m. and each of those days are workless days? Is he entitled to two guarantee payments? The answer is no. With merciless precision, s.28(5) provides that where the amounts worked on each day are not the same, as here, guarantee pay is payable for the day on which the hours are greater and, if they are equal, then it is paid for the second day.

## Calculation of guarantee pay

The complexity of the rules for calculating guarantee pay is out of all proportion to the amounts involved. The basic rule is that the amount is calculated by multiplying the number of normal working hours for that day by the guaranteed hourly rate of pay. The problem is that this is almost bound to produce a figure well in excess of £17.00 and so the calculation is meaningless and it is easier to say that in almost all cases the employee is entitled to £17.00. The only time when this would not be so would be when an employee worked only a few hours and received the minimum rate of pay (see below). If so, they would not be entitled to the maximum and calculations would be needed.

## Claims to guarantee pay

Claims must be brought within three months of the last workless day, with the usual exception allowing tribunals to consider late claims. The tribunal has power to order the employer to make the payment.

## SUSPENSION FROM WORK ON MEDICAL GROUNDS

Employees who have been suspended from work on specified medical grounds are entitled to their normal pay up to a maximum of 26 weeks. This situation arises where the employee is available for work but the employer cannot provide work because of certain requirements in health and safety enactments. These cover employees engaged on work involving exposure to lead, ionising radiations and some other chemicals together with processes hazardous to health. There are certain exclusions from the right to medical suspension pay:

1. employees who have worked for less than one month or are on a fixed-term contract or a specific task contract for less than three months unless they actually work for more than three months;
2. where the employer has offered suitable alternative work or where the employee has failed to comply with the reasonable requirements of the employer to ensure that his/her services are available.

The similarity of these provisions to those governing guarantee pay will be noted. In addition, there is no right to medical suspension pay where the employee is incapable of work through disease or disablement. The point is not that an employee in these cases will not be paid but that the pay will not be medical suspension pay.

An employee who is dismissed rather than suspended on the above grounds may claim unfair dismissal after one month's continuous employment but the dismissal is not automatically unfair.

## NATIONAL MINIMUM WAGE ACT 1998

### ■ The background

The history of statutory involvement in the setting of wages is a long one but it has been piecemeal. The main recent example was the Wages Councils set up in industries where collective bargaining was weak and which were empowered to set wage rates in, for example, the hotel and catering industry. Moreover, the Fair Wages Resolution of the House of Commons required government contractors to pay fair wages. This was rescinded in 1982 and Wages Councils were abolished in 1993. The only exception was the Agricultural Wages Board, which continues to set both minimum wages and terms and conditions for those employed in agriculture and related industries.

However, this bonfire of statutory controls was taking place against a movement in quite the opposite direction. In 1989, all the Member States of the EU, with the exception of the UK, adopted the European Charter of Fundamental Rights and Freedoms, Article 5 of which provides that all workers shall be 'fairly remunerated' and that workers shall be assured of an 'equitable wage'. Although not binding on Member States, it undoubtedly helped to create a climate in which the setting of a national minimum wage was seen as a desirable goal of social policy. The introduction of a national minimum wage was promised in the Labour Party manifesto for the 1997 election and the National Minimum Wage Act was duly passed in 1998. It came into force in April 1999 and the original minimum wage was set at £3.60 an hour for employees aged 22 and over and £3.00 an hour for employees aged 18–21. The rates are now (from October 2002) £4.20 and £3.60 an hour.

A survey in *Labour Market Trends* (December 1998, p.617) estimated that in Spring 1998 up to 2.1 million workers (10.4% of all employees) earned below the national minimum wage (NMW) and part-time workers were more likely to be low paid than full-time workers. Over half of those low paid (i.e. earning below the NMW) were women in part-time jobs and a further 18% were women in full-time jobs. Less than a third were men. The survey concluded that: 'Low pay is predominantly a female and a part-time phenomenon.' The industries where there was a greater incidence of low pay were catering, personal and protective services and sales. Together these accounted for two-thirds of all low paid workers. A further survey (*Labour Market Trends* September 1998, p.463) looked at the experience of countries that already had statutory minimum wages. Although comparisons are not easy because the systems varied, the survey found that, in practice, a NMW need not have an adverse effect on jobs provided that it is set at a reasonable level. This is important, as opponents of the NMW had argued that it could discourage employers from taking on workers. It was also argued by opponents that the introduction of a NMW could have a knock-on effect on other wage rates and thus be inflationary but the survey found that experience abroad was that this was not so.

## The Act itself

The Act sets out the broad framework of the legislation with the Secretary of State being given the power to make regulations. It also establishes the Low Pay Commission. This has no powers of action of its own and can only act when the Secretary of State exercises his powers under s.6 and refers a matter to it. The main ongoing task which has been entrusted to the Commission is the monitoring and evaluation of the impact of the NMW. The Commission has only advisory powers but it is not entirely toothless: if the Secretary of State refers a matter to it concerning the setting of the NMW and associated issues and then subsequently the Secretary departs from any recommendations made by the Commission, the Secretary must lay a report before Parliament giving the reasons why the recommendations have not been complied with.

## Who is covered by the Act?

The Act, by s.1(2), applies to any 'worker' and thus the wide definition is used rather then the narrow one of 'employee'. The term 'worker', it will be recalled

101

from Chapter 4, covers not only those with a contract of employment but also those who undertake to perform work or services personally. Not only this, but the Act specifically applies to agency workers and homeworkers, a point discussed in more detail in Chapter 4. There are certain exclusions, the main ones being workers under the age of 18, workers employed under a contract of apprenticeship, family workers and *au pairs*. The last two were added by the National Minimum Wage Regulations 1999 (NMWR). Furthermore, the Secretary of State is given power, by s.3, to provide that certain classes of workers shall not qualify for the NMW and that differential hourly rates of pay may be prescribed. In the event this has been used to prescribe different rates dependent on age (see below) but s.3 specified that this power shall not be used to set rates of pay which differ dependent on area, type of employment, size of employment or occupation.

## ■ What is the National Minimum Wage?

This is set by the Secretary of State who, as we saw above, should follow any guidance given by the Low Pay Commission or, if not, explain to Parliament why it is not being followed. The rate is an hourly one and was originally fixed (from April 1999) at £3.60 an hour for workers aged 22 or over and at £3.00 an hour for workers aged 18–22. In June 2000 the rate for workers aged between 18–22 was raised to £3.20. As stated above, the present rates are £4.20 an hour and £3.60 an hour. Although further increases will doubtless be made, there is no provision for annual uprating. It should be noted that the lower rate also applies to the first six months of employment for workers aged 22 or over who have agreed to take part in accredited training courses lasting at least 26 days of their first six months of employment (NMWR 1999, Reg.13) but, in order to prevent employers simply paying the lower rate without providing the training, the contract must specify what the training is to be.

Where a worker works, say, four hours a week and is aged 22 or over then the calculation is easy: multiply £4.20 by 4 and the figure of £16.80 is produced. In this situation we are dealing with what the Act and the Regulations call 'time work', where the worker is paid by reference to a set time when the worker actually worked or was available for work. However, matters are not always so simple.

The Act and the Regulations provide the following mechanisms for deciding the hourly rate of pay:

### The pay reference period

This is the interval between payments of wages up to a maximum of a month. Therefore, wages received during this period must, when averaged against the number of hours worked, be such that the NMR was received. Thus, if a worker aged 22 or over is paid monthly then one month is the pay reference period. If in that month the worker worked a 40 hour week for four weeks then the total number of hours worked would be $(40 \times 4)$ 160 hours and the NMR would be $160 \times £4.20 = £672.00$.

## Which payments count towards the NMW?

In the above example it was assumed that all payments counted but this may not be so. The starting point is the actual gross wage and this includes bonuses, incentive payments and any tips paid through the employer. Thus if a waiter or waitress received £2.50 a week but was told by the employer that, as they received at least £10.00 a week in tips there was no obligation to pay them more then that employer would be wrong. If, however, the employer paid the NMW and included in it was a sum representing tips paid into a kitty and shared round by the employer then there would be no objection. The point is that where the money comes from is irrelevant: the NMR must be paid. Two particular categories must be noted:

1. Certain deductions made by the employer count towards the NMW. These are:
   - income tax and NI contributions;
   - deductions to cover an advance of wages or an accidental overpayment of wages;
   - deductions to cover pension contributions or union subscriptions;
   - deductions to pay for shares or securities bought by the worker; and
   - deductions, authorised by the worker's contract, for payments imposed for a disciplinary matter.

   On this last point it should be noted that any deductions would need to be specifically authorised by the contract: the NMW provisions do not make them lawful but only provide that, if they are lawful by another provision, then they still count towards the NMW. Thus in all these cases the NMW must be paid *inclusive* of these sums: the worker *cannot* claim that he/she is entitled to the NMW when these sums have been deducted.

2. However, the following are examples of items which do not count towards NMW:
   - premium payments for overtime and shiftwork;
   - allowances which are attributable to a particular aspect of a worker's working arrangements or personal circumstances and which are not consolidated into basic pay, e.g. London weighting, unsocial hours payments, payments for working in unpleasant or dangerous conditions; tips not paid through the payroll;
   - payments in kind.

   Although payments towards living accommodation is included in the NMW, up to a maximum of £19.95 a week may be offset against it.

## For what time is the NMW to be paid?

There are four categories:

### Time work

This was referred to in the example above, where the worker is paid according to a set time when he/she was working or available for work. Periods spent travelling in connection with work, although not to work, are included but not time spent 'on call' at home. In *British Nursing Association v Inland Revenue* (2002) it was held that employees working from home on an emergency night telephone booking service were working during these shifts even though in between taking calls they could do as they pleased. Accordingly they were on time work.

### Salaried hours work

This is where the worker is paid according to set basic hours in a year in return for an annual salary which does not vary with the hours actually worked. The same rules apply as for time workers except that with salaried workers most of the time during the actual salary period is counted for NMW purposes, for example meal breaks and rest breaks. Therefore, the amount of entitlement to NMW is likely to be higher than with time workers.

### Output work

This is where payment is linked to the amount produced by the worker as in piece work. The worker's time can either be assessed either by a 'fair estimate' or the worker can just be paid for hours actually worked. A worker is protected when a 'fair estimate' is made by a rule that the number of hours agreed as a fair estimate must be not less than four-fifths of the hours that an average worker would take. Any fair estimate agreement must be in writing and made before the work begins.

### Unmeasured work

This is where the work does not fall into any other category, as where workers are available for work when required. The worker is entitled to pay at the rate of the NMW for hours worked or the parties can agree on a daily average of hours to be worked which then must be paid at the rate of the NMW.

## How is the right to the NMW enforced?

The mechanism adopted is that the right to the NMW is a term of each worker's contract and thus s.17 provides that if a worker receives less than the NMW then there is a contractual right to the difference between what was paid and the NMW. This contractual right can either be enforced in a common law action for breach of contract or by a claim under Part II of the ERA as an unlawful deduction from wages and in any proceedings s.28 reverses the burden of proof so that a person is presumed to qualify (i.e. as a worker) for the NMW unless proved otherwise. In addition, an enforcement notice may be issued against an employer requiring that employer to make payments to workers to bring them up to the NMW. If the notice is not obeyed then the employer can be brought before an employment tribunal which, in addition to ordering payments of the amounts due, can also order the employer to pay a fine equivalent to double the underpayment (see ss.19–21). Finally, it is a criminal offence, punishable by a fine not exceeding level 5 on the Standard Scale, for an employer wilfully to neglect to pay the NMW.

# HOURS OF WORK: THE WORKING TIME REGULATIONS

## The background

Statutory regulation of hours of work has, in many ways, a similar history to that of the minimum wage. As with the minimum wage, there have been many legislative forays into this area, most notably the Factories Acts in the nineteenth century and the Shops Act 1950. As with the legislation on minimum wages, legislation here was confined to particular industries and then fell foul of the desire of the 1979–97 Conservative government to deregulate as many statutory controls as possible so that the only legislation remaining dealt with hours worked by those under the school leaving age.

The difference between current legislation on hours of work, contained in the Working Time Regulations 1998 (WTRs) and the National Minimum Wage Act 1998 is that, whereas the genesis of the Minimum Wage Act was domestic political agendas, the WTRs spring from EC law and their gestation was long and complex.

The origin of legislation on working time is found in a Directive (93/104) adopted on 23 November 1993. The interesting point is that the legal basis of the Directive was Article 118A of the EC Treaty, which requires Member States to pay particular attention to encouraging improvements, especially in the working environment, as regards the health and safety of workers. The linkage between working time and health and safety was crucial because Article 118A (now consolidated in Article 137) gives power to adopt measures to improve the working environment in connection with health and safety by qualified majority voting. Thus there was, according to the Commission, no need for a unanimous vote and the Directive could come into operation without the approval of the then UK (Conservative) government. The UK government did not agree and felt that, as the connection between working time and health and safety was tenuous to say the least, a unanimous vote was required. However, in *UK v EU Council (Working Time)* (1996) the ECJ upheld the view of the Commission that the Directive could be a health and safety measure and in any event the incoming Labour government of 1997 was prepared to adopt the Directive.

Discussion of the Working Time Regulations centred on what was said, somewhat inaccurately, to be a maximum 48-hour week. Research (published by the European Commission in an Explanatory Memorandum and quoted in Bercusson, *European Labour Law* (London: Butterworths Law, 1996) at pp.309–310) showed that the average operating hours of plants in the UK was 76 a week, the highest in the EC after Belgium, with 77, but average working hours in UK industry were 37, equal lowest with Belgium. The Commission was concerned that there could nevertheless be pressure on workers to work longer hours, given the gap between plant opening hours and individual working hours. In the retail trade there was also a gap between weekly opening hours (58) and individual working hours (39). In the UK, a survey in *Labour Market Trends* (December 1998, p.599) showed that an average of 29.8% of male full-time employees and 11.6% of female employees worked more than 48 hours. Moreover, 5% of male and 2% of female employees worked more than 60 hours a week. Looking at occupations, the survey found that managers and adminis-trators among men and professional workers among women were most likely to work over 48 hours a week. Indeed, 6% of professional women workers worked over 60 hours a week, the highest proportion of those working these long hours.

It should be noted that, as these rights emanate from a Directive, the question arises of whether the Directive has direct effect in addition to remedies conferred by the regulations. The point arose in *Gibson v East Riding of Yorkshire CC* (2000), where it was held that the right to four weeks' paid annual leave was not capable of direct effect as the Directive did not contain a sufficiently precise definition of working time.

Useful guidance to the WTRs can be found in *A Guide to the Working Time Regulations* issued by the DTI in 1998 and updated in 2000. It is also available on www.dti.gov.uk/er.

## ■ The scheme of the WTRs

Unlike many areas of employment protection law, which set minimum standards which cannot be taken away by the contract of employment, the WTRs set rules which can, in many but not all cases, be modified in a number of ways. Furthermore, it is possible to make what are called 'derogations' in a number of areas, which means that the WTRs will not apply. There is therefore a complex pattern under which the identification of a right will not necessarily mean that that right will apply to a particular worker. However, this should not mask the fact that, for the first time, there is a set of legislative rules governing working time which apply, subject to the modifications and derogations noted above, to all workers and not just to workers in particular sections of industry.

## ■ Modification of the WTRs by agreements

These agreements are known as 'relevant agreements' and can take three forms: collective agreement; workforce agreement; and individual agreement.

### Collective agreement

WTRs can be modified by a collective agreement made between the employer and one or more independent trade unions. However, the terms of any such agreement would have to be incorporated into individual contracts of employ-ment (see Chapter 5).

## Workforce agreement

This type of agreement was included to deal with situations where workers do not have their terms and conditions of employment set by a collective agreement and would otherwise not be able to collectively modify the provisions of the WTRs. A workforce agreement is one that is made either with representatives of the workforce or, if on the date when the agreement is made, the employer employs less than 20 workers, then it may be signed by a majority of the actual workforce. The agreement may either apply to all the workers or to those who constitute 'a particular group' defined as workers who undertake a particular function, work at a particular place, or work in a particular department or unit. The agreement must be in writing, have been circulated in draft beforehand and be signed by representatives of the workforce or by representatives of the particular group except, as stated above, if there are fewer than 20 workers covered by it, then either by all the representatives or by a majority of the workforce. Once made, the agreement lasts for not more then five years. Not only this, but the Regulations lay down detailed provisions on the election of workforce representatives. The employer initially decides the number of representatives to be elected and must ensure that, as far as reasonably practicable, the election is conducted by secret ballot. As the DTI guidance remarks, it would be rare for this not to be possible and it might have been better to have stipulated a secret ballot in all circumstances. The votes must be counted fairly and accurately. Finally, any candidates must be members of the workforce and the employer cannot unreasonably exclude any member of the workforce from standing for election. Before the agreement is eventually signed, copies must be sent to all those affected by it with guidance to enable them to understand it fully.

Workforce representatives are used in other areas such as health and safety and although the same representatives could be used for more than one purpose, the DTI guidance states that it would have to be made clear to those voting that the representatives were being elected for other purposes. Therefore, an employer, having acquired a set of workforce representatives for one purpose could not simply use them for another purpose.

## Individual, legally enforceable, written agreements with workers

The Regulations draw a distinction between agreements individually negotiated between workers and employers which can only apply where it is agreed that the 48-hour a week limit will be excluded (which are not relevant agreements) and agreements contained in contracts of employment with workers but it seems here that such contracts, although made with individuals, would have had to have been agreed by some collective process. It is unfortunate that the Regulations, so detailed in other ways, do not make this clear.

The fact that the WTRs allow use to be made of collective agreements in modifying these rules is noteworthy as representing a departure from UK practice. The aim of the Commission was to set minimum standards but at the same time allow for diversity, and Bercusson (1996) describes the focus on collective agreements as: 'The most daring aspect of the Commission's proposal.' The emphasis on collective agreements certainly gives an indirect push to workers to join unions in that, as we shall see, in some cases it may be to the advantage of both employers and workers to modify the Regulations and, given the complexities of workplace agreements, a collective agreement may be the easiest way of achieving this.

## Who is covered by the Regulations?

The wide definition of worker is adopted, i.e. a worker is a person who either has a contract of employment or who has a contract to personally perform services for another (see s.230(3) of the ERA). However, certain categories are excluded:

- workers in air, rail, road and sea transport together with inland waterways and lake transport;
- sea fishing and other work at sea, e.g. work in the offshore oil and gas industry;
- the activities of doctors in training;
- specific services, e.g. armed services, police, civil protection services.

The Commission has made proposals to amend these exclusions so that all non-mobile workers in transport are included which would, in particular, bring doctors in training within its scope. In *Byrne Brothers v Baird* (2002) it was held that self-employed labour sub-contractors were covered by the definition (see also Chapter 4).

## The 48-hour week

There is no actual rule that hours of work cannot exceed 48 in a week. Instead, Regulation 4 provides that an employer must take all reasonable steps to ensure that a worker's working time, including overtime, does not exceed an average of 48 hours for each seven days in any reference period. The reference period is defined as 17 weeks but it can be raised to 26 or 52 weeks in special cases (see below). Thus it is possible for a worker to work well over 48 hours in a week provided that the average over 17 weeks (or 26/52 weeks) is 48 hours. To enforce this, the employer must keep records, showing whether this rule was obeyed, for up to two years afterwards.

*Example*

X works a basic 38-hour working week. However, in 12 weeks of the 17-week reference period he works ten hours overtime in each week. Therefore, his total hours worked are:

Standard hours (38 × 17) = 646 hours
Overtime (12 × 10) = 120 hours

Total hours worked in the 17-week reference period: (646 + 120) = 766

Average weekly hours: (766 divided by 17) = 45 hours a week. Therefore the limit has been complied with.

A crucial question is: what is working time? This is defined by Regulation 2(1) as any time when the worker is:

1. working at his/her employer's disposal and carrying out his/her duties in accordance with national laws and/or practice;
2. receiving relevant training;
3. at work during any other period which is to be treated as working time under a relevant agreement.

Rest periods are defined as any periods that are not working time. Thus, as the DTI guidance points out, a lunch break would not count unless it was a working lunch.

In the *SIMAP case* (2000) the ECJ held that time spent by doctors on call could be working time if they had to be present at work, as they would be at the disposal of their employer, but not if they could be away from work. As a result of this decision the DTI guidance was amended so that time spent on call only counted where the worker is required to be at his/her place of work.

A particular problem is where a worker has more than one job, as the WTRs impose a 48-hour week on all work which the worker does, not only for one employer. Regulation 4(1) provides that an employer must take all reasonable steps to ensure that the limit is observed and the DTI guidance suggests that an employer should ask the worker if he/she was working elsewhere. If the hours do exceed 48, then an individual opt-out agreement could be made.

There are complex rules dealing with the calculation of average weekly working time. The problem is that account must be taken of days when the worker was absent, for example on sick leave, annual leave or maternity leave, and therefore the basic rule is that an equivalent number of days from the next reference period should be added in to make up for the lost days.

### Example

X works a basic 40-hour five-day week. She also works overtime for eight hours a week for the first ten weeks of the 17-week reference period. In addition, she took five days annual leave in this reference period.

Therefore the total hours worked in the reference period is: 16 weeks at 40 hours = 640 hours. To this is added ten weeks with eight hours overtime: 80 hours. Total 720 hours. To this is added the time worked for the five days of annual leave taken and, as in the first five days of the next reference period there was no overtime worked, one adds $5 \times 8$ (i.e. 5 days at 8 hours a day) = 40 hours. Therefore a grand total of (640 + 80 + 40) = 760 hours. This must be divided by the total number of weeks (17) giving an average number of weekly working hours of 44.7 hours, well within the 48-hour limit.

### To what extent is it possible for the rules on the 48-hour week to be modified or excluded?

Modifications or exclusions are possible in four ways:

### Agreement with employer

An individual worker may agree with the employer that the 48-hour limit will not apply provided that the worker makes a legally binding agreement to this effect. This is the one situation in the WTRs where individuals can agree to opt-out of a particular right. The employer must record the names of those workers who have made such an agreement and the worker can terminate it by giving written notice. The agreement can specify a maximum of three months' notice but, if it is silent on this point, then seven days' notice applies. It should be noted that this provision allowing individual opt-outs applies for seven years from 23 November 1996, after which it will be reviewed by the Commission.

### Special cases

The reference period may be extended to 26 weeks if one or more of the special cases listed in Regulation 21 apply. These special cases are significant under the other parts of the WTRs and the broad principle behind them is that, in these cases, a degree of flexibility is essential on account of the nature of the work. They are set out in Regulation 21 and are as follows:

1. Where the worker is employed a long distance from home or where the worker has different places of work which are distant from each other. The DTI guidance points out that in these cases it may be desirable for them to work longer hours for a short period to complete the task quickly or continual changes in the location of work make it impractical to set a pattern of work.
2. Where the worker is engaged in security and surveillance activities where, for example, there is a need for a 24-hour presence.
3. Where the worker's activities involve the need for continuity of service or production. Regulation 21 sets out a list of examples, although there may be other cases. Among those listed are workers in hospitals, prisons, residential institutions, media work, postal and telecommunications work, public utilities and household refuse collection and incineration.
4. Where there is a foreseeable surge in activity, as with tourism. Thus a hotel which is very busy in, for example, July and August may wish to average the working week over 26 weeks.
5. Where the worker's activities are affected by an occurrence due to unusual and unforeseen circumstances, for example where there has been an emergency.

It must again be emphasised that in all of these circumstances the basic rules relating to the 48-hour week still apply. All that is different is the averaging period.

### Extending the reference period

The reference period may be extended to up to 52 weeks by a collective or workforce agreement.

*Where working time cannot be measured*

The 48-hour limit does not apply at all where, on account of the specific characteristics of the worker's activity, the worker's working time cannot be measured or predetermined even by the worker (Reg. 20). The WTRs give as examples managing executives, family workers and those who officiate at religious ceremonies. The DTI guidance suggests that a useful test is to ask whether the worker has discretion over whether to work on a particular day or if they need to consult their employer. The DTI guidance suggests that the exemption from the 48-hour week only applies where the worker has complete control over working hours. This part was amended by the 1999 Regulations (Reg. 4), which provides that where part of the activities of the worker fall within this category (i.e. they cannot be measured) then the 48-hour limit will not apply to those activities. This area is still not clear, however. What is the position where a worker brings work home at night, such as teachers? Is the time spent at home to be regarded as outside the 48-hour week? The DTI guidance states that one test is whether the worker can decide whether or not to work on a particular day without needing to consult their employer but this is only of help where the worker has a complete discretion and would not apply in the cases of, for example, teachers.

## Enforcement of the 48-hour week provisions

Enforcement of the 48-hour week provisions is by the Health and Safety Executive, which is responsible, very broadly, for enforcement in industry, schools and hospitals, and by local authorities which are responsible for enforcement in retailing and services. Employers are liable to a fine for breach. In addition, in *Barber v RJB Mining (UK) Ltd* (1999) the High Court held that a worker who was made to work in excess of the 48-hour week by the employer could have an action for breach of contract of employment, as it is an implied term of the contract that workers will not be required to work in excess of the limit. Moreover, although for the purpose of criminal proceedings the employer is simply obliged to take all reasonable steps to ensure that the 48-hour limit is observed, this qualifying phrase does not apply to civil proceedings. Thus an employer appears to have an absolute duty where there is a civil action. It was held that a worker could claim a declaration and/or an injunction and could refuse to work beyond the 48-hour limit. It remains to be seen whether other parts of the WTRs will also give rise to civil liability.

## Records to be kept by the employer

The 1998 Regulations required employers to keep detailed records but this was amended by the 1999 Regulations, so that employers only have to record, as mentioned above, which workers have agreed that the 48-hour week limit will not apply to them.

## The limits on night work

An employer is required by Regulation 6 to take all reasonable steps to ensure that the normal hours of night workers do not exceed an average of eight hours for each 24 hours averaged over a 17-week period.

Night work is defined as a period of not less than seven hours which must include the period between midnight and 5 a.m. Beyond this there is some flexibility, as a relevant agreement may specify the actual period; for example, it may specify 10 p.m. and 5 a.m., provided that the period is between 10 p.m. and 7 a.m. If no period is specified then the period of night work is between 11 p.m. and 6 a.m.

A night worker is defined as a worker whose daily working time includes at least three hours of night time (as defined above) on the majority of days when they work, or sufficiently often that they can be said to work such hours as a matter of course, or as defined in a relevant agreement. In *R v A-G for Northern Ireland, ex parte Burns* (1999) a worker was held to be a night worker where the hours worked were between 9 p.m. and 3 a.m. on one week in three.

### Modifications and exclusions of this right

1. The standard reference periods of 17 weeks may be extended by a workforce or collective agreement.
2. These limits on night work may be modified or excluded altogether by a workforce agreement.
3. These rules do not apply at all where the worker falls within one or more of the special cases set out in Regulation 21 (see above) or where the worker's time cannot be measured or determined under Regulation 20 (see above).

However, where the limits on night work either do not apply or are excluded then the worker must be allowed to take a period of equivalent compensatory rest or, if this is not possible, then there is a right to other appropriate protection. However, these rights do not apply where the worker's time cannot be measured or determined.

The limits on night work are enforced in the same way as the 48-hour week.

### Special hazards or heavy mental or physical strain

Where a night worker's work involves special hazards or heavy mental or physical strain, there is a fixed limit, which cannot be modified or excluded, of eight hours' working time. The work that is subject to this limit can either be agreed by a collective or workforce agreement or can be identified as posing a significant risk under a risk assessment conducted by the employer under the Management of Health and Safety at Work Regulations 1992.

## General duty of the employer in organising work patterns

Directive 93/104, the parent of the Regulations provides, under Article 13, a duty on the employer, when organising shift patterns, to take into account 'the general principle of adapting work to the worker' with a view to, for example, alleviating monotonous work and work at a predetermined work rate. This is based on the principle of 'humanisation of work', a concept borrowed from Germany. This is echoed in Regulation 8 which, however, only applies where the monotony of the work puts the health and safety of the worker at risk. In this case the employer must organise regular rest breaks, presumably in addition to those provided under the Regulations (see below).

## Right to a health assessment

Regulation 7 gives a right to a free health assessment to all night workers and to any worker who is about to become a night worker. The purpose is to assess whether the worker is fit to carry out the designated night work and there is also a right to further assessments at regular intervals. There are no circumstances in which this right can be modified or excluded and it is enforced in the same way as the 48-hour week.

## Adult workers' rights to rest periods

An adult worker is one who has attained the age of 18 and there are two provisions:

### Daily rest

There is a right to a daily rest period of not less than 11 consecutive hours in each 24-hour period during which he/she works for the employer (Reg. 10).

### Weekly rest

There is a right to an uninterrupted rest period of not less than 24 hours in every seven-day period. This may be averaged at the discretion of the employer over two weeks so that the worker has 48 hours rest every 14 days (Reg. 11).

### *Modification and exclusion of these rights*

This right does not apply where the worker's working time cannot be measured or determined (see Reg. 20) nor in the special cases set out in Regulation 21. Both of these are dealt with above under the 48-hour week. In addition, a collective or workforce agreement may modify or exclude this right. Where the right is modified or excluded then the worker is entitled to compensatory rest or, if this is not possible, to other appropriate protection. This does not apply to workers whose working time cannot be measured or determined.

## Adolescent workers' rights to rest periods

An adolescent worker is one under the age of 18 and the rights are as follows:

### Daily rest

There is an entitlement to an uninterrupted period of 12 hours rest in every 24-hour period of work unless the day's work is split up or is of short duration (Reg. 10).

### Weekly rest

There is an entitlement to 48 hours rest in every seven-day period (Reg. 11).

#### *Modification and exclusion of these rights*

These rights can only be modified or excluded:

1. in cases of unforeseen or unusual circumstances;
2. where the work is temporary and must be performed at once;
3. where no adult worker is available to do the work.

In addition, these rights do not apply where the worker's time is split up over the day, for example cleaning staff who work in the morning and evening.

#### *Enforcement*

The rights to rest breaks for all workers is enforced by the worker bringing a complaint to an employment tribunal within three months and compensation may be awarded.

## ■ Rights to rest breaks during work

This is contained in Regulation 12 and, as with rest periods, there are different rights for adult and adolescent workers.

### Adult workers

Adult workers are entitled to an uninterrupted break of 20 minutes where daily working time is more than six hours. This is additional to the rest periods. There is nothing in the Regulations about whether workers should be paid and this is a matter for workers' contracts.

#### *Modification and exclusion of these rights*

This right does not apply where the worker's working time cannot be measured or determined (see Reg. 20) nor in the special cases set out in Regulation 21. Collective and workforce agreements may exclude or modify these rights. Compensatory rest may be taken instead under the same rules as apply to daily and weekly rest periods.

### Adolescent workers

Adolescent workers are entitled to a rest break of 30 minutes where daily working time is more than four and a half hours.

*Modification and exclusion of these rights*

These rights can only be modified or excluded in the same circumstances as apply to the entitlement to daily and weekly periods.

*Enforcement*

These rules are enforced in the same way as the entitlement to daily and weekly breaks.

## Right to paid annual leave

All workers are entitled to four weeks' paid annual leave (Reg. 13). There is a minimum period of qualifying employment of 13 weeks and workers must give notice of when they wish to take leave. The notice period must be at least twice the length of the leave period. The employer may refuse permission to take leave at that time. The entitlement to leave arises in a 'leave year', which normally runs from the date when the worker started work. The leave entitlement cannot be replaced by payment in lieu except where the employment is terminated when the worker has not had the leave for that year. It is a common misconception that this right is additional to rights to leave on public and bank holidays. It is not. The four weeks includes these. In *Kigass Aero Components v Brown* (2002) it was held that a worker on long-term sick leave can still claim annual leave under these Regulations, as the only qualification is whether they have been a worker during any part of that year. Thus leave entitlement continues to accrue even though the worker is on sick leave.

### Modification and exclusion of this right

This right cannot be excluded or modified and it is enforced by complaint to an employment tribunal, which may award compensation.

## THE YOUNG WORKERS DIRECTIVE

The DTI has published draft Regulations for implementing the remainder of the Young Workers Directive. These will limit the working time of young workers (those over the minimum school leaving age but under 18) to eight hours a day or 40 hours a week (with longer hours allowed in certain cases); prohibit night work (again except in certain cases); and provide that young workers shall be adequately supervised. There is as yet no date for when these Regulations will become law.

## SUNDAY WORKING

Retail workers are protected from dismissal for refusing to work on Sundays in certain circumstances, which are contained in ss.40–43 and 45 of the ERA.

## ■ Protected shop workers

Shop workers who were employed on 25 August 1994 (when the Sunday Trading Act 1994 came into force) are classified as 'protected shop workers'. They cannot be required to work on Sundays, they cannot be dismissed or selected for redundancy for refusing to work on Sundays and they cannot be subjected to any detriment for refusing to work on Sundays. However, they may lose this protection by:

1. agreeing to work on Sundays; and
2. giving the employer an opting-in notice in writing agreeing to work on Sundays.

## ■ Opted-out shop workers

Shop workers who are not protected shop workers, either because they were not employed on the above date or because they gave an opted-in notice, are known as 'opted-out shop workers'. They may give the employer an opted-out notice stating that they object to Sunday working and then after three months from the date of the notice they acquire the same rights as protected shop workers.

A final point is that these provisions do not apply to employees specifically engaged to work on Sundays, although they still are protected under general unfair dismissal law.

## RIGHTS TO TIME OFF WORK

Details of the various rights to time off work will be found in the appropriate parts of this book but readers might find it convenient to have a shortlist of these rights at this point with an indication of where further details may be found:

1. Right to take time off for trade union duties and activities: see Chapter 13.
2. Right to take time off for employee representatives: see Chapter 12.
3. Right to take time off for public duties: see below.
4. Right to take time off for ante-natal care: see Chapter 10.
5. Right to take time off to care for dependants: see Chapter 10.
6. Right to take time off when under threat of dismissal for redundancy: see Chapter 12.

The right to take time off for public duties is for specified duties such as sitting as a magistrate, or as a member of a local council, health authority, education body, prison visiting committee, statutory tribunal or the Environment Agency (s.50 ERA). Time off must be reasonable and ACAS have given guidance in a Code.

It should be noted that these rights are distinct from the rights to maternity and paternity leave, which are dealt with in Chapter 10.

# Chapter 8

# Health and safety

## INTRODUCTION

The law on health and safety has several objectives:

1. to prevent accidents at work and to prevent injuries developing as a result of events at work;
2. to encourage a positive attitude to health and safety at work;
3. to provide an effective system of compensation for accidents and injuries at work;
4. to provide, where appropriate, for criminal sanctions for breaches of health and safety laws.

These objectives are achieved through a number of different systems:

1. the common law of negligence, which provides compensation for injuries sustained through work;
2. actions for breach of statutory duty which also aim to provide compensation for injuries at work;
3. actions for breach of an implied term in the contract of employment that the employer will ensure that the working environment is reasonably safe for the performance of contractual duties;
4. the system of state benefits for those injured at work;
5. the Health and Safety at Work Act 1974, which aims to encourage good practice in health and safety but which also provides criminal penalties for breach.
6. European Community Regulations together with the Working Time Regulations, which were discussed in Chapter 7.

Each of these will be considered in turn but the diagram below and examples which follow show their interrelationship.

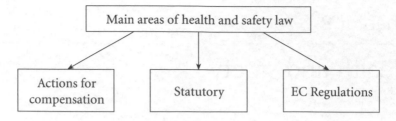

## Example

John is injured at the office where he works by some broken glass in a door. His injuries are not serious but he sustained a badly cut hand.

There will have been a breach of the Health and Safety at Work Act here, although criminal penalties are reserved for serious cases. John may wish to claim some compensation for his injuries under the law of negligence, although the amount would be small, and, if he is away from work, he would receive statutory sick pay (SSP). It is unlikely that he would be away from work for long enough to be eligible for industrial injury benefits. The main result of the accident would probably be a report to the health and safety committee (if there is one) and measures put in place to make sure that this does not happen again.

## Example

Jennifer is very seriously burned when some hot liquid escapes from a container. She is away from work for a year. Clearly Jennifer will be entitled to SSP, but she will also be entitled to compensation for the injuries themselves. She could claim incapacity benefit but it is likely that she will wish to claim a higher sum than the amount of benefit and, in any event, entitlement to benefits is linked to other factors (see below). Thus a common law action for negligence is the obvious avenue, although she will have to prove that the employer was negligent. In addition, there is the prospect that the employer will be fined for a breach of the Health and Safety at Work Act.

The other point to make in this introduction is that an injury at work may also, particularly if it is linked to bullying, lead to an action for harassment on the grounds of sex, race or disability if the reason for the actions which caused the injury was discrimination on any of those grounds. A good example is *Jones v Tower Boot Co. Ltd* (1997) (see Chapter 9). Furthermore, actions which lead to injury can also give grounds for the employee to claim constructive dismissal, although compensation is far more likely to be sought in an action for negligence.

The following statistics, taken from the Annual Report of the Health and Safety Commission for 2000/2001, are useful in setting health and safety in context before starting a detailed examination of the law. The number of fatal injuries was provisionally stated as 291 with an expected final total of 295. This showed a rise of 34% compared with the previous year and was made up of 215 employees and 80 self-employed persons. The number of major non-fatal injuries was 27,303, as compared with 28,652 for the previous year, and the number of injuries classed as over three day was 133,112, as compared with 135,381 in the previous year. The total of all these combined was 160,630 employees and 1,453 self-employed. The message is clear: there is no more vital topic in employment law than this one. (Note that the website of the Health and Safety Commission (www.hse.gov.uk) is a mine of information and really sets the law in context. Frequent visits to it are recommended.)

We will now look in more detail at the various legal systems that apply to health and safety at work.

## ACTION FOR COMPENSATION (DAMAGES) IN A COMMON LAW ACTION FOR THE TORT OF NEGLIGENCE

An action for negligence is not, of course, confined to claims arising out of accidents at work (the most common action for negligence is for damages for injuries resulting from a road accident). Actions for negligence are met with in other areas of employment law as, for example, an action arising from what is alleged to be a negligently given reference (see Chapter 5).

In all negligence actions three points must be proved. In relation to an action by an employee against an employer these are:

1. that the employer owed the employee a duty of care;
2. that the employer broke that duty through negligence;
3. that the employee suffered damage as a result which was not too remote a consequence of the employer's negligence.

The following issues are also relevant:

4. Was the employee guilty of contributory negligence?
5. Did the employee consent to the act which caused the injury?

Finally, we must consider whether the employer, rather than owing a direct duty to the employee, is liable for the actions of other employees. This is known as 'vicarious liability'.

## ▪ The duty of care

The idea of the duty of care is that it defines the situations where the employer *can be* liable to the employee. The standard defines whether there *is* liability. The classic formulation of the duty of care in employment situations is found in *Wilsons and Clyde Coal Co. v English* (1938), where Lord Wright said that the duty was threefold:

1. 'provision of a competent staff of men';
2. 'adequate material';
3. 'a proper system and effective supervision', which is really the general duty to provide a safe system of work.

In addition to these categories there is the more recently recognised duty to safeguard the employee from foreseeable psychiatric injury resulting from work.

These will now be looked in turn, although the duties will be expressed in a more modern way.

## Duty to provide competent fellow employees

This clearly means that the employer must provide the employee with fellow employees who are able to do the job and therefore the employer will be in breach of this duty if he fails to provide proper training so that an employee is injured by the negligence of another employee who was not properly trained for the task. A specific instance of this duty being broken is where an employee is injured by practical jokes played by another employee. In *Hudson v Ridge Manufacturing Co. Ltd* (1957) an employee had engaged in practical jokes for many years by, for example, tripping other employees up. He had been warned by a foreman but, beyond this, no further action was taken. He then tripped up the plaintiff, a disabled man, and injured him. It was held that the employers were in breach of the duty of care owed to the plaintiff as they were aware of the employee's conduct and had not taken proper steps to put an end to it. Therefore, an employer may find that the only way to deal with a practical joker is to dismiss him/her and such a dismissal may then be fair.

## Duty to provide safe plant and equipment

This duty is now one of strict liability, in contrast to the other duties, which require proof of negligence by the employer. In *Davie v New Merton Board Mills Ltd* (1959) the House of Lords held that an employer was not liable for defects in equipment which could not have been discovered on a reasonable inspection of equipment supplied from a reputable source. The effect was that an employee might suffer injury from a piece of equipment but be unable to recover any damages where there was a latent defect.

The law was changed by the Employer's Liability (Defective Equipment) Act 1969, which provides that an employer is liable where the employee:

1. suffers personal injury in the course of employment;
2. in consequence of a defect in equipment provided by the employer; and
3. the defect is attributable wholly or partly to the fault of a third party, whether identified or not.

In this case the injury is deemed to be attributable to the negligence of the employer.

### Example

Ishmael is injured when operating a drill which fractures when in use. His employer bought the drill from a manufacturer who had often supplied this type of drill in the past none of which had ever given any trouble. Under the previous law, Ishmael would probably not have succeeded in a claim against the employer for negligence but now the employer will be liable as the Act creates a presumption that the employer is negligent even though in reality he is not. Had it not been for the Act, Ishmael would have been left to claim against the manufacturer for negligence but if the manufacturer had, for example, ceased business he would have received nothing.

In *Coltman v Bibby Tankers Ltd* (1987) a ship sank with all hands and it was alleged that it had been defectively built due to the negligence of the manufacturer. The House of Lords held that the word 'equipment' could include the actual workplace provided by the employer – in this case a ship – as well as equipment in the more usual sense, such as tools.

## Duty to provide a safe system of work

This duty includes the provision of a safe workplace, safe methods of working, methods of supervision designed to ensure safety and a generally safe working environment. A good general example is provided by *General Cleaning Contractors Ltd v Christmas* (1953), where the employee, a window cleaner, fell when cleaning a window as a result of the sash falling on his hand which made him let go of his hold. Safety belts were provided but there were no hooks to attach them to. The employers were held liable, as it was their responsibility to ensure that there were adequate precautions against injury and the responsibility of deciding how to take precautions should not fall on the employees. The following specific points arise:

### Where safety equipment is provided, how far should the employer go in ensuring that employees use it?

The law has changed a great deal since the remark of Lord Simonds in *Smith v Austin Lifts* (1959), where he deprecated 'any tendency to treat the relationship of employer and skilled workman as that of a nurse and imbecile child'. His point, albeit very unfortunately expressed, was that employees should be expected to look after themselves to a large extent and not expect the employer to be constantly devising safety precautions. This view was upheld in *McWilliams v Arrol* (1962), where a steel erector fell to his death when not wearing a safety belt. Belts were not provided, although they had previously been, but the Court of Appeal found that the employee would not have worn one even if it had been provided. Although there is some truth in what Lord Simonds said, the law has moved on since then. In *Bux v Slough Metals Ltd* (1973) a die-caster lost an eye when a piece of molten metal splashed into his eye. Goggles were provided but the employee, on finding that they misted up, told his superintendent that he would not wear them. No attempt was made to persuade him to do so. It was held that the employers were negligent in not giving instructions 'in a reasonable and firm manner . . . followed by supervision'. The decision in *McWilliams* was distinguished on the basis that there the issue was one of causation, in that the employee would not have worn the safety belt even if it had been provided, and the failure to provide them did not cause the injury, but there is no doubt that the decision in *Bux* represented a change of approach. Even so, the law here is still not clear. Suppose the employee refused to wear safety equipment: would the employer have a duty to suspend him/her unless they did so? Would a failure to do this be negligence? Could an employee ultimately be dismissed in such a case? The answer must be that, as a last resort, an employer, provided that he/she acted reasonably, would be held to have acted fairly in dismissing/suspending if this was the only way to protect an employee from injury. The only other guidance comes from *Crouch v British Rail Engineering Ltd* (1988), where the employee, a fitter, injured his eye when a piece of metal flew into it. Again, the use of goggles would have prevented the injury and here goggles were available in the storeroom five minutes walk away. The Court of Appeal held that the employer had a duty actually to provide the goggles to the employee as part of his tool kit. Finally, it is significant that, under s.7 of the Health and Safety at Work Act (see below), employees have a duty to take reasonable care for their own safety. Could a failure to use safety equipment provided be a breach of this Act? Why not?

### Does the duty extend to activities away from the employer's premises?

The employer will object that this is unfair, as he/she has no control over safety on premises other than their own. However, the courts have held that the duty does apply here as in *General Cleaning Contractors v Christmas* (above). The question then becomes the extent of this duty, a point which is dealt with below under the heading 'Standard of care'. An interesting issue arose in *Reid v Rush and Tompkins Group Ltd* (1989), where an employee was injured in a road accident when working for the defendants in Ethiopia, where at that time there was no requirement to have third party insurance. He argued that his employer had a duty either to provide insurance cover where the employee was working or to advise the employee of the risks of being without cover and advise him to obtain it. It was held that the employer's duties did not extend to these matters as there was no duty to warn against the risk of economic loss alone and, in any event, it would be impossible to formulate such a duty in sufficiently precise terms (see also *Square D Ltd v Cook* (1992) discussed below).

### Duty to safeguard employee from work related upper limb disorder

The duty has recently been held to extend to a duty to safeguard the employee from what was known as repetitive strain injury (RSI) but is now known as work related upper limb disorder (WRULD). The initial decision was that in *Pickford v ICI plc* (1998), where the employee, a secretary, spent a great deal of her time typing and claimed for what was then RSI. It was held that, in principle, such a claim could succeed but on the facts here it failed as the court was not satisfied on the evidence whether the injury was psychogenic (i.e. in the mind) or physical. The employee had to prove that it was physical and she was not able to do so. Subsequently, in *Alexander v Midland Bank plc* (1999), claims for WRULD were brought by encoders at a bank. Their work involved coding in information at very great speed and there was continual pressure to work faster, with league tables and competitions. The claim was for neck, arm and hand strain. The court held that where on the facts the explanation that the injury was psychogenic was unconvincing, then the injury had to be physical, as it was here. Thus claims for WRULD have been accepted in principle and the issue is one of proof.

## Duty to protect the employee from psychiatric injury at work

The existence of this duty was recognised in *Walker v Northumberland CC* (1995), one of the most important recent cases in any area of employment law. Mr Walker was a social worker responsible for a team of four. The workload gradually rose but there was no increase in staffing levels. He eventually suffered a nervous breakdown and, before he returned to work, it was agreed that he would be provided with extra assistance. Although extra assistance was forthcoming, it was withdrawn after a month and Mr Walker suffered a second breakdown and was subsequently dismissed on the ground of permanent ill health. The High Court held that his employers were in breach of their duty of care as, once he had suffered one nervous breakdown, there was a foreseeable risk to his mental health and the employers should not have withdrawn the extra assistance provided. The employers had argued that, as their resources were scarce, they had to take this into account when deciding what assistance to allocate, but the court held that a reasonable local authority would have at least continued the extra assistance until Mr Walker's workload was reduced. Furthermore, any argument that scarce resources were relevant in determining the extent of the duty could only be relevant in tort, being derived from the speech of Lord Wilberforce in *Anns v Merton LBC* (1977), and could not apply if the action was brought in contract for breach of an implied term. Given that the scope of the duties in contract and tort were the same (see below), there would be an injustice in imposing a barrier on recovery of damages in one but not the other. It was unfortunate that the decision in *Walker* was not appealed and, although there were many highly publicised cases of considerable amounts of damages being paid for breach of this duty, these resulted from out of court settlements. At length the matter came before the Scottish Court of Session in *Cross v Highlands and Islands Development Board* (2001), where a training officer had committed suicide, allegedly as a result of stress at work. It was accepted that the duty in *Walker* applied but it could not be shown that the employer was in breach. The court held that, at that date, a reasonable employer would not have conducted a risk assessment on the employee's return to work after being absent due to stress but now the decision would probably have been different in the light of changes in practice due partly to EC Regulations (see below). A significant point was made by Lord Fraser, who held that psychiatric injury should be treated as physical injury and actions should not be confined to the old category of nervous shock cases. A more significant decision was that of the Court of Appeal in *Sutherland v Hatton* (and three other conjoined appeals) (2002). Appeals against three awards of damages for psychiatric injury, two to teachers and one to a machine operator, were allowed, and one, of £175,000 to an administrative assistant, was allowed to stand. Hale LJ laid down the following principles:

1. Claims for psychiatric injury were not to be treated differently from claims for personal injury. Therefore, the basic rules of the tort of negligence apply.
2. Claims could only be brought for injury to health and not for stress as such.
3. The test is the same in all types of employment, in that no types of work are intrinsically dangerous but relevant factors in deciding if a duty exists are the nature and extent of the work done by the employee and signs of impending harm to health.
4. In considering the standard of care, account should be taken of the size of the operation, the magnitude of the risk and the costs and practicability of preventing it.
5. An employer who offered a confidential counselling or treatment service would be unlikely to be in breach.
6. If the only reasonable step was to dismiss or demote the employee and the employee was not agreeable to this, then the employer would not be in breach of the duty by failing to dismiss.

A further question concerning psychiatric harm arose in *White v Chief Constable of South Yorkshire* (1999). The respondents were police officers who had been on duty at Hillsborough Stadium when 96 people were crushed to death and many others were injured. They suffered post-traumatic stress disorder as a result of looking after victims and claimed damages but their claim failed as they were held to be 'secondary victims', i.e. those who fell outside the range of foreseeable injury. In order to recover they would have needed to show that there were close ties of love and affection between them and the victims, which was obviously not the case here. The fact that they were employees was not a reason for treating them as 'primary victims' and allowing them to recover.

### Can the employer claim that the duty of care to employees has been delegated to others with the result that he is not liable?

The courts have rejected this idea, which in effect means that the employer can shift the responsibility for injuries to employees on to someone else. The point was raised in *Wilsons and Clyde Coal Co. v English* (1938) (see also above), where an employee was crushed when a haulage system in a mine was negligently operated and the employers argued that they had discharged their duty of care by appointing a qualified manager. Lord Thankerton said that it was a 'fallacy' to say that the duty was discharged by the appointment of a competent person to perform it.

More recently, the decision in *Square D Ltd v Cook* (1992) has been put forward as a possible example of an employer successfully delegating the duty. The employee was an electronics engineer in Saudi Arabia. Another company occupied the premises where he worked and yet another company was the main contractor. The employee was injured when his foot was trapped in a floor. The court held that, although the duty of care was not delegable, the duty was always to take reasonable care and one needs to look at all the circumstances, including the degree of control which the employer can reasonably be expected to exercise.

The idea that the employer could be responsible for daily events on a site in Saudi Arabia was felt to have an 'air of unreality'. This decision could be considered, despite the words of the court to the contrary, as one where the employer delegated the duty, but it is submitted that a better explanation is that the case only deals with breach of duty rather than the existence of a duty. The court did not suggest that the employer owed no duty at all, only that he did not do so in this particular situation.

## The employer broke the duty through negligence

This question arises only when it has been established that a duty was owed and is generally referred to as the question of the 'standard of care'. In effect, the question when considering the *duty* of care is whether this is a situation where the employer *can* be liable. The *standard* of care decides whether the employer *is* liable. The standard of care is broken by negligence and thus we must first decide what negligence is in the context of the relationship between employer and employee.

In many cases it is difficult to separate the questions of duty and breach, as in *Walker v Northumberland CC* and *Sutherland v Hatton* (above). The judgment of Hale LJ in *Sutherland* inevitably deals with both.

A clear example of where the courts had to assess the standard of care is *Latimer v AEC Ltd* (1953). A large factory was flooded in a very heavy rainstorm and the water then mixed with an oily substance which resulted in the floor becoming extremely slippery. The employers had what they believed was enough sawdust to cover any eventualities but it turned out that there was not enough to cover the whole floor. The plaintiff slipped on an untreated part of the floor and injured his ankle. It was held that the question was whether a reasonably prudent employer would have closed the whole factory down rather than run the risk of injury and on the facts it was found that such an employer would not have done so. The degree of risk was too small and thus an employer is entitled to weigh the extent of the risk against the measures necessary to eliminate it.

On the other hand, the duty owed by the employer to employees is a personal one and the special characteristics of each employee must be taken into account. Where an employee is inexperienced, a higher standard of care is owed. Likewise, a high standard of care is owed where the consequences of an injury to a particular employee are much greater than to most employees. In *Paris v Stepney BC* (1951) an employee who was blind in one eye was employed as a mechanic. He lost the sight of his other eye when a splinter flew into that eye and it was held that, although there might not have been a duty to supply goggles to fully sighted employees, the consequences of the loss of a eye in this case were much more serious and thus a higher standard of care was owed. Therefore, there was a duty to supply goggles and, as the employers had failed to do so, they were liable for negligence.

An application of this principle is the situation where an employee suffers from a medical condition which is either caused or exacerbated by the work which they do. In *Withers v Parry Chain Co. Ltd* (1961) the employee had a severe attack of dermatitis due to the grease used in her job. It was held that her employer was not in breach of duty in employing her on work which it should have known could cause this, as there were no special precautions which could have been taken to protect the employee. In *Pape v Cumbria CC* (1991) the employee was a cleaner and suffered dermatitis through coming into contact with chemical cleaning agents. Employees were provided with gloves but hardly ever used them and they were not warned of the danger of dermatitis occurring in this situation. It was held that the employers were in breach of duty, as the dangers were well enough known to make it the duty of a reasonable employer to warn of the risks but not well enough known for the employer to be entitled to assume that employees would know of the risks. In *Withers* the employers were not obliged to even give a warning yet in *Pape* they were under a duty to warn. Although the cases are distinguishable on the ground that in *Withers* there was no means of ensuring safety, they still represent divergent approaches. Section 25 of the Health and Safety at Work Act 1974 (HSWA) allows inspectors to seize any articles or substances which pose an imminent danger of serious personal injury and here the fact that the process could not be carried in any other way would not be relevant. Although the situation in *Withers* might not be what the drafters of s.25 had in mind, there is a good case that it should apply in such a case. Is an employer under a duty in these cases to dismiss an employee who, in the *Withers* type of situation, cannot do the job without injury? As in cases discussed above where the employee would not wear safety equipment, it is submitted that, provided that the employer acts reasonably, dismissal could be fair but the employer would need to show that there was no other work which the employee could do. This conclusion is supported by the remarks of the Court of Appeal in *Sutherland v Hatton* (above). However, the employee's injuries may have led to him/her becoming disabled under the Disability Discrimination Act 1995 and the employer would then need to consider whether reasonable adjustments could be made to the job to enable the employee to do it without injury.

## The employee suffered injuries as a result which were not too remote a consequence of the employer's negligence

This final element in the law of negligence can, in practice, prove the most difficult of all. A good example is a case where an employee claims to have suffered injury to health as a result of stress at work. It may be that there is evidence that the employee was going through difficult personal circumstances at the time and the employer will say that this was the cause. Employees may be aided by the rule established in *Smith v Leech Brain and Co. Ltd* (1962) that where the defendant can foresee the type of injury suffered by the claimant then there is liability for all damage which results. An employee was, due to the negligence of his employers, splashed on the lip by a piece of molten metal. Some injury was clearly foreseeable but it was not foreseeable that the employee would die of cancer, as happened. The employers were liable, as they could foresee that he would suffer a burn. Therefore, they were liable for all the consequences. This is often known as the 'thin skull' rule, i.e. that if the defendant (e.g. the employer) knows that the other party (e.g. the employee) has a thin skull (or some personal sensitivity to a particular type of injury) then they are liable for all the damage which results even if it may not be foreseeable.

In *Fairchild v Glenhaven Funeral Services Ltd* (2002) an employee claimed that he had suffered from mesothelioma, a form of cancer caused by exposure to asbestos fibres, but, as he had worked for a number of employers during the time when he could have contracted the disease the Court of Appeal held that it could not be proved that it had occurred whilst he was working for his present employer. This decision was reversed by the House of Lords who held that it was contrary to justice in that where two or more people have committed a wrong then the victim should not be deprived of a remedy only because he/she cannot establish which of them was to blame. Accordingly, the victims were allowed to recover from any of the employers, leaving it to them to seek a contribution from other employers shown to be negligent.

## Contributory negligence

Where the employer is liable to the employee for negligence, any damages payable may be reduced as it may be held that the employee has been negligent. This provision is found in the Law Reform (Contributory Negligence) Act 1945, s.1(1) of which states that damages 'shall be reduced to such extent as the court thinks just and equitable having regard to the claimant's share in the responsibility for the damage'.

A good example of an employment case where contributory negligence applied is *Crouch v British Rail Engineering* (above), where the failure of the employee to wear goggles led to a reduction of 50% in his damages although the employers were negligent in failing to provide them.

## Consent

This is often known by the Latin name of *volenti non fit injuria* (to those who are willing no injury is done) and simply means that, if I have consented to what would otherwise be a tort then I lose my right to claim damages for it. A good example is taking part in a game where one consents to running the risks ordinarily associated with it. It differs from contributory negligence in that, if it succeeds, the claimant does not recover any damages at all.

There have been attempts to argue that it should apply in employment cases on the basis that an employee knew of a risk and consented to run it. However, there are two elements in this defence:

1. knowledge of the risk;
2. a free and voluntary consent to run it.

Although knowledge may be present on the part of the employee, it will be difficult to establish that the employee voluntarily consented to run it, as a refusal to do a particular job on the ground of risk could lead to dismissal. In any case there is a strong reluctance on the part of the courts to apply a defence which would result in an employee losing all the damages. In *Bowater v Rowley Regis Corporation* (1944) Goddard LCJ said that the defence would hardly ever apply to acts in the course of normal duty and could only apply where the work itself carried an element of danger. A court today would probably be even less in favour of the defence applying.

The only reasonably modern example of where it did apply is *ICI v Shatwell* (1965), where X and Y were two shotfirers who carried out testing in the open rather than from behind cover in breach of both statutory duties and their employer's instructions. They were injured but it was held that the employers were not liable as the employees knew of the risk and must be held to have consented to it. This is an unusual decision in that the employees had actually *created* the risk rather than agreed to run a risk created by their employer.

## Time limit for bringing actions

Under the Limitation Act 1980, actions for personal injury or death must be commenced within three years of the date when the accident occurred. This period is subject to the following points:

1. Where the claimant only knew of his/her right to bring an action (e.g. if only later did the claimant find out that the defendant was negligent) then the three-year period runs from when the claimant discovered this or ought reasonably to have done so.
2. The court has a discretion under s.33 to allow an action to proceed out of time where it is equitable to do so.

A more detailed account of these rules will be found in works on civil procedure.

## Vicarious liability

In all the above cases we have been concerned with the employer's owing a direct duty to the employee. It is also possible for the employer to be liable to the employee because of the negligence of another employee. This situation is known as one of vicarious liability, in other words, the employee is liable, not for his/her own negligence but for that of another. It can be met with in situations other than employment as where, for example, an employee driving a van whilst carrying out his duties injures a pedestrian by negligence. It can also apply to torts other than negligence.

A good example is *Lister v Romford Ice and Cold Storage Co. Ltd* (1957) (also discussed in Chapter 2), where an employer was held liable to pay damages to one employee, X, for the negligent driving of another employee, Y, which had injured X. The fact that X was the father of Y, although legally irrelevant, gave added interest to the case.

In order for an employer (X) to be vicariously liable two conditions must be satisfied. First, the person who was guilty of negligence (Y) must be an employee of X. Thus where Y is an independent contractor, X will not usually be liable, although in specific situations liability can arise for the actions of an independent contractor. One instance is where the employer specifically tells the contractor to perform a tort.

*Example*

A development company, W, knows that a particular piece of land does not belong to it but it wishes to lay a cable across the land and employs Y, who are independent contractors, to actually lay the cable. This act will be, by itself, a trespass and thus a tort and so W will be liable for the actions of Y even though Y is not an employee. Y could also be sued directly by the owner of the land.

Secondly, the act must be one for which the employer was responsible. The traditional test was to ask whether the employee was performing an act authorised by the employer but doing so in an unlawful manner. This test, which was first suggested by *Salmond on Torts* (now in 21st edition, 1996), was adequate for cases of, for example, negligent driving of the employer's vehicles but was less so in cases of intentional wrongdoing. This point was made by the House of Lords in *Lister v Helsey Hall Ltd* (2001), where the claim was by two pupils at a boarding school for damages resulting from sexual abuse committed by wardens at the school. The employer was held liable and a new test laid down that the employer will be liable if there is a close relationship between the nature of the employment with the wrong. Lord Steyn, in applying this test, considered whether there was a duty owed to the victim by the employer. If so, there would be liability. On the facts here, there was, and so the employer was liable for the acts of the wardens.

## ■ Liability of the employer to independent contractors

We have seen above that an employer is not usually liable for the acts of independent contractors, but is an employer liable to an independent contractor who has been injured in the course of working for the employer? The answer is usually that under the common law of negligence there is no duty but under the HSWA, as we shall see, an employer does owe duties to those other than employees. However, where an independent contractor is working on premises occupied by the employer (although not necessarily owned by them) and is injured, then the employer may be liable for breach of the duty of care owed to all lawful visitors under the Occupiers Liability Act 1957.

## ACTIONS FOR BREACH OF STATUTORY DUTY

These are less common than actions under the common law of negligence. The distinction between them is shown by the following example.

*Example*

Emma works as a secretary for Jones and Co., a firm of solicitors. She is injured when she falls over a bottle of cleaning fluid, which had been carelessly left in the corridor by another employee, Margaret, a cleaner. Emma also suffers injury to her eyesight because of constant exposure to her computer screen and complains that Jones and Co. have failed to monitor the risk or give her proper training. The claim for damages resulting from her fall would be brought in the tort of negligence, but any claim resulting from injury to her eyesight could be under the general law of negligence but could also be for breach of statutory duty based on the employer's failure to comply with the Health and Safety (Display Screen Equipment) Regulations 1992. These Regulations, which will be discussed in more detail later in this chapter, give a right of action the essence of which is that because of the breach of a statute or a Regulation made under a statute, an employee may claim damages. The interesting point is that the statute will usually impose criminal penalties for its breach and will not be primarily concerned with the possibility of a civil action, which is therefore something of a spin-off. The advantage of an action for breach of statutory duty is that the duty will usually be stricter than that at common law for negligence. (Incidentally, this is also an example of where the employer is not only directly liable to the employee (Emma) but also vicariously liable for the acts of another employee. Had Margaret been an independent contractor then the employer would not have been liable for *her* acts but would still have been liable to Emma for breach of the direct duty owed to her.)

How is it possible to tell whether a civil action can be brought for its breach? In *Groves v Lord Wimborne* (1898) it was held that breach of a statutory safety requirement would normally give rise to such an action, although this case concerned sheep on a ship and not employees. This general principle is subject to whether the statute itself gives any indication whether a civil action can be brought for its breach. Section 47 of the HSWA provides that breach of any of the general duties in ss.2–8 of the Act does not give rise to an action for breach of statutory duty but that Regulations made under the Act are to be construed as giving rise to such an action unless the particular Regulation states otherwise. The main Regulations are those made as a result of EC initiatives in 1992 (known as the six pack), which are explored more fully later in this chapter, and discussion will focus on these. However, it should be noted in passing that actions for breach of statutory duty under industrial safety legislation such as the Factories Act 1961 were, until they were repealed, very important. Of the six pack, only one, the Management of Health and Safety at Work Regulations 1992, excludes civil liability. Actions for breach of statutory duty are therefore possible under the other five.

Assuming that an action for breach of statutory duty is possible, the other question is what an employee has to prove to succeed. There are five points:

1. That the statutory duty is owed to the claimant. There is no difficulty with the six pack Regulations, which expressly apply to all employees, even temporary ones.
2. That the duty is placed on the defendant, i.e. in these cases, the employer. This is made explicit in the Regulations.
3. That the defendant is in breach of the duty. The precise standard of care has yet to be clarified under all of the Regulations but in *Stark v Post Office* (2000) it was held that the requirement to maintain equipment imposed in the Work Equipment Regulations is strict, which means that the employer is liable whether or not there was negligence.
4. That the damage suffered by the claimant was of the type which the statute was designed to prevent. So far there is little on how this will be applied under the Regulations but the idea is that damages will not be available where the employee suffers an injury outside the scope of the statute.
5. That the injury was caused by the defendant's breach of the statute. The rules are the same as in the common law of negligence (see above).

In conclusion, actions for breach of statutory duty in health and safety matters are at a crossroads: the well established rules under the old industrial legislation have gone and, although these actions still have a valuable part to play, how the courts will use them in relation to the six pack Regulations is as yet unclear.

## ACTIONS FOR BREACH OF AN IMPLIED TERM IN THE CONTRACT OF EMPLOYMENT

In many cases a claim that the employer is in breach of the duty of care can also be brought as a claim that the employer is in breach of an implied term of the contract of employment to provide a working environment which is reasonably safe for the performance of contractual duties. In *Johnstone v Bloomsbury AHA* (1991) (the junior hospital doctor's case – see Chapter 5) the duty was treated as a contractual one and this was also so in *Waltons v Morse and Dorrington* (1997) (see also Chapter 5). However, there is usually no advantage in bringing the claim in contract and these two cases had features making them more suitable for contractual claims, as we shall see below.

The main reasons for bringing the claim in contract are:

1. Where economic loss is claimed, as in *Scally v Southern Health and Social Services Board* (see also Chapter 2), where the claim was for economic loss (loss here of pension rights) rather than personal injury because a claim for pure economic loss cannot normally be brought in tort.
2. Where the nature of the claim depends on the construction of the terms of the employee's contract as in *Johnstone* (above), where the issue was that the term requiring a certain number of hours of work was alleged to have resulted in injury to the plaintiff.

3. Where the claim is linked with another contractual issue, as in *Waltons* (above), where the claim was for constructive dismissal which is based on contract (see Chapter 11) resulting from the alleged failure of the employer to deal adequately with complaints from the employee about exposure to cigarette smoke.

## STATE BENEFITS FOR THOSE INJURED AT WORK

Only a brief account of these will be given here as the topic lies more in the area of welfare law. However, any discussion of the law on health and safety would be incomplete without some discussion of state benefits.

The system of state benefits for injuries should be seen as part of a larger system providing a comprehensive scheme of benefits when workers are unable to work through sickness or injury. The initial benefit claimed is statutory sick pay (SSP) (described in more detail in Chapter 7), which provides payments for the first 28 weeks of illness. It is not available to the self-employed, who must claim incapacity benefit. This is also the benefit claimed where an employee is no longer entitled to SSP (also explained in Chapter 7).

Where the employee has suffered longer-term disability as a result of an injury at work then a claim for industrial injuries disablement benefit may be made. The following points should be noted in relation to this type of benefit:

1. It is paid only to 'employed earners' and not to the self-employed;
2. It is paid when an accident is suffered as a result of an injury arising out of and in the course of employment;
3. It is also paid when certain prescribed diseases have been contracted;
4. There is no means test for payment;
5. It is not necessary to establish fault on the part of the employer or anyone else.
6. Benefit is paid at set rates and therefore where the employee has a claim for a substantial sum an action for negligence will be necessary;
7. Payment of benefit does not prevent the claimant from bringing an action for compensation for negligence or breach of statutory duty but any compensation awarded may be subject to compensation recovery under the Social Security (Recovery of Benefits) Act 1997;
8. The essence of the compensation recovery scheme is that any final out of court settlement or award by the courts in a personal injury action cannot be made until the defendant has obtained from the Department for Work and Pensions (DWP) Compensation Recovery Unit a certificate giving the figure of total benefit paid to the claimant. The defendant must then deduct this sum from the damages paid and account for it to the DWP.
9. There are various specific benefits: industrial death benefit; disablement pension; constant attendance allowance; exceptionally severe disablement allowance; reduced earnings allowance; and retirement allowance.

## THE HEALTH AND SAFETY AT WORK ACT 1974

### Introduction

This Act has two aims, neatly stated in the Report of the Committee on Safety and Health at Work (1972) (known as the Robens Committee, after its chairman). This recommended that there should be a new, comprehensive Act dealing with health and safety at work. It recommended that 'the Act should contain a clear statement of the general principles of responsibility for safety and health, but otherwise should be mainly enabling in character'.

### A 'clear statement'

The law on health and safety was, prior to the Health and Safety at Work Act (HSWA), in a state of some confusion. There was a mass of legislation, passed at different times and in response to different needs. There were some major pieces of legislation, such as the Factories Act 1961, the Mines and Quarries Act 1954 and the Offices, Shops and Railway Premises Act 1961. Added to this there were detailed Regulations, with the result that health and safety legislation was, in the words of the Robens Report, a 'haphazard mass of law which is intricate in detail, unprogressive, often to difficult to comprehend and difficult to amend and keep up to date'. The committee therefore recommended (and this is one of the few committees to have its recommendations actually implemented virtually in full) that there should be a new Act (the HSWA) which should contain a clear statement of the basic principles of safety responsibility. One particular merit would be that the Act would cover all activities at work, whereas the previous piecemeal system left many areas uncovered. Furthermore, the existing legislation led to a culture in which health and safety was regarded as a matter of following rules rather than a positive duty which concerned all employees.

### An enabling Act

As the proposed Act was to consist of general duties only, there would be a need for detailed regulations and non-statutory codes of practice which would, the committee felt, be the most flexible and practical means of promoting health and safety at work. The previous mass of Regulations would be swept away and be replaced by these new Regulations and codes.

### Machinery of the Act

Although this will be considered in detail later, a mention at this point of the way in which the Act operates may help. As the above introduction has indicated, the emphasis is on self-regulation as far as possible. Nevertheless, the duties in the Act are backed by criminal sanctions and the Health and Safety Executive was set up with overall responsibility for health and safety matters. There is also a system of safety committees and safety representatives.

## Main duties laid down by the Act

Section 2(1) sets out the overriding duty: 'It shall be the duty of every employer to ensure, as far as is reasonably practicable, the health, safety and welfare at work of all his employees.'

Section 2(2) then provides that this duty extends to the following matters, although this does mean that these are the only matters covered:

1. The provision and maintenance of plant and systems of work that are safe and without risks to health.
2. Arrangements for ensuring safety and absence of risks to health in connection with the use, handling, storage and transport of articles and substances.
3. The provision of such information, instruction, training and supervision as is necessary to ensure the health and safety at work of employees.
4. As regards any place of work under the employer's control, the maintenance of it in a condition that is safe and without risks to health and the provision and maintenance of means of access to and egress from it that are safe and without such risks.
5. The provision and maintenance of a working environment that is safe, without risks to health, and adequate as regards facilities and arrangements for welfare at work.

In each case these matters are qualified by the phrase 'reasonably practicable'.

## 'Reasonably practicable'

As with most other safety legislation, the Act does not impose strict liability on the employer. Instead, the above duties require them to do everything reasonably practicable to achieve them. However, where there are criminal proceedings for breaches of the Act, s.40 reverses the burden of proof so that the employer must prove that it was not reasonably practicable to comply with the duty.

The meaning of this phrase, which appeared in s.102(8) of the Coal Mines Act 1911, was considered in *Edwards v National Coal Board* (1949). The issue there was whether the NCB had done everything reasonably practicable to make secure a 'travelling road' along which a miner was walking. He had been killed when a large part of the side of the road had fallen and it was held that 'reasonably practicable' meant weighing the risks of an accident against the measures needed to eliminate them. Here, as the risk was considerable, the court would not be prepared to give much weight to considerations such as the cost of preventing them. Although Asquith LJ observed that reasonably practicable is a narrower term than 'physically possible', it does seem clear that it is wider than 'reasonable care' and thus it is wrong to import ideas from the common law of negligence into this Act, a point made in cases considered below.

## To whom are the above duties owed?

The Act refers to 'employees' and these are defined by s.53 as those who work 'under a contract of employment or apprenticeship'. However, the Act also affects other persons, as we shall see below.

## Other duties under the Act

### Duties to those other than employees

Section 3(1) provides that employers have a duty to persons not employed by them (for example, independent contractors and members of the public) to conduct their undertaking so that they are not exposed to risks to their health and safety and this duty is extended by s.3(2) to self-employed persons. In *R v Associated Octel Ltd* (1996) the House of Lords held that the issue in cases brought under s.3 is 'whether the activity in question can be regarded as part of the employer's undertaking' (Lord Hoffmann). The defendants ran a chemical plant and used a specialist firm for repairs. Indeed, the contractor's eight employees were employed virtually full-time working on the defendant's site. One employee of the contractors was badly burned when, whilst he was cleaning a tank, a light bulb broke causing a bucket of highly inflammable acetone to ignite. It was held that the defendants were liable as the cleaning of the tank was clearly an activity which was part of their undertaking. The House of Lords rejected the view put forward in the earlier case of *RMC Roadstone Products v Jester* (1994), where the court had based its approach on the common law of vicarious liability. It had held that the employer was not liable for the acts of independent contractors and that undertaking here would mean the undertaking of the contractors unless the employer exercised control. This attempt to bring concepts from the common law of negligence into the HSWA was held to be wrong in *Octel*.

The question of risks was considered in *R v Board of Trustees of the Science Museum* (1993), which again shows a conscious break with the principles of the common law. An inspection showed that legionella bacteria in the cooling system of the museum could be dangerous to those outside the building. The museum's defence was that no one had actually been at risk and, in effect, argued that the same rule applied as in actions for negligence: resulting damage must be proved in addition to the breach of duty. The Court of Appeal held that this was wrong: the essence of s.3 is the *exposure* to risk, not necessarily harm resulting from it. Not only this, but the whole philosophy of the HSWA is that of preventing harm and thus it would be wrong to restrict s.3 to cases where harm has actually occurred.

## Duties on controllers of premises

Section 4 places a duty on controllers of premises both to those who work there (other than employees, who are covered by s.2) and to those who use plant or substances provided for their use there. The duty extends to ensuring, so far as is reasonably practicable, that the premises, plant and substances are safe and without risks to health. This duty is outside the scope of employment law except for liability to independent contractors and it is of more significance where there are machines on the premises which the public can use, as in a laundrette. The very existence of this duty is of interest in showing the scope of the HSWA.

## Duties in relation to emissions into the atmosphere

Section 5 imposes duties designed to control and reduce risks resulting from emissions into the atmosphere. This is another example of duties extending beyond the employment relationship. The duty is to use the best means for preventing emissions of noxious or harmful substances and, if any emissions do take place, to render any substances harmless or inoffensive.

## Duties on the designer, manufacturer, importer or supplier of articles for use at work

These are laid down in s.6 and the aim is to ensure that, if possible, threats to safety from these articles are removed at a stage before they reach the workplace. The duty extends to four matters:

1. To ensure, so far as is reasonably practicable, that articles are designed and constructed so that they are safe and without risks to health.
2. To carry out such testing and examinations to comply with the duty in 1 above.
3. To ensure that persons who use the article are provided with adequate information about the use for which it was designed or tested, together with information on the conditions necessary both to use it safely and to dismantle or dispose of it safely.
4. To ensure that persons are also supplied with any revisions of information on the matters referred to in 3 above.

## Duties laid on employees

Section 7, in line with the philosophy of the Act that safety is everyone's concern, provides that employees have a duty to take reasonable care for their own safety and that of others who may be affected by their acts or omissions at work. In addition, there is a duty to co-operate with others who have duties laid on them to enable them to fulfil *their* duties. Section 7 is obviously important where an employee refuses to use safety equipment provided (see above) and could be used as the basis of disciplinary proceedings against those who have acted in breach of safety rules and caused injury to themselves or others. Section 8 then provides that no person shall interfere with or misuse anything provided in the interests of safety.

**Duty not to charge for anything done or provided under these duties**

The final duty, set out in s.9, prevents an employer from charging employees for anything done or provided under the Act or any Regulations under it.

## Can a breach of the Act give rise to civil liability?

The answer is a firm 'no'. Section 47 provides that a breach of any of the above duties shall not give rise to civil liability for, for example, breach of statutory duty.

## Liability of the employer

Given that the Act imposes criminal penalties, can a particular employer argue that they should not be liable to them as they had no knowledge of the breach in question? Under the general criminal law, it has been held that a company can only be liable for the acts of someone who can be regarded as its 'directing mind', but in *R v Gateway Foodmarkets Ltd* (1997) it was held by the House of Lords that this was not appropriate to prosecutions under ss.2 or 3 of the Act and the only issue is whether the company was in breach of the duty. Thus in *Gateway Foodmarkets* a company was convicted as the result of breaches of the Act in one of its supermarkets even though the head office had no knowledge of it. The emphasis then switches to the defence of 'reasonable practicability' and it may be that a company could escape liability for a breach of the Act if it had done everything reasonably practicable through training, instructions and other matters to ensure safety.

## Administration and enforcement of the Act

This is carried out in three different ways:

1. By the Health and Safety Commission and Executive.
2. By enforcement powers of inspectors backed up by criminal penalties.
3. By safety polices, committees and representatives.

## THE HEALTH AND SAFETY COMMISSION

The powers of the Health and Safety Commission (HSC) are set out in s.11. It is responsible to the Secretary of State for the Department for Work and Pensions and to other Secretaries of State for the administration of the HSWA throughout Great Britain. Its functions are:

1. to secure the health, safety and welfare of persons at work;
2. to protect the public generally against risks to health or safety arising out of work activities and to control the keeping and use of explosives, highly flammable and other dangerous substances;

3. to conduct and sponsor research; promote training and provide an information and advisory service;
4. to review the adequacy of health and safety legislation and make proposals to the Government for new or revised regulations and approved codes of practice.

The Commission has general oversight of the work of the Health and Safety Executive (HSE) and therefore, for example, issues an Enforcement Policy Statement to it (see below). It can delegate any of its functions to the HSE.

The Commission is often asked by the government to conduct inquiries into accidents, a recent example being the inquiry into 'Obstruction of Railway Lines by Road Vehicles' set up following the accident at Great Heck, near Selby, on 28 February 2001. A recent development has been the issue of an Offences and Penalties Report, to which reference is made below.

## THE HEALTH AND SAFETY EXECUTIVE

The Health and Safety Executive (HSE) also derives its powers from s.11 and is responsible for enforcing the Act as well as dealing with questions on safety matters and giving advice. For example, guidance is often sought on matters that should be contained in the safety policies of employers and on particular issues such as which employees who come into contact with VDUs are entitled to an eyesight test.

The Act is enforced by inspectors, who offer advice on safety matters but, in addition, have enforcement powers as follows:

1. Issue of an improvement notice (s.21). This is issued where the inspector believes that one of the statutory provisions is being contravened and that this is likely to be repeated or continued. The notice requires the person named to remedy the contravention within a stated period. An appeal against the issue of an improvement notice may be made to an employment tribunal.
2. Issue of a prohibition notice (s.22). This is issued where the inspector believes that activities are either actually being carried out or are about to be and which involve the risk of serious personal injury. The effect is that the activities cannot be carried out until the matters specified in the notice have been remedied. The notice may take effect immediately or after a stated time. There is the same right of appeal as with an improvement notice.
3. To seize articles or substances which are believed to threaten imminent danger of serious personal injury (s.25).

The number of enforcement notices issued (i.e. 1 and 2 above) was 11,058 in 2000/01 as compared with 7,444 in 1996/97; 70% of these were in the manufacturing and construction industries (Annual Report of the HSC 2001).

In addition, there is a power of prosecution and the HSC, as mentioned above, has laid down guidelines for the HSE in deciding whether to prosecute. These include, for example, the need to target by singling out for prosecution any cases where serious risks were run and whether prosecution is proportionate to the seriousness of the offence. In 2000/01 there were 1,493 convictions, with an average fine of £6,250. In *R v F Howe and Son Ltd* (1999) the Court of Appeal held that the general level of fines was too low and any fine must be large enough to bring home the message that the object of prosecutions is to achieve a safe working environment and to protect the public. Even so, in this instance it held that a fine of £48,000 imposed on a small company was excessive, as more weight should have been given to the means of the company. In addition to fines there is the possibility of imprisonment and there have been five cases of this, all since 1996. Most prosecutions are brought against organisations, as it can be difficult to identify the person responsible but there are a few cases of actions against individuals. The Offences and Penalties Report for 2000/01 notes that an additional sanction is the disqualification of company directors where there is a conviction under the Company Directors Disqualification Act 1986.

## SAFETY COMMITTEES AND SAFETY REPRESENTATIVES

One of the objects of the HSWA is, as we have seen, to emphasise that safety is not just a matter of following external rules and then leaving it to the management. One way of achieving this is through the mechanism of safety policies, committees and representatives.

Section 2(3) obliges the employer to issue a general statement of health and safety policy together with arrangements for carrying it out.

Safety representatives are appointed either by trade unions where they are recognised by the employer (see Chapter 14) or, where there are no such trade unions, the employer must consult with elected employee safety representatives. (Note the use of employee representatives in a number of situations in employment law, for instance redundancy consultation.) Safety representatives appointed by trade unions can inspect premises, investigate both accidents and complaints from employees, consult inspectors and receive information. There is a right to time off work with pay to perform these duties. Elected employee representatives have similar powers but they have no right of inspection. Another difference is that while a minimum of two trade union representatives can ask the employer to establish a safety committee, and the employer must comply with such a request if made in writing, elected employee representatives do not have this right. However, they are allowed time off work to perform their functions, as with trade union representatives. The Act does not lay down any specific powers for safety committees and the HSC in guidance issued takes the view that arrangements to enable committees to fulfil their functions should evolve from discussion and negotiations with the employer. Thus it is the representatives who have more teeth.

## EUROPEAN COMMUNITY REGULATIONS ON HEALTH AND SAFETY

The record of the EC in health and safety law has been one of initial inactivity followed by a sudden burst of energy in the late 1980s and early 1990s. The Framework Directive (89/391) was adopted in 1989 and this was followed by the adoption of a Directive on Working Time in 1993, which led to the Working Time Regulations considered in Chapter 7. So far as the Framework Directive is concerned, its adoption led to the adoption of six daughter Directives which came into effect on 1 January 1993. In the UK these were implemented by Regulations, known as the 'six pack'. It was said at the time that 'The European Directives have landed. They have changed the face of British health and safety law' (Hendy and Ford, *Health and Safety* (2nd edn, 1993), quoted in Bercusson *European Labour Law* (1996)).

The Regulations are as follows:

### ■ Management of Health and Safety at Work Regulations 1992

The main duty imposed on employers is that of making assessments of risks to which employees are exposed to at work. Regulations were subsequently made which amended the original ones by requiring employers to identify any special risks to which new or expectant mothers might be exposed to while at work. The Regulations are backed by a Code of Practice, which emphasises that safety arrangements should be integrated with the management system which means that, for instance, when priorities are set any risks are, where possible, eliminated by the careful design of facilities.

### ■ Workplace (Health, Safety and Welfare) Regulations 1992

These set out general requirements for, for example, temperatures, ventilation, lighting, facilities (e.g. toilets) and safe passageways. They are reminiscent of the old Offices, Shops and Railway Premises Act, which they replaced, although too close a comparison should not be drawn.

### ■ Provision and Use of Work Equipment Regulations 1992

These set out minimum standards for work equipment and require that, for example, equipment is suitable for its intended use and is maintained in good repair and that there is protection against hazards such as dangerous machinery.

### ■ Personal Protective Equipment Regulations 1992

These require employers to provide suitable equipment, to ensure that it is properly used and to provide information on its use. (It would be interesting to see how a case such as *Bux v Slough Metals* (above) would fare under this.)

## Health and Safety (Display Screen Equipment) Regulations 1992

Employers have a duty to assess risks caused by use of VDUs and reduce them where possible and to provide proper accompanying equipment such as proper workstations.

## Manual Handling Regulations 1992

These require the employer to avoid the need, where possible, for manual handling where there are risks and, if it does take place, to ensure that there is a proper risk assessment and that risks are reduced to the lowest practicable level.

These regulations do not confer any civil liability beyond liability for breach of statutory duty (above).

# Chapter 9

# Discrimination law

## INTRODUCTION

This topic is sometimes known as 'equal opportunities' but the reason why this term is not used here is that it would imply that the subject matter of this chapter is concerned with equality. In one sense it is, in that the removal of discrimination should ensure greater equality. In another sense, though, there is a gulf between anti-discrimination law and equality as such. Equality, like all abstract concepts, is extremely difficult to pin down. A simple definition would be that it consists in treating everyone in the same way but we know that this is not possible in reality. For example, minors are denied certain legal rights, not in order to discriminate against them but to ensure that they are not taken advantage of. Nor can we say that opportunities are always equal because there will always be cases where some individuals have greater access to particular rights through factors such as birth, wealth and position. This may not be desirable but it is the case.

The approach of UK law has been to focus on particular groups and to enact legislation that provides that if these groups are discriminated against in particular circumstances then they will have a right to a remedy. If a person does not fall within those groups then, even though they may not have been treated equally, they will not have any remedies. There is no concept either of positive discrimination, with one small exception, although, as we shall see, the impact of EC law may be bringing about a change here. Thus for the moment there is no duty in law to take steps to *promote* equality. Instead, the law is essentially reactive: it operates when there is a complaint of discrimination but does not allow steps to be taken to remove the causes of it. For example, if a firm has a very small number of women employees compared with men and it genuinely wishes to ensure a more equal balance between the sexes, it might advertise positions as open to female candidates only. However, if it did so it would be in breach of the law.

It has been argued that the law should take a much more active role in promoting equality. Sandra Fredman, in *Discrimination Law* (Oxford: Oxford University Press, 2002), argues for the development of the law to include,

142

for example, 'mainstreaming', i.e. that the promotion of equal opportunities becomes an integral part of the way in which public bodies carry out their functions. So far, the only example of this is the Race Relations (Amendment) Act 2000 (see below). In a broader context Fredman argues for the adoption of positive duties to promote equality which would fall on the body best placed to achieve this (see especially Chapter 6 of her book for an extended discussion of this).

Turning to the present law, it will be seen from the diagram below that discrimination law operates at present in three areas but that we are on the threshold of major developments.

**Present law**

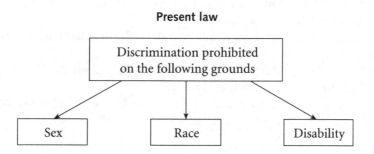

In addition, Regulations have been introduced prohibiting discrimination against both part-time workers and fixed-term employees. These are discussed in Chapter 4, as they concern the status of particular types of people at work.

**Proposed additions to the law**

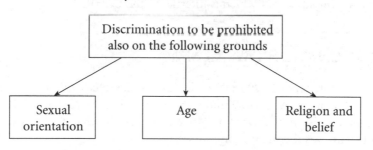

The present laws on discrimination borrow a great deal from US legislation, especially the Civil Rights Act 1964 and subsequent decisions of the US courts, in particular that of the Supreme Court in *Griggs v Dukes Power Co.* (1971), which paved the way for the concept of indirect discrimination which has done so much to extend the boundaries of the law. At the same time as the first legislation outlawing discrimination was being passed, the UK joined the EC and it is EC legislation which has been the driving force behind the later development of sex discrimination law, following the Directive on Equal Treatment (76/207). EC law is now about to have an impact across the whole spectrum of discrimination law following the introduction of Article 13 into the EC Treaties by the Treaty of

Amsterdam in 1997. This provides that the EC may take action against discrimination 'based on sex, racial or ethnic origin, religion or belief, disability age or sexual orientation'. This was followed by a Directive (2000/43) dealing specifically with race equality and a general Framework Directive (2000/78) prohibiting discrimination on the grounds of religion or belief, disability, age or sexual orientation. This must be implemented by 2 December 2003 but there is an extension to December 2006 in respect of age and disability. As a result the following draft Regulations have been introduced, the first two of which deal with entirely new areas and the second two make changes to existing law.

1. The Employment Equality (Sexual Orientation) Regulations, due to come into force on 1 December 2003.
2. The Employment Equality (Religion and Belief) Regulations, due to come into force on 2 December 2003.
3. The Race Relations Act 1976 (Amendment) Regulations 2003, due to come into force in 2003 but with no date as yet.
4. The Disability Discrimination Act 1995 (Amendment) Regulations 2003, also due to come into force on a date to be fixed in 2003.

Regulations dealing with age discrimination are to follow later.

The effect of these changes is not only to add two new areas of discrimination law but to alter the definition of indirect discrimination to bring it into line with the recently changed definition now applicable to sex discrimination and to alter the definition of harassment. Both of these topics are considered below.

In addition the effect of Article 14 of the ECHR must be borne in mind because, as explained in Chapter 3, it contains a very wide-ranging prohibition against discrimination but which is internal to the ECHR.

## DISCRIMINATION LAW CLAIMS

In 2000/01 there were 17,200 claims under the Sex Discrimination Act; 6,586 under the Equal Pay Act; 3,429 under the Race Relations Act; and 2,100 under the Disability Discrimination Act. These statistics all relate to cases where the relevant claim was the main claim.

## SOURCES OF DISCRIMINATION LAW

As discrimination law is derived from a variety of legislative sources, the following list of the main sources may be helpful.

### UK law

- Sex Discrimination Acts (SDA) 1975 and 1986.
- Equal Pay Act (EqPA) 1970.

- Race Relations Act (RRA) 1976.
- Race Relations Amendment Act (RRAA) 2000.
- Disability Discrimination Act (DDA) 1995.
- Disability Rights Commission Act (DRCA) 1999.

*Note*: these Acts will be referred to by the above abbreviations in this chapter.

The SDA and the EqPA form a single code dealing with discrimination on the grounds of sex but, in view of the similarities between the SDA and RRA, these two Acts will be considered together.

## EC legislation

EC Treaty (Rome) 1957, as amended by the Treaty of Amsterdam (1997).

## Articles of the Treaties

- Article 13: discrimination.
- Article 141 (formerly 119 until renumbered by the Treaty of Amsterdam): equal pay.

*Note*: for the sake of clarity, all references in this chapter will be to Article 141 even where the case was decided under what was Article 119.

## Directives

- 75/117 (equal pay).
- 76/207 (equal treatment).
- 92/85 (pregnancy).
- 97/80 (burden of proof in sex discrimination cases).
- 2000/43 (race discrimination).
- 2000/78 (Framework Directive).

## European Convention on Human Rights

- Article 14.

## Other sources

In addition, the International Labour Organisation (ILO) introduced three Conventions dealing with discrimination (in 1958, 1965 and 1980) but they have no binding force. Even so, it was the ILO Convention No. 100 of 1951 which was influential in the framing of the EqPA 1970. Article 2 of this provides for the principle of equal remuneration between men and women for work of equal value and when the EqPA was passed the UK government felt able to ratify Convention No. 100, although it is interesting to note that the ECJ subsequently held that the Act should specifically include equal value as a head of comparison (see below).

We begin our account of the detailed law on discrimination by looking at sex discrimination, but first two preliminary points need to be made:

1. The essential scheme of the SDA is the same as the RRA and therefore examples from the RRA will be used where appropriate in discussing the SDA.
2. The SDA, uniquely, refers to women rather than men and this will be reflected in the discusssion below.

## SEX DISCRIMINATION

First, two preliminary issues:

### ▦ To whom does the SDA apply?

Section 82(1) provides that it applies to employment under either a contract of service or apprenticeship or a contract personally to execute any work or labour. Accordingly, the wider definition of employee applies and the SDA is not confined to those with an actual contract of employment.

### ▦ When does it apply?

Section 6(1) of the SDA makes it unlawful to discriminate in the following ways:

1. In arrangements for deciding who should be offered employment (this covers all selection procedures including the interview).
2. In the terms on which employment is offered.
3. By refusing or deliberately omitting to offer employment.

In *Saunders v Richmond on Thames LBC* (1978) it was held that it is not necessarily discriminatory at an interview to ask a woman candidate different questions from those addressed to a man, provided that there is no discrimination in the interview process. Nevertheless, the effect of discrimination law is that it has become the practice to ask the same questions of each candidate and this is certainly the best practice.

Once the person is an employee then s.6(2) prohibits discrimination:

1. In the way in which she is afforded access to opportunities for promotion, transfer or training or to any other benefits, facilities or services or by refusing or deliberately omitting to afford her access to them.
2. By dismissing her or subjecting her to any other detriment.

The scheme of the SDA is to prohibit the following types of discrimination:

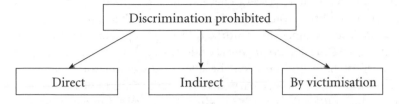

Discrimination on the grounds of marital status is also prohibited.

## ■ Direct discrimination

This is defined by s.1(2)(a) of the SDA as less favourable treatment of a women on the grounds of her sex.

The test is objective and intention to discriminate or motive is irrelevant. Thus in *James v Eastleigh BC* (1990) the council applied different ages to men and women for qualification to use the swimming pool free: 60 for women and 65 for men. This was held to be discriminatory, even though there had been no intention. Nor can discrimination be justified by the payment of some other benefit. In *Ministry of Defence v Jeremiah* (1979) only men were required to do a particularly dirty job and this was held to be discriminatory, even though they were paid extra for the work. This decision has probably laid to rest the much criticised decision in *Peake v Automotive Products Ltd* (1978), where a practice of allowing women to leave work five minutes earlier than men was held not be discriminatory, according to Denning MR, on the ground of chivalry. This was criticised as 'one redolent of all the values that the SDA had sought to lay to rest' (P. Wallington (1978) CLJ 39). In *Jeremiah* Denning MR attempted to justify it on the alternative ground of *de minimis non curat lex* (the law takes no account of trifles), i.e. that five minutes is too small a time to worry about; but the case still remains a blot on the law.

Direct discrimination can also occur when women are treated less favourably because of generalised assumptions based on sexual stereotypes. In *Horsey v Dyfed CC* (1982) a woman was refused permission to go on a training course in Kent as her husband was employed in London and it was thought that she was unlikely to return. This view, based on the idea that women follow their husbands, was clearly discriminatory.

A problem has arisen with dress codes and uniform at work. In *Schmidt v Austicks Bookshops* (1978) it was held that it was not discriminatory for women to be forbidden to wear trousers when there was a dress code for men also, albeit a different one. In *Smith v Safeway Stores plc* (1996) the Court of Appeal held that a prohibition on male employees wearing long hair whilst female employees were permitted to do so was not discriminatory as there were other rules applying to women too in that they had to have their hair tied back. (In the EAT it was held that this rule *was* discriminatory as it affected the employee's appearance outside work as well.) Phillips LJ held that a dress code which made *identical*

147

provision for men and women would have an unfavourable impact, as where men as well as women were required to have 18 inch long hair, lipstick and earrings. Whilst this is doubtless true, it has also been argued that a dress code of the kind in *Schmidt* forces women to conform to an 'appropriate image of femininity' (A. McColgan, *Discrimination Law* (London: Hart Publishing, 2000) p.397).

There must be a link between the alleged discriminatory act and the fact that the complainant was of a particular sex. This seems to be the explanation of *Bullock v Alice Ottley School* (1993), where there were different retirement ages for teachers and domestic staff (60) and maintenance staff (65). In practice the first group was largely female and the second entirely male. A claim under the SDA by an employee from the first group (who had to retire at 60) was rejected on the grounds that the different retirement ages were not discriminatory because there was nothing to stop men from applying for a job in the first group and women in the second. The groups had nothing to do with sex. Although this decision may be correct in theory, it does seem strange as applied in practice.

## ▓ Indirect discrimination

The definition of indirect discrimination in s.1(1)(b) of the SDA has recently changed with the coming into force of the Sex Discrimination (Indirect Discrimination and Burden of Proof) Regulations 2001. The definition is now as follows:

**Where a man applies to a woman a provision, criterion or practice**

$\downarrow$

**which would apply equally to a man**

$\downarrow$

**but which is such that it would be to the detriment of a considerably larger proportion of women than men**

$\downarrow$

**and which is not justifiable irrespective of sex**

$\downarrow$

**and which is to her detriment because she cannot comply with it.**

Each part of this definition will now be examined.

### A provision, criterion or practice

This has changed from the previous wording of a 'condition or requirement' as it was felt that the previous wording was too narrow. For example, in *Perera v Civil Service Commission (No. 2)* (1983) identical wording in the Race Relations

Act was held to mean that there must be an absolute requirement. The applicant, a Sri Lankan, had been refused promotion to a post for which he was qualified because criteria such as command of the English language had been taken into account. It was held that as these were only criteria, their application was not in breach of the RRA. The new definition, which mirrors US law, would mean that the court in a case such as *Perera* would take the criteria into account.

### Would be to the detriment of a considerably larger proportion of women than men

This is the heart of the idea of indirect discrimination and is often known as 'adverse impact'. It has been used to attack rules that disadvantage particular groups of workers. In *Price v Civil Service Commission* (1978) a rule of the civil service that applicants for executive officer grade posts had to be between the ages of 27 and 35 was held to be indirect discrimination against women, as fewer women then men could comply with it because a larger number women of that age group were having, or bringing up, children. In deciding whether a considerably larger proportion of women than men can comply, the correct pool for comparison is often a crucial factor. This is demonstrated by *Jones v Manchester University* (1993), where an advertisement for a post of careers advisor stated that applicants, amongst other criteria, should preferably be between 27 and 35. The applicant, a mature graduate, was not considered, apparently because she was 46. The tribunal held that there was indirect discrimination as the pool was all mature students graduating after 25. Of this group the proportion of women under 35 was considerably smaller than the proportion of men. The Court of Appeal held that this was the wrong pool. The correct one should be all men and women suitably qualified and here there was no great difference between the number of women capable of satisfying the criteria. This was because the post was open to *all* graduates and not just mature ones. The effect of the decision is that applicants need to be careful in choosing the pool and must not narrow it artificially to suit their case (see diagram below).

**The pool for comparison**
**(based on *Jones v Manchester University*)**

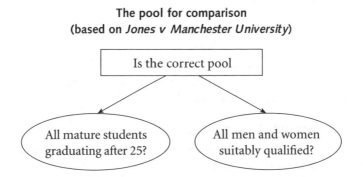

In addition, the question has arisen of what 'considerably smaller' means. Is it something that can be measured with mathematical precision? In *London Underground Ltd v Edwards (No. 2)* (1998) the Court of Appeal held that there was no set number below which the number would not be considerably smaller. Here a complaint that a considerably smaller proportion of women than men could comply with new shift patterns was found to be justified, because out of 2,000 men train drivers all could comply but one woman out of a total of only 21 could not comply. In the USA there has been some attempt by the courts to apply a rule that the success rate of those in the disadvantaged groups should not be more then 80% of those in other groups but there are strong arguments in favour of a broader approach. The concept of indirect discrimination has been applied in a variety of situations. In *Meade-Hill v British Council* (1995) it was held that a job mobility clause in a contract was discriminatory, as a higher proportion of women than men are secondary earners and thus a considerably greater proportion of women than men would find it difficult to move house. A setback was the decision in *Kidd v DRG (UK) Ltd* (1985), where a claim that women found it considerably more difficult than men to work full-time because of domestic responsibilities was rejected and thus a challenge to a redundancy selection procedure which targeted part-time workers first failed. The Part-Time Workers Regulations 2000 will not help here, as they do not give a right to insist on a return to work part-time. The practice of the courts and tribunals in this area has not been entirely consistent. In *Home Office v Holmes* (1984) it was held that a refusal to allow a woman to return to work part-time after maternity leave was indirect discrimination, as she was a single parent and the EAT agreed with the finding of the tribunal that 'despite the changes in the role of women in modern society it is still a fact that the raising of children tends to place a greater burden on them than it does on men'. This decision did not, however, establish as a general principle that it is indirect discrimination to refuse to allow a woman to return to work part-time after maternity leave. Thus in *Greater Glasgow Health Board v Carey* (1987) it was held on the facts that a refusal to allow a employee to return to work after being on maternity leave was justifiable on the grounds of efficiency. The most which can be said is that where an employer is faced with a request to return to work part-time after maternity leave then reasons for any refusal need to be carefully considered. A blanket refusal on the grounds of company policy would be open to successful attack. However, the new rules on flexible working contained in the Employment Act 2002 will make a significant change here as they give an employee a right to ask their employer to consider a flexible working arrangement in circumstances which will include a return to work following pregnancy and this can include a change in working hours (see Chapter 10 for a fuller discussion of this).

### Which is not justifiable irrespective of sex

The defence of justification is now governed by the proportionality test developed by the ECJ in cases such as *Bilka-Kaufhaus v Weber von Hartz* (1986). This states that the practice must be capable of justification by reference to a legitimate objective and that the means chosen must be appropriate and necessary to that end. Two cases on the identical provision in the RRA serve as good examples. In *Panesar v Nestle Co. Ltd* (1980) it was held by the Court of Appeal that a rule which stated that no beards could be worn, thus excluding Sikhs from employment, was justifiable on hygiene grounds. In *Board of Governors of St Matthias CE School v Crizzle* (1993) the restriction of a post of headteacher to communicant Christians was justifiable in fostering the ethos of the school, even though a considerably smaller number of Asians were excluded by it.

### Which is to her detriment because she cannot comply

This means that there must be some disadvantage to the complainant. Thus it is not a narrow term requiring, for example, financial loss. It is best examined in the context of sexual harassment (see below). In *Gill v El Vino Co. Ltd* (1983) the practice of serving women customers at a wine bar sitting at tables whilst men were served standing was held to be discriminatory and the mere fact that customers were treated differently on grounds of sex was accepted as sufficient detriment.

*Note*: First a significant difference between direct and indirect discrimination is that compensation for unintentional indirect sex discrimination is not automatically awarded. This is discussed in the section on remedies. Secondly, the above definition of indirect discrimination is to be used, with minor variations, in cases of discrimination on the grounds of race, sexual orientation and religion and belief. There is no concept of indirect discrimination in disability discrimination.

## DISCRIMINATION BY VICTIMISATION

This is defined by s.4 of the SDA as where a person is treated less favourably because she has brought proceedings under the SDA or the EqPA. Giving evidence is also covered. In the RRA case (under identical provisions) of *Aziz v Trinity Street Taxis* (1989) it was emphasised that the victimisation provisions apply only where the acts of victimisation were connected with actions under the relevant discrimination legislation. A taxi driver thought that he was being treated badly by a taxi drivers' association of which he was a member and that their actions amounted to race discrimination. To assist in his claim for race discrimination he tape-recorded conversations with others whom he thought agreed with his views. He was then expelled from the association for doing so but it was held that the reason for the expulsion was not because of race discrimination but because of the tape recordings.

## DISCRIMINATION ON GROUNDS OF MARITAL STATUS

This is defined as discrimination by s.1(2) but cases on it have been rare. One recent example is *Chief Constable of Bedfordshire v Graham* (2002), where a woman police officer was refused promotion to inspector as her husband was the divisional commander. The reason was that in any criminal proceedings against him she would not be a compellable witness for the prosecution. It was held that this was not sufficient to justify refusing her the post. An earlier example is *Skyrail Oceanic v Coleman* (1981), where a woman was dismissed from her job on her marriage.

## OTHER AREAS

### ■ Sexual harassment

This is an aspect of direct discrimination and was first clearly developed by the Court of Session in *Porcelli v Strathclyde Regional Council* (1986). The test is whether the harassment is on the grounds of sex. If it is not then there may still be an action at common law for a breach of an implied term of the contract (see Chapter 4) or for the tort of negligence (see Chapter 8). In addition, an employee could leave and claim constructive dismissal although in that case the amount of compensation is subject to a statutory ceiling, whereas it is not in the case of contract or tort. In *Porcelli* the applicant was employed as a laboratory technician and was subjected to degrading treatment by two male technicians in an eventually successful attempt to force her to leave. Suggestive remarks were repeatedly made to her, the men deliberately brushed against her, her personal belongings were interfered with, information was withheld from her and equipment was put in a place where she could not reach it. It was held that this would not have happened if she had been a man and her claim succeeded. The fact that she had to transfer to another school was sufficient detriment.

The Equal Treatment Directive was amended in 2000 so that it now contains a definition of sexual harassment which provides that it is unwanted conduct related to sex which affects the dignity of men and women at work and creates an 'intimidating, hostile, offensive or disturbing environment'. The Race Discrimination Directive uses slightly different language and states that it is conduct which violates the dignity of a person and which creates 'an intimidating, hostile, degrading, humiliating or offensive environment' and this has been adopted by the new Regulations, which will come into force in 2003, as the model for the definition of harassment in cases of discrimination on the grounds of disability, sexual orientation, and religion and belief. It will be seen that there are slight and puzzling differences between the definitions, in that the definition as applied to harassment on grounds of sex simply requires the conduct to *affect* dignity whereas the definition for the other areas requires the conduct to *violate* dignity, which seems to make harassment more difficult to prove. On the other hand, the list of what can constitute a harassing environment is longer in the general definition rather than the definition applicable to sexual harassment. Why not have the same definition?

In *Reed and Bull Information Systems Ltd v Stedman* (1999) it was held that the question of whether the complainant suffered harassment is subjective but where a woman appears to be unduly sensitive then the question is whether she has made it clear that she takes exception to such conduct. Accordingly, what may be harassment to one person may not be so to another.

One issue that probably remains unresolved is whether it is necessary to find a male comparator. In *British Telecommunications plc v Williams* (1997) the EAT held that sexual harassment, if proved, would always amount to sex discrimination, as the conduct is itself gender specific. The Court of Appeal rejected this view in *Smith v Gardner Merchant Ltd* (1998), where it was held that there was still a need to show that the act was sex-based. This means that where an act is indeed offensive to a woman then it still will not be sexual harassment if a man would not have been harassed by it. The solution may lie in legislation and indeed a Private Members Bill on Dignity at Work was promoted in the 2001/02 session of Parliament which would make harassment and bullying at work unlawful. This is surely the solution because, although harassment on sexual, racial or disability grounds is repugnant, other forms of harassment are equally unpleasant. Such legislation would, however, need careful drafting. Currently, the Protection from Harassment Act 1997 makes harassment a criminal offence but the Act was passed to deal with stalking and does not refer to harassment on any of the grounds on which discrimination is prohibited.

## Sexual orientation

Discrimination on this ground will be prohibited from December 2003 and the draft Regulations are considered briefly below. For the moment it is not covered by the SDA. In *Grant v South-West Trains* (1998) it was held by the ECJ that there was no discrimination against a female employee who was refused travel concessions for her lesbian partner. As the condition applied to both men and women employees, it was not based on sex, as a male homosexual would also have been refused the concession. The question of sexual harassment has arisen in cases where male homosexuals or lesbians have been harassed on account of their orientation and here the issue has been one of comparison. For example, in *Pearce v Mayfield School* (2001), a claim of harassment by a lesbian teacher who had been forced to resign from her school because of abuse from pupils was held not to fall within the SDA as it could not have been shown that she was treated less favourably than a male homosexual who might have been taunted on account of his sexuality. However, Hale LJ suggested that Article 8 of the ECHR (right to respect for private and family life) could be linked with the general prohibition on discrimination in Article 14, with the result that, in cases involving public bodies, it could be said that there was already a prohibition on discrimination on grounds of sexual orientation. The link with the ECHR was stressed in *Smith and Grady v UK* (1999), where it was held by the ECtHR that a policy of discharging members of the armed forces from service on the grounds of sexual orientation contravened Article 8 of the ECHR, in that it infringed their right to respect for their private life. This, together with the forthcoming implementation of the Framework Directive in respect of sexual orientation (above), marks the end of the exemption from discrimination law of discrimination on the grounds of sexual orientation.

The Employment Equality (Sexual Orientation) Regulations define discrimination in Regulation 2(1) on grounds of sexual orientation, as where a person is discriminated against on grounds of orientation to the same sex, the opposite sex, or both. The definition of indirect discrimination in Regulation 3(1) follows that in the legislation on sex discrimination by providing that it occurs where a provision, criterion or practice which would be applied to a person not of the same sexual orientation puts a person of that sexual orientation at a particular disadvantage and it is not a proportionate means of achieving a legitimate aim.

## Discrimination against transsexuals

In *P v S and Cornwall CC* (1996) it was held that dismissal of a transsexual who was about to undergo gender reassignment was in breach of the Equal Treatment Directive. The ECJ held that the Directive applied not only where there was discrimination on the basis of a person being of one or the other sex but also where the discrimination is based on the *particular* sex of a person. In doing so they seemed to get away from the need to make comparisons which had prevented the law from outlawing discrimination on the grounds of sexual orientation but this further step was not taken. However, the decision in *P v S* might only have protected those employed by the state or emanations of the state (see Chapter 2) (although in *Chessington World of Adventures Ltd v Reed* (1998) it was applied to private sector employees). The Sex Discrimination (Gender Reassignment) Regulations 1999 were passed in order to clarify the position and now direct discrimination against transsexuals is within the scope of the SDA (see also *Chief Constable of West Yorkshire v A* (below)).

## Positive discrimination

This is only allowed in limited circumstances under s.47 of the SDA, where access to facilities for training may be afforded to women only where, at any time in the previous 12 months, the number of women employed in that particular work in Great Britain was nil or comparatively small. In addition, it is lawful under s.47(3) to run courses specifically for those returning to employment after having spent time discharging domestic or family responsibilities. It may be that EC law in this area will move further as a result of the insertion in the EC Treaty of a new Article 141(4), which allows Member States to maintain or adopt measures providing for specific advantages to make it easier for underrepresented sexes to pursue careers. This is a radical departure from previous thinking and it has the potential to take discrimination law forward into a new era of actually *promoting* equality. In *Badeck* (2000) the ECJ ruled that measures intended to give preference to women in areas of the public services where they were underrepresented were not in breach of the Treaty, so long as they did not give automatic preference to women candidates. In *Abrahamsson* (2000), however, it was held that Swedish Regulations were contrary to the Treaty as they *required* university appointments to be from the underrepresented sex. In *Lommers v Minister van Landbouw* (2002) the Dutch Ministry of Agriculture had a policy of making subsidised nursery places available only to female employees except in emergencies and this was held not to breach EC law, provided that the policy was interpreted to make nursery places available on the same terms to men who are single parents. This decision of the ECJ is noteworthy in upholding a policy which would be certainly not be adopted in the UK and a future source of developments is undoubtedly positive discrimination.

## PROOF OF DISCRIMINATION

Assuming that discrimination has taken place the following issues arise:

### How is it proved?

The proof of discrimination can be difficult because, although it may not be too awkward to show less favourable treatment, this will have to be on the ground of sex.

*Example*

Jane is interviewed for a post as a teacher. At the interview she is told that 'we do not usually have women teachers here, you know' and she is not appointed, even though she is the only candidate who holds special qualifications in the main subject which is to be taught. She has been treated less favourably but how can she prove that this was on the ground of her sex? The school may say that, for instance, her performance at the interview did not show any real enthusiasm for the job.

The position is now made easier by the Sex Discrimination (Indirect Discrimination and the Burden of Proof) Regulations 2001, which provide that once the applicant has shown that there is a case to answer then the burden of proof shifts to the employer to prove that there is *no* discrimination. This to some extent builds on the approach of the Court of Appeal in *NW Thames RHA v Noone* (1988) that where the applicant shows less favourable treatment in circumstances which are consistent with discrimination then the tribunal may infer that there has been discrimination unless the employer shows that this was not so. These principles, described by May LJ in this case as 'mere common sense', were restated by Neill LJ in *King v The Great Britain China Centre* (1992) and it remains to be seen whether the new Regulations will make much difference to this approach. It is arguable that they will not: an applicant cannot simply stand up in a tribunal and say 'there has been discrimination'. Some evidence must be adduced and the question is whether the Regulations would make it any easier for the teacher in the above example. It should be noted that the same rules on the burden of proof are to be applied to other forms of discrimination by means of the draft Regulations mentioned earlier in this chapter.

## The need for a comparator

Unlike the EqPA, neither the SDA nor the RRA require that an actual comparator be established. This is because the Acts use the phrase 'treats or *would treat*' (my italics) (see s.1 of both the SDA and the RRA). Instead, there is simply the need to show that the treatment is less favourable than would be given to either an actual or a hypothetical comparator. Although this avoids the difficulties which have arisen with the EqPA, it has thrown up problems of its own. One is that dismissals for pregnancy were not in breach of the SDA as there could be no male comparator, although this problem has largely been solved (see Chapter 10). Another is in the area of discrimination on grounds of sexual orientation (above). It is noteworthy that in the DDA case of *Clark v Novacold* (1999) the Court of Appeal held that in disability cases the comparison should be with an able bodied person and that less favourable treatment is shown merely by the fact that the disability prevented the person from doing the work. This case rescued the law on the DDA from becoming enmeshed in possible comparisons between a disabled person and one who was sick but not disabled under the DDA. In *Balmoody v UK Central Council for Nursing, Midwifery and Health Visiting* (2002) the Court of Appeal held that the construction of a hypothetical comparator was a question of law to be determined by the tribunal in each case.

## Does the employer have a defence?

Section 7 of the SDA sets out the following genuine occupational qualifications (GOQ) which, if proved, will give a defence to an action under the SDA. These are exhaustive and are:

1. Where the essential nature of the job calls for a man for reasons of physiology, (excluding physical strength or stamina).
2. Where being a man is essential for reasons of authenticity in dramatic or other performances.
3. Where the job involves physical contact with men where they might reasonably object to it not being carried out by a woman.
4. Where the holder of the job is likely to work in circumstances where men are likely to object to the presence of a woman as they are in a state of undress or using sanitary facilities.
5. Where the employee is expected to live in a private home and objection might be taken to the employment of a man on the grounds of either the degree of actual contact with others in the home or the knowledge of intimate details of such a person's life which the job entails.
6. Where the employees live in premises provided by the employer and the premises are normally occupied by members of one sex and there are no

separate sleeping facilities for members of the opposite sex and it would not be reasonable to expect the employer to provide them.

7. Where the job is in a hospital, prison or other establishment for persons requiring special care and attention who are all of the same sex and it would not be reasonable to employ women.
8. Where the holder of the post provides personal welfare or education services to individuals which can be most effectively provided by a man.
9. Where the job is in a country where by law the duties could not be performed by a woman.
10. Where the job is one of two to be held by a married couple.

This list has, perhaps because of its detail, caused few difficulties of interpretation. One example is *Etam v Rowan* (1989), where the EAT agreed that a job in a woman's clothing shop could come within (3) above. However, the defence failed because of the provisions of s.7(4). These state that none of the GOQs apply where there are sufficient male employees who are capable of carrying out the duties and whom it would be reasonable to employ on them provided that the numbers are likely to meet the employer's future likely needs without undue inconvenience. In *Etam v Rowan* there were sufficient female employees to do the job. A more recent example is *Chief Constable of West Yorkshire v A* (2002), where the question was whether the need for police officers to carry out intimate body searches was a bar to the employment of a transsexual: it was held that it was not, as the number of such searches was in practice so low.

## ◼ Is the employer vicariously liable for acts of discrimination committed by employees?

Section 41(1) provides that an employer is liable for acts committed by employees in the course of employment. This is known as vicarious liability, as the employer has not committed discrimination himself but is liable for what others have done. Clearly where the employer issues discriminatory instructions or has discriminatory practices the employer is directly liable, but s.41(1) is important where there is an allegation of sexual harassment. Is the employer liable in such cases? Section 41(3) provides a defence where the employer can prove that all reasonably practicable steps were taken to prevent employees from discriminating. The problem in relation to sexual and racial harassment cases in particular has been that the worse the acts of harassment, the more difficult it may be to establish that they were committed in the course of employment. This was recognised in *Jones v Tower Boot Co. Ltd* (1997), where acts of racial harassment had consisted in violent acts, including branding the employee with a hot screwdriver, and there was also verbal abuse. On a traditional view, the employer would not have been liable for these as they fell right outside the course of employment. This would, however, mean that the employee would have no remedy. Thus the Court of Appeal held that the phrase 'course of employment' had to be given a 'purposive interpretation' in line with the spirit of the Act, which meant that the words should bear the same meaning as in everyday speech. Accordingly, the employers were liable. What is the position where the acts are committed by persons who are not employees ? In this case the only way in which the employer can be liable is if it can be found that he/she was in some way *directly* liable. This occurred in *Burton and Rhule v De Vere Hotels* (1997), where waitresses at a dinner were exposed by a speaker to racist jokes. Although the speaker was not employed by the management, so that s.41(1) was inapplicable, it was held that the manager should have ensured that the waitresses were taken from the room if there was a risk of subjection to harassment. In practice it will be very difficult to ensure that this is always done and one wonders if the effect of these two cases is to take us some way along the road to strict liability for employers in cases of harassment on sex, race or disability grounds.

## RACE DISCRIMINATION

This is governed by the RRA 1976 and in many ways the scheme is the same as for the SDA. Indeed, a number of examples in the preceding pages have been from race discrimination law.

### ■ Comparison between the Sex Discrimination Act and the Race Relations Act

*Similarities*

- Same types of discrimination prohibited: direct, indirect and by victimisation.
- Same types of employees covered and same areas.
- Same rules on harassment.
- Same rules on vicarious liability.
- Same remedies.
- Existence of a statutory body to oversee the operation of the Act: here the Commission for Racial Equality (CRE).

*Differences*

- No direct influence from EC law, although this is about to change.
- RRA deals with terms and conditions of employment including pay, unlike the SDA.
- Different definition of indirect discrimination, although this will change with the Race Relations Act 1976 (Amendment) Regulations 2003.
- Different rule on the burden of proof (this will also change with the Race Relations Act 1976 (Amendment) Regulations 2003).
- No compensation for unintentional indirect race discrimination.
- New provisions for 'mainstreaming' in race relations.

It will be noted that the law on race discrimination will soon be harmonised to a much greater extent than previously with sex discrimination law.

# Definition of race discrimination

Section 1(1) of the RRA provides that the Act applies to discrimination on racial grounds which are defined by s.3(1) as grounds relating to colour, race, nationality or ethnic or national origins. Racial group is defined as any group defined by reference to the above grounds.

Two questions arise:

## What is an ethnic group?

In many cases this will be obvious, but what of Sikhs? They are not the inhabitants of a particular country but there seems no doubt that any reasonable person would regard them as an ethnic group. In *Mandla v Dowell Lee* (1981) the House of Lords held that they were and Lord Fraser held that to constitute an ethnic group the group must regard itself and be regarded by others as having certain characteristics, including:

1. A long shared history.
2. Its own cultural tradition.

In addition, he regarded the following criteria as relevant, although clearly not essential:

1. A common geographical origin or descent from common ancestors.
2. A common language, literature and/or religion.
3. Community.

Jews have been held to constitute an ethnic group (*Seide v Gillette Industries Ltd* (1980)) and also gypsies (*Commission for Racial Equality v Dutton* (1989)). Somewhat controversially, it was held in *Dawkins v Environment Department* (1993) that Rastafarians are not an ethnic group because they have only been identifiable for about 60 years.

## What is the meaning of nationality and of national origins?

An instructive case is *National Joint Police Board v Power* (1997), where it was held that there was no discrimination on racial grounds when a complaint of discrimination was brought by Scots against English. England and Scotland were held to be part of one nation, Britain, but it was also held that there could be discrimination in this type of case on grounds of national origin, as England and Scotland were once distinct nations. In *Gwynedd CC v Jones* (1986) the EAT held that there could be no discrimination on the grounds of not being able to speak Welsh, as this in itself could not be a determining factor.

# The lack of a direct influence from EC law

This has not been so great a hindrance in the development of race relations law as it might have been, because many of the developments in sex discrimination have had, or will have, an impact on race relations law. A good example is the lifting of the ceiling on compensation for sex discrimination in 1993 as a result of a decision by the ECJ (*Marshall v Southampton and SW Hampshire AHA (No. 2)* (1993)) that the limit infringed the principle that there had to be adequate remedies for sex discrimination. Clearly, the limit for race discrimination had to be lifted at the same time and it was. However, the Framework Directive brought race relations within the scope of EC law and one consequence has been that the law on race relations has been, and will be, harmonised with that on sex discrimination to a much greater extent.

## The RRA deals with terms and conditions including pay

The difference is simply that under sex discrimination law there are two pieces of legislation, the SDA and the EqPA. In race relations law there is only the RRA.

## Different definition of indirect discrimination

The RRA retains, for the time being, the old formula which requires there to be a 'condition or requirement' which causes adverse impact whereas, as explained above, the SDA now uses the phrase 'provision, criterion or practice'. However, this will change with the Race Relations Act 1976 (Amendment) Regulations 2003 when the new definition which applies to sex discrimination will also apply here.

## No compensation for unintentional indirect discrimination

At present there is no compensation where indirect discrimination is unintentional and so the position is the same as applied to sex discrimination before 1996. However, the government has indicated that it intends to bring race relations law into line with sex discrimination law here also.

## New provisions on 'mainstreaming' race relations

If in other areas race relations law has seemed to lag behind sex discrimination law then this is one instance of where the converse is true. Following a review by the CRE in 1998 which recommended that there should be a positive duty on all public bodies to promote equal opportunity and good race relations, the MacPherson Report into the murder of Stephen Lawrence gave an added impetus to the perceived need to combat 'institutional racism'. This resulted in the Race Relations Amendment Act 2000, which makes it unlawful for a public body to discriminate in areas not covered by the 1976 Act. Therefore, activities such as law enforcement are now subject to the duty not to discriminate and all public bodies must work towards the elimination of discrimination. This involves, for example, monitoring the number of applicants for jobs against the number shortlisted and the number appointed.

## ■ The Commission for Racial Equality

The Commission for Racial Equality (CRE) has similar functions to the EOC, in that it works towards the promotion of equal opportunities and the elimination of discrimination between racial groups. Examples of its work, taken from recent reports, are the elimination of discrimination in education and training, the development of racial equality guidance in youth justice cases and looking at measures to combat the discrimination and poor access to services experienced by racial minorities in rural areas.

## REMEDIES FOR RACE AND SEX DISCRIMINATION

*Note*: the same basic scheme of remedies is to be used in cases of discrimination on grounds of sexual orientation and discrimination on grounds of religion and belief.

## ■ Individual actions

Complaints must be presented by employees or ex-employees within three months of the act complained of, but where the discrimination is continuing then time runs from when the act ends. The remedies as set out in s.65 are:

(a) Compensation. This has not been subject to a statutory ceiling since 1993, and in *Alexander v Home Office* (1988) May LJ set out the heads under which compensation can be awarded:
  (i) for the harm suffered by the complainant including financial loss and other matters including 'inconvenience or the disturbance of an even tenor of life';
  (ii) for injured feelings;
  (iii) exemplary compensation based on punishment of the respondent for anti-social behaviour.
  Head (iii) was overruled by the Court of Appeal in *Gibbons v SW Water Services Ltd* (1993), which held that awards to punish should not be made in cases of discrimination. There was until 1995 a bar on the award of damages in cases of unintentional indirect discrimination but the position is now that such damages can be awarded where it is just and equitable to do so (Sex Discrimination and Equal Pay (Miscellaneous Amendments) Regulations 1996). Despite there being no ceiling on compensation, the average awards are not high: in 2000/01 the average award under the SDA was £5,499, although under the RRA it was considerably higher at £15,484.
(b) An order declaring the rights of the parties.
(c) A recommendation that the respondent takes specified action aimed at reducing or obviating the adverse effect on the complainant of the discrimination complained of.

In practice, (b) and (c) are hardly ever awarded and in 1998 the Commission for Racial Equality proposed that, in relation to (c) and the RRA (which contains identical provisions) there should be a wider power to make recommendations regarding any of the employer's practices and procedures which have been at issue. The Equal Opportunities Commission (EOC) has proposed that tribunals should be given power to order re-employment.

## ■ Enforcement by the Equal Opportunities Commission

The Equal Opportunities Commission (EOC) has wide powers to, for example, conduct investigations, take action against discriminatory advertisements, and seek injunctions to restrain persistent cases of discrimination. It has also sought judicial review where it has believed that, for example, UK legislation was in breach of EC law. The most spectacularly successful example of this was the decision in *R v Employment Secretary, ex parte EOC* (1995) that the rule which at that time stated that part-time employees had to wait five years before bringing an unfair dismissal claim compared with two years for full-time employees was indirectly discriminatory as a far higher proportion of part-time employees were women. This led to the removal of the differential limits. The EOC also provides information and advice and works in general to promote equal opportunities. For example, in its 2000/01 report it mentions its work in trying to ensure that men and women have equal representation at all levels of government and it is also campaigning to eliminate the pay gap between men and women within ten years.

## DISABILITY DISCRIMINATION

This is the most recent area to see a prohibition against discrimination, the relevant legislation being contained in the Disability Discrimination Act 1995. The Act is of great importance, bearing in mind that, according to the Annual Review of the Disability Rights Commission for 2000–01, one in seven people in Britain (8.3 million) suffer from a disability. Although the latest statistics show that there are fewer claims under the DDA than under other discrimination legislation (3,129 in 2000/01 as compared to 17,200 under the SDA), the importance of the Act can be gauged by the number of significant decisions on it which reach the courts. An interim report by Income Data Services on the Act (2000) showed that over 68% of cases concerned dismissal and only 9% recruitment. The Act should be read with the Disability Discrimination Regulations 1996 and the Code of Practice and accompanying Guidance (1996). One feature which does not appear in other discrimination legislation is the exemption for firms employing fewer than 15 employees, although there is power for the Minister to reduce this to two. The effect of this exemption is that 25% of employees are denied protection under the Act and it is estimated that this includes a third of a million disabled employees.

Section 1(1) defines a disabled person as follows:

**Someone who has a physical or mental impairment**

↓

**which has a substantial and adverse long-term effect**

↓

**on their ability to carry out normal day-to-day activities.**

Each of these will now be examined in turn, but it should first be pointed out that this definition has been criticised for using what is known as a 'medical' definition of disability, by concentrating on the nature of the impairment, and not a 'social' one, which would focus on the barriers in society to the inclusion of disabled people.

## Physical or mental impairment

These are not defined, but mental illness only counts if it is 'clinically well recognised'. In *Kapadia v Lambeth London Borough Council* (2000) it was held that depression could count as a disability provided that the other conditions under s.1 are met. Certain conditions are not impairments under the Act, such as dependency on alcohol, paedophilia, kleptomania and, perhaps more surprisingly, hayfever. Liver disease resulting from alcohol abuse would count as an impairment given that, provided that the condition comes within the definition of an impairment, it is irrelevant how it was caused.

In *Morgan v Staffordshire University* (2002) it was held that there are four routes to establish mental impairment:

1. Proof of an impairment recognised in the World Health Organization (WHO) classification.
2. Proof of an impairment mentioned in a recognised medical publication.
3. Acceptance by a recognised body of medical opinion.
4. (Rarely) a state recognised as a medical impairment but which does not result from a known medical illness.

It was held in this case that the terms 'anxiety', 'stress' and 'depression' in medical notes are not enough to amount to medical impairment.

The fact that the Act focuses on the impairment itself led the courts to try to distinguish the *cause* of the impairment from its *effect*. In *Rugamer v Sony Music Entertainment* (2001) it was held that the nature of the illness needs to be considered first. A different approach was taken in *College of Ripon and York St John v Hobbs* (2002), where a lecturer had muscle cramps resulting from a loss of mobility. Although there was no evidence of any organic disease, it was held by the EAT that the condition could still be physical, as its effects were physical.

163

This area will no doubt soon be considered by the Court of Appeal. Clearly, the decision in *Hobbs* will be beneficial where there is undoubtedly some external manifestation of illness but no obvious cause.

## ■ Substantial and adverse long-term effect

The Code of Practice states that 'substantial' means more than trivial and the Guidance issued with the Act suggests that, in deciding if it is substantial, account can be taken of, for example, difficulty in going down stairs and 'inability to carry a moderately loaded tray steadily'. However, 'mere clumsiness' is not enough. In *Goodwin v Patent Office* (1999) an employee suffered from paranoid schizophrenia and as a result his behaviour at work was bizarre but a tribunal had decided that there was no substantial effect on his ability to carry out day-to-day activities, as he could look after himself at home. The EAT held that the tribunal should have considered his behaviour at work, which would have inevitably led to the conclusion that he was disabled. In *Leonard v South Derbyshire Chamber of Commerce* (2001) the EAT held that a tribunal should not balance out what a person can and cannot do when deciding whether the effect of the impairment is substantial. The approach should be to see what the applicant can and cannot do *only with difficulty*. In *Cruikshank v VAW Motorcast* (2002) the applicant had occupational asthma, which was made worse by fumes at work. The EAT held that it was possible to take into account such aggravating factors at work in deciding whether the condition had a substantial and adverse effect. The question was whether the impairment had a substantial and long-term adverse effect on the employee's ability to perform day-to-day tasks both outside work and at work. Accordingly, the EAT rejected the notion that a person is not disabled where he/she can carry out all tasks except very special ones associated with particular employment. The effect, as pointed out by M. Rubenstein ((2002) 29 IRLR 2) is that an employee may be disabled for some jobs but not for others, which is not what the DDA intended.

Long-term effect is defined in Schedule 1 as where the impairment is capable of lasting one year or more or for the rest of a person's life in the case of a terminal illness. Where it ceases but is likely to re-occur then it will be treated as having a long-term effect. An employee who has a progressive condition will be treated as disabled under the Act at the point when the condition has *an* effect on their ability to carry out normal day-to-day activities although at this point it is not substantial. This is to prevent an employer from launching a preemptive strike and dismissing them before the person gains the protection of the Act. In *Mowat-Brown v University of Surrey* (2002) it was held that a person will come within the protection of the Act when the condition is expected to be substantial although is not yet so. In *Greenwood v VAW Motorcast* (2002) the EAT held that a decision on whether an impairment would last for a year should be taken at the time of the action being brought.

## Ability to carry out normal day-to-day activities

There is an 'exhaustive list' of what constitute day-to-day activities in Schedule 1 to the Act. They are defined as activities involving mobility; manual dexterity; physical co-ordination; continence; ability to lift; carry or move everyday objects; speech; hearing and eyesight; memory or ability to learn; concentrate or understand; perception of the risk of physical danger. This must be considered without taking account of any measures to treat or correct the impairment. So a person who has a hearing aid is treated as having a disability even though they may be able to hear very well with it. This is undoubtedly right, as who is to know when the aid might suddenly malfunction?

Under the Disability Discrimination Act 1995 (Amendment) Regulations 2003, a new s.3A is inserted explicitly providing that a difference in treatment cannot be justified if it is not based on a consideration of a person's abilities and is purely because that person is disabled.

A final point on the definition is that, by s.2, it covers those who have had a disability but who have made a full recovery. This is to guard against the person being discriminated against when, for example, applying for a job, as the disability may be revealed on a CV.

## When does the Act apply in employment?

The Act applies to the same types of employees and to the same types of employment as does the SDA. One provision in the DDA (s.11) is unique to discrimination law in that where a job advertisement indicates, or might reasonably be taken to indicate, that the employer might discriminate against a disabled applicant then there is a presumption of discrimination. However, this is not as wide as it sounds, because it only applies where the disabled person has applied for and not been offered the job. Furthermore, the presumption can be rebutted by the employer showing that the reason for the disabled person not being offered the job did not relate to his/her disability.

## Definition of disability discrimination

This is set out in s.5, where it is provided that an employer discriminates against a disabled person where he treats him less favourably than others to whom the definition of disability does not apply. This raises a difficulty: who is the comparator? In *Cosgrove v Caesar and Howie* (2001) the EAT compared the treatment of the applicant, who had been dismissed when absent for over a year through illness, with that of *any* employee who had been absent from work for over a year. This does not seem to be in line with the better decision in *Clark v Novocold Ltd* (1999), where the Court of Appeal held that a comparison should be made with an able bodied person who can do the job. The issue then becomes whether the disabled person had been subjected to a detriment by reason of their disability.

A much canvassed question has been whether the employer needs to have knowledge of the disability to be liable. In *O'Neill v Symm* (1998) it was held that knowledge was required, but the contrary has been held in a number of other cases, including *Clark v Novocold* (above) and *Callaghan v Glasgow City Council* (2002). The disadvantage of requiring knowledge is that, as the Court of Appeal put it in *Clark*, the issue will turn on whether 'ignorant or obtuse employers' have recognised a disability when the issue is whether there is, on an objective basis, a connection between the disability and the less favourable treatment.

The Disability Discrimination Act 1995 (Amendment) Regulations 2003 introduce, by a new s.3B, the definition of harassment which is to be used across discrimination law: that it consists of a violation of a person's dignity and of creating an intimidating, hostile, humiliating or offensive environment.

There are two significant differences from the concepts of discrimination in the SDA and the RRA on the one hand and in the DDA on the other:

1. There is no indirect discrimination as such in the DDA. However, in *Clark v Novocold* the court recognised that the definition of discrimination included indirect as well as direct discrimination and this view is supported by statements made by the Minister in the passage of the Bill.
2. The defence of justification applies to direct discrimination, whilst in the SDA and the RRA it applies only to indirect discrimination. The reason for this is that a person may, through a disability, be unable to do a job, but the danger is that the defence could be applied so as to deprive the DDA of all its force. Section 5(3) provides that a difference in treatment is justified if the reason for it 'is material to the particular case and substantial'. The Code of Practice amplifies this somewhat by providing that the reason must relate to the individual circumstances in question and must not be trivial or minor. In *Baynton v Saurus General Engineers Ltd* (1999) the EAT approved of the idea of applying a balancing exercise between the interests of the disabled employee and those of the employer. Lindsay J in *Clark v Novocold*, in the EAT, whilst not precluding this, felt that the limited requirements of s.5(3) should be borne in mind. He pointed to the words of the section and observed that all that is material is that the reason has to relate to the individual concerned and must not be trivial or minor. The Income Data Services Report (above) showed that the two most common reasons claimed by employers as justification were the employee's health and the amount of sick leave taken.

## ▓ Reasonable adjustment

Once an employee has shown that he/she is a disabled person then s.6 provides that the employer comes under a duty to make reasonable adjustments. Section 6 states that where any arrangements made by the employer or physical features of the premises place the employee at a substantial disadvantage compared to those not disabled then the employer has a duty to make reasonable adjustments. Section 6(3) gives a number of examples of possible adjustments which an employer might make: allocating duties to another employee; transferring the employee to another vacancy; altering working hours; arranging training; modifying instructions or reference manuals; providing supervision; assigning him/her to another place of work; acquiring or modifying equipment, etc. In *Kenny v Hampshire Constabulary* (1999) it was held that the provision of supervision does not extend to providing a personal carer to assist with the personal requirements of the disabled person at work.

Section 6(4) then lists the following factors which shall be considered in deciding if it would be reasonable to take these steps:

(a) the extent to which taking it would prevent the effect (i.e. how much would it actually help?);
(b) the extent to which the steps are practicable;
(c) the cost involved and the extent to which taking these steps would disrupt other activities;
(d) the employer's financial and other resources;
(e) the availability of financial and other assistance to the employer in taking these steps.

Section 6(6) provides that an employer does not have to take these steps if he/she does not know that the employee (or potential employee in the case of, for example, an interview) has a disability.

The Income Data Services Report (above) showed that the most common claim for a reasonable adjustment related to a request to be considered for an existing vacancy.

## Proving discrimination

This will be made easier when the Disability Discrimination Act 1995 (Amendment) Regulations are in force in 2003 as the burden of proof will be reversed. The effect will be that once the employee proves facts from which a tribunal could conclude that discrimination has occurred for which the employer is responsible then it will uphold the complaint unless the employer proves either that he did not commit the act or is otherwise not responsible for it.

## Remedies under the DDA

These together, with the procedures, are the same as under the SDA and the RRA. The average award of compensation in 2000/01 was £12,678 and the highest award was for £71,063.

The Disability Rights Commission (DRC) was set up by the Disability Rights Act 1999 with similar powers and duties to the EOC and the CRE. It is also responsible for other legislation, such as the Special Educational Needs and Disability Act 2001. Among its activities are a helpline, a disability casework service, the giving of policy advice to the government and the support of cases in tribunals. An interesting example of its work is given in its *2001 Review*.

A mobility impaired lady in her eighties was accused of damaging the block of flats where she lived with her motorised wheelchair. She was sent a £60 bill for the damage and she feared that she would have to move out. The intervention of the DRC resulted in an admission that her wheelchair had not caused the damage and she received an apology and £600.

## DISCRIMINATION ON GROUNDS OF RELIGION AND BELIEF

The new Employment Equality (Religion and Belief) Regulations 2003 cover discrimination on the grounds of religion, religious belief and similar philosophical belief (Reg.2(1)). Thus, only belief based on religious grounds or those which are similar, such as humanism, is covered. The Regulations follow the same scheme as the other new Regulations in that they provide for the same extended definition of indirect discrimination and the new definition of harassment. The burden of proof is also reversed, as explained in relation to disability discrimination.

## EQUAL PAY

The legislation on this is contained in the Equal Pay Act 1970 which has, however, been heavily influenced by what is now Article 141 of the European Treaties. As mentioned above, it forms the counterpart of the SDA in discrimination on grounds of sex in dealing with discrimination in terms and conditions of employment. The Act has certainly had an effect in improving the pay of women as compared with men but there is strong evidence that, having had a marked initial effect, it now simply prevents the pay of women from falling further behind that of men. Between 1970 and 1977 women's pay as a proportion of men's had risen from 63% to 75.5% but it is now 81% for women full-time workers. The reason why it is not more is that women tend to work in part-time jobs and in areas which are not as well paid as men. Further advance in the pay of women as compared to men may have to wait for changes in society which are beyond the scope of the law to achieve.

The Equal Pay Act in effect operates alongside Article 141 of the Treaty, which provides for equal pay for equal work. As explained in Chapter 3, where there is a conflict between them then Article 141 prevails. The best example of this is *Macarthays v Smith* (1980) where, as already explained, it was held that Article 141 enabled a female employee to claim equal pay with a previous male employee although the EqPA did not provide for this.

### ▌ The scheme of the Act

Section 1(1) of the EqPA implies an equality clause into the contracts of employees (as with the SDA it refers to women but includes men) in the following cases:

| Like work | Work rated as equivalent | Work of equal value |

The effect is that where a woman is doing any of these types of work with a man in the same establishment or an associated establishment then her contract automatically contains an equality clause enabling her to claim equal pay with a man. Each of these will now be considered in turn.

## Like work

This is defined by s.1(4) as work which is broadly similar, and the differences between the work done by a woman and a man are not of practical importance in relation to terms and conditions of employment. The point is that, to be able to claim equal pay, a woman does not have to show that the work done by her and a man is identical. The courts quickly took this point. In *Capper Pass v Lawton* (1977) it was held that a woman chef who prepared lunches for the company directors and their guests was employed on like work to two male chefs who served in the factory canteen. In *Dugdale v Kraft Foods Ltd* (1976) it was held that the time at which the work is done does not by itself justify a difference in pay, although Phillips J pointed out in *National Coal Board v Sherwin* (1978) that this does not mean that both men and women cannot be paid extra for working at night and at weekends. The phrase 'not of practical importance in relation to terms and conditions of employment' was first considered by the Court of Appeal in *Shields v E Coomes Holdings Ltd* (1978), where a woman counterhand in a bookmakers was paid less than a male counterhand and although the work done by them was virtually the same, the man was there partly to deter troublemakers. However, it was found that he was not trained to do this job and nor had he ever done it. Thus the difference between the work of the woman and the man counterhand was not of practical importance in relation to terms and conditions of employment and a difference in pay was not justified. However, in *Thomas v NCB* (1987) women canteen assistants claimed equal pay with a man who was on permanent night duty and it was held that their claim failed as the added responsibility *was* of practical importance in relation to terms and conditions.

## Work rated as equivalent

This only applies if the work of a woman has been graded as equivalent under a job evaluation scheme. However, where a woman's work is not rated as equivalent then she may challenge the scheme on the ground that it does not fulfil the criteria set out in s.1(5). This provides that the jobs of men and women must have been given an equal value in terms of the demand made on a worker under various heads, such as effort, skill and decision. In *Bromley v H&J Quick Ltd* (1988) Dillon LJ held that any job evaluation scheme must be both non-discriminatory and analytical.

## Work of equal value

This head was introduced into the EqPA by the Equal Pay (Amendment) Regulations 1983 following the decision of the ECJ in *Commission of the EC v UK* (1982) that existing legislation on equal pay infringed the Equal Pay Directive (75/117) in not allowing an equal value claim. This has been the most fruitful area for equal pay claims, as it has enabled women to claim equal pay where there is no similarity on the surface between their job and that of the man.

The first major case was *Hayward v Cammell Laird Shipbuilders Ltd* (1988), where a woman successfully claimed equal pay where she was employed as a canteen cook and her work was held of equal value with that of male painters, thermal insulation engineers and joiners employed by the company. Once her claim succeeded, the court then had to decide whether she was entitled to the same basic rate of pay as her male comparator or a comparison of all the terms of her contract including matters such as meal breaks, sickness benefits and holidays. In fact, when all the terms of her contract were taken into account she was actually better off than her male comparators. However, the House of Lords held that she could simply point to a particular clause in her contract which was less favourable and claim that it should be made equally favourable under the equality clause. In *Pickstone v Freemans plc* (1988) a woman employed as a warehouse operative was not barred from claiming equal value with a man employed as a checker operative even though there was a man employed at the warehouse on the same work as her. The House of Lords held that the fact that other men were doing like work or work rated as equivalent did not bar an equal value claim.

In practice, equal value claims require a complicated procedure which, even after it was simplified by the Sex Discrimination and Equal Pay Regulations 1996, is still lengthy. One reason is that a report from an independent expert is often commissioned by the tribunal and the preparation of this report takes time. The Employment Act 2002 attempts to remedy this by providing in s.42 that the equal pay questionnaire which is used by the applicant to obtain information from the employer is to be shortened and the government estimates that this will result in 10% of applications being withdrawn before a hearing.

Assuming that the woman establishes that she is employed on any of the three types of work outlined above there are two further hurdles to surmount:

170

1. Is there a genuine material difference between the work of the woman and the man?

YES                NO

Claim fails       Claim moves on

2. Are the woman and the man in the same employment? I.e. are they employed at the same establishment or at an another establishment where common terms and conditions are observed?

## ▇ The genuine material difference defence

This is contained in s.1(3) and provides that the equality clause will not apply where a variation in the contracts of men and women is due to a material factor other than sex. Obvious examples are long service and better qualifications.

In *Strathclyde Regional Council v Wallace* (1998) the House of Lords held that where there is no evidence that the difference in pay is due to grounds of sex then there is no need for the employer to be called on to raise the 'genuine material difference' defence at all. Women in a group of 134 teachers, 81 of whom were men and 53 women, were all doing the work of principal teachers, although not promoted to that position. Nine women in the group claimed equal pay with a male promoted teacher but their claim failed on the ground that there was no evidence of sex discrimination at all. Lord Browne-Wilkinson pointed out that the object of the employees was to achieve equal pay for like work, regardless of sex. That, he pointed out, was not the object of the Act.

The following considerations have arisen in these cases:

1. Is 'red circling' justified? Red circling means that the pay of an employee who has been moved to a less well paid type of work is protected by wages still being paid at the higher rate for the work previously done. This could lead to a claim by women that a man was being paid more than them for work which was the same. In *Snoxell v Vauxhall Motors* (1977) the EAT held that where the red circling was due to a factor based on sex (as here, where the women had not been allowed to enter the grades where the men originally were) then there was a valid claim under the Act. However, in other cases red circling has been allowed only on the basis that it will be phased out in time (see *Outlook Supplies v Parry* (1978)).

2. What if the employer says that it was necessary to pay a man more, as this was the only way in which anyone could be induced the take the post? This is known as the 'market forces defence' and in *Clay Cross (Quarry Services) v Fletcher* (1978) it was rejected as a defence under s.1(3), Denning MR robustly remarking that 'the employer cannot evade his obligations under the Act by saying "I paid him more because he asked for more"'. The law was then muddled somewhat by statements by the House of Lords in *Rainey v Greater*

*Glasgow Health Board* (1987) that the remarks in *Fletcher* were 'unduly restrictive' (per Lord Keith) of the purpose of s.1(3), and so a female prosthetist failed in her claim for equal pay with a man who had been employed on a higher grade because it was necessary to pay recruits at a higher rate to match private sector salaries. In *Enderby v Frenchay Health Authority* (1994) the ECJ held that any difference in pay had to be objectively justified and so even if market forces applied in principle, not all of the difference in pay would necessarily be held to be justified on this ground. The effect is that *any* difference in pay must be shown to be attributable to market forces.

3. In *Jenkins v Kingsgate (Clothing Productions) Ltd (No 2)* (1981) the EAT held that the payment of differential wages to part-time workers could only be justified as a genuine material difference if it was intended to achieve an object unrelated to sex. In *Bilka-Kaufhaus v Weber* (1986) the ECJ reached a similar conclusion in holding that the exclusion of part-time workers from an occupational pension scheme, which here affected far more women than men, was only justifiable if it could be objectively justified on grounds unrelated to sex. Here the employer, a store, wished to discourage part-time work because part-timers did not want to work in the late afternoon and on Saturdays. These cases are to some extent academic in view of the Part-time Workers Regulations 2000, although the extent to which differential pay rates to part-timers is justified may be useful guides in the interpretation of the Regulations.

4. Can the fact that pay rates are set in separate bargaining processes justify a genuine material difference in pay? In *Enderby v Frenchay HA* (1994) a woman speech therapist claimed that her work was of equal value to that of male pharmacists and clinical psychologists, but their pay had been set in different negotiations. The ECJ held it was not in itself a justification that pay rates were arrived at in separate negotiations and it is in the actual pay where any justification for a difference must be sought.

Once the claim to equal pay has been made out and it has been established that the defence under s.1(3) is inapplicable, then we move on to the final stage of showing that there is a comparator. Under the EqPA an actual comparator must be found and it is provided by s.1(6) that the comparator must be in the same employment as the applicant or at another establishment at which common terms and conditions are observed either generally or for employees of the relevant classes. Thus it is of no avail for a woman to show that she is paid less than a man doing the same job but working for another employer.

Where the woman and the man are working at the same establishment then the matter is easy: there will be a right to equal pay. Where they are working at different establishments for the same employer then there is the requirement to show common terms and conditions at each establishment. In *Leverton v Clwyd CC* (1989) the House of Lords held that this means that common terms and conditions must be observed at each establishment and not that the terms and conditions of the comparators must be the same. In *British Coal Corporation v Smith* (1996) a claim succeeded where the terms and conditions of canteen workers and clerical officers were contained in agreements which each applied at the establishments where the men and women worked and the fact that there were variations at a local level was not a reason for holding that there were not common terms and conditions.

This area of the law seems likely to move forward as a result of recent decisions. The point is simple: can comparisons be made with other employees working for another employer? The first signs of movement were in *Lawrence v Regent Office Care* (1999), where Mummery J was prepared to go as far as saying that only 'in a loose and non-technical sense' must the employee and the comparator be in the same employment. In *South Ayrshire Council v Morton* (2002) the Court of Session held that a women headteacher could compare her pay with that of a male headteacher employed by a different local authority. The court interpreted Article 141 as only giving as an example the fact that a comparison could be made with those in the same establishment or service and that other factors could be relevant in making a comparison such as whether both employees were covered by the same collective agreement. A ruling from the ECJ is awaited in *Lawrence* (above) on the question of whether a comparison can be made between the pay of an employee working in a service which has now been contracted out with those employees who are still employed in that service.

Once this point has been established the woman can choose the man with whom she wishes to be compared, but in *Evesham v North Hertfordshire HA* (2000) it was held that a woman has the right to equal pay with her comparator and no more. Here a speech therapist established that she was entitled to be placed on the same pay scale as a clinical psychologist but was not entitled, having crossed over to his pay scale, then at once to climb up it on the ground of her greater experience. The Court of Appeal held that the Act simply requires equal treatment and in this context the choice of a comparator is all important.

## What can be claimed?

The Act applies not only to pay and other benefits or 'perks' such as travel concessions (*Garland v BR Engineering* (1982)), but also to occupational pension schemes (see *Bilka v Weber* (above)) and in *Barber v Guardian Royal Exchange Assurance* (1991) it was held that men and women are entitled to pension benefits at the same age. Following *Barber* there has been considerable further litigation in the area of pension schemes.

## Making a claim

Claims must be brought within six months and under s.2(5) back pay is only payable for a period of two years before the claim. In *Jennings v Levez* (1999) the EAT held that this limit was unlawful as it did not correspond to the six-year limit for claiming arrears of pay in contract and so breached the principle of equivalence. In *Preston v Wolverhampton Healthcare Trust* (2001) the House of Lords agreed that there was a breach. Developments are awaited.

# Chapter 10

# Employment rights and the family

## INTRODUCTION

This area has grown in importance in recent years and the following diagram sets out the main rights:

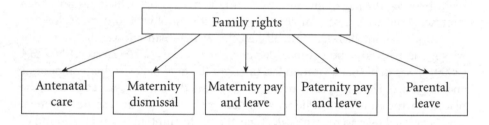

The relationship between these rights is complex and the following example may help:

*Example*

Claire is pregnant. She has the right to time off for antenatal care and if she is dismissed on account of pregnancy then this counts as automatically unfair dismissal. She must take two weeks' maternity leave but she will probably wish to have longer and she can take up to 18 (soon to be 26) weeks' ordinary maternity leave followed by up to 18 (soon to be 26) weeks' additional maternity leave. Her husband, John, will, from 2003, be able to take two weeks' paid paternity leave. Claire is also entitled to maternity pay for the period of ordinary maternity leave. After the child is born, both parents are entitled to parental leave until the child is five but this is unpaid and they are also entitled to time off for dependant care to deal with domestic emergencies.

## ANTENATAL CARE

There is no requirement of a minimum length of service and a woman has a right not to be unfairly denied the right to keep appointments but the employer can ask to see a letter of appointment (s.55 of the ERA 1996).

## THE RIGHT NOT TO BE DISMISSED ON GROUNDS OF PREGNANCY

This right, although originating from UK law, was developed as a result of the EC Pregnant Workers Directive (92/85) (see s.99 of the ERA 1996).

The right is wider than simply one not to be dismissed on pregnancy grounds and applies to dismissal in the following cases:

1. for pregnancy or any reason connected with it, e.g. a miscarriage;
2. that a woman gave birth to a child and the dismissal occurred in the maternity leave period;
3. that she took the benefits of maternity leave or additional maternity leave;
4. that she is suspended from work on maternity grounds;
5. that she is made redundant whilst on maternity leave.

Where a woman is dismissed on these grounds then the employer must, even if not requested to do so, give her a written statement of reasons (s.92(4) of the ERA).

In addition, there is also a right under EC law not to be dismissed on pregnancy grounds as this counts as sex discrimination. Originally, it was not possible for a pregnant women to claim that a pregnancy dismissal was sex discrimination as there was no comparator but in *Webb v EMO* (1994) the ECJ held that a pregnancy dismissal could be sex discrimination as it was gender related. A claim here has the advantage over a claim under s.99 (above) in that there is no ceiling on compensation, whereas s.99 claims are subject to the normal ceiling on unfair dismissal claims. However, a sex discrimination claim under *Webb*, as it is based on case law, is not so clear cut as one made under s.99 and, in particular, may fail if the employment was for a fixed term. This is because of some remarks by Lord Keith in the House of Lords in *Webb* which indicated that the result in that case might have been different had the contract been only for a fixed term. However, an advantage of proceeding under the SDA is that it covers cases other than dismissal and would apply where, for example, a woman claims that she was discriminated against during pregnancy but not actually dismissed.

## THE RIGHT TO MATERNITY LEAVE

This right, from the Maternity and Parental Leave Regulations 1999, has been amended by ss.17 and 18 of the Employment Act 2002, with changes likely to come into force in 2003. There are two periods:

### ▪ Ordinary maternity leave

This will be increased from the present 18 weeks to 26 weeks by the Employment Act. The following points apply:

1. It cannot begin until the 11th week before the expected week of the birth.
2. 21 days' notice must be given (intended increase to 28 days). What if this is not possible? This point is not clear and is an unfortunate gap.
3. All employees are entitled.
4. The employee's contract continues as if she were not absent apart from terms concerning remuneration. This is because she receives maternity pay. The effect is that employees remain entitled to any other benefits, e.g. cheap mortgages and holiday leave, continues to accrue. Continuity is preserved.
5. If leave has not begun but the employee is absent through a reason related to pregnancy at any time after the sixth week before the expected birth then this automatically triggers the beginning of leave. The reason is to stop the taking of sick leave rather than maternity leave at this point.
6. No notice is needed of the intention to return if this is to be at the end of leave but if the employee wishes to return earlier, then 21 days' notice must be given to the employer. If not, then the employer can postpone the return by the length of notice not given.
7. The right is to return to the previous job on the same terms but if the employee's job is redundant when she is away then she is entitled to be offered a suitable alternative vacancy if it exists.
8. Failure to allow her to return is automatically unfair dismissal unless it was not reasonably practicable to allow the employee, on grounds other than redundancy, to return to a suitable job.
9. Failure by the employee to return is treated in the same way as for additional maternity leave (see below).

## ■ Additional maternity leave

Additional maternity leave (Maternity and Parental Leave Regulations 1999, as amended by ss.17 and 18 of the Employment Act 2002) can last until the end of 29 weeks from the end of the week of childbirth, but from 2003 it will be extended to follow on from ordinary maternity leave and to last for a maximum of 26 weeks after the end of ordinary maternity leave. Thus a woman is entitled to a total of one year's leave. Note the following:

1. It is only available to employees who have completed one year's continuous employment by the 11th week before the expected week of childbirth.
2. There is no requirement to give notice that it will be taken.
3. The employer may ask in writing not more than 21 days before the end of ordinary leave if the employee will be taking it and if she does not reply within 21 days then, although the leave may still be taken, she will lose her right to claim for unfair dismissal if she is not allowed to return to work when she ends the leave.
4. The employer and employee remain bound by the implied terms of mutual trust and confidence and the employer must comply with any disciplinary and grievance procedures and terms relating to notice of dismissal. The

employee must comply with any terms relating to disclosure of information and competition as well as terms relating to notice. The rest of the contract is suspended and this means that there is no automatic right to pay.

5. There is no need to give notice of return and thus the employer must assume that an employee who has begun leave is going to take all of it. However, if she does wish to return early then she must give 21 days' notice.

6. On her return she is entitled to either her former job back or to another suitable and appropriate job.

7. If she does not return to work at the end then she must be treated as any other employee who is absent. The significance is that a failure to return does not automatically terminate her contract.

## Compulsory maternity leave

This is for two weeks following the birth and it is a criminal offence for an employer to employ a woman in this period (Maternity and Parental Leave Regulations 1999).

## MATERNITY PAY

This is currently paid for 18 weeks but this will increase to 26 weeks with the Employment Act 2002. The account below assumes that the relevant parts of the Act are in force.

- Only payable to a woman who has worked for a continuous period of 26 weeks before the expected week of the birth.
- Employee can decide when it is to start.
- Paid at an earnings related rate of 90% of average weekly earnings and then for the remaining 20 weeks at a flat rate of £100 a week. The employer can, of course, pay more than this.
- Employer can recover 92% of SMP from the government but small employers (to be defined in Regulations under the 2002 Act) can recover all of it.

## PARENTAL LEAVE

Under ss.76–80 of the Employment Relations the following apply:

- Applies during the first five years of the child's life or until the 18th birthday of a disabled child.
- 21 days' notice to the employer needed but this is likely to be increased to 28 days.
- Available to both parents.
- No statutory right to pay.
- Maximum of 13 weeks.

- Applies to married parents, unmarried mothers and guardians but unmarried fathers must acquire it by a court order.
- Applies to adopters, who must take it within five years of the placement.
- One year's continuous employment needed.
- Employers and employees may agree a scheme but if not the statutory scheme applies.
- Leave under the statutory scheme must be taken in blocks of a week and notice of twice the length of the leave period must be given except that where the period is two weeks or less then at least four weeks' notice is needed. The employer can postpone leave by up to six months on the grounds of the needs of the business.
- In practice, one of the main uses of these provisions will to enable families to go on holiday together, but anecdotal evidence suggests that the takeup of this right has been small.

## PATERNITY LEAVE AND PAY

These new rights under the Employment Act 2002 are likely to begin on 6 April 2003 and will probably have the following features, although at present the government is consulting on the precise details:

- Up to two weeks' leave following the birth.
- 28 days' notice to the employer (probably) needed.
- This will be paid but (probably) only if leave is taken within 56 days of the birth.
- Must have 26 weeks' continuous employment at the 15th week before the birth.
- Will only qualify if average weekly earnings equal or exceed the lower earnings limit for national insurance contributions (at present £72 per week).
- Rate will be the lesser of £100 a week or 90% of average earnings.
- Same rules on recovery as for SMP.
- Right to return to the job after leave: contract continues.

## ADOPTION LEAVE AND PAY

This is also to be introduced from 6 April 2003 and, once again, the precise details are subject to consultation. The broad outlines are:

- 26 weeks' paid leave.
- 28 days' notice to the employer probably needed.
- 26 weeks' unpaid leave (i.e. the maternity leave scheme is mirrored).
- If a married couple adopt, then only one can take leave but the other can take the two weeks' paternity leave.

- Does not apply to step-family adoptions but only where a child is first matched for adoption.
- The rate of pay will be the same as for paternity pay.
- Right to return to the job following leave.

## TIME OFF TO CARE FOR DEPENDANTS

This is a right (ss.57A and 57B of the ERA 1996) given to all employees to take reasonable time off to:

- provide assistance when a dependant is ill, injured, assaulted or gives birth;
- arrange care for an injured dependant;
- deal with matters in consequence of the death of a dependant;
- deal with an unexpected disruption in arrangements for the care of a dependant or the termination of those arrangements;
- deal with an incident involving a child at school.

A dependant is defined as the employee's wife, husband, child, parent or someone who lives in the same household as the employee but is not their tenant, lodger, boarder or employee.

The right is not paid as such but it is expected that employers who have paid in the past will continue to do so. There is no requirement to give notice in advance but the employee should tell the employer the reason for the absence as soon as practicable.

## RIGHT TO REQUEST A FLEXIBLE WORKING ARRANGEMENT

This right, under s.47 of the Employment Act 2002, will be introduced from 6 April 2003 and the details will be in Regulations, but the main features will be:

1. Employers will have a legal duty to consider requests for a flexible working arrangement from those with parental responsibility for a child aged under six or a disabled child aged under 18.
2. The employee can request a change to working hours, change to working times or a change to the place of work.
3. Written request must be submitted to the employer setting out details of the proposed arrangements and making a case for the change.
4. The employer must meet the employee within 28 days to see if a change can be agreed.
5. A 'sound business reason' will be needed for the request to be rejected.
6. There will be a right of appeal.

# Chapter 11

# Termination of employment (I): wrongful and unfair dismissal

## INTRODUCTION

The essence of a claim for wrongful dismissal is that the employee is claiming that the dismissal was in breach of contract. It therefore contrasts with unfair dismissal, where the claim is not based on the contract but on statute. Statistically, unfair dismissal is by far the most important of the two, with 43,590 claims in 2000/01 where the main claim was for unfair dismissal, as compared to 10,187 claims for wrongful dismissal. In addition, there were 2,021 specialised unfair dismissal claims for matters such as pregnancy dismissal and dismissal on the transfer of an undertaking. However, it is often necessary to discuss the two concepts side by side and therefore the following table may be found useful for reference.

| Wrongful dismissal | Unfair dismissal |
| --- | --- |
| Based on the contract | Based on statute |
| Employee must prove claim | Tribunal decides |
| No claim if contractual notice given | Can still claim even if contractual notice given |
| No claim for future loss of earnings | Can claim for future loss of earnings |
| Facts discovered after the dismissal may be used in evidence | Facts discovered after the dismisssal cannot be used in evidence |
| Remedy is compensation | Remedy is compensation or re-instatement or re-engagement |
| No ceiling on compensation | Statutory ceiling on compensation |
| Claim can be brought in the County/High Court or in an employment tribunal if it is for £25,000 or less | Claim must be brought in an employment tribunal |
| No claim if a fixed-term contract is not renewed | May claim if a fixed-term contract is not renewed |
| No qualifying period of employment | One year's qualifying period of employment in most cases |

The other significant differences are found in the procedures of the county court and High Court which, as compared to the procedures of employment tribunals, which tend to be more formal (see Chapter 1).

## METHODS OF TERMINATION

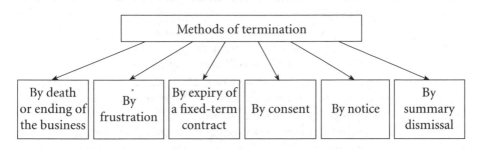

Each of these methods will now be considered in turn under the headings of wrongful and unfair dismissal.

## WRONGFUL DISMISSAL

This section will look in more detail at the methods of termination set out above to see whether they give rise to a claim for wrongful dismissal. It will then look at the remedies on the assumption that there is a claim for wrongful dismissal. The methods of termination set out below are, in general, also relevant to a claim for unfair dismissal and they are also discussed later in the context of an unfair dismissal claim.

### ▓ Termination by death or by the ending of the business

The death of the employer ends the contract of employment at common law but it is important to remember that if the business ends as a consequence of the employer's death then the employees will be entitled to a redundancy payment under the Employment Rights Act 1996 (see Chapter 12). If the business is a company and is wound up compulsorily by the court then this operates as a notice of dismissal to the employees. If it is voluntarily wound up but is to continue in another form, for example by being taken over by another company, then there is no dismissal.

### ▓ Termination by frustration

The doctrine of frustration applies throughout the law of contract and has the effect of discharging the contract (i.e. bringing it to an end). The result will be that the employee is no longer entitled to wages and no claim for wrongful dismissal can be brought, as there has been no dismissal. Any back pay due may be claimed under the Law Reform (Frustrated Contracts) Act 1943, but there will be no right to compensation for future loss of earnings unless an action can be brought establishing that the employer was at fault in some way. This could be where the conduct of the employer is alleged to have caused the illness which frustrated the contract (see below). However, a person who suffers from illness or incapacity may be entitled to statutory sick pay (SSP) and industrial injuries disablement benefit (see Chapter 7). Nevertheless, these sums will not be large and the effect of the contract of employment being ended by frustration will be to deprive the employee of any chance of receiving any lump sum by way of compensation when their employment ceases. This drastic effect of frustration has led some judges to seek to limit the circumstances in which it can apply to contracts of employment, as we shall see below.

A contract is frustrated when performance of it either becomes impossible or where further performance would involve performing something radically different from what was originally intended. Obvious instances from the employment perspective are the illness or incapacity of the employee, but not all such instances will frustrate the contract. In *Condor v Barron Knights Ltd* (1966) the contract of a drummer in a pop group was frustrated when he was unable to fulfil his contract because of the stress of the work and the resulting illness. In *Marshall v Harland and Wolff Ltd* (1972) Sir John Donaldson set out certain matters which should be considered in deciding whether a contract is frustrated and these were added to by the EAT in *Egg Stores v Leibovici* (1976). A composite list from both cases is as follows:

1. The length of the previous employment.
2. The terms of the contract, including any provision for sick pay.
3. How long it had been expected that the previous employment would continue.
4. The nature of the job.
5. The length, nature and effect of the illness or disabling event.
6. The need of the employer for the work to be done and the necessity for a replacement.
7. The risk to the employer of acquiring obligations in respect of redundancy payments or compensation for unfair dismissal to the replacement employee.
8. Whether wages have continued to be paid.
9. Acts and statements of the employer in relation to the employee, including either the dismissal or failure to dismiss the employee.
10. Whether a reasonable employer could have been expected to wait any longer before ending the employment.

The fact that the application of the doctrine of frustration means that the employee may be left without any compensation for the ending of employment has led some judges to seek to restrict its operation to cases of contracts which are intended to last for a long time and not to be determinable by notice. Where the contract is determinable by notice then it is argued that there is no need for the doctrine of frustration, as the contract can be ended by notice. This view was put forward by Bristow J in *Harman v Flexible Lamps Ltd* (1980) but it was rejected by the Court of Appeal in *Notcutt v Universal Equipment Co. (London) Ltd* (1986), where Dillon LJ pointed out that contracts determinable by notice may be intended to last for a long time and thus the distinction drawn by Bristow J between long-term contracts and those determinable by notice was a false one. Not only this, but the decision in *Harman v Flexible Lamps* completely ignored the decisions in *Marshall v Harland and Wolff* and *Egg Stores v Leibovici*.

Even so, in the *Egg Stores* case it was accepted that the doctrine does need to be applied carefully in the case of short-term contracts which can be determined by notice which would at least give the employee the right to wages for the period of notice. This was accepted in *Notcutt* and remains the law. There is a case for looking at whether the doctrine of frustration should apply at all to contracts of employment and to provide that in all cases where the employee is unable to perform the contract through illness or incapacity he/she will be paid wages for the periods of notice to which he/she is entitled. This would avoid requiring the employer to pay a large sum for an occurrence which was not his/her fault, whilst giving the employee some payment.

The other main situation where a contract of employment can be frustrated is where the employee is imprisoned. The problem with applying the doctrine of frustration here is that it can be argued that the act causing the frustration (i.e. the crime for which the employee was imprisoned) was self-induced, in that the employee actually committed the act. Nevertheless, in *Hare v Murphy Bros Ltd* (1974) it was held by Denning MR that a contract of employment was frustrated by imprisonment, although Stephenson LJ held simply that imprisonment ended the contract and he was not concerned about the precise label used to describe why this was so. This left some uncertainty in the law, which was eventually resolved by the Court of Appeal in *Shepherd & Co. Ltd v Jerrom* (1986), which held that frustration can apply where an employee is imprisoned. The difficulty about the fact that the act was self-induced was met by Balcombe LJ who accepted the view of Denning MR that the frustrating event was the actual imposition of the sentence which was not, of course, a matter for the employee. There remains the question of whether frustration applies to all sentences of imprisonment. On principle, and accepting the view of Balcombe LJ, it should do so and this may well be the case with actions for wrongful dismissal. Where unfair dismissal is concerned there may be other considerations, as we shall see.

## ■ Termination by expiry of a fixed-term contract

Termination in this way may give rise to an action for wrongful dismissal where the contract was terminated before it expired. Where the contract simply expired and was not renewed then there can be no action for wrongful dismissal because, as explained above, such an action is based on breach of contract and a failure to renew a fixed-term contract which has ended cannot be a breach of it.

Given these consequences, and the growing use of such contracts, it is clearly vital to know precisely what a fixed-term contract is.

## Example

X is employed as a lecturer by Malvern University for the period 1 September 2002 until 31 August 2003.

This appears to be a fixed-term contract, but what if it also provides that it can be ended by one month's notice on either side during this period?

## Example

Y is employed as a carpenter to work on the construction of a new building until it is completed.

This is fixed-term in the sense that the duration is not unlimited but is limited by the time it takes to complete a task.

The first problem is that the definition of a fixed-term contract in the law on dismissal covers only contracts for a fixed term as measured by time and not task contracts as in the second of the two examples above. This was held by the Court of Appeal in *Wiltshire CC v NATFHE* (1980) but the Fixed-term Employees Regulations, which came into force on 1 October 2002 (see Chapter 4) specifically include task contracts. Similarly, in *Dixon v BBC* (1979) it was held that a contract could still be fixed-term for the purposes of the law on dismissal even if it contained provision for termination by notice, as in the first example above. The reason was related to the law on unfair dismissal, which will be dealt with later in this chapter, but once again it is likely that the definition of a fixed-term contract in the Fixed-term Employees Regulations 2002 does *not* include a contract which can be determined by notice because the definition in Regulation 1(2) is, it will be recalled, that a contract is fixed-term if it is made for a *specific* term which is fixed in advance. It may therefore be the position that, for the purposes of the law on dismissal, a contract can still be fixed-term even if it contains provision for termination by notice, but for the purposes of the Regulations and consequent equal treatment of fixed-term employees, a contract is only fixed-term if it is for a definite period with no provision for termination by notice. On the other hand, the definition of a fixed-term contract under the Regulations does include a task contract, unlike the law on dismissal. Even allowing for the different purposes of the law of dismissal and the Regulations, this all seems unsatisfactory.

The other point is that, as explained in Chapter 4, under the Regulations it will no longer be possible for the employer to contract out of the obligation to pay a redundancy payment and this, together with the fact that under the Regulations fixed timers may have their contracts converted to full-time is likely to make these contracts less attractive to employers anyway.

## Termination by mutual agreement

Where the employer and employee mutually agree that the employment is at an end, then there can naturally be no dismissal and thus no action for wrongful dismissal. The problem is to distinguish a genuine mutual agreement from the 'resign or be sacked' situation, where the employee may argue that there has been a repudiatory breach of contract by the employer sufficient to justify a claim for wrongful dismissal. Voluntary agreements to take redundancy can be good examples of termination by mutual agreement. In *Birch v University of Liverpool* (1985) two lecturers agreed to take early retirement under a scheme which gave very generous compensation in return for employees forgoing their right to (much smaller) statutory payments. They were held to have agreed to terminate their contracts so that it was not open to them to claim later that they had been dismissed. However, each case must be looked at on its own facts. In *Ely v YKK Fasteners Ltd* (1994) the employee told his employers that he wanted to leave his job in order to emigrate to Australia. The employers then arranged for a replacement but subsequently the employee changed his mind and said that he intended to stay. The employers, having made the arrangements for the replacement, insisted that he had already resigned. The Court of Appeal held that he had only said that he intended to resign in the future. This was not a resignation as such and, on the facts, it was the employers who had dismissed him.

## Termination by notice

It is here that the difference between wrongful and unfair dismissal is seen most clearly because, whereas an employee given due notice can still claim unfair dismissal, as the issue is one of fairness, no claim can be brought for wrongful dismissal in such a case because a wrongful dismissal action depends on establishing a breach of contract by the employer and, by giving due notice, the employer has, far from breaking the contract, kept it. However, the main type of wrongful dismissal claim is where it is alleged that *less than* due notice was given and so the claim is for wages for the period of notice or accrued holiday pay to which the employee was entitled but which was not paid.

At common law an employer is entitled to dismiss on giving notice of the length laid down in the contract but this has been overlaid by the statutory notice provisions now contained in s.86 of the ERA 1996. This provides that employees continuously employed for between one month and two years are entitled to one week's notice and this increases by one week for every year of continuous employment with a maximum of 12 weeks' notice where employees have more than 12 years' continuous employment. Employers are only entitled to receive one week's notice where the employee has been employed for at least one week. It must be emphasised that these are only *minimum* periods of notice and, if the contract provides for longer periods of notice, then these must be given. If not, the employee may claim for wages for the period of notice to which he/she was entitled in an action for wrongful dismissal. It is, however, important to establish that notice was actually given. In *Morris v Bailey* (1969), where notice was given, not to the employee personally but to his union, this was held to be insufficient. It is also important that any words used make it clear that the employee is actually being given notice.

*Example*

John works in a newsagent's shop. The owner, Mike, says to him: 'Business is bad. I think that it would be in your best interests to look for another job.' This is not notice and John is still entitled to turn up for work and to receive his wages.

What is the position where the employer wishes to give the employee wages in lieu of notice? In Chapter 7 we saw that a claim for wages in lieu of notice must be brought as a claim for breach of contract (*Delaney v Staples* (1991)). The question here is a more fundamental one: can wages in lieu of notice be paid at all or is the employee always entitled to work out notice? The following situations need to be distinguished:

1. Where the contract expressly allows wages to be paid in lieu of notice. There is obviously no difficulty here: the employer may dismiss and pay wages in lieu of notice. In effect, the employee is dismissed with very little warning but does receive wages for whatever period of notice he/she is entitled to. A variation on this theme is the idea of garden leave clauses, where the employee is given a long period of notice during which they are paid but is not allowed to work for others during that time. These are dealt with more fully in Chapter 5.
2. Where the employer and employee agree that the employment will terminate immediately and the employee agrees to accept wages in lieu of notice. This will be lawful. The only difference between (a) and (b) is that in (a) the contract expressly provided for this, whereas in (b) it was dealt with by an ad hoc agreement.
3. Where the employer dismisses the employee and offers wages in lieu of notice without the employee agreeing. Here the employee will have a claim for wrongful dismissal but may not be awarded any more than the employer offered.

## ■ Termination by summary dismissal

An employer may terminate the contract summarily where the employee has been guilty of a repudiatory breach of the contract of employment. This area has been overtaken by the law on unfair dismissal because where an employee is summarily dismissed an action for unfair dismissal will be preferable. This is because a claim for wrongful dismissal can only lead to damages for wages for the period of notice to which the employee was entitled. The only time when a summarily dismissed employee would choose to claim for wrongful dismissal would be if it was not possible to claim for unfair dismissal (see below). With this in mind, treatment of this topic will be brief.

The leading case is *Laws v London Chronicle Ltd* (1959), where Evershed MR held that 'the question must be – if summary dismissal is claimed to be justifiable – whether the conduct complained of is such as to show the servant to have disregarded the *essential conditions of the contract of service*'. The words which have been italicised correspond to the phrase 'repudiatory breach' on the part of the employer, in that if the employee has *not* broken an essential condition of the contract then any dismissal will mean that it is the employer who has committed a repudiatory breach and will be liable for wrongful dismissal.

Two contrasting cases on this area concern gardeners, both of whom were dismissed following an altercation with their employer during which the gardener used foul language. In the first, *Pepper v Webb* (1969), dismissal was held to be justified as the cause of the dismissal was found to be the failure of the gardener to do the very job which he was employed to do in looking after the garden and greenhouse. This was, to use the words of Evershed MR (above), the disregard of the essential conditions of service. In *Wilson v Racher* (1974) the incident in which the foul language was used was an isolated one and dismissal was not held to be justified. Thus the employer committed a repudiatory breach by dismissing the employee.

The whole topic of when an employer is justified in dismissing because of the conduct of the employee is covered in the section below dealing with unfair dismissal. As a general guide, it can be said that occasions when dismissal is fair will normally be sufficient to justify summary dismissal as well. However, in applying these to the law of summary dismissal, the question must always be asked whether the employee had disregarded an essential condition of the contract of employment.

## Summary

Thus the only cases where an employee can claim for wrongful dismissal will be where:

1. notice was given but it was not of sufficient length;
2. the dismissal was summary;
3. a fixed-term contract was terminated before the expiry date.

## Remedies for wrongful dismissal

Assuming that the employee is able to claim for wrongful dismissal, what remedies may be claimed?

### Damages

The general rule is that damages are awarded only for wages due to employees for the period of notice to which they were entitled but did not receive. These are awarded as damages for the employer's breach of contract. The question of what wages are received a restricted reply in *Laverack v Woods of Colchester Ltd* (1967), where an employee was held not to be entitled to discretionary bonuses payable during the notice period precisely because they *were* discretionary and there was no contractual entitlement to them. Where damages are awarded they may be reduced if the employee has failed to mitigate his/her loss by failing to look for and, if offered, accept alternative work. There are, however, the following exceptions where the employee may recover additional payments as damages.

### Employee dismissed but employer did not go through contractual disciplinary procedures

In *Gunton v Richmond on Thames LBC* (1980) the employee was dismissed without the hearing to which he was entitled under his contract. Damages were awarded for net salary lost for the period for which the procedures should have applied. This will not, however, mean that the employee receives a large extra sum, usually on top of damages for wages in lieu of notice, because the time when any procedures should have operated will not, unless in exceptional cases, exceed a few weeks. The principle in *Gunton* was also applied in *Boyo v Lambeth LBC* (1995) but its application is limited to cases where the contract expressly incorporates a right to have specified disciplinary procedures followed before dismissal.

### Dismissal has meant that employee has lost the opportunity to claim for unfair dismissal

#### Example

Jennifer was employed as a teacher by Barset CC from 1 September 2002 but was summarily dismissed on 1 August 2003. As a result she was unable to claim for unfair dismissal, as she did not have the requisite period of one year's continuous employment. She can bring a claim for wrongful dismissal for damages representing wages for the period of notice to which she was entitled but can she add on a claim for damages for the loss of her statutory rights to compensation for unfair dismissal?

In *Raspin v United News Shops Ltd* (1999) it was held that this was possible, although it has been pointed out that such a claim is not possible where the contract contains a clause expressly allowing the employer to pay wages in lieu of notice and this is done (*Morran v Glasgow Council of Tenants' Associations* (1998)) because here the dismissal is not wrongful at all.

### Employee is claiming damages for loss of reputation

This seems to largely confined to cases of actors and actresses, as in *Marbe v George Edwardes Ltd* (1928), where an actress was awarded damages for loss of reputation when her contract was broken.

There have also been attempts to argue that damages should be payable in the following cases:

*Damages for injured feelings resulting from the manner of dismissal*

These were claimed in *Addis v Gramophone Co. Ltd* (1909) but the House of Lords held that such a claim was inadmissible and this has been the view of the law ever since, despite attempts to argue the contrary. It was thought that the decision in *Malik v BCCI* (1997) might have opened the door to these claims but this was rejected by the Court of Appeal in *French v Barclays Bank plc* (1998).

*Damages (known as stigma damages)*

These are claimed for the stigma suffered by the employee in the labour market due to having been associated with a particular employer. In effect the employee is saying that a prospective employer would look at his/her CV and, seeing that they had worked for Firm X, decide that they did not want to employ anyone who had worked for them. The possibility of such a claim was opened up by the decision of the House of Lords in *Malik v BCCI* (1997), where it was held that a claim for stigma damages could be brought as a result of a breach by the employers of the implied term of mutual trust and confidence (see Chapter 5). However, the effect of this decision was subject to a restrictive interpretation by both the Court of Appeal and the House of Lords in *Johnson v Unisys Ltd* (2001), where it was held that the decision in *Malik* was not authority for the proposition that stigma damages could be awarded in an action for wrongful dismissal. It was pointed out that *Malik* was concerned with an award of damages for breach of an implied term of the contract *during* employment and was not concerned with damages for breach of contract. The result of all this seems to be that the law on what can and cannot be claimed in an action for wrongful dismissal has not moved beyond the situations set out above.

Where damages are awarded, if they exceed £30,000, the excess is taxable (ss.148 and 188 of the Income and Corporation Taxes Act 1988). This does not apply to unfair dismissal compensation.

## Direct enforcement of the contract

Given that the circumstances in which damages for wrongful dismissal are limited, is there more mileage in an action asking that the contract should be directly enforced against the employer?

*Example*

Charles is dismissed from his job as a computer programmer. He is not interested in compensation but simply wants his job back.

As a general rule, such a claim is bound to fail as English law has always set its face against the enforcement of contracts in general and not only employment contracts, preferring to award damages. There are two situations:

(a) The employer wishes to enforce the contract against the employee, i.e. to compel the employee to work.

(b) The employee wishes to enforce the contract against the employer by compelling the employer to continue to give him/her work.

Situation (a) is governed by s.236 of the Trade Union and Labour Relations Act 1992, which provides (in refreshingly straightforward language) that no court shall by way of any specified court order compel any employee to do any work. Thus there is a statutory bar to an action by an employer in (a) above, although s.236 does not cover independent contractors. However, s.236 is simply a reflection of an equitable principle that the courts will not order anyone, whether an employee or not, to perform a contract of personal service.

Situation (b) holds more interest, although it must be said that even here it is unlikely that in any particular case the employee will succeed in getting a contract of employment enforced against the employer. There is, however, some interesting case law on this subject.

The starting point is the decision of the Court of Appeal in *Hill v CA Parsons & Co. Ltd* (1971), where the Court of Appeal held that an injunction would be granted to restrain the dismissal of an employee. The case was unusual, and the circumstances will not re-occur, in that the Industrial Relations Act 1971 was about to come into force. The reason for the dismissal was that Hill refused to join a union where there was a closed shop agreement and the effect of the Act would be to render dismissals for this reason automatically unfair. The effect of the injunction was that Hill remained an employee until the Act came into force and could then claim under its provisions. There was, however, a point of more general interest in that the relationship between the parties had not broken down and mutual trust and confidence remained.

In *Irani v Southampton and SW Hampshire Health Authority* (1985) the employee was dismissed in breach of agreed procedures and an injunction was granted to restrain the dismissal until these had been gone through. The case was similar to *Hill* in two ways: the enforcement of the contract of employment was a means to a particular end and there was no question of the employee actually returning to work; and the relationship between the parties had not broken down. In *Irani* the cause of the dismissal was that Irani and a consultant at the hospital where he was employed could not work together but there was no complaint about his work.

In more recent cases the courts have gone further and actually restrained the employer from breaking the contract. In *Powell v Brent LBC* (1987) the council, having promoted the employee to a more senior post, then revoked this on the grounds that it had been alleged that the council's equal opportunities policy had been broken in making the appointment. The court granted an injunction which restrained the council from re-advertising the post until the main action had been tried. Once more it was emphasised that there had been no breakdown in relationships between the parties.

A more striking case is *Jones v Gwent CC* (1992), where the employee, a lecturer, had been through two disciplinary procedures when allegations of misconduct were found to be groundless but she was still dismissed by the college governors. The reason given was that it was felt that her return to the college would cause a breakdown in relationships due to her past behaviour. The court granted an interim injunction preventing dismissal in breach of the procedures laid down in the employee's contract and a permanent injunction restraining any dismissal on the basis of the governors' decision. It is this second limb of the decision which marks a new departure and it will be interesting to see how far the courts are prepared to travel along this road. The most recent significant instance is the decision of the Court of Session in Scotland in *Anderson v Pringle of Scotland Ltd* (1998), where an employer was restrained from dismissing an employee in breach of an agreed redundancy selection procedure.

## Public law remedies and dismissal

The distinction between public and private law is not easy to state with absolute precision but the basic point is fairly easy to grasp. Whilst private law is concerned with adjusting rights and duties between individuals (including organisations), public law deals with matters which affect either the whole community or at least a sizeable proportion of it. Thus the actions of central and local government are matters of public law, whereas disputes between employers and employees are matters of private law. Nevertheless, there have been numerous attempts, some successful, to argue that an employee has rights under public law and thus to seek judicial review. Why?

There are three main reasons:

1. Public law emphasises that when a decision is taken, the rules of natural justice must be observed. There are two rules:
   (a) that the decision-maker must not be biased; and
   (b) that there must be a fair hearing.
   Although the requirements of a fair procedure loom large in the law of unfair dismissal (see below), they are much less prominent in actions for wrongful dismissal unless, as discussed above, there is a disciplinary procedure incorporated into the contract. Thus a claim in public law can bring in some fundamental procedural safeguards for the employee.
2. The remedies for a breach of public law deal directly with the decision itself, which can lead to the employee being able to enforce the contract. The relevant ones are:
   (a) a quashing order (formerly known as an order of *certiorari*), which would have the effect of quashing a decision to dismiss; and
   (b) a mandatory order, which requires the performance of a duty.
   These could be combined where the court quashes a decision to dismiss because of a flawed procedure and requires the decision-maker to hold any hearing again.
3. Public law remedies do not depend on proving that the claimant is an employee and are thus available to an independent contractor as well.

A clear example of where an employee was able to claim a public law remedy is *R v Liverpool City Council, ex parte Ferguson* (1985), where the council, as part of a dispute with central government, had set a rate that was illegal, as it assumed that the council would be in deficit. Subsequently, the council was compelled to dismiss some employees because it would not have enough money to pay their wages. The court allowed these employees to claim under public law as, although the actual dismissal could be said to be a private law matter, it arose out of decision to set an illegal rate, which was a public law matter.

This is an unusual case and the courts have been reluctant to allow many claims under public law for the simple reason that it gives those who are able to claim them an advantage over those who cannot. For example, the employees in the *Liverpool* case (above) would not have been able to claim in public law if a private employer had employed them. The difficulty has been to draw a clear dividing line between when a claim will be allowed and when it will not.

It appears that an office holder (see Chapter 4) can claim a public law remedy because the very fact that a public office is held makes the matter one of public law (see *Ridge v Baldwin* (1964)). This does not, however, get us very far, given the limited number of office holders. In *R v East Berkshire Health Authority, ex parte Walsh* (1984), a nurse who had been dismissed sought judicial review of the decision, arguing that this was a public law matter because the decision to dismiss was in breach of the procedure in the Whitley Council agreement, which dealt with conditions in the NHS and had been approved by the relevant Minister. The Court of Appeal held that this was not a matter of public law and the termination of a contract of employment was a private law matter, even though the employer was a public body. The crucial factor was that the Whitley Council procedures had been incorporated into the applicant's contract of employment. A clear statement of the principles here was provided by Woolf LJ, who held in *McLaren v Home Office* (1990) that an employee could seek judicial review where there is some body established by statute or under the royal prerogative which has a sufficient public law element. The rationale of this is that it is in the public interest to ensure that such bodies observe the law. Thus it seems that prison officers will be able to seek judicial review of decisions to dismiss them, as in *R v Home Secretary, ex parte Benwell* (1985), where the authority to take action against the officer was based on statute. Unlike *Walsh*, there was no issue of contract, as the matter rested entirely on statute. The other point was that at that date prison officers had no right to claim unfair dismissal (they have been able to do so since 1994) and so judicial review was the only remedy here.

## ▪ Bringing a claim for wrongful dismissal

There is the choice of either a claim in the civil courts or, where the amount claimed is no more than £25,000 (in respect of any one contract of employment), it may be brought in an employment tribunal. What frequently happens is that a contract claim for wrongful dismissal is added on to an unfair dismissal claim where the latter is the primary remedy. One reason for this is that loss due to the employee not having received the correct (or any) notice can be claimed in the wrongful dismissal claim and therefore the unfair dismissal claim (at present subject to a maximum of £52,600) can be used to claim future loss of earnings. Thus in 2000/01, whilst there were 10,187 claims where wrongful dismissal was the primary remedy sought, there were 31,333 wrongful dismissal claims altogether. The other possibility is that it may be that the unfair dismissal claim fails on the facts but the tribunal may still decide that the employee is entitled to pay for notice which was not given. If a wrongful dismissal claim is brought in a tribunal then the normal three-month period for bringing claims applies (see below). It is being increasingly suggested that the £25,000 limit, which has been unchanged since the introduction of this jurisdiction in 1994, should be raised in line with the significant increases in the amount which can be awarded in unfair dismissal claims.

## UNFAIR DISMISSAL

This is the statutory counterpart of the action for wrongful dismissal and was originally introduced by the Industrial Relations Act 1971. The law is now contained in Part X of the Employment Rights Act 1996.

### Methods of termination and unfair dismissal

The methods of termination described above in relation to wrongful dismissal apply to unfair dismissal as follows:

### Termination by death or on the ending of a business

The position is the same as for wrongful dismissal.

### Termination by frustration

The position is essentially the same because s.95 of the ERA 1996, which sets out the circumstances in which an employee is dismissed for the purposes of unfair dismissal, speaks of termination in three ways but the assumption is that the contract is there to be terminated. If the contract has already been frustrated, then it is no longer alive. Nevertheless, it is vital to look at frustration alongside the question of dismissals for sickness which fall under the head of capability dismissals, and this is explored later in this chapter.

### Termination on the expiry of a fixed-term contract

It is here that the first major difference appears between wrongful and unfair dismissal. An unfair dismissal claim can be brought *not only* where an employee is dismissed during a fixed-term contract, as for wrongful dismissal, but also where a fixed-term contract is not renewed. In the latter case there is no action for wrongful dismissal.

### ■ Termination by mutual agreement

The position is the same as for wrongful dismissal but the close relationship between this concept and that of constructive dismissal should be noted. Constructive dismissal does not exist as such in the law of wrongful dismissal but in the law of unfair dismissal a forced resignation may amount to constructive dismissal and give rise to a claim. This is examined below under the discussion of constructive dismissal.

### ■ Termination by notice

The other major change from wrongful dismissal appears here, in that termination, even with due notice, does not bar a claim for unfair dismissal. (This is explained in detail below.)

### ■ Termination by summary dismissal

The law of unfair dismissal does not use the term 'summary dismissal' but instead s.95 of the ERA 1996 speaks of termination *with* or *without notice*. In fact, the law of unfair dismissal has largely taken over this area but the point to note is that here the issue is whether the dismissal is for a fair reason rather than whether there was a repudiatory breach of contract.

### ■ Stages in an unfair dismissal claim

The following are the main stages and the flow chart below should be kept in mind when looking at the law on unfair dismissal.

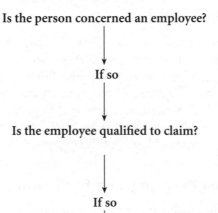

**Is the person concerned an employee?**

**If so**

**Is the employee qualified to claim?**

**If so**

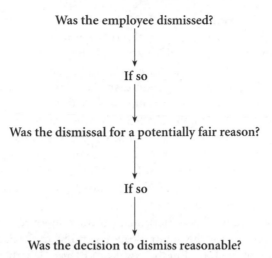

Was the employee dismissed?

If so

Was the dismissal for a potentially fair reason?

If so

Was the decision to dismiss reasonable?

## Is the person concerned an employee?

This topic does not call for greater elaboration here, as the distinction between employees and independent contractors was dealt with in Chapter 4. However, it is vital to reiterate that the right not to be unfairly dismissed only applies to employees, as the foundation of the law here, s.94 of the ERA, states that: 'An *employee* has the right not to be unfairly dismissed by his employer' (my italics). Thus an independent contractor is left to claim for breach of contract where, as the relationship is akin to employment, the matter will generally be decided according to the principles of wrongful dismissal.

## Is the employee qualified to claim?

The starting point is the phrase 'the effective date of termination'. Section 97 of the ERA provides that this means:

(a) where notice is given, the date on which it expires;
(b) where there is no notice (i.e. summary dismissal), the date when termination takes effect;
(c) where the employee is employed under a fixed term, the date on which the term expires.

The cases where the employee is not qualified to claim are set out below and thus, if the employee is *not* within any of these classes, it can be assumed that he/she is qualified:

1. Where at the effective date of termination the employee had not been continuously employed for one year. (Note that in cases of automatically unfair dismissal there is no qualifying period of a year and claims can be brought from day one of employment except in cases of dismissal on the transfer of an undertaking and for spent convictions (see pp.208–9).) This was reduced to one year in 1999 (and thus applies to dismissals occurring on or after

1 June 1999). Previously, from 1985 onwards, it had been two years and before that, from 1979, one year; before 1979 it had been six months. The reason for the changes was the feeling of the 1979–97 Conservative government that employers were inhibited from taking on employees because of fear of the consequences of an unfair dismissal claim. The change to one year was dictated by a change in the political climate and also the two-year limit had been subject to a lengthy challenge in the courts on the ground that it was sexually discriminatory, as it indirectly discriminated against female employees who were more likely than men to be in jobs for a short time. This litigation (finally under the name of *R v Secretary of State for Employment, ex parte Seymour Smith* (1995)) eventually failed but it did build up a certain head of steam against the two-year limit.

2. Where at the effective date of termination the employee was either over the normal retiring age for the job or, if there is none, over 65. This provision is found in s.109 of the ERA, but there was doubt as to whether it meant that in all cases an employee over 65 could not claim. However, in *Nothman v Barnet LBC* (1979) the House of Lords held that there are two rules and thus an employee over 65 but under the normal retiring age (e.g. 70) could claim. Equally, an employee dismissed where the normal retiring age is *under* 65 could not claim. Problems can arise in establishing what the normal retiring age is and these are illustrated by *Hughes v DHSS* (1985), where the normal retiring age was 60 but employees were then allowed as a matter of policy to stay on until 65. The policy then changed again and the age was lowered to 60. The House of Lords held that the age was now 60 and thus an employee over that age could not claim. These limits may be subject to change when legislation outlawing age discrimination comes into force by December 2006 (see Chapter 9). Meanwhile there was an attempt in *Taylor v Secretary of State for Scotland* (1999) to argue that a dismissal beyond the normal retirement age was discriminatory as being in breach of an equal opportunities policy which included age discrimination. The attempt failed, as it was held that the employers still retained a discretion as to when the employment of those over the normal retirement age should be terminated. (This case is also dealt with, from a different perspective, in Chapter 5.)

3. Where the employee is either a share fisherman (s.199 of ERA) or is employed in the police service (s.200 of ERA).

4. Where the employee is governed by a dismissal procedures agreement which has been approved by the Secretary of State as operating in substitution for the statutory scheme (s.110 of ERA). The only one in existence is the agreement between the Electrical Contractors Association and the Electrical Electronic Telecommunications and Plumbing Union in 1979.

## Was the employee dismissed?

This is the next hurdle which the employee has to surmount and the definition of dismissal for the purposes of the law on unfair dismissal is set out in s.95 of the ERA. Dismissal occurs when:

1. The contract is terminated by the employer with or without notice.
2. A fixed-term contract expires without being renewed under the same contract.
3. The employee terminates the contract, with or without notice, in circumstances where he/she is entitled to terminate it without notice because of the employer's conduct. This has come to be known as constructive dismissal but it is important to remember that the Act does not use this phrase and so it is important to apply the statutory phrase.

Category 1 above includes both summary dismissal and dismissal with or without notice and the discussion above under wrongful dismissal of when employment can be said to be terminated and when the employee really leaves by mutual agreement is of particular relevance here. Fixed-term contracts (2 above) have also been dealt with under wrongful dismissal but the significant point here is that where a fixed-term contract expires and is not renewed, then the employee will have to show that the reason for non-renewal was a fair one. In *Terry v East Sussex CC* (1976) it was held that a failure to renew a fixed-term contract could come under dismissal for some other substantial reason (see below) and it may be that it is easy for an employer to justify non-renewal as where the need for the services of the employee have ended.

The main category for discussion here is that of constructive dismissal (3 above). The legislation gave no guidance on the meaning of the phrase 'entitled to terminate it' and it was not until *Western Excavating v Sharp* (1978) that it was established that this meant that the employee was contractually entitled to terminate the contract. In this case Denning MR held that: 'if the employer is guilty of conduct which is a significant breach going to the root of the contract of employment, or which shows that the employer no longer intends to be bound by one or more of the essential terms of the contract, then the employee is entitled to treat himself as discharged from any further performance.'

This contract test, rather than a more general test of whether the employer has behaved unreasonably, might have been thought to be unduly restrictive. There was undoubtedly a fear that the concept of constructive dismissal might get out of hand and be used whenever, for example, the employer and the employee had a disagreement. In *Western Excavating* itself the employee resigned when his employer refused to give him an advance against accrued holiday pay. As Denning MR pointed out, there was no breach of contract by the employers at all. The merit of the contract test is that, by focusing on the contract, it provides a means of distinguishing between situations where, in Lawton LJ's phrase in this case, 'the employer is the kind of employer of whom the employee is entitled without notice to rid himself' and an employer with whom the employee simply happens to disagree.

In the event, the imposition of a contract test has still enabled the law of constructive dismissal to be fruitfully developed. The courts have recognised that an employee will be contractually entitled to terminate for breach of an implied as well as an express term, and have extended the range of implied terms to include a term that the employer will treat the employee with trust and respect, which is really a variation of the implied term of mutual trust and confidence. This was dealt with in Chapter 5 and reference should be made in particular to the judgment of Browne-Wilkinson J in *Woods v WM Car Services Ltd* (1981). Examples where conduct by the employer has been held to be in breach of this implied term are: *British Aircraft Corporation Ltd v Austin* (1978) (failing to investigate a justified health and safety complaint); *BBC v Beckett* (1983) (unjustifiable demotion for a minor disciplinary offence); *TSB Bank plc v Harris* (2000) (misleading reference); *Wigan BC v Davies* (1979) (failure to protect the employee from harassment by other employees). In addition, in *Woods v WM Car Services Ltd* (above) it was held that it is possible for a series of incidents over a period of time to amount to a breach. (See *Rossiter v Pendragon plc* (2002) (Chapter 12) for an unsuccessful attempt to claim constructive dismissal in connection with transfer of an undertaking.)

There may also be a breach by the employer of an express term of the contract giving rise to a claim for constructive dismissal. Obvious examples are a failure to pay wages and a unilateral decision by the employer to change the employee's place of work.

There are, however, two points to bear in mind which may act against the success of a constructive dismissal claim:

1. As the matter is essentially one of contract, the claim cannot succeed if the employer was allowed under the contract to do what was done. For example, where the contract contains a mobility clause then it will not be a breach to require the employee to move. However, even here it may be that this power is exercised in such a way as to breach the implied duty of trust and confidence and thus amount to a breach. Thus in *United Bank Ltd v Akhtar* (1989) it was held that the giving of very short notice of a move could be a breach (see also Chapter 5).
2. Where the employee does not resign or at least complain in strong terms soon after a breach by the employer then it is likely to be held that he/she has accepted the breach and so cannot complain in respect of it.

A final and very important point is that even though the court may find that the employer has been guilty of a breach it may also find, in accordance with the general law on unfair dismissal, that the employer acted reasonably under s.98(4) (below). One example is that a unilateral change in contract terms may be held to be justified under the 'some other substantial reason ground' (see below).

Before considering the question of the actual fairness of the dismissal, two other points should be noted:

1. Can it be said that the employee has dismissed himself/herself by his/her conduct and as a result there is no dismissal at all by the employer? This was suggested by Denning MR in *London Transport Executive v Clarke* (1981), where a bus driver took seven weeks' absence from work without permission.

Although the employee knew that this conduct would result in his being dismissed, the majority of the Court of Appeal held that it was still open to the employer to elect whether to treat the contract as continuing or to repudiate it. The result of applying this elective theory of contract termination is that the courts and tribunals are not debarred in advance of considering the merits of a claim, even though, as here, it was bound to fail.

2. The employee cannot agree in advance not to claim for unfair dismissal. Section 203(1) of the ERA renders void any agreement 'to exclude or limit the operation of any provision of any part of this Act' and this has been held to include cases where the employee agrees in advance that he/she will be taken to have resigned in particular circumstances. A good example is *Igbo v Johnson Matthey Chemicals Ltd* (1986), where the employee signed an agreement that if she did not return from holiday by a stated date then her employment contract would be deemed to be automatically terminated. This was held to be void under s.203(1), because what was in essence an agreement for self-dismissal was clearly an attempt to exclude the unfair dismissal provisions of the Act.

## Was the dismissal for a reason that is potentially fair?

Once it has been established that the employee was dismissed, the claim moves on to two more stages:

1. The employer must show what the reason for the dismissal was.
2. The tribunal must be satisfied that the employer acted reasonably in treating *that* reason as a sufficient reason for dismissing the employee (see s.98(4) (below)).

A distinction is therefore drawn between the *reason* (in 1 above) and *reasonableness* (in 2 above). It is for the employer to show the reason but the tribunal decides reasonableness. Therefore, in 1 the burden of proof is on the employer and he/she must begin by bringing evidence to show the reason, whereas in 2 the burden of proof is said to be neutral in that neither side has to prove or disprove reasonableness and instead the tribunal decides.

## The reason for the dismissal

The employer does not have a free choice in deciding which reasons to bring forward in support of his/her contention that the dismissal is fair. Instead, s.98(1) and (2) of the ERA provide a list of five reasons which are 'potentially fair'. This means that if the employer fails to show that the dismissal was for any of these reasons, then the employee's claim for unfair dismissal will succeed without the tribunal having to consider the issue of reasonableness at all. Furthermore, it may be that the reason for the dismissal was one which statute provides is automatically unfair, as explained above, in which case there will automatically be a finding of unfair dismissal. If, however, the employer shows that the dismissal was for one or more of those reasons then the action moves on to the question of reasonableness. Thus no reason for dismissal can be considered automatically fair, and therefore justified, in advance.

There are therefore three possibilities:

1. If the employer fails to show that the reason was one of the potentially fair reasons, the employee's claim will normally succeed.
2. If the reason was one which is automatically unfair, the employee's claim will automatically succeed.
3. If the employer shows that the reason was for one of the potentially fair reasons, the action continues to the reasonableness stage.

The five potentially fair reasons set out in s.98(2) of the ERA are widely drawn and in most instances an employer will have no difficulty in showing that the dismissal was for one or more of them. There is, however, an additional requirement that they must be substantial and thus a trivial instance would not be enough. They are as follows:

1. A reason relating to the capability or qualifications of the employee for performing work of the kind he/she was employed to do.
2. A reason related to the employee's conduct.
3. The employee was redundant.
4. The employee could not continue to work in the position he/she holds without breaking a statutory provision.
5. Some other substantial reason of a kind justifying dismissal.

These will be dealt with below.

It is also relevant to mention that under s.92 the employee is entitled to be provided on demand with a written statement of the reasons for dismissal and, if this is not given within 14 days, the employee is entitled, on complaint to a tribunal, to be awarded an extra two weeks' pay. The significance here is that once the employer has stated the reason in writing then this is admissible in evidence at any hearing and, although the employer is at liberty to give a different reason later, it will be necessary to explain why there was a change. In *Abernethy v Mott, Hay and Anderson* (1974) Cairns LJ gave some examples of where a tribunal might accept a different reason from that given at the time, such as where a different reason is given out of kindness, or where the employer misdescribes the reason so that although in reality it falls within the five reasons set out above, it did not appear at first to do so and as a result it is later clarified. A more robust approach was taken in *Hotson v Wisbech Conservative Club* (1984), where the reason given in the employer's notice of appearance to the tribunal was that the employee was inefficient but it became clear at the hearing that it was because the employee was suspected of dishonesty. It was held to be unfair to dismiss for a reason which was not the real reason.

These reasons will be examined in detail later but we will first examine the relationship between these reasons and the question of reasonableness.

## Was the dismissal reasonable?

This is the heart of the law on unfair dismissal and it is contained in s.98(4) of the ERA 1996 in words which should be very carefully noted by anyone connected with employment law:

> the determination of the question whether the dismissal is fair or unfair (having regard to the reason shown by the employer) –
>
> (a) depends on whether on the circumstances (including the size and administrative resources of the employer's undertaking) the employer acted reasonably or unreasonably in treating it as a sufficient reason for dismissing the employee, and
>
> (b) shall be determined in accordance with equity and the substantial merits of the case.

The following points arise.

### Facts discovered afterwards cannot be relied on

It is the reason shown by the employer when dismissing which is considered and it is not possible for the employer to rely on facts discovered afterwards to justify the fairness of the dismissal. This was established by the House of Lords in *W Devis and Sons Ltd v Atkins* (1977), in contrast to the position in a wrongful dismissal claim, where facts discovered afterwards can be relied on.

### Example

Joan is dismissed on suspicion of pilfering from the shop where she works. After she was dismissed, proof comes that she was indeed pilfering. This cannot be used to justify the fairness of the dismissal, although it may well be relevant to the amount of compensation that Joan will receive. If Joan had brought a claim for wrongful dismissal then the employer would have been able to rely on the facts discovered afterwards as a defence to her claim.

### Did the employer act reasonably?

The issue is whether the employer acted reasonably and not injustice suffered by the employee. This means that the focus is on the conduct of the employer and is why correct procedures are so important. The genesis of the emphasis on procedure can be traced to early cases such as *Earl v Slater and Wheeler (Airlyne) Ltd* (1973). The employee was off sick and when he was away it was discovered that he seemed not to be carrying out his work satisfactorily. When he returned he was handed a letter of dismissal but he had no opportunity to answer the allegations. The tribunal held that the dismissal was fair, as the allegations appeared to be true and so no injury had been done to him. Donaldson P held that this was not the point: 'Good industrial relations depend on management not only acting fairly but being manifestly seen to act fairly.' Here in a nutshell is the present law.

This branch of the law has not, however, had a straightforward passage. In *British Labour Pump Co. Ltd v Byrne* (1979) it was held that in spite of the failure by an employer to use the proper procedures, the dismissal would still be fair if it could be proved on a balance of probabilities that, even if they had been properly followed, the employee would still have been dismissed. This decision was mush criticised for allowing the employer the benefit of hindsight and the House of Lords in *Polkey v AE Dayton Services Ltd* (1988) overruled it. Here the employee was made redundant without warning and the tribunal held that his claim for unfair dismissal failed, as it could not be shown that consultation would have made any difference. The House of Lords held that this was the wrong approach and instead the question should be whether the employer acted reasonably in deciding not to issue any warning. Mackay LC emphasised that a failure to follow the procedure laid down need not make a dismissal unfair provided that a decision not to follow a particular aspect of the procedure (for example to consult the employee) was a reasonable one. He envisaged circumstances where a failure might not be unfair, such as when failure to consult was caused by an impending redundancy situation. On the other hand, it is difficult to see how the failure in the *Earl* case (above) could ever be considered fair.

The *Polkey* test has been such a feature of employment law that one might naively have imagined that it was impregnable. However, its effect will be severely limited by the provisions of the Employment Act 2002. Sections 29–34, which are due to come into force in 2003, lay down statutory dismissal and disciplinary procedures (DDPs) and statutory grievance procedures (GPs). These will become implied terms of all contracts of employment and provide, in particular, a shortened disciplinary and dismissal procedure. These procedures will be an irreducible minimum, and a new s.98A of the ERA provides that a dismissal in breach of them will automatically be unfair, although the Secretary of State is given power to grant exemptions from some of the requirements of the statutory procedures in certain circumstances. The details of the procedures will be considered later in this chapter but what is significant here is that, provided that the employer has complied with the DDP, the *Polkey* test will not apply. Instead, the *British Labour Pump* test is effectively resurrected and the new s.98A provides that failure to follow the procedures laid down can be ignored if to have followed them would not have affected the outcome.

The reason for this change is that the government felt that tribunals have been concentrating too much on the minutiae of procedures and not enough on the merits of the case. It has also pointed out that many firms do not have internal disputes procedures and these changes will at least ensure that all employees will have certain basic procedural safeguards in their contracts. One reason for the change must be the rise in the number of unfair dismissal applications, rising from 41,914 in 1998/99 to 49,401 in 2000/01. All governments are concerned about costs and it must be hoped that these changes do not sacrifice justice on the altar of budgets.

### Tribunal must not act as an appeal court

The tribunal is not to act as an appeal court in deciding whether the reason for the dismissal was a fair one. Instead, the 'range of reasonable responses test' applies. This was expressed by Browne-Wilkinson P in *Iceland Frozen Foods Ltd v Jones* (1982) as the tribunal having to start from the words of the statute (now s.98(4)) and 'in many (though not all) cases there is a band of reasonable responses to the employer's conduct within which one employer might reasonably take one view, another quite reasonably take another'.

### Example

Joanne is dismissed because she has been late for work on a number of occasions. Joanne states that this is because she has a young child to look after who is often ill. After considering the matter carefully, the tribunal decides that, although many employers would have given a final warning, dismissal is not outside the band of responses which a reasonable employer might make as a result of her actions. Thus the dismissal is for a fair reason.

(It must, however, be emphasised that the reasons are only one aspect and the questions of procedure must also be considered, as in the flow chart on pp.194–195 above.)

This test was criticised as allowing a decision to dismiss to be fair even though it may have been at the very edge of fairness. In *Haddon v Van der Bergh Foods Ltd* (1999) the test was swept aside by the EAT, which felt that, instead, the words of the statute were enough in themselves and that a gloss such as this test was wrong. This phase did not last long and in *Post Office v Foley* (2000) the band of reasonable responses test was restored. Even so, this test remains subject to criticism in that it allows a dismissal to be fair for being within the band of reasonable responses, whereas under the law of wrongful dismissal it might not be held to be a breach of contract. The other criticism is that it arguably allows the reason for a dismissal to stand unless it was perverse in the sense that no reasonable employer would have decided to dismiss for that reason. The concept of only allowing a decision to be questioned unless it is perverse arises in public law, where the actions of bodies such as local authorities can be challenged in this way. However, these are bodies entrusted by statute with a good deal of discretion and so the concept of only allowing perverse decisions to be challenged makes sense. Here we are dealing with a dispute between individuals, where it is suggested that different considerations should apply.

### Procedural considerations

Given that under s.98(4) of the ERA 1996 any decision to dismiss must be reasonable, how has this been applied? The starting point is the ACAS Code of Practice on Disciplinary and Grievance Procedures, reissued in September 2000. This does not take the place of a disciplinary or grievance procedure but recommends what should be contained in one. Although it does not have legal force, s.207 of TULRCA 1992 provides that it is admissible in legal proceedings and any relevant parts shall be taken into account. In effect, any departure from its provisions will have to be justified. However, where there is a DDP or GP under the Employment Act 2002 (see above) then the employer has to observe the following procedures otherwise a dismissal is automatically unfair:

## DDP

The procedure to be followed is:

- a statement of the grounds for the action which has led the employer to consider disciplinary action or dismissal which must be sent to the employee;
- a meeting which must take place before action is taken, although there will doubtless be provision for where the employee does not attend;
- a right of appeal;
- where the employer wishes to dismiss for extreme cases of gross misconduct, the procedure is shortened so that the employer can dismiss and send out the reasons to the employee, who has a right of appeal. There is no requirement of a meeting.

There is no indication in the Act of how the employer is expected to decide which procedure to use. Although guidance will be given in Regulations, employers will be well advised to use the standard procedure rather than the shorter procedure in all but the most obvious cases of gross misconduct.

The employer is not to regard this is as the only procedure: the rest of the procedural requirements (see below) remain but, as explained above, they are downgraded so that a failure to follow them can be justified if it would have made no difference to the outcome.

## GP

The procedure follows the same pattern except that the employee takes the initiative with a statement of the grievance which is followed by a meeting and an appeal if necessary. Where the grievance is raised by a former employee then there is no requirement for a meeting and instead the employer must respond in writing.

The significance of GPs is that Regulations will be made under which employees will be debarred from bringing certain types of claim unless the subject has first been raised with the employer in a grievance procedure. An obvious example is a constructive dismissal claim.

These new provisions should be considered alongside the ACAS scheme for voluntary arbitration (see Chapter 1) as a further means of encouraging the settlement of unfair dismissal claims without recourse to tribunals. It will be interesting to see what effect they have on the figures for dismissal applications to tribunals.

### The ACAS Code

The ACAS Code itself provides that disciplinary procedures should not be viewed as a means of imposing sanctions but as a means of helping and encouraging improvement amongst workers whose performance is unsatisfactory (para. 8). The main features are as follows:

*Oral and written warnings*

Oral warnings are appropriate for minor offences but for more serious matters a formal written warning should be given. This should set out the nature of the offence and state that a final written warning will be considered if there is no 'satisfactory sustained improvement or change' (para. 15). A note of oral warnings should be kept, but paragraph 15 suggests that they should be disregarded after six months. A warning given for one offence should not normally be used in a disciplinary procedure in relation to another offence, although there may come a point where different warnings can be taken together, as in *Auguste Noel v Curtis* (1990). Here a number of warnings for different offences could be said to be part of an overall pattern of misconduct. The need to be careful about when warnings were given and when they expire was illustrated in *Bevan Ashford v Malin* (1995). A final written warning was given, to last 12 months, but the employee was dismissed for a similar act on the very day *after* the warning had expired. The dismissal was held unfair.

*Disciplinary proceedings*

Where disciplinary proceedings are needed then the Code recommends that suspension without pay should be considered (para. 15). Commission of a criminal offence outside work is not suggested as an automatic reason for dismissal and the issue is whether it makes the employee unsuitable for the work.

*Worker's companion*

At a disciplinary hearing at which a penalty could be imposed or confirmed, the worker should have the opportunity to be accompanied by a 'worker's companion'. This is a statutory right contained in ss.10–15 of the Employment Relations Act 1999. Under it, a worker may request to be accompanied by a fellow worker, a union official employed by the employer or by a union official who has been certified by the union as having received training in acting as a worker's companion. The companion may address the hearing and confer with the worker during it but will not be able to answer questions on behalf of the worker.

*Proportionality of penalty*

Any penalty imposed should be proportionate to the nature of the offence, the degree of wilfulness and the position of the employee, including seniority. The final step should be dismissal, disciplinary transfer or demotion (paras. 15–18).

## The fairness of the dismissal

The fair reasons were set out briefly on p.200 and are in s.98(2) of the ERA, they are any of the following, although it is emphasised that they must be, according to s.98, substantial ones. The application of them is very much a matter of practice and not strict precedents.

### Capability or qualifications

'Capability' is stated by s.98(3) of the ERA to be assessed by reference to 'skill, aptitude, health or any other mental or physical quality'. The most common instance under this head is ill-health. In *East Lindsey DC v Daubney* (1977) it was held that consultation with the employee should be the first step and cases have emphasised that the employer should weigh the needs of the business for the employee's job to be done against the expected time when the employee is likely to be away and the prospect of a full recovery. The doctrine of frustration is relevant in that where there is no prospect of a recovery at all then the contract is frustrated and automatically ends, with no issue as to the fairness of the dismissal. Where the issue is incompetence and the employee was dismissed for not being able to do the job then the question of what training was given is vital. In *Davison v Kent Motors* (1975) dismissal for assembling 471 out of 500 components in the wrong order was unfair as there was no evidence that training had been given in how to assemble them correctly. 'Qualifications' is defined by s.9 as refering to academic, technical or professional qualifications and dismissal could be fair where an employee is required to obtain certain qualifications but does not do so. Even so, the question of reasonableness is relevant because the employee may argue that he/she was not given time off work to enable him/her to study for the relevant qualifications.

### Conduct

The ACAS Code gives examples of where an employee may be dismissed for gross misconduct including (para. 7) theft, fraud, violence at work, harassment, serious negligence or breach of confidence and deliberate damage to property. In *BHS v Burchall* (1978) it was held that an employer should first show that he/she honestly and on reasonable grounds believed that the employee had committed the offence and that at that stage he/she had carried out as full an investigation as was reasonable. The employer is not bound to wait for the outcome of a criminal trial before dismissing, although it is common practice to wait until then and suspend beforehand. It has been pointed out that the *Burchall* test can lead to confusion, as the burden of proof states that the employer must show a reasonable belief in the guilt of the employee. In *Boys and Girls Welfare Society v McDonald* (1996) it was emphasised that the application of this test did not alter the statutory rule that the burden of proof rests neither with the employer nor the employee but is neutral. What is the position where the employer is not certain which of the members of a group were guilty of dishonesty? Can they all be dismissed? In *Whitbread & Co. v Thomas* (1988) the EAT held that, provided the act would justify dismissal if committed by one employee, then dismissal of the whole group can be fair so long as a proper investigation has been made to try to identify who was individually responsible and that the act was committed by one or more members of the group.

## Redundancy

See Chapter 12.

## Continued employment would be a breach of the law

Examples where the employee could not work in his/her position without contravention of a legislative provision have been few. However, an obvious example would be where an employee who is employed to drive a vehicle is disqualified and there is no alternative work.

## Some other substantial reason (SOSR)

This category of potentially fair reasons for dismissal is a residual one which can include any reason not included in the other four specific reasons. It has been used in cases involving reorganisations (see Chapter 12) and other aspects are considered here.

In *RS Components v Irwin* (1974) Sir John Brightman explained the rationale as follows:

> Parliament may well have intended to set out ... the common reasons for a dismissal but can have hardly have hoped to produce an exact catalogue of all the circumstances in which a company would be justified in terminating the services of an employee.

Furthermore, he held that this head is to be considered as an independent head of dismissal and is not to be confined to reasons which are *ejusdem generis* (i.e. of a similar kind) to the specific reasons.

There are, in effect, two issues to consider when deciding if a dismissal is fair under this ground although clearly these are interrelated:

1. Was the reason a substantial one? In *Harper v National Coal Board* (1980) Lord McDonald said that what he called 'a whimsical or capricious reason which no person of ordinary sense would entertain' would not be substantial.
2. Did the employer have a genuine belief that the reason was substantial? In *Harper* Lord McDonald said that one factor would be whether 'most employers would be expected to adopt' the view that the reason was a substantial one.

In practice, a number of decisions on SOSR have had the effect of widening the powers of employers to dismiss. Some of these are dealt with in Chapter 12, which looks at dismissals on reorganisations, and this includes *RS Components v Irwin* (above). The operation of SOSR has been criticised (by J. Bowers and A. Clarke in (1981) 10 ILJ 34) who feel that: 'Other substantial reason could not fail to be a wide categorisation but that it would provide so wide a ragbag of gateways to fair dismissal surely could not have been foreseen, nor that so few employers would fail to prove that their reason was substantial.' They suggest that a more extensive definition of reasons could mean that the need for SOSR disappeared. However, this suggestion was made in 1981 and SOSR is still with us.

The following are the main types of situations where SOSR has been held to be a potentially fair reason for dismissal:

*Refusal by an employee to agree to changes in the contract of employment*

See Chapter 12.

*Dismissals arising out of reorganisation falling short of redundancy*

See Chapter 12.

*Personality differences between the dismissed employee and other employees*

In *Treganowan v Robert Knee & Co. Ltd* (1975) the working atmosphere in an office had become intolerable due to a difference of opinion between Treganowan and other employees about the merits of the permissive society. This was affecting the company's business and it was held that the dismissal of Treganowan was for SOSR. However, in *Turner v Vestric Ltd* (1981) it was held that an employer should make every effort to improve the working relationship before considering dismissal.

*Dismissal because of pressure from a third party*

The third party might, for example, be a major customer. The justification put forward by the employer will be that the business would be affected if the customer withdrew their custom and therefore there was no alternative to dismissing the employee. However, in *Dobie v Burns International Security Services (UK) Ltd* (1984), the Court of Appeal held that an employer must also take into account injustice to the employee, looking at, for example, the length of service of the employee and the employee's record.

*Dismissal of a temporary employee where it was made clear that the employment was temporary*

This may be the explanation of *Priddle v Dibble* (1978), where the applicant, a farm worker, was dismissed to make way for his employer's son. The dismissal was held fair. Bristow J found that the applicant had known that the son would be likely to work on the farm and it was 'natural and reasonable for a farmer to want to employ his son'. One could add that this is not in doubt, but, with respect, it should not be seen as a justification for dismissal. A decision of this kind could be seen as supporting the argument of Bowers and Clarke (above) that this head of dismissal should be reconsidered.

## ■ Automatically unfair reasons for dismissal

In the following cases the dismissal is automatically unfair and so there is no room for the test of reasonableness. However, it is for the employee to establish that the reason fell within these grounds:

- Reasons related to trade union membership or activities (see Chapter 13).
- Reasons related to the assertion of a statutory right (s.104 of the ERA), e.g. where the employee has asserted any right in the ERA, the Working Time Directive and the right to minimum notice of termination of employment.
- Where the employee has taken leave for family reasons (see Chapter 10).
- Reasons related to health and safety, e.g. where the employee was carrying out duties as a health and safety representative or a member of a health and safety committee (see Chapter 8).
- Refusing to work on Sundays (s.35(5) and (6) of the ERA 1996).
- Making a protected disclosure under the Public Interest Disclosure Act 1998 (see Chapter 5).
- Taking part in protected industrial action (see Chapter 14).
- Dismissal in connection with the transfer of the undertaking (see Chapter 12).
- For spent convictions (Rehabilitation of Offenders Act 1974).
- For carrying out the functions of pension fund trustees (s.102 of the ERA).
- For carrying out the functions of employee representatives in relation to redundancy or transfers of undertakings (see Chapter 12).
- Where the employer had failed to follow the DDP in dismissing an employee (Employment Act 2002).

### Time limits for bringing a claim

Section 111 of the ERA 1996 provides that claims for unfair dismissal must be brought within three months of the effective date of termination of the contract but there is power to extend this where the tribunal considers that it was not reasonably practicable for the complaint to be presented in that time. In addition, s.33 of the Employment Act 2002 allows the Secretary of State to make Regulations which will allow the time limit to be extended where one of the statutory procedures (Disciplinary and Dismissal Procedures or Grievance Procedure) has been followed. The object is to make the use of such procedures more attractive.

## ◼ Remedies for unfair dismissal

There are three:

1. Compensation.
2. Re-engagement.
3. Reinstatement.

Remedies 2 and 3 are often known together as re-employment.

Compensation is the remedy sought in nearly all cases. In 2000/01 the number of cases where re-employment was ordered was 15 out of 11,565 cases proceeding to a hearing. Of these 6,712 were dismissed and compensation was awarded in 1,993. However, when the law of unfair dismissal was introduced in 1972, re-employment was intended to be the primary remedy. This has not been the case because employees generally do not wish to go back to a firm where they have been badly treated and in any case tribunals are often reluctant to make an order.

## Re-employment orders

The orders are made under ss.114 and 115 of the ERA and the effect of a reinstatement order is that the complainant must be treated as if he had never been dismissed. Back pay must be made for the period when he was not employed and in all respects he must be treated as if the dismissal had never taken place. Re-engagement involves being re-employed in a job which is comparable to the previous one. The award is discretionary and it is only made if the tribunal is satisfied not only that it would be practicable for the employer to comply but also that it would be just. Thus re-employment has not been ordered where the parties were in a close personal relationship which has broken down (see *Enessy v Minoprio* (1978)).

An employer cannot be compelled to comply with an order for re-employment: instead, an order can be made that he/she is ordered to pay an additional award to the complainant equivalent to between 26 and 52 weeks' pay in addition to the basic and compensatory award.

## Compensation

This consists of the following:

### A basic award

This is calculated on the same basis as redundancy compensation (see Chapter 12) and is awarded for loss of accrued continuity of employment rights consequent on the dismissal. The current maximum is £7,000. It is reduced by the amount of any redundancy payment received but where the employee is dismissed in circumstances that he/she does not qualify for a redundancy payment then two weeks' basic pay is payable. There is a minimum amount of £3,400 where the employee is dismissed through trade union membership or activities. It may be reduced where the employee has contributed by his/her conduct to the dismissed and this may be so even where the misconduct is only discovered *after* the dismissal. It will be recalled that in *Devis v Atkins* (1977) it was held that misconduct discovered after the dismissal could not affect the decision on whether the dismissal was fair but it can be taken into account here and it may be that the employee receives nothing.

### Example

John is dismissed for suspected pilfering at work. The tribunal finds that at the time of the dismissal this was not fair on the evidence available. However, ten minutes after the dismissal, proof comes to light that John was indeed guilty. Although John's dismissal was held unfair he may well not receive any compensation under either the basic award or the compensatory award (below).

### Compensatory award

The current maximum is £52,600, and by s.123(1) of the ERA it must be such an amount as the tribunal considers 'just and equitable having regard to the loss sustained by the complainant in so far as that loss is attributable to action taken by the employer'.

The heads of loss were set out in *Norton Tool Co. v Tewson* (1973) as follows:

## Immediate loss of wages up to the time of the tribunal hearing

This includes net wages and overtime if worked regularly, together with bonus payments and tips. It is therefore a wider calculation than is made for damages for wrongful dismissal. Earnings from another job which the employee has now obtained can be deducted as well as social security benefits.

## Manner of dismissal

An award will only be made under this head if the manner of dismissal made it more difficult to find another job.

## Future loss of earnings

These will be awarded on the basis of the difference in wages between the job from which the employee was dismissed and any new job already obtained. If the employee is still out of work then the tribunal must have some evidence based on the labour market and local conditions taking into account the employee's age and state of health.

## Loss of future employment protection rights

The employee has lost any continuity of employment. As this is also compensated in the basic award, a sum of £100 is normally awarded here.

## Loss of pension rights

This head was added subsequently.

As stated earlier, the award can be reduced to take account of the employee's conduct.

Under the new provisions in the Employment Act 2002, compensation will be *increased* by 10–50% where an employer unreasonably fails to follow the DDP or GP set out in the Act. Where the failure to follow it is the fault of the employee then the award may be *reduced* by the same figure.

# Chapter 12

# Termination of employment (II): dismissal for economic reasons

## INTRODUCTION

This chapter looks at dismissals where the reason for the dismissal is, broadly speaking, not a personal one connected with the employee *per se* but results from the ending of the employee's job, the reorganisation of the business, or the transfer of the business to another employer. These three reasons correspond, in general terms, to the three areas that will be examined in this chapter. However, the principles of the law on unfair dismissal which were outlined in Chapter 11 are also relevant and will be referred to extensively here.

## REDUNDANCY

### ■ Social significance of redundancy

Each year over 200,000 people are made redundant. The latest full survey (*Labour Market Trends* June 2001, pp.315–321) showed that the total number of redundancies remained roughly constant between spring 1995 and spring 2000, with 181,000 redundancies in spring 1995 compared with 180,000 in the similar period in spring 2000. In the spring of 2000, half of redundancies were due to staff cutbacks with the business still continuing and 32% were due to the business actually closing down. In each spring quarter since 1995 the survey showed that about two-thirds of those made redundant were men. This may be due to the fact that the highest incidence of redundancy is amongst workers in male dominated industries: manufacturing and construction. Over half of all those made redundant were aged between 25 and 49, with those aged 50 and over making up about a quarter. A final point of interest is that in spring 2000, 46% of workers received redundancy pay and of these 42% also received pay in lieu of notice. Another 15% of those made redundant received pay in lieu of notice but no redundancy payment, and a third received no payment at all, presumably because they did not qualify for one. We will consider the significance of these statistics later in this chapter.

## Purpose of redundancy legislation

The core idea of redundancy is, as P. Davies and M. Freedland put it (*Labour Legislation and Public Policy* (Oxford, 1993), pp.145–146), that 'the employer had ceased to have a business need for the job that the employee in question had being doing and had accordingly decided to dismiss the employee'. The original legislation was the Redundancy Payments Act 1965, but the law is now contained in Part XI of the Employment Rights Act 1996.

The Redundancy Payments Act 1965 has been described as 'crossing the Rubicon as far as employment protection legislation was concerned' (P. Davies and M. Freedland, *Labour Law Text and Materials* (2nd edition 1984), p.528). The reason is that this was the first piece of statutory regulation of the employment relationship itself. Previous legislation, as we have seen, tinkered with the edges of the contract of employment (see Chapter 4), whereas in the 1965 Act, for the first time, Parliament enacted a comprehensive code dealing with a particular area. It has never been clear whether Parliament meant this to be the forerunner of the flood of statutory regulation which then followed, marking the end of 'voluntarism', or whether it was seen simply as a response to a particular problem.

The answer may well be the latter. It was felt in the early 1960s that industrial change needed to happen more rapidly and that one way of doing this was to encourage greater labour mobility. There were already voluntary schemes in existence whereby workers who had been made redundant were given lump sum payments but these were not especially generous, nor did they cover many workers. Accordingly, the Redundancy Payments Act made it a statutory requirement to make these payments. What then happened was doubtless unforeseen at the time. In 1971 Parliament passed the Industrial Relations Act, which gave a statutory right to protection from unfair dismissal and, ever since, the redundancy payments legislation has been a poor relation of it mainly because the compensation levels are so much greater with unfair dismissal. This is particularly so at present, with the maximum compensation for unfair dismissal standing at £52,600, whereas that for redundancy is £7,500. Accordingly – and this is of crucial importance in appreciating the relationship between different areas of law here – an employee will prefer to argue, if possible, that he has been unfairly dismissed, whereas an employer will argue instead that the employee has been made redundant. A good recent example is *High Table Ltd v Horst* (1997), discussed below. When considering the cases, one needs to distinguish between those decided in the golden age of redundancy payments legislation from 1965 to 1971, when it held the field unchallenged and was the only means of dismissed employees gaining any statutory compensation, and those decided after the coming into force of the Industrial Relations Act 1971 when it became, and has remained, a decided second best to unfair dismissal.

Redundancy payments legislation has been described by a leading authority (C. Grunfeld, *The Law of Redundancy*, 3rd edition (London: Sweet & Maxwell, 1989) p.3) as having 'helped, in some degree . . . to enable British industry and commerce to take on the growing international competition'. Be that as it may, the Act was strongly criticised by R. Fryer ('The Myths of the Redundancy Payments Act 1973' (1973) 2 ILJ 1) as having perpetuated several myths adding up to the belief that the Act 'has done something, even too much, to redress the gross imbalance between capital and labour'. In Fryer's view, the Act did not, in spite of a 'myth' to the contrary, restrict managerial discretion.

One point stressed by both Grunfeld and Fryer is that the Act did not confer any kind of job security. It simply gives compensation for loss of a job through redundancy. The purpose of the Act was described by Denning MR in *Lloyds v Brassey* (1969) as 'in a real sense compensation for long service'. He also stressed that: 'It is not unemployment pay. Repeat "not". Even if he gets another job straightaway he is nevertheless entitled to redundancy pay.'

## Impact of European Union law

The main impact of EU law has been in the area of redundancy consultation procedures and not on the substantive law of redundancy.

## Role of the courts

In *Moon v Homeworthy Furniture (Northern) Ltd* (1977) the EAT decisively rejected an attempt to make the courts the arbiters of whether a redundancy was justified. A factory had been closed down and the whole workforce was made redundant. The employees argued that the employer's contention that the factory was not economically viable was wrong. The EAT held that, provided there was a cessation of work, which there was here, the court could not investigate whether this could have been avoided. As Kilner-Brown put it: 'The employees were and are seeking to use the industrial tribunal and the EAT as a platform for the ventilation of an industrial dispute.' One can see this attitude as an example of the unwillingness of the courts to interfere in matters considered to be within the scope of managerial prerogative, a point to which we shall return in the discussion of dismissals resulting from a reorganisation (see later in this chapter). It has been suggested in K. Ewing (ed.), *Working Life* (London: Lawrence & Wishart, 1996), p.298, that a court should be able to refer the question of whether a redundancy was necessary to a Labour Inspector. However, as things stand at present, the role of the courts is confined to dealing with whether a factual situation actually constitutes redundancy.

## ▤ Summary

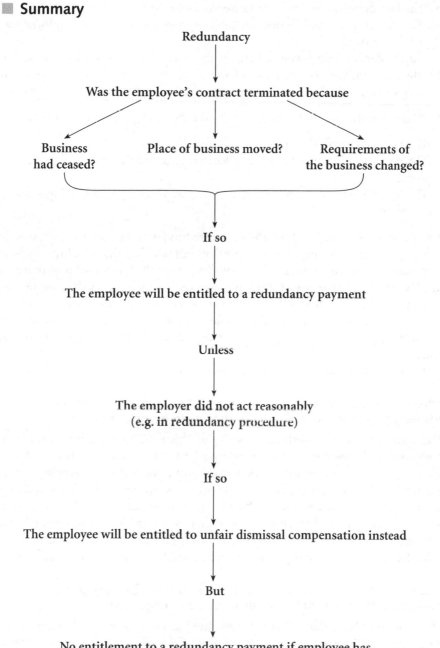

Redundancy

↓

Was the employee's contract terminated because

Business had ceased?     Place of business moved?     Requirements of the business changed?

If so

↓

The employee will be entitled to a redundancy payment

↓

Unless

↓

The employer did not act reasonably
(e.g. in redundancy procedure)

↓

If so

↓

The employee will be entitled to unfair dismissal compensation instead

↓

But

↓

No entitlement to a redundancy payment if employee has
unreasonably refused an offer of suitable alternative employment

## ▤ Definition of redundancy

Redundancy is defined in s.139 of the ERA 1996 as where a dismissal is wholly or mainly attributable to:

(a) the fact that the employer has ceased or intends to cease:
  (i) to carry on the business for the purposes for which the employee was employed,
  (ii) to carry on the business in the place where the employee was employed,
(b) the fact that the requirements of the business for employees to carry out work of a particular kind have ceased or diminished or are expected to.

It will be seen that the Act envisages redundancy occurring in three situations:

1. The business closes down.
2. The business continues but the employee is required to move his/her place of work.
3. The business continues but the need for work done by that employee ceases or diminishes.

It must be emphasised that, in all cases of redundancy, the issue is not, strictly speaking, whether an employee is redundant but whether that employee's *post* is redundant. The focus is not on the employee personally but on the post that that employee holds. Furthermore, this emphasis on the post rather than the person reminds us that a redundancy situation must not be used as a cover to get rid of an employee whom the employer wants to be rid of for other reasons, for example allegations of misconduct. The way to deal with this is by a dismissal procedure.

We will look at each of these situations in turn.

### Where the employer has ceased or intends to cease to carry on the business for the purposes for which the employee was employed

The term 'business' is defined by s.235 of the ERA as including a trade or profession and any activity carried on by a body of persons whether corporate or incorporate. The only other point worthy of note is that the employer does not have to be the actual owner of the business. In *Thomas v Jones* (1978) a sub-postmistress retired and, as a result, the post office which she ran closed. An employee who had worked in the post office was held to be entitled to a redundancy payment because the actual business of running that particular post office had ceased even though the post office itself, of course, still continued.

### Where the employer has ceased or intends to cease to carry on the business in the place where the employee was employed

The situation here is that either the entire business has moved or that there is no longer any need for the employee's services at the place where he/she worked. The courts originally evolved a contractual test for deciding this but now what can be called a 'geographical test' holds sway.

#### The contractual test

This asked whether an employee could be contractually bound to move his place of work. Therefore, if there was an express term in the employee's contract that, for example, an employee could be required to work anywhere in the United Kingdom, then an employee who worked in London could not claim a redundancy payment if his/her place of work was moved to Manchester. (Note, however, that the employer must act reasonably when requiring the employee to move: see *United Bank v Akhtar* (1989).) Suppose that there was no express mobility clause. In that case the courts would ask whether a term could be implied into the employee's contract that, for example, the employee should be employed within daily travelling distance of home. If so, and employees were being required to travel beyond this, then they would be entitled to refuse to do so and claim a redundancy payment. Conversely, if the distance was within daily travelling, then, if they refused, they would themselves be in breach of contract. In *O'Brien v Associated Fire Alarms* (1968) employees who were employed in Liverpool were required to work in Barrow, about 150 miles away. The Court of Appeal held that they were redundant, as Barrow was clearly not within daily travelling distance of their homes. This approach was confirmed in *Coutaulds Northern Spinning Ltd v Sibson* (1988), where the Court of Appeal, in a case involving a claim for constructive dismissal (see Chapter 11), upheld the decision in *O'Brien* and rejected an attempt by the industrial tribunal to impose a requirement that a request to the employee to move must be reasonable.

### The geographical test

This looks at where the employee actually works rather than at where he/she could be required to work under a mobility clause. This approach was first applied in *Bass Leisure Ltd v Thomas* (1994). The applicant worked at a depot in Coventry and her employer, in accordance with a term in her contract, required her to work at another depot 20 miles away. She did not wish to do so. The EAT held that she was entitled to a redundancy payment as her actual place of work could not include a depot 20 miles away. The Court of Appeal approved this approach in *High Table Ltd v Horst* (1997). The respondent was employed as a waitress by the appellant, which provided waitress services for a number of firms in the City of London. Her letter of appointment specified that she was appointed as a waitress to a particular firm but after five years, cuts in the budget of that firm meant that she was no longer needed there. The appellant's staff handbook, which formed part of the respondent's contract of employment, gave the appellant the right to move the respondent to another location, which would, wherever possible, be within daily travelling distance of work. The court held that the respondent was redundant. Peter Gibson J held that the contract of employment cannot be 'the sole determinant' of where the employee's place of work is and the question of where the employee works 'is one to be answered primarily by a consideration of the factual circumstances which obtained until the dismissal'. There is a slight difference in approach between this decision and that in *Bass Leisure*, which appeared to reject any reliance at all on a mobility clause. Here the Court of Appeal simply relegated such a clause to *evidence* of the position and held, on the facts, that the respondent's place of work was the actual firm where she worked.

The decision in *High Table* is interesting for two further reasons:

1. Peter Gibson J mentioned that a mobility clause could still be invoked by an employer to require employees to move their place of work and, if an employee refused to move under the terms of a mobility clause, then this may be grounds for a fair dismissal. He observed that 'the issues of dismissal, redundancy and reasonableness in the actions of an employer should be kept distinct'.

2. The decision neatly illustrates how redundancy now works in the opposite way from what was originally intended. The employee (the respondent) did not want to be made redundant but wished to claim unfair dismissal, presumably on the basis that the employer should have redeployed her. The employer wished to claim redundancy, as the amount of compensation payable is less.

In the result, employees lose under both the above tests. Mobility clauses can be used against employees but the courts are not now prepared to use the existence of a mobility clause to say that there is no redundancy and therefore open up a claim for unfair dismissal.

### Where the requirements of the business for employees to carry out work of a particular kind have ceased or diminished or are expected to do so

This has proved to be the most difficult part of the definition of redundancy to apply. It also seems from the statistics quoted at the beginning of this chapter to be very common in practice, as these showed that over half of redundancies were due to staff cutbacks rather than the actual closing down of the business. The typical situation is where the business is continuing but the need for employees whose work is of a particular kind has either ceased or is diminishing. Although this may not have been so in all of the cases referred to in the above figures, it will have been so in a considerable number.

#### The nature of the problem

*Example*

X has worked as a typist for Y Ltd for 25 years. His work is excellent. Y Ltd require all their typists to use word processors but X refuses, saying that 'he will not get used to new tricks'.

This situation neatly illustrates the relationship between redundancy and unfair dismissal. If Y Ltd failed to act reasonably by, for example, offering training and otherwise attempting to meet X's concerns, then X could have a claim for redundancy under s.98(4) of the ERA. If, however, Y Ltd has acted reasonably then the focus switches to whether X was redundant on the ground that the requirement for typists was 'work of a particular kind'.

#### The approach of the courts

The first major case to deal with this issue was *North Riding Garages Ltd v Butterwick* (1966). The applicant had been employed at a garage as a workshop manager in charge of the repairs workshop. He also spent some time in actual mechanical work on vehicles. The new owners wished him to do more work on the sales side and more paperwork. They also introduced new working methods to which the applicant found it difficult to adapt, and he was dismissed. Widgery J held that 'an employee who remains in the same kind of work is expected to adapt himself to new methods and techniques'. However, 'if new methods alter the nature of the work required to be done' then employees may be redundant. In this case no particular kind of work had ceased or diminished and therefore the applicant was not redundant.

Similarly, in *Vaux and Associated Breweries Ltd v Ward* (1968) a barmaid in a hotel was dismissed because it was felt that she would not fit in with a new image which was being introduced in the hotel. It was held that she was not redundant, as the requirement for her work had not changed: her replacement did the same work as she did.

Once again, in *Hindle v Percival Boats Ltd* (1968), a highly skilled boatbuilder was dismissed as he was 'too good and too slow'. The Court of Appeal held that he was not redundant, as the requirement for his work had not ceased or diminished. The fact that he had not been replaced did not assist him because, as Sachs LJ put it: 'an employer is entitled to come to a genuine conclusion that despite the requirements of his business he prefers to have a vacancy in his staff rather than to take on an unsuitable replacement.'

All these three cases show a broad view being taken by the courts as to what is work of a particular kind and a corresponding emphasis on the duty of employees to adapt to new methods of work. A slightly different approach was seen in *Murphy v Epsom College* (1984). The applicant was one of two plumbers employed by the school. The school modernised its heating system and decided that it needed a heating technician rather than two plumbers. The applicant was selected for dismissal and it was held that he was redundant, as plumbing was a particular kind of work and this had diminished. The irony was that the applicant wished to claim unfair dismissal but was thus unable to do so, whereas in the three earlier cases the applicants who were held not to be redundant might have had a good chance of succeeding in an unfair dismissal claim but at the time that remedy was not, of course, available.

### The position where the employee's contract enables the employer to require the employee to move to other work if the present work ceases or diminishes

Until recently, the law appeared to be that in such a situation the employee was not redundant. In *Nelson v BBC* (1977) the employee's contract required him to work 'when how and where' the BBC required. Therefore, he was not redundant when the Caribbean service in which he worked was cut back, since he could be transferred to another post. In effect, the Court of Appeal preferred the 'contract' test to the 'function' test, which asks what work the employee was required to do and actually did. In *Cowen v Haden Ltd* (1983) this approach was approved but the Court of Appeal managed to achieve a different result on the facts. A divisional contracts surveyor's own contract enabled his employer to require him to perform any duties 'which reasonably fall within the scope of his capabilities'. It was held that these wide words only related to work that reasonably came within the function of a divisional contracts surveyor. Therefore, he was held to be redundant because there was, in fact, no longer work of this particular kind.

This emphasis on the words of the employee's contract was decisively rejected by the House of Lords in *Murray v Foyle Meats Ltd* (1999). The applicants were employed as meat plant operatives. They normally worked in the slaughter hall but, under their contracts of employment, they could be required to work elsewhere and occasionally did so. Fewer employees were required in the hall due to falling business and the applicants were dismissed. They brought proceedings for unfair dismissal and the employers contended that the dismissals were due to redundancy as there was a diminution in the requirements for employees to carry out work of a particular kind, i.e. in the slaughter hall. (The relevant statute was the Contracts of Employment and Redundancy Payments Act (Northern Ireland) 1965, with identical wording to what is now the Employment Rights Act.)

Irvine LC, with whom the other Law Lords agreed, held that both the contract and the function tests miss the point. He considered that:

> the language of [s.139(1)(b)] is simplicity itself. It asks two questions of fact. The first is whether one or other of various states of economic affairs exists. In this case, the relevant one is whether the requirements of the business for employees to carry out work of a particular kind have diminished. The second question is whether the dismissal is attributable, wholly or mainly, to that state of affairs.

Applying this test, he held that 'the tribunal found on the facts that the requirements for employees to work in the slaughter hall had diminished. Secondly, they found that that state of affairs had led to the applicants being dismissed. That, in my opinion, is the end of the matter.' Accordingly, the applicants were redundant.

The difficulty with this deceptively simple approach is that, as has been pointed out (by Catherine Barnard (2000) Cambridge Law Journal 38), it 'effectively air brushes the words "work of a particular kind" from the statute: the statute does not say "there is a redundancy whenever a dismissal is attributable to a diminution in the employer's requirement for employees" but that is the effect of the Lord Chancellor's approach.'

Another view is to regard the decision as bringing welcome clarification to this area by saying, in effect, that an employee whose dismissal is attributable to redundancy has been dismissed by reason of redundancy. The effect of the decision is that in cases where the employee's contract covers a wider range of duties than those actually performed, then the work actually performed will, in effect, be 'work of a particular kind'. The practical result will be to make it more difficult for employees to claim unfair dismissal and easier for employers to say that they are redundant.

*Example*

X's contract requires her to work 'in any capacity' for her employers, Y, who run a garden centre. X has worked for many years selling garden furniture but Y decide to discontinue this and dismiss X. X claims that she has been unfairly dismissed. Y claims that she is redundant. Under the law as established in *Nelson v BBC*, X could argue that she was not redundant as she could, under the terms of her contract, be required to work elsewhere. Therefore, by dismissing her, Y is liable for unfair dismissal. However, the effect of *Murray v Foyle Meats* is that because the requirement for X to work in the section selling garden furniture has ceased she is therefore redundant.

The decision in *Murray v Foyle Meats* means that *Nelson v BBC* is now no longer good law but that *Cowen v Haden* is probably still correct on its facts.

In *Shawkat v Nottingham City Hospitals Trust (No. 2)* (2001) the applicant was employed as a thoracic surgeon but, following a reorganisation, he was required to carry out cardiac work as well as thoracic work. He declined to do so. The Court of Appeal held that he was not redundant because there was no diminution in the requirements for the work of a particular kind which the applicant was doing, i.e. thoracic surgery. The reorganisation did not result in the applicant's redundancy. This decision can be seen as an application of Irvine LC's words in *Murray* when he emphasised that a redundancy must be attributable to a diminution in the requirements for employees to carry out a particular kind of work. Here the requirements had not declined. Instead, the applicant was left to claim that unreasonable duties had been imposed on him and therefore he was unfairly dismissed.

### Bumped redundancies

*Example*

In *Safeway Stores v Burrell* (1997) Judge Peter Clark gave the following example:

> An employee is employed to work as a fork-lift truck driver, delivering materials to six production machines on the shop floor. Each machine has its own operator. The employer decides that it needs to run only five machines and that one machine operator must go. Selection for dismissal is done on the LIFO [last in first out] principle within the department. The fork-lift truck driver has the least service. Accordingly, one machine operator is transferred to driving the truck: the short service truck driver is dismissed. Is he dismissed by reason of redundancy? The answer is yes.

(*Note*: redundancy selection procedures are dealt with later in this chapter.)

The reason given by the judge was that there was a diminution in the requirement for employees to carry out the work of operators and this caused the dismissal. Therefore, there does not have to be a diminution in the requirement for the work actually done by the dismissed employee.

This reasoning was applied in this case where the applicant, a petrol station manager, lost his post in a reorganisation where all posts of petrol station managers were replaced by petrol filling station controllers. He was told that he could apply for one of these posts but he declined. It was held that he was redundant. As was pointed out by Judge Clark, the Act refers to 'employees' and not 'employee' and the fact was that a redundancy had come about and, as a result, he was redundant.

This reasoning was rejected in *Church v West Lancashire NHS Trust* (1998), also a decision of the EAT. It was held that the phrase 'work of a particular kind' means work of a particular kind which the actual employee was employed to do and therefore in a bumping situation the bumped dismissal will not be redundancy. In the fork-lift truck example, the truck driver would not be redundant because there was no diminution in the requirement for *his* work.

This controversy seems to have been settled by *Murray v Foyle Meats* (above) and it is within this context that the decision makes most sense. The words of Irvine LC clearly indicate that the test in *Safeway Stores v Burrell* is correct. As will be recalled, he stated that, provided the requirements for work of a particular kind have ceased or diminished *and* the employee is redundant as a result, then that is redundancy.

### Redundancies, terms of the contract and reorganisations

A number of cases have dealt with the situation where employers have altered the terms on which employees were employed and these employees have claimed that this change amounted to redundancy. A straightforward decision is *Chapman v Goonvean and Rostrowrack China Clay Co. Ltd* (1973), where the withdrawal of free transport to work was held not to make affected employees redundant. The argument that the requirements of the business for their work would have ceased if this change had not been made was rejected. Denning MR pointed out that the requirements for their work continued as before.

This was followed by *Johnson v Nottinghamshire Combined Police Authority* (1974), where a change in shift patterns was similarly held not to amount to redundancy. In *Lesney Products v Nolan* (1977) a change in shift systems resulted in reduced opportunities for overtime but, once again, this was held not to amount to redundancy. Although the actual decision was fairly straightforward, Denning MR's emphasis on the right of employers to reorganise their business was an important indicator of judicial attitudes in an area to which we shall return later in this chapter: 'it is important that nothing should be done to impair the ability of employers to re-organise their work force and their times and conditions of work so as to improve efficiency.'

## ■ Redundancy selection procedures

Assuming that the dismissal of an employee falls within the definition of redundancy then that employee will be entitled to a redundancy payment. However, as has been pointed out, the maximum compensation for unfair dismissal is far higher and it is this which makes redundancy selection procedures so significant. Therefore, an employee will seek, if possible, to bring the claim under unfair dismissal rather than redundancy.

## Relationship between redundancy and unfair dismissal

### Example

X works in a shop owned by Y. X's contract simply states that he is employed by Y. Y decides that the shop does not need so many employees as business is falling off and issues X with a notice of dismissal by reason of redundancy.

X may decide to:

- Challenge the need for redundancy at all on the basis, for example, that the shop was profitable. However, as we have seen, the courts will not concern themselves with this issue (see *Moon v Homeworthy Furniture* (above)).
- Argue that the definition of redundancy does not apply to him. This will involve a consideration of whether the requirement for X's particular kind of work had ceased or diminished. If it has, then X is redundant. If not, then X will have a good claim for unfair dismissal.
- Argue that, although his post *may* be redundant, the redundancy selection procedure was unfairly carried out. For instance, Y may have decided to make 20 employees redundant and X objects to the fact that he was chosen. Here X's claim will be founded on unfair dismissal.

It is the last of these points to which we will now turn. In the following cases an employee whose dismissal was due to redundancy will nevertheless be held to have been dismissed unfairly and thus entitled to compensation for unfair dismissal.

### Redundancy as an excuse

This provision deals with where an employee is selected for dismissal ostensibly because of redundancy but in reality for another reason. Redundancy is just the excuse.

The employee is unfairly dismissed where all the following conditions are satisfied:

1. the employee is dismissed by reason of redundancy; and
2. he/she can show that the circumstances constituting the redundancy applied equally to other employees in similar positions in the undertaking who were not dismissed; and
3. the dismissal was for one of the following reasons:
   (a) trade union membership or activities;
   (b) non-membership of a trade union;
   (c) on the grounds of pregnancy or childbirth;
   (d) making health and safety complaints;
   (e) asserting a statutory right;
   (f) being a protected shopworker;

    (g)  acting as a pension fund trustee;

    (h)  acting as an employee representative; or

    (i)  exercising rights under the Minimum Wage Act, Public Interest Disclosure Act or Working Time Regulations.

(*Note*: these areas have been explained more fully in other chapters; the statutory basis of these provisions is in ss.99–105 of the ERA 1996 and s.153 of the TULRCA 1992.)

### Selection procedure was unfair

The employee may claim in broader terms, as in the above example, that the redundancy selection procedure was unfair. In *British Aerospace plc v Green* (1995) Millett LJ explained that criticism of the redundancy selection procedure may take two forms:

1. A challenge to the fairness of the selection system, e.g. selection criteria or consultation procedures.
2. A challenge to the fairness of the manner in which the system was applied.

The basis of the law here is s.98 of the ERA 1996. As will be recalled, s.98(2)(c) provides that redundancy is a potentially fair reason for dismissal and s.98(4) provides that, as in other cases, the determination of whether the dismissal is fair or unfair depends on whether 'in the circumstances (including the size and administrative resources of the employer's undertaking) the employer acted reasonably . . .' Therefore, the issue is the reasonableness of the employer's conduct. This was emphasised in *Polkey v Dayton* (see also Chapter 11), where the House of Lords held that it was wrong to say that a failure to consult the employee did not matter as he would have been made redundant anyway. The issue was not injustice to the employee but the reasonableness of the employer's conduct. A useful summary of the approach of the courts was given by Waite LJ in *British Aerospace plc v Green* (1995). He observed that 'the employer who sets up a system of selection which can reasonably be described as fair and applies it without any overt sign of conduct which mars its fairness will have done all that the law requires of him'.

## Main guidelines on fairness

These are not rules as such but, in line with the words of Waite LJ above, simply guidelines.

    These were set out by Browne-Wilkinson J in the EAT in *Williams v Compair Maxam Ltd* (1982):

- Employers must give as much warning as possible of impending redundancies.
- Employers must consult unions on the redundancy procedure and will seek to agree the selection criteria with the union.
- Any criteria must be capable of being objectively checked against, for example, attendance records, efficiency records and length of service.

- Selection must be made fairly in accordance with the criteria and employers must consider any representations made by the union as to the selection procedure.
- Employers must seek to offer alternative employment, if possible, rather than redundancy.

Browne-Wilkinson J summed up the approach by saying that:

> The basic approach is that, in the unfortunate circumstances that necessarily attend redundancies, as much as is reasonably possible should be done to mitigate the impact on the workforce and to satisfy them that the selection has been made fairly and not on the basis of personal whim.

(*Note*: these requirements have since been added to by statute (see below).)

## Other points to note on redundancy procedures

### Changes in selection criteria

Initially many selection criteria were based on 'LIFO' (last in, first out). This was often favoured by unions as a less unfair way of selection but the emphasis has now switched to more sophisticated criteria, such as ones based on skills audits of employees, and their efficiency. This will often lead to employees being assessed on a points system.

### Right to see evidence of correct application of criteria

Where an employee has been selected for redundancy, is there a right to see evidence relating to other employees to check whether the criteria has been correctly applied? In *British Aerospace v Green* (above) the Court of Appeal held that 'Documents relating to retained employees are not likely to be relevant in any but the most exceptional circumstances'. However, this approach was not applied in two later cases. In *FDR Ltd v Holloway* (1995) the court ordered disclosure of documents on employees not selected and in *John Brown Engineering Ltd v Brown* (1997) the Scottish EAT held that where disclosure of scores on a points system has not been made by employers then an industrial tribunal was entitled to find that the relevant employees had been unfairly dismissed. The law on this area is, for the moment, uncertain but it is hoped that a less rigid approach than in *British Aerospace* may eventually be adopted. Indeed, it may be that *British Aerospace* could eventually be confined to its own facts, as that case involved very large redundancies: 530 employees out of a total of 7,000.

### Lower standards of procedure for smaller firms

In smaller firms a lower standard of procedure is set because of the reference in s.98(4) of ERA to size and administrative resources but, even so, any selection must be based on objective criteria (*Gray v Shetland Norse Preserving Co.* (1985)).

## Effect on employer of failing to observe procedure

A failure to observe the procedure may not be fatal to an employer, as in *Lloyd v Taylor Woodrow Construction* (1999), where a failure to inform the employee of the selection criteria was cured at the appeal stage when he was allowed to challenge the criteria. However, the court emphasised that a defect could only be cured at an appeal which was a complete rehearing rather than simply a review of the decision. This area is not, however, yet settled. Some confusion has derived from the speech of Lord Bridge in *Polkey v Dayton* (above), where he said that an employer might act reasonably in taking the view that 'in the exceptional circumstances of the particular case, the procedural steps normally appropriate would have been futile, could not have altered the decision to dismiss and therefore could be dispensed with'. The difficulty was that this left the door open to the sort of interpretation which actually occurred in *Duffy v Yeomans and Partners Ltd* (1994), where it was held that an objective test applied, i.e. did the employer, in deciding not to follow a particular procedure, do what a reasonable employer might do? In *Polkey* the test was deliberately subjective and looked at what that *particular* employer did. The danger is that the interpretation in *Duffy* could take us back to the now discredited approach in *British Labour Pump v Byrne* (see Chapter 11).

## Infringement of equal opportunities legislation

A redundancy selection procedure is open to challenge on the ground that it infringes equal opportunities legislation. In *Clarke v Eley (IMI) Kynoch Ltd* (1982) redundancy criteria which involved making part-time workers redundant first was held to amount to indirect sex discrimination, as the great majority of employees were female. This area has not yet been clarified; for example, are LIFO criteria in breach of the Sex Discrimination Act because women are statistically less likely to have long service than men because of career breaks? The point was left open in the *Clarke* case but in *Brook v London Borough of Haringey* (1992) it was felt that the fact that LIFO was widely used would tend to negate any finding of discrimination. However, LIFO is less widely used now. Would a sudden switch to LIFO when other more sophisticated selection methods had previously been used be discriminatory? The other possibility is that redundancy selection procedures may infringe the Part-time Workers (Prevention of Less Favourable Treatment) Regulations 2000, which prohibit discrimination against part-timers unless there is objective justification (see Chapter 4). This may prove to be more effective than a challenge under the Sex Discrimination Act, as there is no need to prove that there was adverse impact.

## Advance consultation

In *Elkouil v Coney Island Ltd* (2002) the EAT held that where a redundancy dismissal is unfair through a failure to consult in advance then the starting point should be what the likely outcome would have been if there had been proper consultation. Here the consultation process should have started ten weeks before the notice of dismissal and thus the applicant would have had ten weeks to look for another job. Therefore, the applicant lost the chance of being re-employed much earlier than he was and an award of ten weeks' pay was made.

## Statutory consultation procedures

In addition to the above rules on consultation and, to some extent, running parallel with them, there are statutory procedures which apply when an employer is proposing to make 20 or more employees redundant. The origin of these rules is in European Community law and specifically in Directive 75/129 of 1975. The impetus for this was, according to Bercusson (*European Labour Law* (London: Butterworths Law, 1996), p.219) the 'economic dislocation of Western Europe consequent on the rise in oil prices following the 1973 Middle East War'. The same reason applied to the legislation on transfer of undertakings (see later in this chapter). The current EC Directive is 98/59. The UK legislation is in s.188 of the Trade Union and Labour Relations (Consolidation) Act 1992, supplemented by the Collective Redundancies and Transfers of Undertakings (Protection of Employment) (Amendment) Regulations 1995 and 1999.

There is an extended definition of redundancy, which is only applicable here, and which is now contained in s.195 of the Trade Union and Labour Relations (Consolidation) Act 1992. This provides that redundancy is a 'dismissal for a reason not related to the individual concerned or for a number of reasons all of which are not so related'. The effect is to include within the definition of redundancy dismissals from reorganisation of a business and could have applied in, for example, *Shawkat v Nottingham City Hospital NHS Trust* (above). There is also a statutory presumption that any dismissal is for redundancy (s.195(2)).

## Relationship between the statutory consultation procedures and redundancy selection procedures

Breach of the statutory procedures can lead to the making of a 'protective award', which results in a payment of wages to employees concerned (see below). However, unlike breach of the selection procedures, it does not lead to a finding of unfair dismissal, although in *Rowell v Hubbard Group Services Ltd* (1995) the EAT felt that in an unfair dismissal case a tribunal should follow the general approach of the statutory procedures and therefore indirectly they can be said to be relevant to an unfair dismissal claim.

### The statutory consultation procedures in detail

These apply when an employee is proposing to dismiss as redundant 20 or more employees at one establishment within 90 days or less. Section 188 provides that, in deciding the number involved, no account shall be taken of those in respect of whose dismissals consultation has already begun.

The employer is required to consult appropriate representatives of affected employees. These are:

1. Representatives of an independent trade union recognised by the employer if the employees are 'of a description' in respect of which the union is recognised by the employer. The employees do not have to actually be members of the union, a point stressed in *Governing Body of the Northern Ireland Hotel and Catering College v NATFHE* (1995).
2. If 1 above does not apply then the employer must consult employee representatives who have already been elected or appointed and who have authority from the employees to act in this case or, if none exist, then employee representatives must be specifically elected for this purpose.

The consultation must begin in good time and in any event not less than 30 days before the first dismissal takes effect. However, where the employer proposes to dismiss 100 or more employees, the 30-day period is increased to at least 90 days.

The consultation must be genuine, as s.188 specifically provides that it 'shall be undertaken by the employer with a view to reaching agreement with the appropriate representatives'. In *R v British Coal Corporation and Secretary of State for Trade and Industry, ex parte Price* (1994) Glidewell LJ said that any consultation must be at an early stage, adequate information provided, adequate time allowed for responses and conscientious consideration of these responses. It is common for a meeting to be held when unions or employee representatives put forward their reasons why the redundancies should not happen and the effect of this decision is that an employer should then take time to consider these reasons rather than respond at once. In *Middlesbrough BC v TGWU* (2002) the employers had already decided that there would be redundancies before the redundancy consultation began and it was held that this meant that the consultation could not be genuine.

The consultation must include ways of avoiding the dismissals, reducing the numbers to be dismissed and mitigating the consequences of dismissals. The following information must be disclosed to the unions or representatives:

1. Reasons for the proposals.
2. Numbers and descriptions of employees to be made redundant.
3. Total number of such employees at the establishment.
4. Proposed method of selection.
5. Proposed method of carrying out the dismissals and over what period they are to take effect.
6. Proposed method of calculating redundancy payments.

It may be that in a particular case extra information should be provided in line with Glidewell LJ's remarks above that 'adequate information should be provided'. This could include details of employees not selected for redundancy, as discussed above.

The following issues have arisen in the interpretation of these provisions:

## When exactly must consultation begin?

There is a conflict between the words of s.188, which says that it must be when the employer is 'proposing to dismiss', and Directive 75/129 (the mainspring of these rules), which uses the words 'contemplating redundancies' a wider term. In *APAC v Kirvin Ltd* (1978) it was held that the word 'proposing' meant that consultation need only begin when the employer has formed a definite view that redundancies are needed. In *ex parte Price* (above) Glidewell LJ accepted that there was a conflict and, if that view prevails, s.188 will need amending. However, in *Griffin v South West Water Services Ltd* (1995) Blackburne J disagreed with Glidewell LJ that there was a conflict and so the point remains open. In *MSF v Refuge Assurance plc* (2002) Lindsay J in the EAT considered that there is indeed an inconsistency between these two provisions and therefore it seems that legislation may be needed amending s.188 to bring it into line with EC law.

## Does the term 'employer' include associated employers?

This may be important when deciding how many employees have been made redundant. In *E Green & Son (Castings) Ltd v ASTMS* (1984) it was held that, even though three firms were all subsidiaries of the same holding company and they all operated from the same premises, they were separate employers and so it was not possible to aggregate the total numbers to, in this case, increase the total consultation period from 30 days to 90.

## What is meant by 'establishment'?

The point arose in *Clarks of Hove Ltd v Bakers' Union* (1977) where a factory, a bakery and shops were all held to constitute one establishment. This enlightened decision is curiously at odds with that under the previous heading above.

## Failure to consult

### Protective award

A failure to consult can lead to the unions or employee representatives involved or, where there was no consultation machinery, the employees themselves, seeking a protective award from an employment tribunal. This is an order that the employer shall continue to pay wages for a protected period (ss.189 and 190 of TULRCA). The length of the period is such as the tribunal considers just and equitable having regard to the seriousness of the employer's default in complying with the statutory requirement with a maximum of 90 days. In *Talke Fashions v Amalgamated Society of Textile Workers and Kindred Trades* (1977) the EAT held that the approach should be compensatory and should initially look at how much the employee has lost through the employer not consulting in time. However, in later cases the EAT has allowed other matters to be taken into account so that a punitive element is, in effect, added. In *Spillars-French (Holdings) Ltd v Usdaw* (1979) Slynn J pointed out that there were 'degrees of different gravity'; for example, the fact that some information was given orally to employee representatives when it should have been in writing would not be treated as seriously as a failure to give reasons at all.

Note two other points:

1. A complaint that an employer has failed to comply with the consultation requirements must be presented to the employment tribunal within three months of the date when the last of the dismissals to which it relates takes effect unless it is not reasonably practicable to do so.
2. An employee may not be entitled to a protective award if he/she unreasonably resigns during the protected period or unreasonably refuses suitable alternative employment.

### Special circumstances defence

The employer may argue that there were special circumstances which made it not reasonably practicable to comply with the consultation requirements (s.188 (7)). If so, the employer is obliged to take only such steps as are reasonably practicable. If this defence succeeds then there will either be no protective award or, possibly, a reduction in it. In *Clarks of Hove v Bakers' Union* (1978) the employer had been in financial difficulty and, instead of initiating the consultation procedure, sought a buyer for some of its shops to enable it to continue trading. When a potential buyer pulled out, it made all its employees redundant. The Court of Appeal held that insolvency is not by itself a special circumstance; it depends on the cause. Sudden disaster striking a company could be, but if the insolvency was due to a gradual run down of the company (as happened in this case), then it would probably not be. As Geoffrey Lane LJ put it, 'to be special, the event must be something out of the ordinary, something uncommon.'

### Notification of redundancies of the Secretary of State

In addition to the consultation requirements, an employer who proposes to dismiss as redundant 20 or more employees at one establishment within 30 days must give the Secretary of State written notice of the proposal at least 30 days before the first dismissal takes effect. Where 100 or more employees are to be dismissed within 90 days then notification must be 90 days before. The special circumstances defence applies here also. The penalty is a fine and a copy of the notice must be sent to the employee representatives.

## TIME OFF TO LOOK FOR WORK

Section 52 of the ERA 1996 gives an employee under notice of dismissal for redundancy the right to time off work to either look for new employment or to make arrangements for training for new employment. This right only applies to employees with at least two years' continuous employment and it is enforced by complaint to an employment tribunal, which can order the employer to pay the employee an amount equivalent to the pay which would have been received had the time off been allowed but subject to a maximum of two-fifths of a week's pay (usually in practice two days' pay).

## REDUNDANCY COMPENSATION

The whole object of the law on redundancy is, of course, to enable employees to claim redundancy compensation. This is calculated according to a formula, as laid down in s.162 of the ERA 1996, and is as follows:

- One and a half week's pay for every year of continuous employment in which the employee was 41 years old and over.
- One week's pay for every year of continuous employment in which the employee was 22 years old but not over 41.
- Half a week's pay for every year of continuous employment in which the employee was 18 years old but not over 22.

The maximum amount of pay which can be counted is at present £250.00 and the maximum number of years' continuous employment which can be counted is 20. Thus the maximum is £250 × 20 × $1^1/_2$, i.e. 20 years at $1^1/_2$ weeks' pay for every year = £7,500.

Note that where an employee is made redundant after the age of 64, the amount of redundancy pay is progressively reduced so that, for example, if the employee is made redundant at 64 years and nine months, the employee receives one quarter of the payment for that year.

### ■ Who is not entitled to a redundancy payment?

The following employees are not entitled to a redundancy payment (all references are to the ERA 1996):

- Those with less than two years' continuous employment (s.155).
- Those aged under 20. This is the effect of s.211(2) because no years' service are taken into account before 18 and two years' continuous employment are needed.
- Those who have reached normal retiring age or, if there is none, 65 (s.156).
- Those employed under a fixed-term contract for two years or more who have renounced their rights to a redundancy payment (s.197(3)). (Soon to be abolished by the Employment Act 2002.)
- Share fishermen (s.199(2)).
- Persons ordinarily working outside Great Britain unless at the relevant time they were working in Great Britain on the employer's instructions (s.196(6)).
- Crown servants and certain public officials (s.159).
- Those employed as a domestic servant by a near relative (as defined in s.161).
- Classes of employees excluded by order of the Secretary of State in cases where a collective agreement covers the issue of redundancy (s.157).
- Those dismissed for misconduct (see below).
- Those who refuse a suitable offer of alternative employment (see below).

## ■ Making a claim for a redundancy payment

By s.164 of the ERA 1996 the claim must be made in writing to the employer, although no special form is laid down. An employee will (subject to the exception below) lose the right to a redundancy payment unless within six months of the date of termination of employment one of the following occurs:

1. The payment is agreed and paid.
2. The employee has claimed by notice in writing.
3. A question as to either the right to payment or the amount of payment has been referred to an employment tribunal.
4. The employee has presented a complaint of unfair dismissal to an employment tribunal.

The exception referred to above is that even if the six-month period is not observed then a tribunal may, if it considers it 'just and equitable', still award a redundancy payment if the complaint is made in ways 2 to 4 above in the six-month period immediately following the initial six-month period. There is no requirement that the actual application to the tribunal should be made within any particular time; only that the above rules are observed. An unfortunate rule is that an employee who claims early, i.e. before the actual termination of employment, is prejudiced in that this claim is invalid (*Watts v Rubery Owen Conveyancer* (1977)). This rule does not apply to unfair dismissal claims by virtue of the express words of s.111(3) of the ERA.

If the employer refuses to make a redundancy payment after the employee has taken all reasonable steps, short of actually taking proceedings in an employment tribunal, or if the employer is insolvent and the whole or part of the payment is unpaid then the employee may apply to the Secretary of State for a payment (s.166 ERA).

## ■ Cases where an employee dismissed by reason of redundancy may not be entitled to a redundancy payment

### An offer to renew the employee's contract or to re-engage him/her is unreasonably refused

Where the employer makes an offer to the employee, before the termination of employment, to either:

1. renew the contract of employment on the same terms; or
2. re-engage the employee under different terms and conditions and the offer constitutes suitable employment;

then the employee is not entitled to a redundancy payment if the offer is unreasonably refused, provided that it was to take effect not later than four weeks after the end of employment.

Renewal of the contract is straightforward but re-engagement needs some discussion. Two points must be considered and should initially be kept separate, although Neill LJ in *Spencer v Gloucestershire CC* (1985) said that too rigid a distinction should not be made, as the same factors might be common to both.

### Was the actual offer of employment suitable for the employee?

In *Carron Co. v Robertson* (1967) it was that held that suitability must be looked at objectively and is a question of fact for the tribunal. In *Taylor v Kent CC* (1969) Parker LCJ said that suitability means 'employment which is substantively equivalent to the employment which has ceased.' Relevant issues have been pay, location and how long the employment is expected to last. In *Taylor* it was held that an offer to a redundant headteacher of a post as a supply teacher was not suitable because of the loss of status involved.

### Offer is found to be unsuitable

If the offer is found to be unsuitable then the matter ends and the employee is entitled to the redundancy payment. If, however, the offer is found suitable then the further question arises of whether the employee unreasonably rejected it. This is a subjective question and personal reasons which relate to the employee must be considered. In *Spencer v Gloucestershire CC* (1985) school cleaners were asked to accept fewer hours work as an economy measure and they refused saying that the job could not be done properly in the time allowed. It was held that this could be a reasonable reason for refusal. In *Thomas Wragg & Sons Ltd v Wood* (1976) an employee under notice for redundancy found another job but, one day before his redundancy notice was due to expire, he was offered an alternative job by his employers. His refusal of his job was held reasonable. Other cases have dealt with, for example, family commitments.

### Trial period

An employee who accepts an offer of renewal or re-engagement is, by s.138(2) of the ERA, automatically allowed a trial period of at least four weeks from the end of the old contract. The advantage to the employee is that, merely by starting the new job he/she is not taken to have accepted it, as it may be difficult to say whether it is suitable until it has been tried. If the employee terminates the employment during the trial period for any reason connected with, for example, its unsuitability, then the employee is treated as having been dismissed at the date of termination of the old contract. Although the employer can still argue that the employment was suitable, at least the employee is able to argue that it was not and this is the significance of the trial period.

An employee who has been constructively dismissed because the employer sought to impose a new contract on him/her also has the right to the same trial period. However, a complication has arisen because at common law it had been held, before the statutory trial period was introduced, that an employee has a trial period of a reasonable length unless a specific period was agreed. In *Air*

*Canada v Lee* (1978) the EAT held that the statutory period was additional to the common law one, but it is uncertain how one tells when the common law period has ended and the statutory trial period has started.

## The employee is guilty of misconduct

These provisions are, unfortunately, extremely complex and care is needed in their application. In principle, there seems no need for these rules since an employee dismissed for misconduct is not entitled to redundancy compensation. However, s.140 predates the unfair dismissal legislation and we seem to have a classic case of subsequent legislation failing to dovetail with earlier legislation.

### Example

X is employed by Y. Y gives X three months' notice on 1 January that he is dismissed for redundancy. X is then discovered to have been stealing and is dismissed on 1 February. Section 140(1) applies.

This provides that X will lose his entitlement to a redundancy payment provided that Y dismissed X in any one of the following ways:

1. Without notice.
2. With shorter notice than X is entitled to.
3. With full notice but with a statement that the employer would have been entitled to dismiss without notice.

There is also a distinction between a single and a double dismissal. A single dismissal is where an employee could have been dismissed for redundancy but is in fact dismissed for misconduct. A double dismissal is illustrated in the above example. It was held in *Simmons v Hoover Ltd* (1977) that where there has been a double dismissal then s.140(3) comes into play and the tribunal has the discretion to award an 'appropriate payment' to the employee, presumably all or part of the redundancy payment. This does not apply where there has been a single dismissal. The EAT, in *Simmons*, set out seven situations where s.140 could apply and further discussion of s.140 can be found in the decision of the NIRC in *Sanders v Ernest A. Neale Ltd* (1974) .

## Dismissal of employees on strike

The effect of s.143 and s.140 is that where an employee is under notice of dismissal for redundancy and then goes on strike and is dismissed for going on strike, the entitlement to a redundancy payment is not affected, although the employer may serve a notice on the employee (a notice of extension) requiring him/her to make up the time lost by going on strike. Note that the definition of a strike is the same as for continuity purposes and is in s.235 of the ERA (see Chapter 6). If the employee fails to comply with the notice, a guaranteed right to a redundancy payment is lost, although a tribunal retains a discretion to order an 'appropriate payment' nonetheless. In *Simmons v Hoover* (1977) the converse applied and the employee first went on strike and was *then* issued with a redundancy payment. It was held that what is now s.140(2) did not apply and there was no right to a redundancy payment. Therefore, in order to have a right to a redundancy payment the redundancy notice must come before the strike. A final point is that these provisions date from the time when an employee on strike had no right to complain for unfair dismissal and today the idea of a strike as misconduct sits oddly with the provisions of the Employment Relations Act 1999 (see Chapter 14), where in some circumstances the dismissal of an employee on official strike is automatically unfair.

## The position of employees laid off or on short time

Is some cases an employee laid off or on short time may be able to claim a redundancy payment. Again, the provisions, in ss.147 and 148 of the ERA, are complex. The following points arise:

- Does the employer have the right to lay the employee off or put the employee on short time? If not, such an action is likely to constitute an unfair dismissal and the employee will be able to claim for this.
- If the employer does have the right to do either of these then a right to a redundancy payment may arise, provided that the lay-off or short time satisfies the statutory definition.
- Lay-off is defined as where the employee for a whole week receives no remuneration under the contract.
- Short time is defined as where during a whole week the employee receives less then half the normal week's pay.
- An employee who is laid off or on short time as defined above for a period of four or more consecutive weeks may claim a redundancy payment provided that this is done by serving a notice within four weeks of the end of the period.
- An employee who is laid off or on short time for a series of six or more weeks in a period of 13 weeks (of which no more then three were consecutive) may also claim a redundancy payment, provided that the notice is served within four weeks of the last date in the series.
- The employee must actually terminate the contract by giving the required notice.
- The employer can contest the claim by serving a notice within seven days of the employee's notice stating that within four weeks there will be a period of 13 weeks without any lay-offs or short time.
- Where the lay-off or short time is wholly or mainly attributable to a strike or lock out, these provisions do not apply (s.154).

## DISMISSAL ON A REORGANISATION

### Introduction

Dismissal of an employee on a reorganisation of a business can lead to any of the following consequences:

(a) a finding that the employee was redundant because there was no longer work of the particular kind which the employee was employed to do, as explained above;

(b) a finding that the employee was unfairly dismissed;

(c) a finding that the employee was fairly dismissed as the reason for the dismissal fell within the category of dismissal 'for some other substantial reason'.

It is with category (c) and its relationship with categories (a) and (b) that we are concerned in this section. Although the concept of SOSR dismissals has been explained earlier in general terms, SOSR has had a particular impact in this area.

*Example*

X is employed as a manager of a small supermarket and is asked by her employer, Y, to stay behind for an hour after the other staff have gone in order to stack the shelves and to be responsible for personnel matters. Neither of these duties were in X's contract but Y tells X that the national firm which runs the supermarket is in financial difficulties and X , along with all the other managers, will need to perform these extra duties in order that staffing costs can be saved.

X is clearly not redundant because her job has not altered: her particular kind of work remains the same. (See *Chapman v Goonvean and Rostrowrack China Clay Co. Ltd* and *Johnson v Nottinghamshire Police Authority* earlier in this chapter.)

X will argue that she has the right to refuse to perform the extra duties because her contract cannot be altered without her consent. As a matter of contract law this is true but it may be that, if she refuses, Y could dismiss her and, instead of X having a good claim for unfair dismissal, Y could argue that X's dismissal was for a fair reason, in particular, some other substantial reason.

## ◾ Dismissal for refusing to agree to changes in the terms of the contract of employment

Although dismissal on a reorganisation covers wider issues than simply refusing to agree to changes in contract terms, this topic is a useful starting point, not least because the first case on it involved this matter. In *R S Components Ltd v Irwin* (1974) the employers, who manufactured electrical components, found that a number of their employees were leaving and soliciting customers of the employers to deal with them instead. As a result, the employers were losing business and therefore they required employees to sign a restrictive covenant which prevented them from soliciting customers of their employers for 12 months after leaving their employment. The employee was one of four who refused to accept the covenant and he was dismissed. It was held that the dismissal was fair on the ground that dismissal was for a substantial reason. Brightman J considered that it would be 'unfortunate for the development of industry' if an employer who was considering embarking on a new technical process was unable to require employees to agree to some 'reasonable restriction' on the use of their knowledge. In *Irwin* it appears to have been assumed that the restriction was, in itself, reasonable, as clearly a failure to agree to an unreasonable restriction should not be a ground for a fair dismissal.

## Reorganisational redundancy

### The idea of reorganisational redundancy

This is really a separate topic from that above and the word redundancy is, of course, strictly incorrect in this context as the situation is not redundancy but possible unfair dismissal. As Bowers and Clarke point out (in 'Unfair Dismissal and Managerial Prerogative: a Study of Some Other Substantial Reason' 10 ILJ 34): 'It is difficult to pinpoint precisely when this notion of "reorganisational redundancy" crystallised.' The initial thinking of the courts was simply to ask whether an employee's work had been reorganised so that he/she was redundant or not. If not, then there was the possibility of a claim by the employee for unfair dismissal (see e.g. *Delanair Ltd v Mead* (1976)). Nevertheless, the courts soon began to talk in a way which blurred the line between redundancy and straightforward dismissal. In *Gorman v London Computer Training Centre* (1978) Phillips J said that an employer who was overmanned could say that, even though for 'technical reasons the employees were not redundant nevertheless a dismissal could be for some other substantial reason'.

The first case in which reorganisational redundancy was recognised and applied appears to be *Ellis v Brighton Co-operative Society* (1976). The employee was required to work longer hours and his duties were increased as a result of a reorganisation of the business. He was not contractually bound to accept these changes and, when he refused to do so, he was dismissed. It was held that his refusal to accept them justified dismissal for some other substantial reason. The EAT held that 'Where there has been a properly consulted-upon reorganisation which, if it is not done, is going to bring the whole business to a standstill, a failure to go along with the new arrangements may well – it is not bound to but may well – constitute some other substantial reason'.

### When will a dismissal in cases of 'reorganisational redundancy' be justified?

Although there has been much discussion as to the precise terminology to be used, there is no doubt that the employer must show that the situation was dictated by the needs of the business. The debate has been about the precise threshold to be applied with some judges stressing the requirement for a pressing business reason and others emphasising the need to uphold managerial prerogative.

The first major case was *Hollister v NFU* (1979). Hollister was one of the NFU's group secretaries and the union reorganised its insurance business so that Hollister no longer received any commission on insurance sold. It was found that the total package offered on the reorganisation did not mean a drop in salary but Hollister refused to accept it because taken as a whole it diminished his existing rights. The Court of Appeal held that he was fairly dismissed. Denning MR felt that the test in *Ellis* (above) of whether if there was no reorganisation the business would be brought to a standstill was too restrictive and preferred the test of Arnold J in the EAT in *Ellis* of whether 'there was some sound, good business reason for the reorganisation'.

In later cases the courts have expressed further different formulations of the test. In *Banerjee v City and East London AHA* (1979) the EAT used an even looser test than that in *Hollister*: would the proposed changes bring discernible advantages to the organisation and were they 'matters of importance'?

### The question of reasonableness

Some emphasis has been placed by the courts on the need for the employer to have acted reasonably and this has, to some extent, acted as a check on the stress laid upon the employer's right to manage. The problem is that the decisions conflict. In *Evans v Elementa Holdings Ltd* (1982) the EAT held that the matter should be looked at from the perspective of the employee and a tribunal should ask whether the terms offered were 'objectionable and oppressive'. However, in *Chubb Fire Security Ltd v Harper* (1983) the EAT held that the question of reasonableness should be considered from the point of view of both parties: were the employers acting reasonably in deciding that the advantages to them of the proposed reorganisation outweighed any disadvantage which they should have contemplated that their employees might suffer?

In *Richmond Precision Engineering Ltd v Pearce* (1985) the approach in *Chubb* was in turn criticised and it was held that the question of weighing advantages and disadvantages was not the only task for a tribunal. Purely because there was a disadvantage to the employee did not mean that the employer had acted unreasonably. It held that the test is whether the terms offered are ones which a reasonable employer could offer in the changed circumstances of the employer's business. In *St John of God (Care Service) Ltd v Brooks* (1992) it was pointed out that this was wrong in law: the issue is whether the decision to dismiss is reasonable and does not concern a reasonable employer's offer. Not only this, but circumstances surrounding the offer also needed to be considered. In this case the fact that the vast majority of employees had accepted new, and much less favourable, terms and conditions when NHS funding for a care service was reduced was 'highly significant'. One might sum up this area by saying that, given the need for some criteria as in (a) above, the question is, as always, one of reasonableness and no factor should be excluded.

### The need for consultation with the employee

In *Hollister v NFU* the Court of Appeal held that this was only one of the relevant factors and therefore there was no absolute requirement to consult. As Denning MR put it: 'Negotiation is only one of the factors which has to be taken into account'. In fact Mr Hollister was not consulted at all. However, it is submitted that this no longer represents the law and indeed in the previous case of

*Ellis v Brighton Co-operative Society* the court had referred to a 'properly consulted-upon reorganisation'. Certainly it seems that the emphasis on fairness to the employee in *Polkey v AE Dayton Services Ltd* (1988) (see Chapter 11) means that some degree of consultation is required in cases of reorganisation.

## DISMISSAL ON THE TRANSFER OF AN UNDERTAKING

The common law position has been overlaid by the Transfer of Undertakings (Protection of Employment) Regulations 1981. The following diagram attempts to show the position.

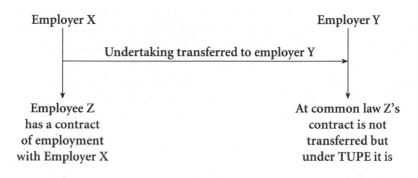

The above example is slightly oversimplified, in that it is not certain that contracts of employees will be transferred under TUPE, but it does illustrate the dramatic difference which TUPE has made when a business is transferred.

The common law position was set out in *Nokes v Doncaster Amalgamated Collieries Ltd* (1940), when the question arose as to the position of employees in two companies which had been amalgamated. Atkin LJ held that the contracts of employment were not transferred and emphasised that: 'the servant was left with his inalienable right to choose to serve his new master or not.'

This approach was rooted in the contractual idea that obligations under a contract were between the parties and that rights and obligations under them could not be transferred to third parties. The effect was that employees could find that, when the undertaking for which they worked changed hands, their contracts were not taken on by the new owner and their employment was ended without any redress. Even if they were taken on, they had lost continuity of employment. In a world where takeovers and mergers were becoming increasingly common, the continued existence of the common law rule represented a grave threat to job security.

The position changed with the enactment of TUPE, which was passed in order to implement the Acquired Rights Directive (77/187). These were amended by the Trade Union Reform and Employment Rights Act 1993 and now further change is in the air with the need to implement the revised Transfer of Undertakings Directive.

(*Note*: when decisions of the ECJ are discussed in this chapter references will be to the Directive and when the decisions are to those of UK courts references will be to TUPE.)

The cornerstone of the present law is Regulation 5(2), which provides that a relevant transfer shall not operate to terminate the contract of employment of anyone employed by the transferor in the undertaking transferred but any such contract shall have effect after the transfer as if it was originally made between the transferor of the undertaking and the employee.

Thus the common law position is reversed and the transfer of an undertaking does not terminate contracts of employment but merely transfers them. Regulation 5(2) should be read in conjunction with Regulation 8, which provides that any dismissal of an employee in the transfer of an undertaking is automatically unfair if the reason or principal reason for it was the transfer or a reason connected with it. Accordingly, if Employer Y in the example on p.236 had refused to take Employee Z on then this would have been an automatically unfair dismissal and Z would have had a claim against Y.

There is, however, a defence provided by Regulation 8(2) which states that where the reason or principal reason for the dismissal is an economic, technical or organisational one, entailing changes in the workforce, then the dismissal is deemed to be for a substantial reason and therefore attention switches to s.98(4) of the ERA (see Chapter 11) to determine whether the employer acted reasonably. This is known as the ETO defence. In *Berriman v Delabole Slate Ltd* (1985) the applicant was employed as a quarryman in a business which was transferred. The transferee wished to bring in new conditions of employment so as to bring the contracts of the transferred employee into line with existing employees. The Court of Appeal held that the ETO defence did not apply, as it only covered situations where there are changes in the number or functions of the workforce. Therefore, transferred employees are entitled to retain their existing conditions of employment and the effect is that firms which have absorbed a number of other firms may have employees on a bewildering variety of different conditions. The obvious answer is to harmonise them but legally this can only mean levelling up to the most favourable terms. An interesting attempt to challenge a change in working conditions failed in *Rossiter v Pendragon plc* (2002). The employee's contract had been transferred under TUPE but one result was that the commission scheme was much less favourable than before the transfer, resulting in a loss of income of about £3,000 a year. He claimed constructive dismissal but his claim failed, as there was no repudiatory breach of contract (see *Western Excavating v Sharp*, Chapter 11). The fact that he had suffered a detrimental change in his working conditions was not enough in the absence of a repudiatory breach. To hold otherwise would, by extending the law of constructive dismissal in TUPE situations, give an employee a new right which had not been intended.

The one exception to the rule that contractual rights are transferred is Regulation 7, which provides that there is no transfer of that part of a contract of employment which includes an occupational pension scheme but in *Beckman v Dynamco Whichloe Macfarlane Ltd* (2002) it was held by the ECJ that this exception does not cover enhanced benefits on the grounds of early retirement through redundancy and thus the liability to pay falls on the transferee. This decision will be of great significance where TUPE applies to employees who have had their contracts transferred when a service is contracted out to the private sector, as the private sector will be liable to pay terms on a redundancy which was negotiated in the public sector. These are likely to be much more generous than would often be paid by private sector employees.

The ETO defence did apply in *Whitehouse v Chas. Blatchford & Sons Ltd* (1999). The transferee of a business had successfully bid for a contract to supply appliances to a hospital but the bid was made conditional on a reduction in staffing costs. As a result the applicant was made redundant along with 13 others and it was held that the ETO defence covered this. The applicant was still entitled to a redundancy payment but not to a (probably) greater amount of compensation for unfair dismissal.

In *Wilson v St Helens BC* (1998) employees were dismissed before a transfer and were subsequently re-engaged on new contracts which were less favourable. In the House of Lords it was held that the dismissals before the transfer were effective in law even though they breached Regulation 8(1). Thus the variations in the contracts were effective. However, there seems to be no reason why the employees in such a case could not claim unfair dismissal from their contracts with the transferor in an action against the transferee employer, as Regulation 5 states that the transferred contract shall have effect as if *originally made* between the transferee and the employee.

A transferee employer may well wish to find a way in which he is not liable to take on the whole workforce of the old employer. *Litster v Forth Dry Dock Engineering Co. Ltd* (1989) illustrates an attempt to avoid this. Under Regulation 5(3) the Regulations only apply where the employee was employed *immediately* before the transfer and here all the 12 applicants were dismissed one hour before the transfer. The House of Lords held that they were still protected and read into Regulation 5(3) the words 'or would have been so employed if they had not been unfairly dismissed'. A decision otherwise would have left a gaping hole in the protection afforded to employees.

It is worth noting that TUPE does not only apply to transfers of liability but it can also transfer liability in tort. In *Bernadone v Pall Mall Services Group Ltd* (2000) liability to an employee injured at work was transferred.

It may be that an employee does not wish to transfer to a new employer and the right not to do so was recognised by the ECJ in *Katiskas v Konstantinidis* (1993), which held that an employee may object to a transfer. As a result of this decision, paras. 4(A) and (B) were inserted into Regulation 5, confirming the existence of the right to object.

A different and fundamental issue was raised in a decision of the European Free Trade Area Association (EFTA) Court under the similar provision in the Business Transfers Directive. In *Viggosdottir v Islandspostur HF* (2002) the applicant was a post office worker but was held to have the status of the UK equivalent of an office holder so that she was not an employee and so the Directive did not apply to her.

## TUPE and continuity of employment

The concept of continuity of employment was dealt with in Chapter 6, but there is an overlap with TUPE transfers which is best considered here. Section 218 of the ERA 1996 provides that continuity of employment is preserved where a trade, business or undertaking is transferred. Problems arose in determining precisely what was meant by these terms and it was held in *Woodhouse v Peter Brotherhood Ltd* (1972) that there would be no transfer of the business where there was only a transfer of the physical assets. Section 218 seems to overlap with TUPE, although TUPE does not expressly refer to whether continuity of employment is preserved. However, it is likely that it does do so, as Regulation 5(2)(a) refers to the transfer of rights under or in connection with the contract and it is submitted that continuity is a right in connection with the contract. In the event that this is not so then s.218 plugs the gap.

## The need for the transfer of an undertaking

In order for TUPE to apply there must be an *undertaking* which is *transferred*. The requirement of a transfer was fatal to the employee's claim in *Askew v Governors of Clifton Middle School* (1999), where a teacher at a school which ceased to be maintained by the local authority was made redundant. He applied to work at the school which replaced his old school but was not employed and then claimed that he had been unfairly dismissed as TUPE applied. His claim failed on the simple ground that there had been no change of employer, which remained the local authority. Where there are transfers between subsidiary companies in the same group then it was held in *Allen v Amalgamated Construction Co. Ltd* (1999) that TUPE applied provided that the companies were distinct legal persons with separate employment relationships with their employees.

A more intractable problem has been defining what is meant by the term 'undertaking', particularly when a service is contracted out. The starting point is two decisions of the ECJ. In *Dr Sophie Redmond Stichting v Bartol* (1992) the ECJ held that the Acquired Rights Directive applied to a non-commercial body, in this case one which provided services to drug addicts. This led to the amendment of TUPE so that it now refers to any trade or business, whereas before it only applied to commercial ventures. The other decision was that in *Daddy's Dance Hall* (1988), which held that there did not have to be a direct contractual link between the transferor and transferee. With the expansion of contracting out of public services in the UK the question was the extent to which TUPE would apply so that an organisation which successfully tendered for a service would also have to take on the employees.

In *Spijkers v Gebroeders Benedik Abatoir* (1986) the ECJ held that the Acquired Rights Directive applies whenever a business retains its identity when transferred. Thus, as applied to the situation in *Woodhouse v Brotherhood* (above), it is quite clear that it would not apply, because all that was transferred were the assets. In *Spijkers* the ECJ held that a variety of factors were relevant, such as the extent of the similarity between activities carried on before and after the transfer and whether the customers were transferred. It was also relevant that the employees and the physical assets were transferred, although transfer of assets alone would not be enough. The first UK case to apply TUPE to contracting out was *Dines v Initial Health Care Services* (1994), where a hospital cleaning contract was awarded on re-tendering to another firm and it was held that TUPE applied.

However, the ECJ then began a subtle change of tack in *Rygaard v Stvø Mølle* (1996) and *Süzen v Zehnacker* (1997). In *Rygaard* a building contract which had been sub-contracted to Firm X was, by agreement, then sub-contracted to Firm Y and it was held that the Acquired Rights Directive did not apply because it was held that a transfer must relate to a stable economic entity which was not limited to performing a one-off contract. This decision seemed clearly correct on its facts, but it was followed by *Suzen*, which held that employees dismissed when a cleaning contract for a school was transferred from one contractor to another could not claim as 'the mere loss of a service contract to a competitor cannot . . . by itself indicate the existence of a transfer'. It was held that 'an entity cannot be reduced to the activity entrusted to it' and that where a service contract was lost to a competitor, the 'service undertaking previously entrusted with the contract does not, on losing a customer, thereby cease fully to exist'. The essential difference from this case and *Spijkers* was the move away from the more factual approach in *Spijkers* to an emphasis on the notion of a stable economic entity.

One can see the point that the court was making: Firm X loses a contract to Firm Y but Firm X may still exist. How can it be said that there has been a transfer of an undertaking? But from the point of view of those employed, there will be a loss of employment. In addition, it meant that the position of workers where physical assets were transferred was significantly better than in labour intensive occupations such as in *Süzen*. The matter is still not yet settled, but in the UK the courts have, from initially applying a stricter test in line with *Süzen*, more recently gone back to the *Spijkers* approach. In *Betts v Brintel Helicopters* (1997) it was held, applying *Süzen*, that there was no transfer where a contract to provide helicopter transport to workers on oil rigs was transferred, one significant feature being that no employees were taken on and that no assets were transferred. The obvious point here is that it appeared that a transferee could avoid TUPE by the simple method of refusing to take on workers employed by the transferor. *ECM (Vehicle Delivery Service) v Cox* (1999) signalled a move back to the wider approach in *Spijkers*. The workers were employed as drivers and yardsmen by a firm which had a contract to deliver cars imported into the UK. The contract was then lost to another firm and it was held that there was a transfer. None of the employees had been taken on by the transferee but this was held to be irrelevant, as one needed to have regard to why this was so. Here the reason was that the employees were claiming unfair dismissal on the basis that

TUPE applied and the transferee did not want to be saddled with liability for this claim.

The most recent UK decision is in line with the approach in *ECM v Cox*. In *RCO Support Services v Unison* (2002) it was held that TUPE could apply where cleaning services in hospitals were transferred, although no assets were transferred and no employees were taken on. Although this decision may be welcome, the uncertainty in this area is clearly unacceptable and it is understood that among the proposed changes in TUPE there will be a special definition of service transfers.

## Consultation on the transfer of an undertaking

Regulation 10 of TUPE provides that where there is a relevant transfer there is a duty to inform and consult 'appropriate representatives', which means either employee representatives elected by the employees or representatives of an independent trade union recognised by the employer. If there is no trade union and no representatives are elected then the information must be provided individually.

The following information must be provided:

1. When the transfer is to take place and the reasons for it.
2. The legal, economic and social implications for the employees.
3. The measures which the employer envisages he will take in relation to the employees.
4. If the employer is the transferor, the measures which the transferee envisages he will be taking.

The appropriate representatives may complain to a tribunal of a failure to consult, and affected employees may be awarded a maximum of four weeks' pay. The employer may, as with redundancy consultation, put forward the 'special circumstances' defence to a complaint of failure to consult.

# Chapter 13

# Trade unions: their status and their members

## INTRODUCTION

The final two chapters of this book have a different flavour from the rest. Whereas the focus of the other chapters has been primarily on individual employment rights, the focus here is on collective aspects. Thus we consider, in the final chapter, the law on collective action taken by trade unions but in this chapter we deal with the relationship between a union and its members. This introduction serves as an introduction to both chapters.

The history of the legal relationship between the law and trade unions has not been a happy one. When, at the time of the Industrial Revolution, trade unions in the modern sense began to be formed, they were outlawed by the Combination Acts of 1799 and 1800. This was partly because of fear of bodies of organised labour, inspired to some degree by the French Revolution, partly no doubt because of a general feeling that trade unions as such interfered unduly with the powers of employers, and partly because, from the strictly legal point of view, a trade union was seen as acting in restraint of trade. Thus it came within the definition of criminal conspiracy which, as we shall see later, could make an agreement to do a particular act a criminal offence even though the act was not in itself criminal. This last point retains its significance today for, even though long ago it was declared by statute that the purposes of a union were not unlawful, although technically in restraint of trade (by the Trade Union Act 1871), the fact remains that some of the very activities of a union, such as the calling of a strike, bring it into conflict with the law. Why, then, is there this continued uneasy relationship between the law and trade unions?

A full answer to this question can only be given in a book devoted to history and industrial relations, rather than in a legal textbook such as this, but certain points can validly be made here. The law has traditionally been keen to protect the rights of individuals when these are opposed to a large organisation, but, although this may go some way to explaining what is sometimes perceived as hostility of the law to trade unions, it does not go far enough.

There is in fact a noticeable difference between the attitudes of the courts to issues explored in this chapter where, to some extent, the law and unions have worked alongside each other, as compared to the next chapter, where collective industrial action is considered. Not only this, but in the early part of the twentieth century what has been called 'the long sleep of public law' meant that the courts were most reluctant to intervene on the side of individuals in actions against public bodies and this did not really change until *Ridge v Baldwin* (1964).

It may well be that the real explanation can be found in a class analysis, where the judges' attitudes were conditioned by class hostility to unions. Certainly unions have believed this. Memories still exist of the case of the Tolpuddle Martyrs who, in 1834, were convicted and transported to Australia on a charge of taking an illegal oath contrary to the Unlawful Oaths Act 1797. The underlying reason for their conviction was seen as the fact that they were organising a union of agricultural workers. The problems with the law and trade unions has often been contrasted with the way in which the law took up the notion of a company and, by a series of statutes passed in the nineteenth century, gave companies a secure legal framework in which to operate. In fact, it was suggested at that time that unions should also become companies and this was also suggested by the Royal Commission on Trade Unions and Employers Associations (The Donovan Commission) in 1968. The unions rejected this idea. The Industrial Relations Act 1971 provided that unions who registered under the Act would have corporate status but the consequence of registration was seen by unions as also leading to an unacceptable degree of interference in their internal affairs. The result was that very few unions registered and the idea of corporate status was unnecessarily linked with a political agenda. Is it not time, at a period when, unlike in the 1970s, the subject does not arouse so much heat, to look afresh at a proper legal status for trade unions?

## HISTORY OF TRADE UNIONS AND THE LAW: A BRIEF REVIEW

The Combination Acts, which effectively banned trade unions, were repealed in 1825 but this did no more than remove the threat of prosecution for criminal conspiracy. In *Hornby v Close* (1867) it was held that the activities of unions were in restraint of trade and it was not until the Trade Union Act 1871 that, as we saw above, this was reversed. This Act was the first piece of legislation to deal with the affairs of unions but it was followed by the Conspiracy and Protection of Property Act 1875, which in effect provided that those engaged in strike action would no longer be liable to prosecution for criminal conspiracy. The interesting point is that the first Act was passed by a Liberal government but the second was passed by a Conservative one. This illustrates the point that, whilst on the whole it has been Liberal and, later, Labour, governments who have been more favourable to unions, this is not universally true. On the other hand, Labour governments, and, in particular, the present one, have not always enjoyed a cosy relationship with trade unions.

It was, however a Liberal government which acted to remove the next threat to unions, which came about as a result of the decision of the House of Lords in *Taff Vale Railway Co. v ASRS* (1901). This had held that a union could be sued in tort for the acts of its officials and thus the funds of the union could be at risk from an action by an employer for damages caused by a strike called by those officials. The result was the Trade Disputes Act 1906, which gave immunity to trade unions from actions in tort. (The law on immunities is explored in the next chapter.) There matters rested for many years as, although it was felt by some that there was a need to look afresh at trade unions and their place in modern society, there was a disinclination to take any action. This state of affairs was particularly prevalent in the early days of the 1951–64 Conservative government, when Walter Monckton was Minister of Labour (see the chapter on Monckton in A. Roberts, *Eminent Churchillians* (London, 1994)), and the general attitude of the period to industrial relations is also captured in Chapters 2 and 3 of P. Davies and M. Freedland, *Labour Legislation and Public Policy* (Oxford, 1993).

The setting up of the Donovan Commission in 1965 was a harbinger of changing times and its report was followed by a White Paper, *In Place of Strife* (1968, Cmnd. 3623), which went beyond the recommendations in the report and proposed an Industrial Relations Act with, for example, strike ballots and powers to enforce a 'conciliation pause' where a strike had been called without adequate discussions between employers and unions. These proposed powers were backed by legal sanctions and as such were anathema to the majority of the unions, coming in particular from a Labour government. They were withdrawn and replaced by a set of voluntary proposals but the episode, in addition to the political damage done to the Labour government, led to the introduction by the Conservative government elected in 1970 of a more far reaching Industrial Relations Act. The details of this are history but the Act attempted a detailed regulation of trade unions and their affairs with, for example, provision for the imposition of emergency 'cooling off procedures' in industrial disputes and a presumption that collective agreements were legally binding. Trade unions were made liable for 'unfair industrial practices', some of which corresponded with the 'economic torts' so that, to trade unions, the spectre of *Taff Vale* (above) emerged from the shadows of 1901. The requirement on unions to register under the Act proved to be a disastrous mistake, as unions made the campaign against registration the cornerstone of their opposition to the Act. At the same time, the Act introduced new laws giving employees protection against unfair dismissal and these have, of course, survived. In one way, and presumably quite unintentionally, this introduction of new individual employment rights by the Industrial Relations Act turned out to be a far more effective method of changing the nature of trade union action than any of the complicated provisions in the Act relating to industrial disputes. This was because, with the flood of new employment rights of which this was really the precursor, employees have increasingly turned to tribunals and, more recently, arbitration as a means of settling grievances rather than resorting to industrial action.

The Conservative government fell in February 1974 in the middle of a miners' strike, and the incoming Labour government not only repealed the Industrial Relations Act but introduced legislation which greatly buttressed the position of trade unions. In particular, the law on the closed shop was strengthened, unions were given the right to be consulted on impending redundancies and the right to appoint safety representatives with wide powers. This marked the apogee of trade union power, as the Conservative government elected in 1979 embarked on a gradual programme of legislation with major statutes in 1980, 1982, 1984, 1989, 1990 and 1993. Unlike the Industrial Relations Act, the emphasis was not on one all-embracing piece of legislation but on a gradualist approach. There were two themes: first, either bringing what were seen to be unacceptable practices under control or prohibiting them (for example, the outlawing of secondary picketing) and, secondly, giving increased rights to individual union members. A great deal of this legislation is still with us because the Labour government elected in 1997 passed one major employment law statute, the Employment Relations Act 1999, which left most of the legislation of the previous government intact, and made it clear that it would not introduce any more major legislation in this area. The position was expressed by the Prime Minister in his forward to the White Paper *Fairness at Work* (1998, Cmnd. 3968), which preceded the Employment Relations Act: 'The days of strikes without ballots, mass picketing, closed shops and secondary action are over.'

At the same time, and initially almost unnoticed by the protagonists, the impact of both the European Convention on Human Rights and of European Community law was gradually making itself felt in the field of collective employment law and these may prove to be the most significant influences in the future.

## DEFINITION AND LEGAL STATUS OF TRADE UNIONS

### ■ Definition of a union

Section 1 of the Trade Union and Labour Relations (Consolidation) Act 1992 (TULRCA) defines a trade union as an organisation consisting wholly or mainly of workers of one or more descriptions and whose principal purposes include the regulation of relations between workers of that description or descriptions and employers or employers' associations. The key elements are that it must be an organisation of workers concerned with relations with employers. Thus in *Midland Cold Storage v Turner* (1972) a shop stewards committee in the London docks which acted as a pressure group was not a union as it did not enter into bargaining with the employers.

## Legal status of unions

Section 10 of TULRCA states that a union is not a corporate body but that it can be sued and be sued in its own name; it can make contracts; and criminal proceedings can be brought against the union itself. Unions are in a unique legal position: they are theoretically unincorporated associations, which is the same legal status as that possessed by countless small sports and social clubs, yet s.10 of TULRCA then gives them most of the legal powers and duties of corporations, in allowing them to sue and be sued, etc. This position had already been reached by the courts in *Bonsor v Musicians Union* (1956), where it was held that a union was liable to compensate a member who had been expelled wrongly. (See later in this chapter for a further discussion of this case.) However, they do not possess one power of a corporation, as they cannot hold property which must, by s.12, be vested in trustees to be held on their behalf. If a union is sued then that property can be taken in satisfaction of a judgment just as if the union was a corporation.

*Example*

A union is sued for damages by an employer for calling a strike without holding a secret ballot as required by law. The union is held liable to pay damages and these will come from property held by the trustees.

An important provision is contained in s.11 of TULRCA, which continues the rule first introduced in the Trade Union Act 1871 that the activities of a union are not to be regarded as unlawful simply because they may be technically in restraint of trade. This applies not only to the actual purposes of the union but also to its rules. The reason for this was to avoid the possibility, canvassed by Sachs LJ in *Edwards v SOGAT* (1971), that the courts could intervene and strike down a union rule on the grounds that it was oppressive and therefore possibly in restraint of trade. (The relationship between union rules and restraint of trade is dealt with later in this chapter.)

One should also note that, by s.160 of TULRCA, a trade union may be joined in an unfair dismissal action by either the employee or employer where it is alleged that the union put pressure on the employer to dismiss the employee because of non-membership of the union.

## Listing of unions and certificates of independence

Section 2 of TULRCA provides that the Certification Officer shall keep a list of trade unions. There is no legal requirement on unions to be listed but there are a number of advantages: entry on the list is, by s.2(4), conclusive evidence that the organisation is a trade union and there are a number of tax advantages. Moreover, ss.13 and 14 of TULRCA provide for a simplified procedure for the vesting of property in trustees where the union is listed. There is no similarity between listing and the requirement to register under the Industrial Relations Act and so the vast majority of unions are listed. The main inducement to be listed is that listing is the essential prerequisite to the granting of a certificate of independence, which is essential for the granting of a large number of statutory rights: these are too numerous to list in full here but many rights granted to unions are only granted to those who have certificates of independence. Thus only unions with such a certificate are entitled to be consulted about impending redundancies and other matters and only members of independent trade unions are protected from dismissal on the grounds of union activities.

Applications for certificates of independence are made to the Certification Officer under s.6 of TULRCA and s.5 sets out the definition of an independent trade union. This is one which is not under the domination or control of an employer or an employer's association and is not liable to interference by the employer or employer's association tending towards control, whether this interference is by the provision of financial or material support or by any other means. The object is to weed out organisations which may appear to be representing the employees but which in fact are simply pawns of the employer.

The criteria for the granting of certificates were set out by the Certification Officer in 1976 and can now be found in their Annual Report. They were approved by the EAT in *Blue Circle Staff Association v Certification Officer* (1977) and are as follows:

## The strength and sources of the union's finances

Clearly a union which receives finance from the employer will not be considered independent.

## The extent of any assistance given by the employer in either establishing or running the organisation

The word 'extent' should be emphasised: it is common practice and good industrial relations for the employer to provide the union with facilities such as notice boards and, if necessary, an office and this is recommended in the ACAS Code of Practice on Time Off for Trade Union Duties and Activities. If, however, the extent of the assistance is such that the union would not be able to function without it then the independence of the union is likely to jeopardised.

## Whether the constitution allows for interference by the employer in the affairs of the union

In the *Blue Circle* case (above) the rules originally allowed management representatives to sit on the committee and, even though this was changed, these representatives helped in the drafting of the new rules. This indicated that the organisation was not independent. In *Squibb UK Staff Association v Certification Officer* (1979) the EAT held that where a staff association had been dominated by the employer then it might take some time before it was able to demonstrate that it had shaken this off sufficiently to be granted a certificate of independence.

### Is the union a single company one or does its membership come from a broader base?

This is also relevant when considering the extent of any assistance given by the employer (above) because, as the Certification Officer has pointed out in the Guidance on Applications for a Certificate of Independence, if a single company union receives facilities from an employer then it would find it very difficult to survive if those were cut off, whereas a broadly based union which also received them could survive. An instance of a single company union failing to gain a certificate is provided by *Government Communications Staff Federation v Certification Officer and CCSU* (1993), where the continued existence of an organisation representing staff at GCHQ (who were not at that time allowed to join a union) depended on the approval of the Director. The EAT felt that the words 'liable to interference' in s.5 meant 'vulnerable to interference' or exposed to the risk of interference so that any matters which indicated a possibility of interference by the employer would mean that the union would not be granted a certificate. Nevertheless, there have been many instances of single company unions which were undoubtedly independent, such as the railway unions.

### Does the union have a robust attitude in negotiations with the employer?

The negotiating record of the organisation will be looked at, although the amount of industrial action which the organisation has been involved in is not by itself a criterion.

## RECOGNITION OF UNIONS

The idea of recognition is that an employer is prepared to negotiate and otherwise deal with a union on matters covered by collective bargaining. In very many cases this has been happening for many years and will happen for a long time in the future. However, it is also true to say that, with the decline in union membership and the shift from national collective bargaining to bargaining on a company basis, union recognition has been in decline.

There are four preliminary points to be made.

### ■ Voluntary or statutory recognition

Recognition can be voluntary under an express agreement, or it can, under provisions introduced by the Employment Relations Act 1999, be introduced as a result of a statutory procedure. Section 178(3) of TULRCA provides that a union is recognised 'to any extent' for the purposes of collective bargaining which means negotiations covering:

1. terms and conditions of employment;
2. engagement or non-engagement or termination or suspension of either employment or the duties of employment;
3. allocation of work or duties of employment between employees;
4. disciplinary matters;
5. membership or non-membership of a trade union;
6. facilities for union officials;
7. machinery for negotiation or consultation on any of the above matters.

The phrase 'to any extent' means that there must be a clear agreement to recognise but that it need not be for all of the above matters. It should be noted that a collective agreement is, by s.179 of TULRCA, presumed not to be legally binding. Where a union is recognised as a result of the statutory recognition procedure in the Employment Relations Act, then it only covers negotiations relating to pay, hours and holidays.

## Other forms of recognition

Recognition can also be for various purposes scattered around the legislation, such as the receipt of bargaining information, consultation on impending redundancies, consultation on TUPE transfers and appointment of safety representatives. None of these is, of course, covered by the statutory recognition procedure.

## Recognition for disciplinary and grievance procedures

An employer may agree to recognise a union only for the purpose of representing its members in disciplinary and grievance procedures. This type of recognition will not entitle the union to claim that it is recognised for the purposes of collective bargaining or any of the matters discussed in 'Other forms of recognition', above (see *USDAW v Sketchley Ltd* (1981)).

## THE STATUTORY RECOGNITION PROCEDURE

The statutory recognition procedure is extremely detailed and operates by way of insertion by the Employment Relations Act into TULRCA 1992 of a new Schedule A1.

## The procedure in outline

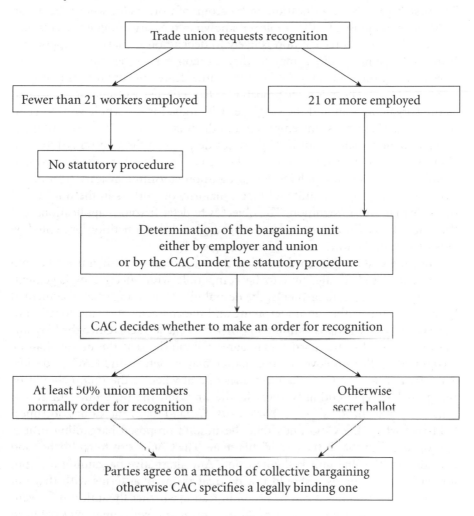

Trade union requests recognition

Fewer than 21 workers employed

21 or more employed

No statutory procedure

Determination of the bargaining unit
either by employer and union
or by the CAC under the statutory procedure

CAC decides whether to make an order for recognition

At least 50% union members
normally order for recognition

Otherwise
secret ballot

Parties agree on a method of collective bargaining
otherwise CAC specifies a legally binding one

## The procedure in detail

This begins with a request by a trade union (or unions, as a joint request may be submitted) for recognition on behalf of a group of workers known as the 'bargaining unit'. There is one vital precondition: the statutory recognition procedure only applies where the employer employs at least 21 workers, although the proposed bargaining unit may be smaller than this. It should also be noted that there is nothing to prevent an employer entering into a voluntary recognition agreement with a non-independent union but the statutory recognition only applies to recognised unions. If the parties agree on recognition at that stage (i.e. voluntary recognition, known in the legislation as 'agreements for recognition') the matter ends. If not, the statutory procedure continues.

## Identification of the bargaining unit

The first stage is the identification of the group of workers for whom the union seeks to be recognised by the employer, known as the bargaining unit. This may be a crucial stage, as recognition is likely to depend on the level of support for it in the bargaining unit. It may be that a union has strong support amongst a particular group but does not have the same degree of support amongst the whole workforce. The union will probably try to get the particular group recognised as the bargaining unit and the employer will argue for the whole workforce to be the unit. The parties (the employer and the union) will try to agree what the bargaining unit shall be but if they cannot do so, then the Central Arbitration Committee (CAC) decides. However, the CAC can only act if it is satisfied that members of the union applying for recognition constitute at least 10% of the workers in the proposed unit and that a majority of workers in the unit would be likely to favour recognition. The object is to deter frivolous applications and the White Paper *Fairness at Work* (1998) suggested that a petition presented by at least 10% of the workers would be strong evidence.

Once the CAC begins to determine the bargaining unit, it must take into account the need for the unit to be compatible with effective management, existing bargaining arrangements, the desirability of avoiding small fragmented bargaining units within an undertaking and the characteristics and location of the workers in the proposed unit and other relevant workers. Once the bargaining unit is decided, the parties may agree voluntarily that the union shall be recognised by the employer or the matter may be left to the CAC to decide. The question for the CAC then becomes one of whether the union should be recognised as representing workers in the unit and the procedure for this is outlined below. In *R v CAC, ex parte Kwik-Fit Ltd* (2002) the Court of Appeal held that where the CAC finds that the union's proposed bargaining unit is appropriate then that is the end of this stage. The CAC is not to go further and consider whether the unit is the best one. Any alternative bargaining unit put forward by the employer should not be treated on equal terms with that put forward by the union but can be useful in testing whether the unit put forward by the union is appropriate. In *Graphical Paper and Media Union v Derry Print Ltd* (2002) it was held that the statutory recognition procedures can only be used to gain recognition for a bargaining unit covering one employer but where there are two firms which are really one then an exception will be made and recognition can be sought in respect of both of them in one procedure.

## Order for recognition

Once the bargaining unit is determined, the question is then whether the union shall be regarded as representing workers in it. The CAC therefore decides whether to make an order for recognition, although it must be emphasised that at any time in the procedure the parties may reach a voluntary agreement. There are two ways in which the CAC can decide whether the union should be recognised:

1. If the CAC is satisfied that at least 50% of the workers in the unit are union members then there will be a declaration that the union shall be recognised unless there are significant doubts about the evidence of union membership, or a significant number of members tell the CAC that they do not want collective bargaining, or the CAC itself considers that a ballot should be held in the interests of good industrial relations.
2. If less than 50% of workers are union members then a secret ballot of the workers in the bargaining unit must be held. If the result of the ballot is that a majority of those support union recognition *and* those voting constitute at least 40% of the workers in the bargaining unit then the application succeeds. If not, it is dismissed.

## Method of collective bargaining

Following a declaration of recognition, the parties should agree on a method of conducting collective bargaining but, if they cannot do so, then the CAC may, as a last resort, specify a method which takes effect as a legally enforceable agreement between the parties. The Trade Union Recognition (Method of Collective Bargaining) Order 2000 specifies a model method with a six-stage process, starting with the submission by the union of a claim and ending with the involvement of ACAS if the parties cannot agree. The model also makes provision for the setting up of a Joint Negotiating Body.

## Changes in the bargaining unit

Where either party believes that there have been changes in the bargaining unit after the declaration of recognition then they can apply to the CAC for a determination that the bargaining unit is no longer appropriate. Such an application can only be made if there is evidence that the present unit is no longer appropriate because of changes in the structure of the business or its activities or where there has been a substantial change in the number of workers in the present unit.

## Application for derecognition

An application for derecognition can be made after a minimum of three years from the declaration of recognition. This application can only be made on the grounds that:

1. The employer contends that the size of the workforce has fallen to below 21.
2. The employer or workers believe that there is no longer majority support for the collective bargaining arrangements.
3. The original declaration of recognition was made on the basis of 50% union membership and the employer believes that this is now below 50%.
4. The workers wish to end voluntary recognition of a non-independent union.

## DISCLOSURE OF BARGAINING INFORMATION TO INDEPENDENT RECOGNISED TRADE UNIONS

Section 181 of TULRCA provides that an employer has a general duty to disclose information to trade unions, for the purpose of collective bargaining, which is either information without which the union would be impeded in carrying out collective bargaining or information which ought to be disclosed in the interest of good industrial relations. The contrast with the provisions discussed above could not be starker: whilst it might be said that they are over-detailed, these are virtually meaningless. Fortunately, there is a Code of Practice (on Disclosure of Information to Trade Unions for Collective Bargaining Purposes) which gives details of information which should be disclosed. Examples are details of pay and benefits, conditions of service, analysis of the workforce, the performance of the organisation and financial information. Section 182 lays down certain information that need not be disclosed: that which has been communicated to the employer in confidence; information relating specifically to an individual (e.g. details of performance-related pay received by a named individual); and other information which, if disclosed, could cause substantial injury to the undertaking. The Code gives, as examples of the last category, details of marketing and pricing policies and details of how tender prices are made up. A failure to disclose information as required can lead to a complaint by the union to the CAC. If conciliation through ACAS fails then the CAC may hear a claim by the union that the contracts of specified workers should include specified terms and conditions. The CAC cannot, however, give guidance on what should be disclosed in future.

## THE RIGHT TO FREEDOM OF ASSOCIATION

### ▇ Background

The right to freedom of association can be said to date from the repeal of the Combination Acts in 1825 but, as always in UK law, the right was couched in negative terms: it was simply provided that a union was not liable in the criminal law for existing. No positive right to form one was given and the legislators at the time would have been astonished at the suggestion that it should be. Even today, the right to associate is protected in UK law by statutory provisions giving the right not, for example, to be subjected to any detriment on the grounds of union membership. Before these detailed provisions are considered, however, it should be noted that international and specifically European legislation does recognise a positive right to associate:

#### Under international standards

The constitution of the International Labour Organisation (ILO), first established in 1919 and whose constitution was revised in 1946, asserts that freedom of association is essential to sustained progress. This right is also given expression in the Universal Declaration of Human Rights, adopted by the United Nations General Assembly in 1948, which declares that 'everyone has the right to form and join trade unions for the protection of his interests'. These statements are not, of course, legally enforceable, although they do set a standard to which states should aspire and, arguably, they could be said to have paved the way for the European principles in this area.

## Under European principles

The ECHR states in Article 11(1) that: 'Everyone has the right to freedom of peaceful assembly and association with others, including the right to join and form trade unions for the protection of his interests.' It then states in Article 11(2) that no restrictions shall be placed on this right other than are prescribed by law and are necessary in a democratic society in the interests of public safety, for the prevention of disorder or crime, for the protection of health or morals or for the protection of the rights and freedoms of others. The effect of Article 11 was considered by the EctHR in *X v Ireland* (1971) where it was held that any intimidation of employees to make them give up their functions within a union was in breach of Article 11. As such, this adds nothing to existing UK law and this impression is strengthened by remarks of the judges in *UKAPE v ACAS* (1980), where Lord Scarman, whilst prepared to recognise the effect of Article 11, even though at that date it was not incorporated into UK law, felt that it did not give a right to a union to seek recognition from an employer, a right now provided by statute. Thus it seems that, given that UK law has comprehensive provisions protecting union membership and activities, Article 11 may not add anything beyond possibly applying to self-employed persons who are victimised by employers on the grounds of union membership. This is because UK legislation refers only to 'employees', whereas the Convention has no such restriction. Given the increase in the number of persons who are self-employed this may not be quite as insignificant a point as it seems. The ECtHR has itself adopted a restrictive interpretation of Article 11 and has stated that it does not give a right to trade union recognition or a right to strike (see *Swedish Engine Drivers Union v Sweden* (1980) and *Schmidt and Dahlstrom v Sweden* (1976)). Moreover, the ECtHR has stated that Article 11 is an area where states should enjoy 'a wide margin of appreciation in the choice of means to be employed'. Finally, one must not forget the link between the ECHR and EC law because Article 6 of the Treaty of European Union commits the EU to respect fundamental rights, amongst which those in the ECHR are mentioned. The right of freedom of association was recognised by the ECJ in the *Bosman* decision in 1995 and the ECJ is prepared to extend the right of association to allow a staff association to do anything which protects the interests of their members (*Union Syndicate v EC Council* (1974)). It will be interesting to see whether the ECJ, rather than the ECHR, explicitly rules, as it has already come close to doing, that there is a right to strike.

## ■ The right of association in UK law

The right of association is protected by UK law in the following ways.

### Protection against being refused employment on grounds of union membership or non-membership

Section 137 of TULRCA makes it unlawful to refuse employment on the grounds of union membership. The term 'refused' is defined widely as refusals to entertain applications, making a person withdraw an application, refusing to offer employment and offering it on such terms that no reasonable employer would offer. It will be noted that the right to associate (i.e. not to be refused employment on grounds of union membership) is coupled with the right to disassociate (i.e. the right not to be refused employment on grounds of *not* belonging to a union) and this second aspect is related to the closed shop, which is considered below. The likelihood is that s.137 only applies to refusals on the grounds of union *membership* rather than *activities* because the decision of the EAT that it *could* apply to activities (*Harrison v KCC* (1995)) may be suspect in view of the later decisions of the House of Lords in *Associated Newspapers Ltd v Wilson* and *Associated British Ports v Palmer* (1995), which are considered below. Thus an employer who refused employment to a person on the grounds that they were known as union activists would almost certainly not be caught by s.137. A complaint of a breach of s.137 lies to an employment tribunal, which can order compensation up to the limit of compensation for unfair dismissal.

### Protection against dismissal on trade union grounds

Section 152(1) of TULRCA provides that a dismissal of an employee will be automatically unfair if the reason, or principal reason, is that the employee:

1. Was, or proposed to become, a member of an independent trade union.
2. Had taken part, or proposed to take part, in its activities at an appropriate time (defined as either outside working hours or within working hours with the employer's agreement).
3. Was not a member of a trade union or had refused to become or remain a member. (This is an instance of the right to disassociate and is considered below under the closed shop.)

Note that, as with all cases of automatic unfair dismissals, there is no qualifying period of employment before an application can be brought under s.152.

Suppose that a job applicant was a union activist in a previous employment and gains a position with a new employer by concealing this. This is precisely what happened in *City of Birmingham DC v Beyer* (1977), where the employee was dismissed when his past as a union activist was found out (about an hour after he started work!). It was held that because he had concealed his activities the dismissal was fair on the ground of the employee's deceit. However, in *Fitzpatrick v British Railways Board* (1990) it was held by the Court of Appeal that where an employer dismisses on the ground that an employee was a union activist in a previous employment then this by itself could be dismissal on grounds of trade union activities. The distinction between the two cases is really the deceit of the employee in *Beyer*. Note that if either of the employees in these cases had been refused employment on the grounds of union activities then s.137 of TULRCA would apply when the distinction between membership and activities has been considered in other cases (above).

The remedies on a complaint that a dismissal was for a s.152 ground are the same as for other unfair dismissal actions (see Chapter 11), except that:

1. There is a minimum basic award of £3,400, unlike the normal unfair dismissal cases where there is no minimum.
2. An employee can apply for interim relief under ss.161–166 of TULRCA where the tribunal, if it thinks that the complaint is likely be upheld at the full hearing, must first ask the employer if they are willing for the employment to continue until the hearing. If the employer is willing then an order is made that the employment shall continue until then. If not, then the second option is for the tribunal to order that certain parts of the contract of employment shall continue so that the employee will continue to be paid and pension rights and continuity of employment will be preserved. However, other parts of the contract will not continue, such as the employee's obligation to work and the effect is that an employer who does not comply with the initial request to continue employment will end up paying the employee for doing nothing. A request for interim relief must be made within seven days of the dismissal and where it is for trade union membership or activities it must be supported by a certificate from a union official stating that in their opinion the dismissal was for this reason.
3. Section 160 of TULRCA allows employers or employees to ask the tribunal to join a trade union or other person to the proceedings where it is claimed that the employer was induced to dismiss the employee as a result of pressure exerted by them because the employee was not a union member. This could work where, for instance, the employer gives in to union pressure and dismisses the employee who then complains of unfair dismissal and joins the union as a co-defendant. Complaints under s.152 must be presented within three months of the dismissal (with the usual proviso for an extension of time beyond this at the employment tribunal's discretion).

## Protection against being subject to detriment

Section 146(1) of TULRCA provides that employees have the right not to be subjected to action short of dismissal (detriment) for the purpose of:

1. Preventing or deterring the employee from being, or seeking to be, a member of an independent trade union or penalising him/her for doing so.
2. Preventing or deterring the employee from taking part in the activities of an independent trade union at an appropriate time or penalising him/her for doing so.
3. Compelling the employee to be or become a member of an independent trade union. (This is again an example of the right to disassociate.)

### Action short of dismissal

What follows is complex and you should keep the following in mind:

1. X Ltd tells its employees that they cannot belong to a trade union and if they do so they will be dismissed. This is covered by s.152 and dismissal would be automatically unfair.
2. Y Ltd tells its employees that if they give up their rights to be represented by the union in collective bargaining (not give up actual union membership) then they will be granted a pay rise. It is this area which forms the battle-ground described below.

The phrase 'action short of dismissal' was inserted into s.146 by Schedule 2 to the Employment Relations Act 1999 as a result of the decisions of the House of Lords in *Associated Newspapers v Wilson* and *Associated British Ports v Palmer* (1995). In both these cases the employer had offered pay increases to employees who gave up their rights to have their contracts negotiated through collective bargaining and changed to individual contracts. It was held that the employer's decision not to give pay rises to those who did not agree to the new contracts was not an act but just an omission and, as s.146 only then covered situations where the employer actually took action, the acts in these cases were not covered by s.146. On this point these cases are now only of historic interest because of the above amendment to s.146 which, by inserting the words 'action short of dismissal', would now mean that the action taken by the employers in those cases came under s.146.

However, these decisions are still of importance because of the consideration which was given by the courts to the word 'purpose' in s.146. To put it simply, it may be that the *effect* of the employer's actions will be to subject an employee to a detriment on trade union grounds but was this the *purpose* of the employer's actions? If not, then the action will be outside s.146. In the *Wilson* and *Palmer* cases the issue was whether the purpose of the employers in offering a pay rise only to those who signed individual contracts was to penalise those employees who had not signed or to change the system of bargaining from collective to individual agreements. It was held by a majority of the House of Lords that it was the latter. Furthermore, the then government introduced an amendment (known as the Ullswater amendment) to s.148 of TULRCA in the Trade Union and Employment Rights Act 1993 in response to the decision of the Court of Appeal that the purpose of the employer's actions *was* to deter union membership. The amended s.148 provides that where there is evidence that the employer's purpose was:

(a) to further a change in its relations with employees; or
(b) to prevent or deter union membership,

then the tribunal *must* regard the reason as (a) unless no reasonable employer would have acted in this way. The result is that *any* evidence that the purpose was (a) must be taken as conclusive that the employer's purpose was (a), even though there is ample evidence that it was (b), subject to the saving clause about the reasonable employer. The effect is to make it very difficult to argue that any action by an employer is to deter union membership and thus within s.146. This change was not reversed by the Employment Relations Act but now the ECtHR has ruled in *Wilson and others v UK* (2002) that the giving of 'sweeteners' as in *Wilson* and *Palmer* to induce employees not to make use of the union's services was in breach of Article 11 of the ECHR because, as the ECtHR observed, no real distinction can be drawn between membership of a union and use of its services. The government will now need to amend the law to ensure that employees are not deterred from seeking union representation in the way which occurred in the *Wilson* and *Palmer* cases.

Another issue, which is relevant to both s.152 and s.146, is the meaning to be given to the words 'membership of a trade union'. Does it cover just membership or the *benefits* of membership? In *Discount Tobacco v Armitage* (1995) an employee was dismissed after her union had written to her employer asking for her to be given a written statement of terms and conditions of employment. The EAT found that she had been dismissed on the grounds of trade union membership, Knox J sensibly pointing out that to confine the term 'union membership' to in effect no more than possession of a membership card would be to 'emasculate the provision altogether'. This wider view can be seen as at variance with the decisions in *Wilson* and *Palmer* because the effect of *Armitage* was to hold that there was no distinction between membership of a union as such and the benefits of membership, yet that was precisely what the employees in the other two cases had lost. Although the decision in *Armitage* was accepted in *Wilson* and *Palmer* as correct on its facts, the House of Lords declined to lay down a general principle that membership of a union should be given the same meaning as using its facilities and so the robust approach of Knox J in *Armitage* has not been followed.

A complaint by an employee of detriment under s.146 must be presented to an employment tribunal within three months (or later if the tribunal finds that it was not reasonably practicable for it be presented within the time limit) and the tribunal may award compensation which is just and equitable. This can include compensation for injury to feelings, for example, as well as financial loss.

## Other protection

Section 144 of TULRCA provides that a provision in a contract for the supply of goods or services that only non-union labour should be used is void. There is also a statutory duty under s.145 of TULRCA not to exclude a person from a list of approved suppliers on the ground that it is unlikely that they would be unlikely to meet a requirement to use only non-union labour.

## THE RIGHT TO WORK

The recognition by the courts of a 'right to work' can be seen as a counterpart to the right to associate because, if there is no right to work, then the right to associate when at work is meaningless. In *Nagle v Fielden* (1966) the claimant had been refused a licence as a trainer by the Jockey Club because she was a woman. As the club had a monopoly over flat racing, this meant that the claimant could not engage in her profession as a trainer. The Court of Appeal held that she was unlawfully denied a licence. Lord Denning said that 'the common law . . . has for centuries recognised that a man has a right to work at his profession without being unjustly excluded from it'.

This case is also important in the context of the jurisdiction of the courts over union rules and should also be considered in the light of the statutory rules on exclusion from unions. Both of these are dealt with later in this chapter.

## THE CLOSED SHOP

The idea of the closed shop is that an agreement is made between an employer and a trade union that the employer will not employ anyone who is not a member of that union. The fact that such an agreement can be made is an instance of the law supporting the right to associate, but equally the fact that such agreements can no longer be enforced is in fact an example of the law upholding the right to disassociate.

There are two ways in which closed shops operate: the *post-entry* closed shop, under which existing employees must belong to a particular union and the *pre-entry* closed shop, where belonging to a union is a condition of employment. There is nothing unlawful in the making of such an agreement; the issue is whether and how it can be enforced. The high water mark of enforcement of closed shops came with the legislation of the 1974–79 government, culminating in the Trade Union and Labour Relations (Amendment) Act 1976. This made dismissal automatically fair where the reason was that the employee was not a member of an independent trade union unless the employee had a genuine religious objection to membership of any trade union whatsoever. At that time almost 25% of all employees were covered by closed shop agreements, and they were particularly prevalent in the nationalised industries.

The 1979 Conservative government was hostile to the idea of the closed shop and added strength was given to this view by the decision of the ECtHR in *Young, James and Webster v UK* (1981). This concerned whether a closed shop agreement in the railway industry was in breach of Article 11 of the ECHR, which provides, as we saw above, that there is a right to join a trade union. A majority of the judges considered that this implied a right *not* to join. On the facts of the case it was held that Article 11 had been violated. The closed shop agreement had been introduced after the employees had begun employment, the employees objected to union membership on principle and the consequence of refusal to join (dismissal and consequent loss of livelihood) were judged particularly harsh. Thus it would seem that the enforcement of a closed shop agreement by dismissal of those who refused to join would be in breach of the ECHR.

The possibility of the ECtHR being asked to rule on a closed shop is most unlikely now that enforcement of closed shops has ceased as a result of legislation. The present Prime Minister has explicitly ruled out the reintroduction of legislation enforcing the closed shop (in his preface to the White Paper *Fairness at Work*, quoted above). The relevant legislation was first contained in the Employment Act 1988, which prevented enforcement of a post-entry closed shop (now in s.152 of TULRCA) and the Employment Act 1990, which prevented enforcement of a pre-entry closed shop (now contained in s.137 of TULRCA, which is noted above). The position now is that it is unlawful either to refuse a person employment or to dismiss an employee on the grounds of failure to be a member of an independent trade union.

## RIGHTS TO TIME OFF WORK FOR UNION DUTIES OR ACTIVITIES

These rights are contained in ss.168 and 169 of TULRCA (duties) and s.170 (activities), together with s.43 of the Employment Act 2002 and are supported by an ACAS Code of Practice.

### ■ Right to time off for union duties

This right is with pay and is given to officials of recognised independent trade unions. The right only applies to time off for three purposes:

1. Negotiating with the employer.
2. Acting on behalf of employees.
3. Training which is relevant to the above duties and which is approved by the union or by the TUC.

The ACAS Code of Practice gives guidance on what can be within the scope of the right: negotiating on terms and conditions of employment; consultation on redundancies and transfers of undertakings; and disciplinary and grievance procedures. The Act requires that the duties must be concerned with negotiations with the employer and the courts have held that attendance at meetings and conferences and other activities can be covered if there is a close connection between the activities and the negotiations. Thus in *London Ambulance Service v Charlton* (1992) attendance at meetings of a district committee of the ambulance service to prepare for negotiations in connection with collective bargaining were held to be covered and in *Adlington v British Bakeries (Northern) Ltd* (1989) attendance at a meeting to discuss the implications of a government proposal to repeal a statute regulating hours of work in the baking industry were also covered. Kerr LJ in the Court of Appeal, said that there was an 'exceptionally close connection' between the meeting and a bargaining matter with employers. Although this case was decided under the previous law, which had more generous provisions relating to time off, it is likely that it is still good law.

Section 169 of TULRCA provides that the employee is entitled to be paid the amount which they would have received had they worked at the time. This seems straightforward but what is the position where the duties are performed by a part-time worker at a time when they are not actually at work? In *Hairsine v Hull City Council* (1992) it was held that there was no right to paid time off but this may be in conflict with the decision of the ECJ in *Arbeiterwohlfahrtder Stadt Berlin v Botel* (1992). This held that a part-time worker was indirectly discriminated against by a decision that she should receive less pay while on a training course than a full-time worker would. However, the matter is not entirely clear, as the decision of the ECJ was under what is now Article 141, which refers to 'work' and, although attendance at a training course will count as work in view of the above decision, could the same be said of a negotiating session? The point is not dealt with in the Part-Time Workers (Prevention of Less Favourable Treatment) Regulations 2000.

The remedy is for the tribunal, on a complaint by the employee, to award the amount of pay which should have been received.

## Right to time off for union activities

This is without pay and is given to members of recognised independent trade unions. The ACAS Code gives as examples attending union conferences and other meetings as a union representative, voting in union elections, and attending meetings with union officials to discuss matters relevant to the workplace. In *Luce v Bexley LBC* (1990) a refusal to allow a teacher time off to attend a lobby of Parliament against the Education Reform Bill was held justified as the lobby was concerned with political objections to the Bill and not with specifically union activities.

The remedy is for the tribunal, on a complaint by the employee, to award just and equitable compensation taking into account the blame attaching to the employer and any loss to the employee.

## Rights to time off for trade union learning representatives

These are introduced by s.43 of the Employment Act 2002 and give rights to paid time off to trade union learning representatives who are members of independent recognised trade unions. The right covers time off for analysing training needs, providing information and advice on them, arranging learning and training, promoting the value of it and preparing for learning and training. The representative must have undergone training to prepare for this role and the union must certify to the employer that this has taken place. The government hopes that this new right may be taken up by members of groups who are underrepresented among shop stewards who can claim rights to time off for union activities. Groups mentioned are ethnic minority groups, older men and part-time workers.

## RIGHT TO TIME OFF FOR EMPLOYEE REPRESENTATIVES

Section 61 of the ERA 1996 provides that employee representatives are entitled to reasonable paid time off during working hours to perform their functions and to undergo training. The right is thus the same as that given to trade union officials but is, of course, restricted to the specific functions which representatives may perform under statute. There is, unfortunately, no code of practice governing this right, but it is suggested that where the functions of employee representatives parallel those of union officials, the time off should be the same. This is especially important with redundancy consultation. There is the same remedy if time off is refused as for trade union officials.

## UNION RULES

Many of the cases to be considered below deal with disciplinary hearings conducted by unions against their members. It is vital to appreciate that there are also statutory provisions governing these, which will be considered after the common law rules, and the two sets of rules have to be understood together.

### ■ Basis of the courts' approach

The courts may be asked to intervene when it is alleged that a union has acted in breach of its rules. A preliminary, but important, issue is the way in which the courts construe these rules. It has often been emphasised that the rules should not be subjected to the same minute scrutiny as, for example, statutes. In *Heatons Transport (St Helens) Ltd v TGWU* (1972) Lord Wilberforce pointed out that 'union rule books are not drafted by parliamentary draftsmen. Courts of law must resist the temptation to construe them as if they were.' In *Jacques v AUEW (Engineering Section)* (1986) Warner J said that the rules of unions are not to be construed like a statute 'but so as to give them a reasonable interpretation which accords with what in the court's view they must have been intended to mean'.

The effect is that the courts will look not only at the rules of the union but also at custom and practice and the result of this approach is to give the courts a good deal of freedom in how they interpret and apply union rules. What seems clear is that when looking at the disciplinary powers of unions the courts favour the rights of the individual member. Lord Denning went further in *Edwards v SOGAT* (1971) and put forward the 'by-law theory', under which the rules of the union will be construed as a legislative code and can be struck down if unreasonable. Indeed, he referred to construing the rules *against* the makers, i.e. the union itself. The by-law approach, with its attendant presumptions (which, it must be said, has not found favour with other judges), could be said to be in conflict with the decision of the ECtHR in *Cheall v UK* (1985). Here it was held that, although the right of unions to expel or admit members was not unfettered (see below), provided that the union acted according to the principles laid down by the court, they should be free to decide questions of expulsion and admission.

## ■ The contract of membership

This is founded on the rules of the union, subject to the above considerations. One obvious point is that it will not, therefore, apply when a person is *applying* to become a member, which is why the court in *Nagle v Fielden* (above) rested the common law on membership applications on a right to work.

In *Bonsor v Musicians Union* (1956) the contract doctrine was applied to a case of expulsion. Bonsor had failed to pay his subscriptions to the union for a year and a rule provided that if a member was more than six months in arrears with subscriptions then a branch committee could resolve that he be expelled. Instead, Bonsor was told by the branch secretary that he was expelled and this was held to be unlawful, as the rule book was a contract and the expulsion was in breach of the rules.

The courts have intervened on many other occasions, examples being: refusal of a right of appeal given under the rules (*Silvester v National Union of Printing, Bookbinding and Paper Workers* (1966)); irregularities in the holding and conduct of meetings (*MacLelland v NUJ* (1975)); and a strike call in breach of the union's rules (*Taylor v NUM (Derbyshire Area) (No. 1)* (1984)).

The view was taken that the courts would not imply a power into the rules to discipline or expel a member. However, in *McVitae v Unison* (1996) the court held that such a power can be implied where there are compelling reasons for this. Disciplinary proceedings had been taken by NALGO against some of its members for alleged racial and sexist acts but NALGO then merged with NUPE to form UNISON. There was no express power in the rules of UNISON to take disciplinary proceedings against members for acts committed before amalgamation but the court held that a power would be implied, especially as the conduct alleged was contrary to the rules of UNISON.

Where there are disciplinary rules then the courts can, in some cases at least, examine both the rule and the action taken under it to see if the action was justified. In *Esterman v NALGO* (1974) a ballot of NALGO members was held during a dispute with local authorities which showed that 49% were in favour of industrial action. The union then instructed its members not to co-operate in the holding of local government elections. The claimant disobeyed this and was invited to attend a meeting at which her expulsion would be considered on the ground that she was 'unfit for membership'. The court granted an injunction to stop the hearing on the ground that the failure to obtain a majority meant that there was doubt whether the union had power to instruct its members to take action and therefore the claimant could not be 'unfit for membership' in disobeying this instruction. The result of *Esterman* is that the union will not be allowed even to consider the matter at all, as distinct from the court simply reviewing a decision already taken. The draconian nature of this case was somewhat mitigated by the Court of Appeal in *Longley v NUJ* (1987), where it held that an injunction to stop a hearing in advance would only be granted in 'exceptional circumstances' where no reasonable tribunal acting *bona fide* could possibly find against the claimant.

Does a claimant have to exhaust all internal remedies before making an application to the court? In *Leigh v NUR* (1970) the claimant was nominated as a candidate in the election for president of the union but the general secretary refused to approve his candidature. The claimant took action in the courts to rescind this action and the union contended that he should first exhaust the remedies in the union's rule book before taking legal action. Goff J, in the High Court, held that an express clause in the rules that a claimant must first exhaust legal remedies cannot oust the jurisdiction of the courts to hear claims that the rules have been broken, but a claimant must show a good reason why a court should intervene *before* the remedies in the rule book are exhausted.

A related issue is whether the rule in *Foss v Harbottle* (1843), which is applied to companies, also applies to trade unions. The effect of this rule is that if something is done which can be ratified by a simple majority of members then no action can be brought by an individual in respect of it. The rule does not apply where it is alleged that the rights of individuals have been infringed and this obviously means that in many of the cases discussed above the rule could not be applied. In *Taylor v NUM (Derbyshire Area) (No. 3)* (1985) the claim was that expenses incurred on a strike were unlawful as the strike was *ultra vires* the union, having been called without a ballot. Accordingly, it was claimed that these expenses should be repaid by the officials concerned. It was held that repayment would not be ordered, partly because a simple majority of the union's members could resolve not to seek repayment and, in effect, ratify the decision to call a strike. Vinelott J observed that: 'The courts are, in principle, reluctant to intervene in the affairs of any association, corporation or unincorporated association . . . you can please yourself whether you call that the rule in *Foss v Harbottle* or not.' The point has been urged that this decision is wrong: if the payments were *ultra vires* then the decision to make them could not be ratified because an *ultra vires* act cannot be ratified (*Ashbury Railway and Carriage Co. Ltd v Riche* (1875)).

Section 63 of TULRCA has an impact on the above situations by providing that where a member applies to the union to have a matter determined then if the union has failed to determine it within six months the court must ignore any rule requiring internal remedies to be exhausted in deciding whether or not to hear the action. This rule would not prevent a claimant going to the courts *before* six months were up and in this situation the remarks of Goff J in *Leigh v NUR* (above) are still relevant.

## The rules of natural justice

The rules of natural justice are:

1. The rule against bias.
2. The right to a fair hearing.

These rules have been applied to the decisions of trade unions and the following cases serve as good examples of when this has been so.

### Rule against bias

In *Taylor v National Union of Seamen* (1967) the general secretary of the union had dismissed an official and had then presided over the appeal made by him. Not only this but, during the appeal, he had made interventions which were prejudicial to the official's case. It was held that this was a clear case of bias. (See also *Roebuck v NUM (Yorkshire Area) (No. 2)* (1978).)

In *White v Kuzych* (1951) the union member objected to the inclusion on a panel hearing a disciplinary charge against him of a member known to be hostile to his views. It was held that this was not by itself evidence of bias. Lord Simon said that members with strong views on policy could still sit on a tribunal, so long as there is 'a will to reach an honest conclusion'. This is an important and realistic decision because where there is an issue on which there are strong feelings (such as, here, the closed shop) then members with views on it can still sit as long as they keep those views out of the meeting. If they were not allowed to sit at all, it could be very difficult at times to find a tribunal able to sit because all potential members would have views one way or the other.

### The right to a fair hearing

A good example of the right to a fair hearing is *Radford v NATSOPA* (1972). Radford was facing a disciplinary hearing and refused to reveal to the union in advance the nature of his discussions with his own solicitor. He was then expelled forthwith for wilfully taking action against the union. It was held that, as there was no hearing on this charge, the decision to expel him would be quashed as it was in breach of natural justice.

A final point to note is that there is no automatic right to legal representation (*Enderby Town FC Ltd v Football Association* (1971)) although, on a practical level, it would be wise to think carefully before deciding whether to turn down a request for this. A request for *some* representation (not necessarily legal) should always be granted on a disciplinary charge especially as this is in line with the right to be represented by a 'worker's companion' at disciplinary hearings conducted by employers (see Chapter 11).

## STATUTORY RULES ON EXCLUSION, EXPULSION AND OTHER DISCIPLINARY ACTION TAKEN BY UNIONS AGAINST THEIR MEMBERS

From the passage of the Trade Union Act 1984 onwards a new theme emerged in the legislation introduced by the 1979–97 Conservative governments on trade unions. This was that of 'giving the unions back to their members' and it led to many new rules, not only on disciplinary matters but also on related topics such as union elections.

The rules on disciplinary matters appear in two places: in ss.64–66 of TULRCA 1992 (dealing with unjustifiable disciplining) and in s.174 of TULRCA (dealing with the right not be excluded or expelled from a union). There is an overlap between the two, as one of the forms of unjustifiable disciplining is expulsion. The reason for this is that s.174 is the successor to legislation which had its genesis in the Employment Act 1980 and which was designed to deal with where an employee had been excluded or expelled where there was a closed shop. Now that closed shops are no longer enforceable, there is a strong case for having a single code of legislation dealing with disciplinary action. Before dealing with the details, three preliminary points should be noted:

1. Section 64(5) expressly preserves the existing common law rights where disciplinary action has been taken by a union. In some cases it will be a question of choice whether to use statute or common law.
2. Where a person is *excluded* from a union then only s.174 can apply.
3. Where there is a complaint of unjustifiable expulsion then s.66(4) provides that the bringing of proceedings under either s.174 or s.66 will bar proceedings under the other head.

## ◼ Exclusion or expulsion under s.174 of TULRCA

Exclusion means where a person is refused admission to membership. In *NACODS v Gluchowski* (1996) the claimant was suspended from membership of the union but it was held that s.174 only applies to refusal of membership or expulsion and not to suspension.

Section 174(2) provides that the exclusion or expulsion of an individual shall only be permitted on any one of the following grounds:

(a) that the individual does not satisfy, or no longer satisfies, an 'enforceable membership requirement' contained in the rules of the union;
(b) that the individual does not qualify for membership, or no longer qualifies, because the union only operates in a particular geographical area;
(c) that the union is a single employer union and the individual either is not, or is no longer, employed by that employer;
(d) that the exclusion or expulsion of the individual is entirely attributable to the conduct of the individual.

The term 'enforceable membership requirement' in (a) above is defined as one which restricts membership by reference solely to the following criteria, which are set out in s.174(3):

(a) employment in a specified trade, industry or profession;
(b) occupational description;
(c) possession of specified qualifications or work experience.

Accordingly, it is unlawful for a union to refuse to admit a person on ground (a) who satisfies any of the above criteria as laid down by the union.

The other significant provision is that found in (d) in s.174(2) (conduct) and here again the Act leaves nothing to chance.

Section 174(4) provides that conduct does not include any of the following:

(a) being, or ceasing to be, a member of another trade union or political party or where the individual is employed by a particular employer or at a particular place;
(b) conduct of a type which is specified in s.65 as one where the individual is protected from unjustifiable discipline.

The effect is that a union is not allowed to refuse to admit to membership or exclude from membership on the ground of conduct if the ground is any one of these matters specified in s.174(4). As we will see, there are other constraints on expulsion in ss.64–65.

The remedy for a breach of s.174 is ultimately an award of compensation but the provisions are exceedingly complex. The essence of them is that a complaint is made to an employment tribunal which, if it upholds the claim, makes a declaration to this effect. The union then has a period of time in which to admit the person to membership or rescind the expulsion. If it acts in accordance with the declaration then compensation is awarded by the tribunal, the maximum being the same as for unfair dismissal (at present £56,000 (£3,400 basic award and £52,600 compensatory award)). If it does not act in accordance with the ruling then the matter goes direct to the EAT (a most unusual procedure), which can award compensation with the same maximum but with a minimum of £5,600. (See *Bradley v NALGO* (1991), discussed below under s.65, for a case dealing with the amount of compensation.)

Note the effect which s.174 has had on the TUC's Bridlington Principles (below).

## ■ Unjustifiable disciplining under ss.64–66 of TULRCA

Section 64 sets out the disciplinary sanctions which are caught by these provisions and s.65 sets out the actions by an individual which can lead to these sanctions. The effect is that if a member commits any of the acts listed in s.65 then the union cannot take any of the actions listed under s.64 as a disciplinary measure.

The following are the unjustifiable disciplinary sanctions listed in s.64(2):

(a) expulsion from the union or a branch or section of it;
(b) that a sum should be paid to the union or a branch or section of it;
(c) sums paid as subscriptions shall not be treated as having been paid or as having been paid for a different purpose;
(d) deprivation of some or all of the benefits, services or facilities enjoyed by members;
(e) encouraging or advising another union not to accept the person in question as a member;
(f) subjecting the person to any other detriment.

In *NALGO v Killorn* (1996) union members who had crossed a picket line during a strike were suspended and their names were advertised in a circular. The suspension was held to amount to a deprivation of benefits under (d) above and the advertisement of names was held to be subjecting them to a detriment under (f), as it caused them acute embarrassment.

Section 65(2) then lists the actions by individuals that can lead to the imposition of these sanctions. It must be emphasised that in any of these cases the sanctions listed above will amount to unjustifiable discipline.

(a) failing to take part in or support a strike or other industrial action whether the strike or other action is called by the member's own union or another union;

(b) failing to contravene, for the purpose of the strike or other industrial action, a requirement imposed by the employer under the contract of employment or any other agreement with the employer;

(c) asserting that the union or its officials or trustees have broken the law;

(d) encouraging another to act in the ways set out in (b) or (c) above;

(e) contravening an requirement of the union which is itself an infringement of s.64;

(f) failing to agree to the deduction of membership subscriptions from wages;

(g) resigning or proposing to resign from a union or refusing or proposing to refuse to become a member of a union;

(h) working or proposing to work with persons who are not union members;

(i) working or proposing to work for an employer who uses non-union labour;

(j) requiring the union to fulfil its duties to members under TULRCA, e.g. dealing with ballots.

In addition, seeking assistance from the Certification Officer is also an action for which the disciplinary sanctions listed in s.64 are unjustifiable under s 65(3)

Although this list might be thought to contain everything which a union member might do, certainly in the course of an industrial dispute, this is not so. In *Knowles v Fire Brigades Union* (1996) a firefighter was expelled for having accepted a 'retained' contract to be available in his spare time although it was against union policy to accept these contracts. The Court of Appeal held that neither (a) nor (b) above were broken as there was no industrial dispute. The matter was simply one of union policy. In this case there would probably be no remedy either under s.174 above because expulsion for conduct cannot be on the grounds defined in s.65, which then leads us back to the point that s.65 did not apply here. The only possible remedy would be at common law.

It is possible that the provisions of s.174 are in breach of Article 11 of the ECHR and of Articles 3 and 5 of ILO Convention No. 87 on freedom of association. Article 11 gives a right of freedom of association (see above) and in *Cheall v UK* (1985) the ECtHR held that where a union excluded or expelled a person and the decision was in breach of its rules, or was arbitrary, or the result was that the person lost employment or otherwise suffered exceptional hardship, then the decision could be in breach of the ECHR. It is arguable that these are the only grounds for exclusion or expulsion under the ECHR and that the grounds in s.174 and ss.64–65 should be interpreted in accordance with the ruling in *Cheall*.

The remedies for a breach of ss.64–65 are similar to those laid down for breach of s.174 and are set out in s.66. In *Bradley v NALGO* (1991) members who had been expelled for not taking part in a strike were held to have been unjustifiably disciplined but were only awarded the minimum, as there was no evidence that as a result of their expulsion their future job prospects would suffer.

## AMALGAMATIONS BETWEEN UNIONS AND DISPUTES BETWEEN UNIONS

Sections 97–106 of TULRCA provide detailed procedures for amalgamations between unions and transfers by one union of its members and assets to another. The details are beyond the scope of this book but what is of more significance are the 'Bridlington Principles' which have, since 1939, governed disputes between unions over membership. (They are known as the Bridlington Principles as they were first drawn up at the TUC conference held there in 1939.) These originally provided that unions would not accept as members those who were or had been members of another union without making enquiries from that union about the status of the applicant. If a member was found to have been admitted to membership in breach of these rules, the TUC Disputes Committee could either order a union not to admit that person or, if they had been admitted, to expel them. These rules then ran foul of what is now s.174 of TULRCA (above), dealing with the circumstances in which a person can be expelled from a union, and so the principles were revised in 1993 so that, if a person is admitted in breach of them, the remedy is the payment of compensation to the person's former union by the union which admitted that person, and there is no longer a power to order the union to expel the member.

## POLITICAL FUNDS OF TRADE UNIONS

Trade unions have traditionally engaged in political activity, one of the main areas being support for Labour Party candidates at elections. These activities are governed by legislation, which was first made necessary by the decision of the House of Lords in *Amalgamated Society of Railway Servants v Osborne* (1911), where it was held that expenditure on political objects was *ultra vires* the union. This decision is yet another example of the anomalous status of trade unions, as the *ultra vires* doctrine belongs to company law and unions are not, of course, companies. However, the House of Lords drew an analogy with companies and held that the doctrine applied.

This decision led to the Trade Union Act 1913, which allowed a trade union to establish a political fund, separate from its other funds, and from which individual members would be allowed to opt out. The present legislation is contained in ss.71–87 of TULRCA. This provides that union funds can only be applied to political objects if the members have approved the setting up of a political fund by passing a 'political resolution' in a secret ballot which has to be held every ten years. The rules for the ballot must be approved by the Certification Officer, voting must be by post, and an independent scrutineer must oversee the ballot.

Section 72 defines 'political objects' as expenditure of money on any of the following matters:

(a) any contribution to the funds of, or on payment of expenditure incurred by, a political party;
(b) the provision of services or property for the use of a political party;
(c) in connection with the registration of electors, the candidature of any person, the selection of a candidate or the holding of a ballot by the union in connection with election to any political office;
(d) the maintenance of any holder of any political office;
(e) the holding of political conferences or meetings;
(f) the production, publication or distribution of literature, film, sound recording or advertisements designed to persuade people either to vote or not to vote for a political party or candidate.

A vital point is that if the expenditure falls within any of these categories then it must be paid for out of the political fund. If there is no money in the fund then the expenditure cannot be made.

In *Paul and Fraser v NALGO* (1987) it was held that publication by NALGO of leaflets and posters in a campaign just before the 1987 general election against government spending cuts and their effect on the public services was within (f) above. Browne-Wilkinson J felt that a campaign to change the government itself was within (f) but a campaign just to change the *policy* of the government was not. The distinction between these two is not always easy to draw.

Where a 'political resolution' has been passed then s.82 of TULRCA provides that a set of rules must be established relating to the fund stating that, for example, any payments under the above categories must come from the political fund and that members who have opted out from making contributions shall not be discriminated against for that reason nor barred from holding any office other than one which relates to the management of the fund.

Whenever a political resolution is passed or renewed then union members must be told of their right to opt out of paying the political levy. Opting out can take place at any time and s.84 provides that if notice of opting out is given within one month of the political resolution being passed or renewed then there is no liability at all to pay the political levy. If notice is given later then the liability ceases from the following 1 January.

## ELECTIONS OF UNION OFFICIALS

These are dealt with in ss.46–56 of TULRCA. The object is to ensure that elections are held at regular intervals, that voting is by secret ballot and that no one is unreasonably excluded from standing for union office. Thus s.46 provides that elections must be held at least every five years for the following offices: all members of the executive, whether voting or not; president; and general secretary. Section 47 provides that no person shall be unreasonably excluded from standing for election, but it was held in *Paul and Fraser v NALGO* (1987) that a union can require that a candidate must have a certain level of support from the membership as a condition of standing. Section 47 also states that no candidate shall be required to be a member of a political party, but it does allow for the rules of the union to exclude members by class. The effect is that the union could not require candidates to be, for example, members of the Labour Party but it could lay down the negative requirement that no member of the Conservative Party could stand. There are detailed requirements for the conduct of elections: there must be a postal ballot and each candidate must be given the opportunity to have an election address produced and distributed by the union (s.48). The election must be supervised by an independent scrutineer (s.49).

# Chapter 14

# Collective action

## INTRODUCTION

The central point of the law on collective action by trade unions is that the taking of such action almost inevitably involves the commission of a tort and, possibly, a crime. The history of the law on collective action is one of the law attempting to strike a balance between the right to engage in collective action and the rights of others, notably employers and employees who do not wish to take part in such action. The way in which this has been done is to provide that trade unions and others engaging in collective action shall enjoy certain immunities from being sued in tort or prosecuted under the criminal law. This is a typically British way of doing things. There is no broad principle guaranteeing the freedom to take strike action. The torts and crimes that may be committed remain unaltered. There is simply a limited immunity. However, this may change, as we shall see later in this chapter, when the effect of the ECHR is felt to a greater extent.

One consequence of this lack of thinking from first principles is that UK law has never thought through precisely what, for legal purposes, industrial action is, and when it amounts to a breach of contract. This point is well worth noting at the outset and will be considered more fully later in this chapter in the section on individual employees and industrial disputes. In the discussion on collective action which follows it will generally be assumed that the action involved is a strike, which does obviously amount to a breach of contract, although, as we shall see, there have been attempts even here to argue in some instances that it may not be.

*Example*

The Union of Nuts and Bolts Operatives decides to call its members out on strike and issues notices to them with the instruction that they are to withdraw their labour from a certain date. The union at this point may have committed three torts:

1. The tort of conspiracy, by deciding to call a strike, although this is doubtful in view of the decision of the House of Lords in *Crofter Hand Woven Harris Tweed Co. Ltd v Veitch* (1942).
2. The tort of inducement of a breach of contract. This has certainly been committed, as the instruction to members to withdraw their labour is an inducement of a breach of contract (see below).

3. The tort of intimidation will have been committed if the union issued a threat to the employer that it would call a strike.

*Note*: the above torts are together known as the 'economic torts'.

Accordingly, the employer could sue the union for torts (2) and (3) and possibly (1) under the principle in *Taff Vale Rly Co. v ASRS* (1901), which held that a union could be sued in tort and its assets taken in satisfaction of a judgment. The effect of this would be that the union could be made bankrupt. Suppose, for example, that the workers at a factory went on strike for two months. Their employer loses £5m in lost orders and sues the union in tort for this. The union cannot pay, it is made bankrupt and it ceases to exist. The right to strike would, for all practical purposes, not exist.

The law prevents this from happening by granting immunity from all of the above torts provided that the action is taken 'in contemplation or furtherance of a trade dispute'. The meaning of this phrase will be considered later, but it can be said for now that the strike call by the union in the above example would have immunity as a trade dispute.

There is, however, one further hurdle which the union will have to surmount in order to gain immunity: the strike must have the support of a ballot which satisfies the statutory requirements.

The following flow chart shows the relevant factors in deciding whether a union is liable for the economic torts.

**Has the union committed any of the economic torts?**

**If so**

**Was the tort committed in contemplation or furtherance of a trade dispute?**

**If so**

**Did the action have the support of a secret ballot conducted according to the statutory rules?**

**If so**

**The union will have immunity from an action for the economic torts provided that:**

**(a) the action is not secondary action**

**and**

**(b) the action is not taken for a prohibited purpose**

## THE LIABILITY OF TRADE UNIONS IN SPECIFIC TORTS

### ■ The tort of inducement of a breach of contract

This tort can be committed either by a direct inducement of a breach or by an indirect one.

#### Direct inducement

The following diagram shows how this tort can be committed:

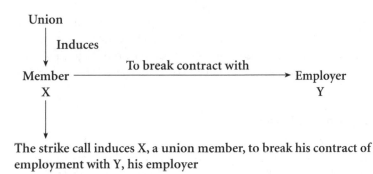

The strike call induces X, a union member, to break his contract of employment with Y, his employer

This is where X induces Y to break a contract which Y has made with Z. Its origin is in the decision in *Lumley v Gye* (1853), where the owner of a theatre (X) was liable for inducement by persuading a singer (Y) to break her contract with the manager of another theatre (Z) so that she could sing for X instead. The organisers of industrial action which amounts to a breach of contract will be liable for inducement by calling on employees to take the action.

An essential point is that the actual inducement is aimed at one or more of the parties to the contract. In *Middlebrook Mushrooms Ltd v TGWU* (1993) mushroom growers were in dispute with a union and the union distributed leaflets outside supermarkets supplied by the growers asking customers not to buy the growers' mushrooms. An action for inducement of a breach of contract failed, as the leaflets were not directed at the supermarket, in order to induce it to break its contract with the growers, but only at the customers.

The following points, which derive from the judgment of Jenkins LJ in *DC Thomson & Co. Ltd v Deakin* (1952), must be proved for an action for inducement to succeed:

#### *Defendant must intend to interfere with contractual rights of another*

First it must be proved that the defendant (the inducer) intended to interfere with the contractual rights of another. It seems that precise knowledge of the actual terms of the contract is not needed, so long as the defendant knows that a breach of the contract will result from the inducement. In *Emerald Construction Ltd v Lothian* (1966) a building workers' union advised its members, on safety grounds, to take industrial action to force main contractors on sites to cease using sub-contractors. However, if the main contractors did so, they would be liable to the sub-contractors for breach of contract. The union argued that it would not be liable for inducing this breach of contract as it did not know that the only way in which main contractors could end contracts with sub-contractors was by breach. The Court of Appeal held that although the union may not have had precise knowledge of the terms of the contracts, it did have the means of finding out what the terms were and from this it has been argued that recklessness as to whether a breach is induced is enough. This is supported by the county court decision in *Falconer v ASLEF and NUR* (1986), where the union was sued by a season ticket holder for calling strike action which induced a breach of contract by British Rail in not running trains. The county court judge rejected the union's argument that they intended to harm British Rail and not the claimant, as the breach of the claimant's contract was a foreseeable result of the strike action.

### Evidence of actual inducement

There must be evidence of actual inducement, such as direct instructions to union members to withdraw their labour, and that these were then acted upon so that a breach resulted. This element could not be proved in *D and C Thomson & Co. Ltd v Deakin* (above). The union (NATSOPA) had a recognition dispute with X Co., who were printers and publishers. X was supplied with paper by Bowaters and NATSOPA asked other unions to help in supporting action against X. As a result, lorry drivers employed by Bowaters told their employer that they would object to delivering paper to X and therefore Bowaters did not ask them to do so. X sued NATSOPA for inducing a breach of their contract with Bowaters but the union was not held liable. The union had only asked other unions for help and – a crucial point – they had not induced Bowaters' employees to stop delivering paper.

### Indirect inducement

The following diagram shows how this tort can be committed:

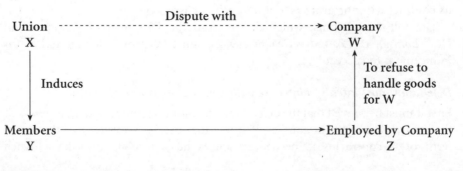

This is where X induces Y to break a contract (e.g. by going on strike) with Z and as a result Z breaks a commercial contract with W. A simple way of appreciating the difference between direct and indirect inducement is to remember that in direct inducement there are three parties but in indirect inducement there are four. Indirect inducement is generally known as secondary action, i.e. where a union (X) has a dispute with W and induces its members (Y) employed by Z to refuse to handle goods delivered for W so as to put pressure on W. The breach of contract between Z and W is indirectly induced by X. This was the situation in *JT Stratford and Sons Ltd v Lindley* (1965), where the union induced its members to break their contracts of employment with the result that their employer broke a commercial contract with another firm. The union was held liable to that firm for inducement. The effect of an exclusion clause in the commercial contract was considered in *Torquay Hotel Co. Ltd v Cousins* (1969). The defendant, a union official, told Esso that supplies of oil to the hotel would be met by a picket line, as the union was in dispute with the hotel. There was a *force majeure* clause in the contract between the hotel and Esso which excluded the liability of Esso for breach of contract where the failure to deliver oil was due to an industrial dispute. However, Russell LJ, in the Court of Appeal, pointed out that the clause excluded liability *for* a breach of contract; it did not mean that there was no breach. Therefore, the union was liable for inducing a breach of contract between the hotel and Esso. The reasoning of Denning MR was different. He held that the tort of inducement is committed even when a third person only prevents or hinders the performance of a contract, as well as when an actual breach is induced. It is not easy to envisage the circumstances when this will occur and it is submitted that the approach of Russell LJ is to be preferred. Nor is it clear whether this extension of the tort applies to direct as well as indirect inducement. (See also the discussion below on the tort of interference with trade or business, with which the remarks of Denning MR are connected.)

## Defence of Justification

This defence applies to the tort of inducement but there is only one reported case where it has succeeded in actions involving industrial disputes. This was *Brimelow v Casson* (1924), where chorus girls who worked for the claimant were paid such low wages that some of them resorted to prostitution in order to earn a decent wage. The union persuaded some theatre owners to refuse to honour contracts with the claimant in an attempt to put pressure on him and it was held that the union had a moral duty to do this and was not liable for inducing a breach of contract. But in *South Wales Miners Federation v Glamorgan Coal Co.* (1905) the defence of justification failed where the union persuaded its members only to work intermittently so that less coal would be produced. The argument was that as coal became scarcer its price would rise, the mine owners would make more money and wages would then increase as a result. Although the union thought that this action was justified as being in the best interests of both workers and employers, the court did not agree and held that the defence of justification did not apply.

## Immunity from actions for the tort of inducing a breach of contract

Section 219(1)(a) of TULRCA provides that an act done in contemplation or furtherance of a trade dispute is not a tort only on the ground that it induces another to break a contract. The immunity applies to breaches of any contract, not just contracts of employment, and so in principle the immunity covers both direct and indirect inducement although, as we shall see, immunity for inducement for what constitutes secondary action is severely curtailed by statute. The phrase 'contemplation or furtherance of a trade dispute' is considered after all the economic torts have been outlined.

## ◼ Liability for inducement of a breach of other legal rights

Although this is a relatively modern development, the potential for an extension of the tort of inducement to areas other than breach of contract was laid down by Lord Macnaghten in *Quinn v Leatham* (1901) when he pointed out that any 'violation of a legal right' was a cause of action. Thus in *Meade v Haringay LBC* (1979) a school was closed by the local authority as a result of strike action by caretakers and other staff. It was said *obiter* by Denning MR, with whom Eveleigh LJ agreed, that the union involved had induced the local authority to act in breach of its statutory duty by closing the schools and that the statutory immunity (above) did not cover this (as it only applies to breaches of contract). In *Associated British Ports v TGWU* (1989) the Court of Appeal agreed that the tort of inducement of a breach of statutory duty could be committed provided that there was an independent right of action to sue for the breach of duty. Some breaches of statutory duty are actionable by individuals (as in *Meade*) but others are not. Discussion of this question more properly belongs in books on administrative law but the general rule is that it is a question of construction of the statute. The position is made clear in relation to one area by the Telecommunications Act 1984, s.16 of which expressly provides that where a licensed operator is in breach of its licence then the Director-General of Telecommunications may issue an enforcement order to the operator. If the operator breaches this order then any person who suffers loss where the contravention was due to industrial action may sue the organiser of that action (e.g. the union involved).

In addition to breach of statutory duty, the tort of inducement has been extended to inducements of equitable obligations, such as the obligation to account as in *Prudential Assurance Co. v Lorenz* (1971), where a union induced agents involved in an industrial dispute not to submit premiums, which they had collected, to the company. However, in *Wilson v Housing Corporation* (1997) it was not extended to inducing a breach of contract. The significant point is not so much that the tort of inducement exists in these cases, as there is clearly no reason why it should not, but that a union who commits it other than when inducing a breach of contract in circumstances covered by the statutory immunity will be liable. Therefore, whilst the statutory immunity (above) remains, it is gradually being reduced in scope by the development of this part of the law.

# The tort of interference with trade or business

The notion of inducement has recently been extended to situations where there is no actual inducement of a breach but instead there is an interference not amounting to a breach. The origin of this may be seen in the words of Denning MR in *Torquay Hotels v Cousins* (above), when he referred to acts which hinder or prevent the performance of a contract. The extension of liability to these acts was approved by the House of Lords and, in particular, by Lord Diplock, in *Merkur Island Shipping Corporation v Laughton* (1983). The precise scope of this tort remains uncertain and there have been suggestions that a new 'super-tort' is emerging which will embrace not only inducement and interference but also intimidation, which is dealt with below. The problem is that there is no express immunity from interference with a contract as distinct from breach.

# The tort of intimidation

This is an old tort, dating from *Tarleton v McGawley* (1793). It has traditionally been committed where there is a threat of physical violence to make a person do or not do something but in *Rookes v Barnard* (1964) the House of Lords surprisingly extended it to industrial disputes. Rookes (a non-union member) was lawfully dismissed with proper notice as a result of an ultimatum by the union that there would be a strike if he was not. The tort of inducement was not committed, as the dismissal was lawful, but the tort of intimidation *was* held to have been committed, as there was a threat (the intimidation) to break contracts of employment by a strike and this amounted to an unlawful act which was intended to injure Rookes by causing his dismissal. The extension of this tort to industrial disputes was justified by Lord Devlin, who likened threats to clubs and observed that all that matters 'is that, metaphorically speaking, a club has been used'. It did not matter what it was made of, whether it was a physical club or an economic club. The effect is that a union which threatens strike or other industrial action in breach of contract will commit this tort.

This decision caused alarm among trade unions, as the tort of intimidation in this context was not covered by the statutory immunities, although this was swiftly remedied by the Trade Disputes Act 1965.

## The immunity from actions for the tort of intimidation

Section 219(1)(b) of TULRCA 1992 provides that an act done in contemplation or furtherance of a trade dispute is not actionable solely on the ground that it consists in threatening that a contract will be broken or that its performance will be interfered with. This applies, as with the immunity for inducement, to any contract and not just to contracts of employment.

## ■ The tort of conspiracy

This can be committed in two ways:

### Conspiracy to injure another

Here the essence of the tort is the combining together rather than what is proposed, but it must be proved that the predominant purpose of the combination is to injure a third party and not to advance the interests of the conspirators. It was used in *Quinn v Leathem* (1901) to render a union liable for conspiracy where it had initiated a boycott of an employer's produce in the course of an attempt to enforce a closed shop. It was held that the union's purpose was not to advance the interests of their members but to injure the employer. This development was dangerous to the activities of unions as it struck at lawful activities (a boycott is not by itself unlawful) by labelling them as conspiracy on the basis of their motive. A wider view of the purpose of industrial action was taken in *Crofter Hand Woven Harris Tweed v Veitch* (1942). The claimant was a producer of cloth on the island of Lewis who obtained yarn (raw material) from the mainland rather than on the Hebrides, as it was cheaper. The union instructed dockers to refuse to handle this yarn because the imports were threatening the jobs of island workers who also produced yarn but it was held that the union was not liable for conspiracy as its purpose was not to injure the claimant but to protect the interests of their members. On this basis, it is very unlikely that a union would be liable for this type of conspiracy, as the purpose of industrial action is almost always going to be the advancement of members' interests or some other lawful motive, even though damage is caused to the employer's business in the form of lost business. For instance, in *Scala Ballroom (Wolverhampton) Ltd v Ratcliffe* (1958), conspiracy was not committed when a union's object was to force an employer to end a colour bar. Thus a strike call will almost always not be an actionable conspiracy.

### Conspiracy to injure another by using unlawful means

The difference between this and conspiracy to injure (above) is that here the actual means proposed are unlawful, whereas there the tort was committed by the combination itself. This form of conspiracy would be committed by, for example, conspiring to cause personal injury and it is part of the general law rather than having a particular application to industrial disputes.

### The immunity from actions for the tort of conspiracy

Section 219(2) of TULRCA 1992 provides that an agreement or combination to do an act in contemplation or furtherance of a trade dispute is not actionable provided that the act would, if done by one person, not be actionable. Thus there is immunity from conspiracy to injure another but not from conspiracy to injure another using unlawful means. In any event, in the light of the decision in the *Crofter* case, it is unlikely that a union would commit this tort.

## The possibility of actions against unions for economic duress

Actions for economic duress have surfaced since the 1970s and the essence of the action is that a party to a contract was forced to enter it by some form of pressure that went beyond normal commercial pressure. It can be applied to industrial disputes, although its main use is obviously between businesses. An example of its use in industrial disputes is found in *Universe Tankships Inc. of Moravia v International Transport Workers Federation* (1982). The ITWF was conducting a campaign against the use of flags of convenience ships and, in pursuance of this, members of the National Union of Seamen refused to handle a ship belonging to the claimant. The union lifted this action only when the claimant made a substantial payment to its welfare fund. It was held that this payment was made as a result of economic duress and therefore the claimant was entitled to restitution of it. The difficulty with economic duress – and not only in cases involving industrial action – is drawing the line between legitimate and illegitimate pressure. The action for restitution for sums paid as a result of economic duress is not in tort and none of the statutory immunities outlined above applies.

## Summary of the position on whether action is covered by a statutory immunity

There is statutory immunity for the torts of inducing a breach of contract, intimidation and conspiracy, provided that they are covered by the 'golden formula', explained below. There is no immunity from any other action. It has already been pointed out, but deserves further emphasis, that, as time goes on, the position of trade unions with regard to immunity in tort is gradually weakening. The situations described above, where there is no immunity, show how the law has developed over the last 30 years and how the immunities of unions in tort are thus being gradually eroded.

## Does the action take place in contemplation or furtherance of a trade dispute?

The immunity granted from actions for the torts of inducing a breach of contact, intimidation and conspiracy only applies where the action takes place in contemplation or furtherance of a trade dispute. This is the celebrated 'golden formula' and the effect is that two questions have to be asked:

1. Was there a trade dispute?
2. If so, was the action which resulted in one or more of the above torts being committed in contemplation or furtherance of it?

## Was there a trade dispute?

The term 'trade dispute' is defined by s.244 of TULRCA as a dispute between workers and their employer which relates wholly or mainly to one or more matters (see below). Before looking at these matters, there are four significant points to be made:

### Definition of 'worker'

The term 'worker' is defined in s.296 of the Act and is the wider definition which includes not only those employed under a contract of employment but also those who undertake to perform work or services personally (see Chapter 4).

### Former workers

The dispute can concern former workers if the dispute concerns the termination of their employment (s.244(5) of TULRCA).

### Dispute must be between workers and present employer

The dispute must be between workers and their present employer. Thus sympathy strikes are not covered by the statutory immunities, as sympathy strikers do not have a dispute with their employer. In *University College Hospital NHS Trust v Unison* (1999) a dispute about the terms which would be offered to employees when the undertaking was transferred to private employers was held not to be covered by the Court of Appeal as it was not a dispute with present employers but with potential future ones. This was partially reversed by the ECtHR in *Unison v UK* (2002), where it was held that the restriction on the right to strike had to be justified under Article 11 but in this case it was, as Article 11(2) allows restrictions which are proportionate and necessary in a democratic society. The ECtHR agreed with the UK government that the restriction did not prevent strike action being taken when actual steps were taken to downgrade conditions. Even so, this case is of general interest as an example of the application of the ECHR to collective rights.

This issue also arose in *Dimbleby and Sons Ltd v NUJ* (1984), in which the House of Lords refused to hold that there was a trade dispute where there were associated companies and one of these was engaged in a trade dispute but not the other. This reluctance of the courts to concern themselves with where economic power lies and willingness to look only at legal ownership of the organisation has been criticised. For example, T. Novitz and P. Skidmore in *Fairness at Work* (London: Hart Publishing, 2001) point out that workers employed by interconnected companies may wish to take action to establish transnational standards in a group of companies and at present such action would not be covered by the statutory immunities. K. Wedderburn, who is similarly critical of the present position, has referred to the process of restricting immunities rigidly to disputes with an employer party as 'enterprise confinement' ((1998) 18 ILJ 27–30). Moreover, the ILO has argued that workers should be able to participate in sympathy strikes so long as the actual strike is lawful (see Novitz and Skidmore

(2001) pp.139–140). So far, the UK government has shown no sign of deviating from the position taken in the White Paper *Fairness at Work* (1998) that the days of sympathy strikes are over and it must be said that if the law were to be changed to allow *unrestricted* secondary industrial action then unions would soon lose a great deal of goodwill. Is the solution one which, whilst recognising that the days of mass secondary picketing are over, still recognised that the present law does not take sufficient account of the economic realities of business organisation today? Possibly the development of the jurisprudence surrounding Article 11 may take us further.

### Matters which can be the subject of a trade dispute

Section 244(1) lists the matters which can be the subject of a trade dispute as follows:

1. Terms and conditions of employment, or the physical conditions in which workers are required to work. In *BBC v Hearn* (1977) Denning MR held that the phrase 'terms and conditions' could cover terms which actually applied in practice without their ever being formally incorporated into the contract, but the scope of this is unclear.
2. Engagement or non-engagement, or termination or suspension of employment or the duties of employment of workers. This has been held to include a dispute about possible job losses (*Hadmor Productions Ltd v Hamilton* (1982)). However, it does not include cases where the action is in support of the reinstatement of workers who have been on unofficial strike (see below).
3. Allocation of work or the duties of employment between workers or groups of workers. Therefore, demarcation disputes are covered provided that all the workers are employed by the same employer. This was the element that was not present in *Dimbleby v NUJ* (above).
4. Matters of discipline.
5. A worker's membership or non-membership of a trade union. However, action taken to enforce union membership is not covered (s.222 of TULRCA (below)).
6. Facilities for union officials.
7. Machinery for negotiation and consultation and other procedures relating to these matters including union recognition.

The final requirement is that the dispute must relate 'wholly or mainly' to any of the above matters. Therefore disputes which are political will not be covered. In *BBC v Hearn* (1977) threatened disruption of the broadcasting of the FA Cup Final (because the broadcasting of it to South Africa would infringe the anti-apartheid policy of the union) was not covered. However, if it can be shown that the action, although having political overtones, is fundamentally concerned with any of the above matters then it will be covered. In *Wandsworth LBC v NASUWT* (1994) the issue was whether a boycott by teachers of testing under the national curriculum was covered. The Court of Appeal held that it was because, although the union was opposed to the principle of testing, the fundamental cause of the dispute was the extra workload which would be placed on teachers. An instance of where the dispute was the other side of the line is *Mercury Telecommunications v Scott-Garner* (1984), where action taken to try to prevent the privatisation of British Telecom was held to be motivated by the opposition of the union to privatisation as such rather than to fear of job losses as a result of privatisation.

### Is the action in 'contemplation or furtherance' of a trade dispute?

This is the other hurdle which industrial action must surmount in order to be protected under the statutory immunities.

'In contemplation' of a trade dispute means that the dispute, although not actually occurring, must be imminent. In *Health Computing Ltd v Meek* (1980) a union sent out a circular instructing its members not to deal with a private company which was attempting to win contracts with health authorities. The reason was that the union feared job losses among its members if this happened. The court accepted the argument of the union that the object of the circular was to prevent a dispute if health authorities did in fact award contracts and so the action was covered. However, in *Bent's Brewery Co. Ltd v Hogan* (1945) the union sought information from managers of public houses about their takings prior to formulating a wage claim. The giving of this information would have been a breach of the managers' contracts of employment and it was held that the action by the union was not covered because there was no dispute, although clearly if any claim was not conceded there might be.

'In furtherance' of a trade dispute means that the dispute must actually be happening and thus if it has ended the immunities also end. One example of where the immunities would not apply is where action is taken during a dispute but is motivated solely by personal spite against, for instance, the employer as an individual.

Whether the action is in contemplation or furtherance of a trade dispute is a matter for the subjective judgement of those involved in organising it. The reasonableness of the belief that it *is* is irrelevant. This position was reached in *Express Newspapers v McShane* (1979), where the House of Lords overruled the objective test proposed by the Court of Appeal which, by making the courts to some extent the judge of whether the action came within the 'golden formula', had opened up a potentially wide field for judicial involvement in this area and one which was viewed with apprehension by the unions.

## ■ Summary of the position so far

Assuming that the actions of the union fall within the statutory immunities and that they are within 'contemplation or furtherance of a trade dispute' one might then assume that the union could safely conclude that it had immunity from actions in tort. Not so, however. Before going on to investigate the further possible legal pitfalls awaiting the organisers of industrial action, it might be helpful to look an example of how the law works thus far.

*Example*

The Toilers Union calls a strike amongst its members at the premises of Gradgrind and Co. over a proposed reduction in wages and an increase in working hours. The strike call is a tort as it is an inducement of a breach of contract but, as the action is concerned with terms and conditions of employment, it is one of the matters which can be the subject of a trade dispute and the strike call is clearly in furtherance of this.

## ■ Situations where the statutory immunities are lost

The union cannot rest assured that it is safe from legal action because, in the following circumstances, a union can still be liable in tort for having called a strike or other industrial action:

1. Where the action is viewed as 'secondary industrial action'.
2. Where the action does not have the support of a secret ballot conducted according to the statutory requirements.
3. Where the action is taken for a purpose prohibited by statute.

These will now be considered in turn.

### Secondary industrial action

This covers what are popularly known as 'sympathy strikes' and is defined by s.224(2) of TULRCA as where a person induces another to break a contract or interferes or induces another to interfere with its performance, or threatens to do so, and the employer who is a party to the contract is not a party to the dispute.

*Example*

Employees of the Great Worcestershire Railway Company are on strike over a proposal by the management to reduce overtime payments and the dismissal of certain employees for alleged breaches of safety rules. These come within the definition of a trade dispute (categories 1 and 2, p.285 above) and the action will have the statutory immunities. Employees of the Herefordshire Railway Company come out on strike, also in support of their fellow workers, but this will not attract the statutory immunities, as there is no dispute between them and their employer.

(Note that if there was a likelihood that the action by the Worcestershire Railway Company would be a prelude to similar action by other railway companies then the question would be whether the action by the employees of the Herefordshire Railway Company was sufficiently in contemplation of a trade dispute to bring it within the 'golden formula'.)

The removal of the statutory immunities from secondary industrial action was originally contained in legislation passed by the 1979–97 Conservative government but it has remained and the present Labour government has no plans to remove it. The present position has already been discussed above (under the heading 'Dispute must be between workers and present employer').

The only situation where secondary industrial action will be protected is where it arises in the course of picketing. Suppose that there is peaceful picketing which is within the law (see below). The pickets persuade a lorry driver who is about to deliver supplies to the factory to turn back. This will result in a breach of the driver's own contract of employment as he/she will have been contractually obliged to make the deliveries. However, the pickets will not be liable for having induced this.

## Action which does not have the support of a ballot

The requirement to hold a ballot before industrial action was another change introduced by the last Conservative government which has remained unaltered in essence under the present Labour government. The law is contained in ss.226–235 of TULRCA, supported by a Code of Practice on Industrial Action Ballots and Notification to Employers (2000), which covers 'desirable practices' on ballots. It is generally accepted that ballots are here to stay. Even Novitz and Skidmore (2001), who are critical of much of the present legislation, agree that ballots are right in principle, but they make the valid point that the requirements should not be so complex as to invite frequent legal challenges by employers. Furthermore, the ECtHR accepted in *NATFHE v UK* (1998) that the requirements in the legislation on some of the details of the ballot are not in breach of Article 11 of the ECHR (right to freedom of association) and thus by implication it accepted the legitimacy of the requirement of a ballot in itself. Nevertheless, if the procedural requirements are too onerous then this could be a breach of Article 11. In fact, despite some changes made by the Employment Relations Act 1999, the balloting requirements are undeniably complex.

The basic position, as stated by s.226 of TULRCA, is that any act done by a trade union to induce a person to take part, or continue to take part, in industrial action is not protected (i.e. from action in tort) unless the action has the support of a ballot. The phrase 'industrial action' means that action other than a strike, such as an overtime ban or a ban on rest day working, is covered (*Connex South Eastern Ltd v RMT* (1999)). The basic rule is that a failure to comply with any of the requirements set out below will result in the ballot having no effect and the consequent loss of the statutory immunities in any resulting action. This is subject to one exception, contained in s.232B of TULRCA, which provides that accidental failure to comply with the rules on entitlement to vote and the sending of ballot papers will not invalidate the ballot if the failure is on such a small scale as not to affect the result. One example would be the putting of the wrong address on the envelope containing the ballot paper.

The statutory requirements and other relevant points are set out below.

### *All members will be entitled to vote*

Every member who it is reasonable to believe at the time of the ballot will be induced (i.e. by the union) to take part in the industrial action will be entitled to vote (s.227). The courts have shown some liberality in the interpretation of this provision. In *BRB v NUR* (1989) the Court of Appeal held that an inadvertent failure to allow a member to vote by, for example, not supplying a ballot paper, did not invalidate the ballot. The test, imported from s.230, is one of reasonable practicability. In *London Underground v RMT* (1995) a particular problem arose: what is the position regarding members who have joined the union since the ballot? Can they still be called on to take industrial action? The Court of Appeal sensibly said that such action would still be protected, pointing out that the words in s.227 refer to those who the union reasonably believes to be entitled to take part. As Millett LJ put it: '[the union] cannot identify future members.' There is also a requirement in s.228 for separate workplace ballots so that the proposed action must be supported by a majority in each workplace in order to make the action at that workplace protected from liability in tort. The reason is that workers in different workplaces may have different views on whether action should be taken. 'Workplace' is defined by s.228 as premises with which the worker's employment has the closest connection. Nevertheless, it is possible to have one ballot for more than one workplace in the following situations (s.228A):

1. Where there is a common interest across workplaces.
2. Where there is a common occupation amongst those balloted even though there is more than one employer.
3. Where there is a single employer across different workplaces.

### Ballot paper must comply with statutory requirements

The ballot paper must comply with the following requirements and a failure to do so will invalidate the result of the ballot:

1. It must contain at least one of the statutory questions, which are whether the member is prepared to take part in a strike or in other industrial action short of a strike. If both types of action are contemplated then the ballot must ask both questions.
2. It must, by s.229(4) of TULRCA, contain what has become known as a 'health warning' which must be in these words:

   **If you take part in a strike or other industrial action, you may be in breach of your contract of employment. However, if you are dismissed for taking part in a strike or other industrial action which is called officially and is otherwise lawful, the dismissal will be unfair if it takes place fewer than eight weeks after you started taking part in the action, and depending on the circumstances may be unfair if it takes place later.**

The intention behind this is admirable: to ensure that there is no doubt in the minds of those considering voting in favour of what the legal consequences might be. The problem is that too many of these words are incomprehensible (as it may be to readers of this book as the relevant law is explained later in this chapter). However, given the need to make the position clear, it is difficult to see what else could have been done. The statement cannot be commented upon in the voting paper and has to go in even if it is likely that the action will not involve a breach of contract such as a ban on working voluntary overtime (*Power Packaging Casemakers Ltd v Faust* (1983)). The ballot paper need not give any details of what the dispute is about, although the Code of Practice recommends that it does.

3. It must give the name(s) of those entitled to call the action in the event of a majority voting in favour. The reason is to prevent a strike call, for example, being made by local officials before the union's head office has given approval.
4. It must contain the name of the independent scrutineer. The scrutineer must report on the ballot within four weeks, stating whether he/she is satisfied with the arrangements for its conduct, although the scrutineer does not oversee the actual ballot (i.e. the counting of votes etc.) itself.
5. The union must provide the employer of those entitled to vote with a sample of the ballot paper at least three days before the voting begins (s.226A(1) of TULRCA). The object is to enable the employer to challenge the ballot if he/she believes that there is an irregularity in it.

### Ballot must be conducted according to statutory rules

The ballot must be conducted according to the following rules:

1. It must be by post.
2. Members must be allowed to vote without interference from the union, its members, its officials or its employees (s.230(1) of TULRCA).
3. Voting must be in secret.
4. So far as is reasonably practicable, those voting must incur no direct cost.
5. All votes must be counted fairly and accurately.
6. Voting must be in secret (although the requirement of secrecy will not apply if this is not reasonably practicable).
7. The union must, by s.226A of TULRCA, give seven days' notice of the ballot to employers of those entitled to vote and this notice must also give such information to employers as will help the employer 'to make plans'.

The extent of the details which the union should supply to the employer has been a particularly controversial area. The original legislation (contained in the Trade Union Reform and Employment Rights Act 1993) required the union to describe the employees in the notice to the employer. In *Blackpool and Fylde College v NATFHE* (1994) this was held to amount to a requirement that the union should supply the employer with the names of all those who were to be balloted. Moreover, as the words of the legislation were unambiguous, the court did not feel able to interpret the legislation so as to give effect to the right to privacy in Article 8 of the ECHR so that the names were not disclosed. The law was changed by the Employment Relations Act 1999 to the present phrase of 'information needed to make plans' and the decision in the *NATFHE* case was overruled by the provision in s.226A(3A)(c) of the Trade Union and Labour Relations Act 1992 as amended by the Employment Relations Act 1999 that a failure to supply names of employees would not be a ground for holding that the ballot was invalid. The reason for this requirement is that it is felt that an employer needs to know what might happen so that, for example, disruption to customers is minimised. However, in the House of Lords' debates on this clause Lord Wedderburn considered that this was a 'most extraordinary provision' (quoted in Novitz and Skidmore (2001) at p.146) as he felt that it simply provided the employer with the ammunition to reduce the impact of a strike. The Code of Practice states that the information should be such as to enable disruption to customers to be avoided if possible and to ensure health and safety and safeguard equipment which might suffer from being shut down if left without supervision. It should be noted that the same rules on the information to be disclosed to employers apply when the union gives notice that industrial action will be called and clearly the same objections to this apply also.

### Action must begin within time limit

If the ballot has resulted in a vote in favour of a strike or other industrial action then the action must begin by a certain date otherwise the ballot loses its effectiveness and another will have to be held. The usual period is four weeks but the employer and the union can agree on an extension of up to another four weeks (s.234(1) of TULRCA). The vital point is that the industrial action must commence within the time limit even though it might continue beyond then. In *Monsanto plc v TGWU* (1986) the action was suspended for two weeks to allow negotiations to take place and then resumed when these broke down. However, this was by then beyond the four week time limit. The Court of Appeal held that as the action had commenced within the time limit there was no need for a fresh ballot as the resumption was merely a continuation of the action.

### Action must be called by specified person

The actual call for a strike or other industrial action must, as mentioned above, be by a specified person (s.233 of TULRCA). In *Tanks and Drums Ltd v TGWU* (1992) the Court of Appeal held that where the specified person was the general secretary of the union then it was lawful for him to instruct a local official that he could actually take the decision to call the strike if negotiations with the employer were unsuccessful. However, the court felt that a decision by the specified person simply to delegate in advance all decisions to call industrial action would be unlawful. Specific delegation in each situation is needed.

### Notice must be given

The union must, by s.234A of TULRCA, give at least seven days' notice in writing to the employer of any industrial action following on from a ballot. Notice can be given at any time from the day on which the employer is informed of the result of the ballot. The same rule as to the information to be given applies as in cases where the employer is informed of the intention to hold a ballot: it must be such as to enable the employer to make plans. Moreover, if the action is intended to be continuous then the notice must state when it is to start and if it is to be discontinuous (i.e. only on certain days of the week or certain weeks) then the notice must state all the dates when it is to take place. An exception is where the employer and the union have agreed on a suspension of the action to enable negotiations to take place. In this case it can be resumed without the need for a fresh notice (s.234A(7B)). If a particular employer is not notified then the statutory immunities are lost as against him but not against other employers who *have* been given notice.

### Failure to comply with rules

If a union fails to comply with all of the above rules then who can take action? Obviously there is the loss of the statutory immunities but, in addition, any union member can restrain the calling of any industrial action without the support of a ballot (s.62 of TULRCA). An employer who is affected by a ballot called in breach of the statutory requirements can act by seeking an injunction once the action has begun and can use s.235 (below) so long as they are not companies because s.235 refers to 'individuals'. Section 235 is especially aimed at allowing a third party to claim an injunction. If such a party can show that the likely effect of unlawful industrial action would be to prevent or delay the supply of goods or services to them or to reduce the quality of goods or services supplied, they may seek an injunction to prevent it. This applies to any action which amounts to a tort and which is not protected by the statutory immunities (e.g. action not in contemplation or furtherance of a trade dispute, secondary action etc.) and also to any action taken without the support of a ballot.

### All procedures have been exhausted

The Code of Practice exceeds even the extensive requirements described above and, although not legally binding, breach of its provisions may be relevant when a court is deciding whether to grant an injunction in the circumstances described above. The Code suggests that no industrial action should take place until all the agreed procedures have been exhausted and that no industrial action should take place until the report of the scrutineer has been received. In addition, the Code recommends that ballots should not be used simply as a tactical means of, for instance, getting the employer to improve on an earlier offer, and should only be used when industrial action is really contemplated.

## Where the action is taken for a prohibited purpose

This is the third way in which industrial action which is taken in contemplation or furtherance of a trade dispute may nevertheless lose the protection of the statutory immunities. In effect, these are actions which the legislation so strongly disapproves of that those who take them lose the protection of the statutory immunities. This will arise in the following cases:

1. Where one or more of the reasons for the action is the fact or belief that the employer has dismissed an employee who took part in unofficial industrial action (s.223 of TULRCA). This is part of the strategy of removing protection from unofficial industrial action. Precisely what such action is will be explained below.

2. Where one or more of the reasons for the industrial action is the fact or belief that the employer has employed or might employ a non-union member or has failed, is failing or might fail, to discriminate against a non-union member (s.222 of TULRCA). The object of these provisions was originally to withdraw immunity from action to enforce the closed shop but the legislation has the effect of removing immunity from any action at all for reasons of non-membership of a union.
3. Where the industrial action is taken in order to induce a person to incorporate a requirement in a (commercial) contract that a union shall be recognised (s.225 of TULRCA). Therefore, industrial action cannot be used as a means of getting union recognition for workers employed by another employer, as distinct from the employer with whom the union is dealing.

## PICKETING

The word 'picketing' conjures up a certain image to most people: that of workers, during a strike, standing outside the entrance to a workplace with banners trying to persuade fellow workers and others such as lorry drivers not to enter the workplace. Some readers may remember the mass picketing during the 1970s: for example, in the miners' strike. However, in order to begin a discussion of the legal issues surrounding picketing, it would be helpful to have a more precise definition. Unfortunately, this is what we do not have. The only way forward is to start with s.220 of TULRCA (dealt with in detail later in this chapter), which refers to the 'attendance' of pickets. Nevertheless, the actions of pickets *when* attending may involve breaches of the law and this section is concerned with precisely what pickets can lawfully do and when their actions will be unlawful. The area is a complex one, involving not only statute and common law but also the Code of Practice on Picketing. In addition, the ECHR needs to be considered. In essence the law needs to balance the right of pickets to assemble and put their point of view against the need to prevent civil disorder.

There is no right in English law to picket. However, s.220 of TULRCA provides that the attendance of pickets is lawful provided that the following conditions are satisfied:

1. The picketing is in contemplation or furtherance of a trade dispute.
2. The pickets are attending at or near their place of work (although trade union officials may attend at or near the place of work of their members).
3. Their purpose is only peacefully to obtain or communicate information or peacefully persuade a person to work or not to work.

Section 220 does not define what is meant by 'place of work' but the Code of Practice (para. 17) states that 'lawful picketing must be limited to attendance at, or near, an entrance or exit from the factory, site or office at which the picket works'.

The effect of s.220 is that any activities *outside* peacefully persuading or communicating in the circumstances set out above may incur civil or criminal liability.

### Example

There is a strike at the firm of Nuts and Bolts Ltd and a number of employees are picketing the entrance to it by standing outside. They ask those employees who are going into work not to do so and try to persuade them to join the strike. Some agree to join the strike but others decide to go into work. The activities of the pickets, were it not for s.220, might amount to the following:

(a) The crime of obstruction of the highway.
(b) The torts of public and private nuisance.
(c) The tort of inducement of a breach of contract (committed by inducing others to break *their* contracts of employment by joining the strike). This would also apply if the pickets persuaded an employee of another organisation (e.g. a lorry driver) not to cross picket lines by making deliveries and thus he broke his contract of employment.

However, the protection given to picketing goes no further than this. As Lord Salmon put it in *Broome v DPP* (1974): '. . . it is nothing but the attendance of the pickets at the places specified which is protected; and then only if their attendance is for one of the specified purposes.' Thus in this case the actions of a picket in standing in front of a lorry to stop it entering a site were not protected and he was convicted of obstruction. In *Tynan v Balmer* (1967) the actions of pickets in continually walking round in a circle were also outside the immunity. Thus the refusal of the defendant (a union official) to obey the order of a police officer to order this to stop was held to be a wilful obstruction of a police officer in the execution of his duty.

Accordingly, the activities of pickets can give rise to liability in the following ways.

## ▨ Under the civil law

### Inducement of a breach of contract

It is interesting that this is the one occasion when the law still allows what amounts to secondary industrial action because, as the example above showed, the effect of the picketing can be that an employee (in this case the lorry driver) breaks a contract (his own) with *his* employer, who is not a party to the dispute.

### Nuisance

This is a doubtful area. There are two torts: public nuisance and private nuisance. Private nuisance is an unlawful interference with a person's (in this context, the employer's) use or enjoyment of land but the courts have differed on the question of whether picketing can constitute a nuisance. In *Hubbard v Pitt*

(1975) Denning MR had no doubt that 'picketing is not a nuisance in itself'. However, he pointed out that it can be a nuisance when it is 'associated with obstruction, violence, intimidation or threats'. If any of these are committed then it is likely that there will be prosecutions for specific criminal offences rather than simply an action for the tort of private nuisance. Is there any place for actions in private nuisance as in industrial disputes?

In *Mersey Dock and Harbour Co. v Verrinder* (1982) it was held that the actions of pickets in standing outside the employer's premises could be a nuisance if these amounted to putting improper pressure on the employer, but since then the Code of Practice has put a virtual maximum of six on the number of pickets, which can hardly be considered improper pressure. The most important decision is that in *Thomas v NUM (South Wales Area)* (1985), where Scott J held that mass picketing could amount to a nuisance and that harassment of workers who did wish to go into work could be what he called a 'species of private nuisance'. This extension of private nuisance went against the traditional view that actions for nuisance can only be brought by those with an 'interest in the land' (i.e. an owner or a tenant). This covers employers but not employees and this orthodoxy was reasserted by the House of Lords in *Hunter v Canary Wharf Ltd* (1997). Thus actions for nuisance arising out of picketing can, it seems, only be brought by employers. However, the wider question of whether there is an independent tort of harassment is not settled, although actions may now be brought under the Protection from Harassment Act (1997) (below).

Public nuisance is a tort which covers any activities which can cause inconvenience or damage to the public, and an individual who has suffered damage over and above that suffered by the public at large can sue. It is rarely used in relation to picketing but was in *News Group Newspapers Ltd v SOGAT* (1986), where the conduct of pickets at large demonstrations at Wapping extending over a considerable time was found to constitute public nuisance and *The Times* newspaper, which had lost journalists as a result, was entitled to claim.

## Trespass

The tort of trespass is very rarely used in cases involving picketing and the likelihood of it being used at all has decreased since the decision of the House of Lords in *Jones v DPP* (1999) (which did not concern picketing but a protest near Stonehenge), that peaceful assemblies could amount to reasonable use of the highway. Previously, it had been thought that any use of the highway other than for passage could be a trespass, and that would have covered picketing, although the s.220 immunity would often have protected it anyway.

## Harassment

The statutory tort of harassment, contained in the Protection from Harassment Act 1997, is primarily aimed at activities such as stalking but can also be applied to picketing. It is committed by a course of conduct which amounts to harassment of another and could have applied, for example, in cases such as *Thomas v*

*NUM* and *News Group Newspapers v SOGAT* (above), where large numbers were involved.

## ▮ Under the criminal law

### Obstruction of the highway

Obstruction of the highway, contrary to s.137 of the Highways Act 1980, occurred in *Broome v DPP* (above) and the difficulty is, of course, to determine when a use of the highway becomes an obstruction. The presence of anyone standing on the pavement, for example, is an obstruction in that others will have to walk round that person to continue on their way. However, the courts take the view that to amount to an obstruction the use must be unreasonable and it is probable that picketing within the scope of s.220 and the Code of Practice would not be an obstruction.

### Obstructing a police officer

Obstructing a police officer in the execution of his duty (s.89(2) of the Police Act 1996) amounts to a crime where, for example, pickets refuse to obey the instructions of the police to prevent a breach of the peace. In *Piddington v Bates* (1960) the police limited the number of pickets outside premises to two and it was held that Piddington had been correctly arrested for obstructing a police officer in the execution of his duty when he repeatedly tried to disobey this instruction in order to join the picket line. In *Moss v McLachlan* (1985) police stopped a convoy of miners, coming to join picket lines, about a mile and a half from the actual lines and, when they refused to obey an instruction to turn back, they were arrested. It was held that they had obstructed the police in the execution of their duty, as the police feared that there would be a breach of the peace if the convoy continued.

### Specific offence under s.241 of TULRCA

This was originally introduced by the Conspiracy and Protection of Property Act 1875 and makes it an offence for a person, with a view to compelling another to do or not to do an act which they have a right to do, wrongfully and without legal authority to:

(a) use violence to or intimidate that person or his wife or children, or injure his property;
(b) persistently follow that person about from place to place;
(c) hide his tools, clothes or other property or deprive or hinder him in the use of them;
(d) watch or beset his house or other place where he resides, works, carries on business or happens to be;
(e) follow that person with two or more other persons in a disorderly manner along a street or road.

This can be seen as the counterpart of s.220 in that, whilst s.220 confers the one kind of specific immunity which pickets have, s.241 creates the one specific crime which pickets can commit.

It appears that the words 'wrongfully and without legal authority' mean that the act must amount to a tort before it can amount to a crime under s.241. Indeed, in *Ward Lock and Co. v Operative Printers Society* (1906) Fletcher Moulton LJ said that s.7 of the Conspiracy and Protection of Property Act 1875 (the predecessor of s.241) 'legalises nothing, and renders nothing wrongful that was not so before'. The most common charge under s.241 is 'watching and besetting' but this will only be committed if the picketing is outside the immunity in s.220.

## Public order offences

The Public Order Act 1986 introduced a number of specific offences which can be committed in industrial disputes. They can be grouped into two types:

### Those which relate to the control of public meetings, assemblies and processions

Thus s.11 requires that advance (usually six days') notice of public processions is given to the police; s.12 allows the police to impose conditions on public processions; and s.13 allows the banning of them altogether if the powers in ss.11 and 12 are considered insufficient to prevent serious disorder. In the case of public assemblies (defined as those consisting of 20 or more persons in a public place wholly or partly in the open air), the police can impose conditions as to their duration, place and maximum numbers where the purpose of the organisers is considered to be intimidatory to others or where the assembly may result in serious public disorder, disruption to the life of the community or serious damage to property. Although these provisions are applicable to all public order situations, they clearly have an impact on picketing and this is especially so of s.14.

### Those which relate to actual offences which may be committed as a result of public disorder

These are (in descending order of seriousness):

1. riot (s.1), which requires a common purpose on the part of at least 12 persons;
2. violent disorder (s.2), which requires the presence of three or more persons;
3. affray (s.3), which has no minimum number and is simply the use or threat of unlawful violence;
4. threatening, abusive or insulting words or behaviour (s.4);
5. intentional harassment (s.4A); and
6. disorderly behaviour (s.5).

Note that 4 and 5 above are treated equally seriously.

## The Code of Practice on Picketing

This, as with all codes of practice, is not legally binding as such but is taken into account by the courts. The best known provision is the suggested maximum number of six pickets for each entrance to premises, and this has led to six being considered as the normal maximum by the courts (see, for example, Scott J in *Thomas v NUM* (above)). Some other main provisions are that where an entrance is used by workers at other firms then the pickets should not ask them to join the strike; picketing should be confined to locations as near as possible to the place of work; pickets should be only be designated as official if trade union is prepared to accept responsibility for their actions; and pickets should ensure that essential supplies and services get through.

## Picketing and the Human Rights Act 1998

Article 11(1) of the ECHR provides that: 'Everyone shall have the right of freedom of peaceful assembly.' This right has been held to apply to peaceful assemblies but not where the organisers intend disorder to result nor, clearly, where disorder does result (*G v Germany* (1989)). This balance between the right of assembly and the need to prevent public disorder is reflected in UK law and so it seems unlikely that the general thrust of the provisions explained above could be considered in breach of the ECHR, especially in view of 'the margin of appreciation' given to states in the area of public order. However, some particular aspects could be open to challenge; for instance, the way in which the limit of six pickets in the Code seems to have become solidified into an absolute maximum. Suppose that there was a peaceful assembly of ten pickets. A police officer requires four of them to go in order to bring the number down to six. They refuse and are arrested for obstructing a police officer in the execution of his duty. What duty? The answer would be 'to prevent breaches of the peace'. But no breach is likely. The other issue is that there is no clear guarantee in UK law of peaceful assembly and indeed the law on what constitutes an obstruction, for example, is so vague that it could, if strictly interpreted make it impossible to hold an assembly. The decision of the House of Lords in *Jones v DPP* (above) is a welcome clarification of the fact that trespass to the highway is not committed by peaceful assemblies, and this seems to bring the law into line with the requirements of the ECHR, although it should be noted that the minority (Lords Hope and Slynn) held that the right was confined to reasonable use as a highway and did not extend to assemblies. This view could well be at variance with the ECHR.

## GENERAL LIABILITY OF TRADE UNIONS IN TORT

The discussion above has concentrated on the specific torts which trade unions are likely to commit when organising industrial action. This should not obscure the fact that trade unions are liable in tort as such and, outside the specific immunities dealt with above, they have no immunity at all and are, with regard to liability, in the same position as anyone else. This did not apply from 1906 until 1982, when trade unions had a complete immunity from actions in tort but this immunity, originally conferred by the Trade Disputes Act 1906, was removed by the Employment Act 1982. Thus injunctions can be sought against unions and they can be liable for damages. This brings the risk that the amount of damages awarded could be such as to bankrupt the union where the employer sues for losses due to a stoppage in production caused by a strike.

To meet this problem, s.22 of TULRCA provides limits on the amount of damages, based on the number of members which the union has, as follows:

- Less than 5,000 members: maximum award £10,000.
- Between 5,000 and 25,000 members: maximum award £50,000.
- Between 25,000 and 100,000 members: maximum award £125,000.
- Over 100,000 members: maximum award £250,000.

Moreover, any award of damages may not be met from the political fund. However, these limits do not apply where the union is sued for damages for personal injury nor where it is sued for breach of duty in connection with the ownership, occupation, possession, control or use of property. The effect is that the limit applies whenever the union is sued in connection with an industrial dispute but not otherwise. For example, if the union owned a vehicle which was involved in a crash whilst being used on union business and driven by an employee of the union, then the union could be liable for the full amount of damages if the negligence of the driver was found to be the cause of the crash.

This example also illustrates another point: for what actions will the union be liable? Given that the union can only act through individuals, this is of crucial importance. The position is that there are two tests for establishing whether a union is liable for the individual's acts.

## Where the action is brought for one or more of the 'economic torts'

Here s.20 of TULRCA provides that a union will be liable for acts authorised or endorsed by it where the act was done, authorised or endorsed by any of the following: the union's principal executive committee, general secretary or president; any other official or committee; any other person empowered by the rules to do, authorise or endorse these actions. There are detailed rules (contained in s.21) on when and how a union may repudiate actions so as to escape liability. In summary, they are that any one from the executive, general secretary or president must give written notice of the repudiation in writing as soon as reasonably practicable to the officials or committee whose actions are repudiated. They must also give notice of repudiation to every union member who might take part in the action which is now repudiated as well as to their employers.

## ■ Where the action is brought in respect of any other tort

In this case the test of whether the union is liable is whether the act was authorised by the union, either expressly or by implication. In *Heatons Transport (St Helens) Ltd v TGWU* (1972) the House of Lords held that custom and practice meant that a union was bound by the actions of shop stewards who had instituted the blacking of lorries in the course of an industrial dispute.

## THE POSITION OF INDIVIDUAL EMPLOYEES IN EMPLOYMENT DISPUTES

At the outset of this discussion one small but significant point must be made: the legislation on collective action has, up to now, spoken of 'workers' as defined by s.296(1) of TULRCA, which adopts the wider definition contained in s.230(3) of the ERA 1996. Thus it includes not only those who work under a contract of employment but also those who undertake personal services. However, from now on, in relation to the law on unfair dismissal the narrower definition of employee in s.230(1) of the ERA is used, which refers only to those working under a contract of employment. It is suggested by Morris and Archer (*Collective Labour Law* (Oxford: Hart Publishing, 2000) p.531) that this may be in breach of Article 11 of the ECHR, which states that the right to join a trade union for the protection of their interests is available to everyone. It is argued that a court may in future regard the use of the term 'employee' and not 'worker' in unfair dismissal legislation relating to industrial action as a restriction on this right under Article 11 and amending legislation will be required.

The foundation of much of the law outlined above is the simple fact that a strike is a breach of the contract of employment. In *Morgan v Fry* (1968) Denning MR put forward a different view: that provided that the length of notice of strike action is of at least the length of the notice required to terminate contracts of employment then the strike only suspends the contract and does not break it. This view was not accepted in the later case of *Simmons v Hoover Ltd* (1977), where the orthodox view that a strike is a breach of contract was restated and this has gone unchallenged since then.

It is worth noting the suggestion of P. Elias (in *The Strike and Breach of Contract: Essays for Paul O'Higgins* (London: Mansell, 1994)) that strikes which are called in response to repudiatory breaches of contract by the employer (e.g. changes in the contract of employment imposed by the employer) should *not* be considered to be breaches of contract by the employees. The breach is that of the employer and not the employees. This view, which seems to accord with orthodox contract principles as well as justice, was not accepted in *Simmons v Hoover Ltd* (1977) (see also *Wilkins v Cantrell and Cochrane (GB) Ltd* (1978)). However, it does have merit. The law on unfair dismissal treats some breaches of contract by employers as repudiatory so as to entitle employees to resign and, on an individual basis, to claim that their contracts have been terminated, thus leading to liability on the employer for constructive dismissal. Why should not repudiation by the employer also entitle employees to make, in effect, a collective resignation? The fact that this is labelled as a strike is irrelevant.

Before considering in detail the position of employees dismissed for taking part in strikes or other industrial action, we need to look at precisely what these terms mean, as this is an area where there is an unfortunate lack of clarity.

## Strikes

Strikes are defined by s.246 of TULRCA as 'any concerted stoppage of work'. This may have made redundant the curious decision in *Lewis and Britton v E Mason and Sons* (1994) that action by one employee can constitute industrial action, although this will depend on whether the action in this case (a refusal by a lorry driver to drive an unheated lorry to Scotland in winter) was a strike or other industrial action. Note that there is a different definition of a strike for continuity purposes in s.235(5) of the ERA 1996 (see Chapter 6).

## Industrial action short of a strike

The first question is whether particular industrial action short of a strike is a breach of contract. If it is, then the employer will have the right to withhold wages for the time during which the employee was engaged in the action (see Chapter 7) and may be able to fairly dismiss the employee (see below). What if it is not? In *Faust v Power Packing Casemakers Ltd* (1983) the Court of Appeal held that industrial action need not amount to a breach of contract where the action consisted of the employee 'applying pressure on his employer or of disrupting his business'. The reason given by Stephenson LJ was that to hold otherwise would involve the courts adjudicating on the merits of industrial disputes in unfair dismissal applications. The unhappy result is that whilst any action involving a breach of contract *will* amount to industrial action, one cannot say that the absence of a breach of contract means that there is no industrial action. Nor does the reasoning of Stephenson LJ seem convincing, even adopting his own words. For if the courts are to examine the motives for the action, which is what his words quoted above must inevitably mean, then surely this must involve the courts looking at what the dispute is about, which is not far distant from looking at the merits of the dispute.

Given this confusion, the best way forward is to look at particular forms of industrial action. The following are the main types.

1. Refusal to perform duties expressly laid down in the contract.
2. A go-slow.

3. A ban on overtime.
4. A work to rule.
5. A withdrawal of goodwill.

Whether any of these are breaches of contract will depend on several factors:

### Whether the action was a breach of an express term of the contract

Where the employee refuses to perform terms expressly laid down in the contract this will be a breach, as in *Miles v Wakefield MDC* and *Wilusynski v Tower Hamlets Borough Council* (both cases on withholding of wages – see Chapter 7). Whether a go-slow amounts to a breach is more problematic but it was held to be one in *General Engineering Services Ltd v Kingston and St Andrews Corporation* (1988). If overtime is voluntary then one would have thought that such a refusal would not be industrial action but in *Faust v Power Packing Casemakers Ltd* (above) it was held, applying the view of the law in that case, discussed above, that refusing to work voluntary overtime could be industrial action even though not a breach of contract. The other two situations are unlikely to involve express breaches of contract, but may be breaches of an implied term (below).

### Whether the action amounts to a breach of an implied term of the contract to serve the employer faithfully

The nature of this term was explained in Chapter 5 but it is of particular significance in this context. In *Secretary of State for Employment v ASLEF (No. 2)* (1972) the Court of Appeal held that work to rule was a breach and in *Ticehurst v British Telecommunications plc* (1992) a withdrawal of goodwill by a manager was also held to be a breach. The deciding factor seems to be the intent with which the act is done. Thus in the *ASLEF* case Denning MR observed that an employee 'can withdraw his goodwill if he pleases. But what he must not do is *wilfully* obstruct the employer' (my italics). In *Ticehurst* Ralph Gibson LJ said that there would be a breach if the employee did or omitted to do an act where there was a discretion in the matter 'not in the honest exercise of choice or discretion . . . but in order to disrupt the employer's business or to cause the most inconvenience that can be caused'.

### Lock-outs

This type of situation deserves special mention. Lock-outs are not defined for the purposes of collective employment law but, as we saw in Chapter 12, they are defined for redundancy and continuity of employment purposes by s.235(4) of the ERA and this definition will probably be used in the context of collective disputes.

### Was the employee taking part in the action?

A further consideration is whether the employee is actually taking part in the strike or industrial action. If not, then there can, of course, be no breach of contract. In *Coates v Modern Methods and Materials Ltd* (1982) a strike was called and an employee turned up for work but saw pickets at the entrance. She did not go in to work, as she said that she feared abuse if she crossed picket lines, so returned home. She was suffering from back trouble and her doctor gave her a sick note which covered the next two weeks. It was held that she had taken part in the strike as the fact was that she had not crossed the picket lines. Stephenson LJ held that employees must be judged by what they do and not by why they do it: 'those who stay away from work with the strikers without protest' are to be regarded as having taken part in the strike. An interesting example is provided by *Rasool v Hepworth Pipe Co. (No. 2)* (1980), where attendance at an unauthorised one-hour union meeting was held not to be taking part in industrial action because the meeting was not called with the purpose of putting pressure on the employer. This is an odd decision, illustrating the lack of clear thinking in this area, because taking time off to attend an unauthorised meeting was undoubtedly a breach, although the context was whether employees had been taking part in union activities.

## STRIKES AND OTHER INDUSTRIAL ACTION AND DISMISSAL

*Note*: in the discussion that follows, the word 'strike' will be used to cover both strikes and other industrial action.

The law of contract allows an employer to summarily dismiss an employee who is taking part in a strike, as the strike is a repudiatory breach of contract. Similarly, payment of wages to those taking part in strikes and other industrial action can be withheld (see Chapter 7).

The law on unfair dismissal originally regarded dismissal of employees on strike or taking part in other industrial action as being in a kind of halfway house. Under the Industrial Relations Act 1971, tribunals had no jurisdiction to hear a complaint of unfair dismissal when striking employees were dismissed rather than the dismissal being held fair or unfair, although this was subject to qualifications, as described below. This legislation was, rather surprisingly, continued by the Labour government of 1974–79 and the effect was that dismissal was treated in exactly the same way as if the legislation had said that it was fair, because the employees were not entitled to any remedy. The Conservative government tightened the law in the Employment Act 1990 by removing all protection from employees who were on unofficial strike. The Labour government returned in 1997 was committed to changing the law to give greater protection from dismissal to striking employees but what resulted in the Employment Relations Act 1999 was, in the eyes of many, a somewhat half-hearted gesture in fulfilment of this commitment. The effect is that, *in some circumstances only*, dismissal of striking employees is automatically unfair. The position now is that there is a distinction between official and unofficial industrial action *and* a distinction between certain types of official industrial action. This complex position is the result of the intervention of successive governments in a piecemeal fashion without ever going back to first principles.

## SUMMARY OF THE PRESENT LEGISLATION

1. If the action is official which is also protected under s.238A of TULRCA then dismissal is automatically unfair if the circumstances set out in s.238A (3), (4) and (5) apply. (This is the change made by the Employment Relations Act 1999.)
2. If the action is official which is also protected under s.238A of TULRCA but the circumstances set out in s.238A(3), (4) and (5) do not apply then the employees will not be able to make a complaint of dismissal if the employer has dismissed all the employees taking part, otherwise it may be unfair. (This is the position as it originally was in the Industrial Relations Act 1971.)
3. If the action is official but not protected then the position is the same as in 2 above.
4. If the action is unofficial then employees who are dismissed have no remedy in any circumstances. (This is the change made by the Employment Act 1990 and left as it is by the current Labour government.)

These will now be looked at in detail.

### ■ Dismissal of employees who are on official industrial action which is also protected

There are two vital questions: is the action official and, if so, is it protected?

#### Official

The legislation defines 'official' negatively, in that s.237(2) of TULRCA provides that action is unofficial in relation to an employee unless *either* the action is authorised or endorsed by the union of which the employee is a member *or* the employee is not a member but others taking part in the action are members of a union which has authorised it. However, if no one taking part in the action is a union member then it is not to be regarded as unofficial. The reason for this last provision is that otherwise, if there was no union representation, then all action would be unofficial, which would, as we shall see, have unfortunate consequences. If action is not unofficial then it must be official and so one needs to look at the converse of the above situations.

#### Protected

This means that the union authorising or endorsing the action has, by virtue of s.219 of TULRCA, immunity in tort for so doing. This means that:

1. The act involves the commission of one or more of the economic torts (see above).
2. The act is in contemplation or furtherance of a trade dispute.
3. The union has complied with the statutory procedures on balloting.

4. The action is not secondary industrial action.
5. The action is not taken for purposes prohibited by statute.

(The reason for these provisions is that it is felt that it would be wrong if the union was immune from an action in tort for calling the strike but employees could have action taken against them for taking part in it.)

If the action amounts to official protected industrial action then s.238A(2) of TULRCA provides that any employee shall be regarded as unfairly dismissed if the reason or principal reason for the dismissal is that they took protected industrial action and any one of the following three conditions are satisfied:

1. The dismissal took place within eight weeks beginning with the day on which the employee started to take protected industrial action.
2. The dismissal took place after the end of the eight-week period but the employee had stopped taking protected industrial action. (This is to protect the employee from being subjected to victimisation by the employer after returning to work.)
3. The dismissal took place after the end of the eight-week period and the employee was still taking protected industrial action but the employer had not taken reasonable procedural steps to resolve the dispute. The following factors are laid down by s.238A(6) for deciding whether reasonable steps have been taken by the employer:
   (a) Did the employer or a union comply with procedures laid down in any collective agreement which is applicable?
   (b) Did the employer or a union, after the start of the protected industrial action, offer or agree to commence or resume negotiations or unreasonably refuse a request that conciliation or mediation services be used?

   However, in determining whether the employer has taken any of these steps, the tribunal shall not take account of the merits of the dispute (s.238A(7)). Thus there will be no point in the employer arguing that the reason why none of the procedural steps was taken was that the strike was so completely unreasonable that there was nothing to negotiate about.

## Example

The Toilers Union call a strike among its members at Gradgrind & Co. in support of a pay claim. The strike is official as it is called by the union and the action is protected as the strike call amounts to an inducement of a breach of contract for which the union has immunity in tort under s.219 of TULRCA. The action is not secondary industrial action, nor was it called for a prohibited purpose and it had the support of a ballot. Gradgrind dismisses Joan, an employee who was taking part in the strike, two days after it started. The dismissal of Joan is *automatically* unfair.

(Readers may find that it helps to understand a complicated area if the situations 2 and 3 above are applied to this example.)

## ▨ Dismissals where the action was official protected industrial action

Where the action was official protected industrial action but the circumstances in 1, 2 and 3 above did not apply, the rules are the same as for dismissals under the heading below.

## ▨ Dismissals where the action is official but not protected

Where the action is official but not protected, the circumstances in 1, 2 and 3 cannot apply.

The rules are the same under this heading and the one above. As mentioned above, this is the law as it was before the Employment Relations Act 1999 came into force and the basic position is that if all employees taking part in industrial action were dismissed and not re-engaged then s.238 of TULRCA provides that the 'tribunal shall not determine whether the dismissal was fair or unfair'. Stated slightly more precisely, s.238 provides that the only cases where a tribunal can hear complaints of unfair dismissal are:

1. Where one or more relevant employees were not dismissed ('relevant employees' is defined by s.238(3) for these purposes as employees at the establishment where the employee works who were, at the date of the dismissal, taking part in the strike or other industrial action).
2. Where a relevant employee was, before the expiry of three months beginning with the date of his/her dismissal, offered re-engagement but the complainant was not.

In these cases the dismissal is neither automatically fair nor unfair but the tribunal will consider fairness in the ordinary way. Therefore, the employer must show that the reason for the dismissal was one or more of the potentially fair ones (see Chapter 11) and the tribunal will then proceed to decide reasonableness in accordance with s.98(4) of the ERA. However, if the only reason given by the employer for the dismissal is that the employer was on strike then the dismissal will be unfair, as this is not a potentially fair reason within s.98(4). If the dismissal is held unfair then the House of Lords held in *Crosville Wales Ltd v Tracey (No. 2)* (1997) that compensation cannot be reduced by the mere fact that the employee was participating in the strike, although it was stated *obiter* that conduct apart from participation might go to reduce damages. This could be, for example, where their behaviour was 'over-hasty and inflammatory' (per Lord Nolan).

Where, however, the reason for the selection of the striking employee for dismissal was union membership or activities then the dismissal is automatically unfair (s.152 of TULRCA) and the same applies where the dismissal was for specified health and safety activities, reasons relating to family leave, grounds of pregnancy or childbirth or acting or standing for election as an employee representative (s.238(2A) TULRCA (1992)).

## ■ Where the action is unofficial

Here, as stated above, dismissed employees have no remedy even where the dismissal was selective, except that dismissal on the grounds specified in s.238(2A) above will be automatically unfair.

## LOCK-OUTS

Lock-outs require separate discussion because, although they are clearly different in nature from strikes and other industrial action, they are treated in the same way under unfair dismissal legislation.

The definition of a lock-out in s.235(5) of the ERA is, as stated above, probably applicable to lock-outs in industrial disputes, although it is found in a part of an Act dealing with entitlement to redundancy payments. It will be recalled that it defines a lock-out in terms of action taken by an employer rather than action by an employee as in all other cases of industrial action. Such action can, by s.235(5), be the closing of a place of employment, the suspension of work or the refusal by an employer to continue to employ certain employees in consequence of a dispute. As such, a lock-out may well amount to a breach of contract by the employer. The question of whether the lock-out is a repudiatory breach will depend on its length, amongst other factors. The curious point is, however, that employees who leave and claim that they have been dismissed because of the lock-out will find that they are in exactly the same position as employees who are dismissed for taking industrial action where the conditions listed on p.302 above did not apply or where the action was not protected.

Therefore, the protection afforded by s.238A of the Employment Relations Act 1999 to strikers dismissed within the first eight weeks etc. does not apply to those dismissed as a result of a lock-out and they are left in the position which applied to all official strikers before 1999. Thus an employer can dismiss all employees locked out but if there are selective dismissals then there may be liability for unfair dismissal. The matter is complicated by the fact that the definition of 'relevant employee' differs for lock-outs as compared with strikes or other industrial action. For lock-outs, s.238(3) defines relevant employees as those 'who were directly interested in the dispute'. In *Fisher v York Trailer Co. Ltd* (1979) the employers sent a letter to all 34 employees on a shift, as they were concerned that they were 'going slow'. They required all of them to undertake that they would work at a normal pace but seven did not do this and were dismissed. The EAT held that *all* 34 employees were 'directly interested' in the dispute and so they could all be dismissed under the provisions outlined above. This could be a double-edged sword for employers: an employer might see it as an advantage to be able to dismiss all employees involved but then care must be taken actually to dismiss *all*, as if any relevant employees are not dismissed those dismissed could claim that they have been selectively dismissed under s.238 of TULRCA.

The other problem with this area is that the boundary between a strike and a lock-out may be a thin one.

*Example*

Gradgrind & Co. decide to increase working hours of employees from 40 to 42 a week, together with a new shift pattern consequent on the introduction of new machinery. The company says that the cost of the new machinery has been such that it must be used more intensively than the machinery it replaced. Existing hours of work and shift patterns are written into contracts of employment. The employees decide that they will not return to work until Gradgrind & Co. agrees to negotiate on these matters but Gradgrind reply by saying that the employees will not be allowed into work unless they agree to the new arrangements. If this is a strike then, if it also amounts to official protected industrial action (see above), Gradgrind will not be able to dismiss anyone on strike for the first eight weeks. If it is a lock-out then Gradgrind can dismiss all those 'directly involved' and will be safe from any action for unfair dismissal provided that *all* are dismissed.

## THE FUTURE OF THE LAW ON DISMISSAL FOR TAKING PART IN STRIKES, LOCK-OUTS AND OTHER INDUSTRIAL ACTION

This branch of the law has always been controversial and remains so. There is pressure for it to be changed so that, as suggested by Novitz and Skidmore in *Fairness at Work* (Oxford: Hart Publishing, 2001), p.178, 'the dismissal of any workers engaged in lawful industrial action is treated as a nullity'. Yet, at the same time, as the authors recognise, the whole idea of strikes, lock-outs and other industrial action is viewed as an anachronism, not least by the present government, with its emphasis on partnership in industrial relations.

Of one thing we can be sure: this part of employment law, like all others, is not static. It will go on developing, sometimes at an alarming pace (especially for those who write books on employment law!). Yet the subject will not cease to fascinate, beguile and, when the courts and the legislators between them have left us in a state of total confusion, as in the law discussed above, infuriate. But dull and predicable employment law will never be and this is one reason among many for studying it.

# Specimen examination questions and points for inclusion in the answers

### Question 1

Ron is a mechanic and has been employed by Mike's Motors, a small lawnmower repair firm, for two years. On 1 February 2001 Mike said to Ron:

> From 1 March you'll be on your own legally. You'll be self-employed. I'm fed up with all of these new employment laws and so I'd like you to sign this, but remember that things won't change bar a few small details. It's all in here.

Mike then gives Ron a document which states:

> I agree that I am a self-employed mechanic. My wages will be paid gross but I will continue to tender my services exclusively to Mike's Mowers. If I am unable, due to sickness, to work on any day then I may engage a substitute. I will provide my own tools and equipment. In consideration of signing this agreement I become entitled to a bonus of £100.

Ron signed the document.

On 1 April Mike came up to Ron and said: 'Sorry old chum but my son is coming into the business and I can't afford to employ you and him. You'll have to go from the end of the week.' Ron asks you for advice on whether he is able to claim compensation for dismissal.

### Question 2

Sarah is employed as a salesperson by Mouse Ltd, which sells highly specialised computer equipment to large international firms. She earns £50,000 p.a. A clause in her contract states that:

> On termination of your employment for whatever reason you shall not be engaged directly or indirectly in the business of designing or marketing computer equipment anywhere in the world for a period of two years.

Sarah resigns and sets up in business on her own doing the same kind of work as she had done for Mouse Ltd. Mouse Ltd also suspects that, before she left, she copied confidential details of customer accounts.

Advise Mouse Ltd on:

(a) Whether the above clause in Sarah's contract is enforceable.
(b) Whether any action can be taken against her if it is found that she has copied details of customer accounts.

(c)  Would it make any difference to your answer if Sarah had been wrongfully dismissed?

## Question 3

Jane works at a firm of solicitors. Two months ago she was involved in a car accident which has left her with recurring back trouble and also spells when she finds it difficult to concentrate. Medical reports indicate that these conditions will continue for some time.

She has asked to be allowed to work flexible hours and to reduce her total working hours from 38 a week to 30. She has also asked to be provided with a special chair to ease the pain in her back.

Her employers have agreed to provide a chair when the staff move to new offices next year but have refused to agree to the changes in working hours on the ground that all employees need to be at work at the same time and for the same number of hours so as to provide an efficient service to clients.

Advise Jane on any claim which she may have under the Disability Discrimination Act.

## Question 4

Catherine is interviewed for a teaching post at a small primary school. She is asked at the interview how many children she has and, when she answers 'five', she is asked 'how will you manage to get them all off your hands in time for you to get to work?' She says that this will be no problem, but she is not appointed. She has now learnt that a man was appointed who was not asked questions about his children.

Advise Catherine on whether she has any claim under the Sex Discrimination Act.

## Question 5

Edith has been appointed as a secretary at a local authority school on a salary of £13,000 for a 21-hour week. She has just learned that, although her predecessor, a woman, was on the same salary, the man who was secretary before her received £13,000 for a 20-hour week. She also finds that a male secretary at a neighbouring school, run by the same local authority, receives £14,000 for a 21-hour week.

Advise Edith on any claim which could bring.

## Question 6

Barry works in a bank in the City of London. He has a team of five but his deputy leaves and is replaced by a junior clerk. Barry complains to Terry, his line manager, that his workload is becoming excessive as he is now doing the work of two but Terry tells him that times are bad and there is no funding for anyone on the salary of a deputy. Barry then sees his doctor, who certifies that he is suffering from hypertension brought on by stress, but Terry simply says: 'Wait a year and then things may improve and we'll look at the situation again.' A week later Barry has a nervous breakdown.

Advise him on the possibilities of success in any claim against the bank.

## Question 7

'It is important that the operation of the legislation in relation to unfair dismissal should not impede employers unreasonably in the efficient management of their business, which must be in the interests of all.' (Phillips J in *Cook v Thomas Linnell and Sons Ltd* (1977).)

(a) Do you agree with this statement?
(b) Do you consider that it accurately reflects the aims of the legislation and the attitudes of the courts when interpreting it?

## Question 8

Danny worked as a school meals supervisor for Barset County Council. The school meals service was then contracted out to a private firm, Best Burgers, and Danny was told two weeks after the change that his post was redundant but that he could apply for a post as a van driver delivering pre-cooked meals to schools. Danny is unhappy about accepting this job as it will mean working further away from home and he needs to be near home as he cares for his elderly mother.

Advise Danny on whether he should accept the new post and, if not, whether he has any claim against Barset County Council and/or Best Burgers.

## Question 9

'Without the threat of recourse to industrial action, collective action would amount to little more then "collective begging". Given this, there is a strong case for reform of the current extensive restrictions on industrial action.' (Novitz and Skidmore, *Fairness at Work* (Oxford: Hart Publishing, 2001))

Do you agree with these statements?

## Question 10

Consider the impact which the Human Rights Act 1998 has had on employment law up to the present time and estimate the potential which the Act has to bring about further change.

## SUGGESTED POINTS FOR INCLUSION IN ANSWERS

There are two types of questions set out above: the problem type and the essay type. With each there is a golden rule about answering them.

### Problem questions

Concentrate on *analysing* the problem and take each point separately, setting out the relevant law (and *only* the relevant law) and then applying it to the question.

*Do not* on any account succumb to the temptation to set out vast quantities of information on the topic in general, but what information is given must be used by applying it to the question.

## ▩ Essay questions

Answer the question directly and never use it as an excuse to simply write all that you know about a topic. The author has read hundreds of answers where students have done this and marks have been thrown away. It is the commonest reason for low marks in an examination apart, of course, from not knowing the law at all! Look at the guidance given below on answering the specimen essay questions for ideas on how to tackle specific questions.

### Question 1

This question deals with two points:

1. Is Ron an employee? Start with the statutory provisions, which do not take us far, and then move on to the tests used by the courts. Consider the significance of the right to engage a substitute, the provision of tools and equipment and the description of Ron as self-employed, etc. Mention relevant cases on each of these. At the end you may be uncertain about the answer. Do not worry! This is often a sign of strength rather than weakness: the poor candidate is more likely to take refuge in black and white statements.
2. If Ron is an employee he may be able to claim for wrongful dismissal or for unfair dismissal as he has one year's qualifying employment. The question does not ask whether he will succeed in a claim but only whether he is *able* to bring one and so a detailed account of the law on unfair dismissal is not required. A good example of the necessity of reading the question carefully!

### Question 2

(a) Contract in restraint of trade. Does it protect an enforceable interest? If not, void. If it does, move on to consider whether it is no wider than reasonably necessary to protect that interest. Possibility of severance. Remedies of the employer.

(b) Common law duty of confidentiality. Has it been broken? Significance of high salary – does the employee owe a higher duty?

(c) Whole clause probably unenforceable.

### Question 3

Disability Discrimination Act 1995. Look carefully at all parts of the definition and apply to the situation. Duty to make reasonable adjustments. What could this mean here? Remedies.

## Question 4

Sex Discrimination Act 1975. Does it apply? If so, has there been direct or indirect discrimination? Was the questioning justifiable irrespective of sex? Has Catherine suffered a detriment? Remedies.

## Question 5

Equal Pay Act 1970. Is it like work? If so, does it enable a comparison to be made with a former employee? Second situation: is it like work? If so, can a comparison be made with a worker at another establishment? Remedies.

## Question 6

Possible breach of the duty of care in negligence. Discussion of cases – this is a question where a very careful comparison between the facts of the problem and the two leading cases can gain very good marks. The question is deliberately open-ended as it does not ask specifically about liability in negligence and therefore credit will be gained for a mention of other possibilities, e.g. action for breach of an implied term of the contract and resignation followed by a claim for constructive dismissal.

## Question 7

This essay question deals with two issues and *both must be addressed separately*. The first asks for the opinion of the candidate on the statement: beware of simply uttering generalities. There is a real issue here: the efficient running of a business is of course in the interests of all, not just the employer. The point is whether this consideration should be allowed to interfere with a legitimate right of an individual employee. The second part asks whether the statement reflects the attitude of the courts. Rather then ranging superficially over a vast area, it would be better to look at a few cases in detail and evaluate the statement in the light of them.

## Question 8

Has the contract of employment been transferred? Application of TUPE. If so, does the ETO defence apply to the dismissal? If not, then will it be automatically unfair? What of the offer of alternative employment? Is it reasonable to refuse it?

## Question 9

Look at the statement in the quotation first. Do you agree with it or not? Then go on to look at the present law on industrial action, e.g. ballots, immunities etc. and consider whether they unduly impede industrial action. Try to give a lawyer's answer rather then one based on general prejudices and ideas. This is a question where it would be very tempting to fall into the trap of giving just a general account of the law. Resist it!

## Question 10

Again a two-part question. You need to be aware of the current impact of the Human Rights Act 1998 on, for example, the law on collective action and other areas too and to have read widely enough to be able to look ahead. Once again, mere generalities are tempting but must be avoided.

# Glossary of legal terms

**Acts of Parliament**  Laws made by Parliament.

**Appellant**  The party bringing an appeal.

**Applicant**  The person(s) who bring(s) an action in an employment tribunal.

**Civil law**  That part of English law which regulates the relations between individuals, including companies, as distinct from criminal law, which regulates the relations between individuals and the state.

**Claimant**  The person(s) who bring(s) an action in the civil courts. Until 2000 the term was the 'plaintiff' and law reports until this date use that term.

**Codes of practice**  These are generally issued under the authority of a statute but they are not legally binding. They are, however, taken into account by the courts and in practice one should be prepared to explain and justify a failure to observe the provisions of a code.

**Common law**  That part of English law which has been developed by decisions of the courts as distinct from statute law which is made by Parliament.

**Contracts**  Legally binding agreements.

**Crown**  In practice, this means the executive arm of the state, which administers the country, the term having its origin in the fact that executive acts are carried on in the name of the monarch.

**Defendant**  The person(s) against whom a civil law action is brought.

**Delegated legislation**  This is where an Act of Parliament gives authority for laws to be made under its authority by, for example, government ministers.

**Ex parte**  Literally 'from one party' and meaning where only one party is represented on the initial application. This term is used in cases where applications have been made for judicial review against public bodies but the term used for cases brought today is 'from one side' rather than *ex parte*.

**Force majeure**  Where a person acts under an irresistible compulsion.

**Injunction**  A court order which commands a person to do or not to do an act which, if committed, would amount to a crime or a tort.

**Obiter** (in full, *obiter dicta*)  This is used to refer to words spoken by a judge in a judgment which are not strictly necessary for deciding the case but which are said as an indication of the judge's views on a related point. The literal meaning is 'words on the way'.

**Regulations**  In UK law this means laws made under the authority of an Act of Parliament by what is known as delegated legislation. It also means a particular type of EC law (see Chapter 2).

**Respondent**  This term has two meanings: the person against whom an action in an employment tribunal is brought and the party against whom an appeal in a civil action is brought.

**Statute law**  A statute is another name for an Act of Parliament and therefore statute law is simply another name for Acts of Parliament.

**Torts**  Wrongs which involve a breach of the civil law rather than the criminal law and therefore normally lead to an action for damages (compensation).

**Ultra vires**  'Beyond the powers'. Means where a public body has acted beyond the powers given to it by statute. The result is that such an act is generally void.

# Index